ENGLISH RECUSANT LITERATURE
1558–1640

Selected and Edited by
D. M. ROGERS

Volume 258

RICHARD SMITH
Of the Author and Substance
of the Protestant Church and Religion
1621

RICHARD SMITH

Of the Author and Substance
of the Protestant Church and Religion
1621

The Scolar Press
1975

ISBN 0 85967 254 9

Published and printed in Great Britain by
The Scolar Press Limited, 59-61 East Parade,
Ilkley, Yorkshire and
39 Great Russell Street,
London WC1

1868446

OF
THE AVTHOR
AND
SVBSTANCE
OF THE
PROTESTANT CHVRCH
AND RELIGION,

TWO BOOKES.

Written first in Latin by R. S.
Doctour of Diuinity,

AND

Now reuiewed by the Author, and transla-
ted into English by VV. Baſ.

Euery thing muſt be reduced to its beginning.
Tertull. Præſcript. cap. 20.
Permiſſu Superiorum, M.DC.XXI.

The Scope of this Worke.

IF both Luther *himselfe*, and the famousest Protestants of all sorts, haue many wayes most plainly and most freely confessed, that Luther was the Author and Beginner of the Protestant Church and Religion (*as in this worke doth manifestly appeare*) *then vndoubtedly he was so*.

And if Luther were the Author and Beginner therof, assuredly, it is not the Church and Religion of Christ.

Read therefore and iudge indifferently; and thereby an end may be made of all Controuersies in Religion betwixt the Catholiks and Protestants.

THE

THE
PREFACE OF
THE AVTHOR TO
the Reader.

Wherein the manner and profit of this Worke
is declared.

THERE are two kinds of questions (gentle Reader) which
are in controuersy betwixt the
Catholikes and Protestantes;
the one kind is of fact, to wit,
Whether Luther was the Author,
and beginner of the Protestants Church and Religio;
whether before him it were visible and had Pastours;
whether he and the first Protestant Preachers were
sent to preach Protestancy, and the like : The other
kind of question is of Christs doctrine or law :
For example, *whether Christ taught good workes*
do iustify, be necessary to saluation, meritorious, and

* 2
such

Why a
a queſtion
ot Fact is
handled
rather thē
of doctrin

ſuch others . At this preſent I treate not of this
ſecond kind of queſtion, but only of the former
and that for three cauſes . Firſt the queſtions of
Doctrine are innumerable, but the queſtions of
Fact, few . And many haue handled them, and
that moſt exactly, but theſe, few haue touched,
and (for ought that I know) none of purpoſe
hath hitherto written of the Authour of Proteſtancy, and in that manner as I intend to write.

1.

2.

Secondly there are few queſtions of doctrine of
that nature, that all other controuerſies of faith
depend vpon them ; but the moſt queſtions of
Fact are ſuch, as if they be well decided, al other
Controuerſies of religion are at an end . Such
kind of queſtion this eſpecially is , which now
I handle, *VVhether Luther were Author and beginner of the Proteſtant church and Re.igion* For if it
be made manifeſt , that he was the Author and
Beginner of it, euery one will ſtraihgt ſee that it
is not Chriſts Church & Religion, but Luthers
deuiſe and inuention . Thirdly in queſtions of
doctrine, or law, Proteſtants want not ſome
pretext of Scripture (as neither any Heretikes
wanted)and therfore diuers tymes they are ready to debate theſe kind of Queſtions, in which

3.

(as Tertullian ſayth) *they pretend Scriptures, and
with this their boldnes ſhake ſome, and in the diſpute
weary the conſtant, catch the weake & ſend away the
middle ſort with ſcruple and dou.ts .* But in queſtions

ons of Fact they are destitute not only of al pre-
tence of Scripture, vnles it be some most vaine,
but also of all testimony of men and help of reason, and stand only vpon their owne sayinges,
& are conuinced by the testimonies of the whol
world, and sometyme also by their owne confessions, and therefore are brought to debate
these kind of questions no more willingly, then
is a theefe to his tryall. Neither do they in these
disputs either weary the constant, or catch the
weake; but shew their owne weaknes and wil-
fullnes vnto all kind of men. And this is the
cause why Ministers are so loath to dispute of
the Church, because the Church, being a company of men, includeth many questions of fact,
as of antiquity, succession, continuance, visibility, mission, ordination of Pastours, and such
like; in which points there is little colour, or
shew on their part.

2. Fourthly, Protestants exact more diffi-
cult poofes in questions of doctrine, then they
can demand in matters of Fact. For in matters
of Fact, wherof the scripture speaketh nothing,
they must be content with testimonies of men,
against whome no iust exception can be made,
or they must refuse all triall of these kind of
questions. But in controuersies of doctrine,
they account those only to be lawfull proofes,
which are taken out of the scripture. Neither

doe thefe fatiffie them, vnleffe they be plaine &
(a) *expreffe, and* (as they fay) word (b) *for word
containe that which is in queftion, or at leaft be fo
pregnant and ftrong, that they* (c) *ftopp all mens
mouths that they can gainfay nothing.* For it is the
common fault of Proteftants, which S. Auguftin faith, himfelfe was guilty of, whiles he
was an heretike, that *they will be as certaine of all
things as that feauen and three make ten.* Nay they
yield not alwayes to thefe kind of proofs: For
what can be fayd more expreffly, more plainly,
more literally, then the fcripture faith, that
man is iuftified by workes, and not only by
faith; that, that which our Sauiour gaue with
his hands to his Apoftles after his laft fupper,
was his very body and bloud, and fuch like: &
yet the Proteftants yield not to thefe kind of
teftimonies, but deuife figures and fhiftes to
delude them. Catholiques proofes in contro-
uerfies of doctrine are certainly Theological de-
monftrations, becaufe they are clearly drawne
from the proper principles of Diuinity, to wit,
from cleare words of God confirmed by the
tradition of the Church and vnanimous expofi-
tion of the Fathers; which kind of proofe is as
great and ftrong, as either Diuinity or law, or
any Science whatfoeuer which is founded in
words either doth affoard, or the nature of any
law or fcience which is grounded in words (as

Diuinity

(a) *Melan.
& Brent.
in Hofpin.
fol.* 107.
*Colloq.
Ratisb.feff.*
11.
(b) *Vorft.
refponf. ad
Slad.*
(c) *Luth.
de feru.
arbitr.fol.*
440.
Lib. 6.
confeff. c.
4.

Diuinity is) can beare or affoard . And as the Philosopher saith well, it were starck madnes to exact any other kind of proofes of any Profession, then the nature therof can affoard. But because heretiques expound what words soeuer as they list, and litle set by the authority of the Church or Fathers, and the vnlearned hardly perceaue what kind of proofe is a Theologicall demonstration, & such as Diuinity can affoard no greater, or which is the true sense of Gods word, or how great the authority of the Churh and Fathers ought to be; therefore with them, Catholiks proofs in points of doctrin, albeit in truth they be Theological demonstrations, take litle effect. Wheras on the other side Catholique proofes in matter of Fact, are not only Theologicall, but also (that I may so speake) Mathematicall demonstrations, because they consist of one principle which is grounded not only vpon the foundations of Diuinity, to wit the word of God together with the expositiō of the Church and Fathers, but also is manifest by the light of reason : which kind of principles these are , *That Gods Church hath alwayes bin: that it is one : that it is the auncientest of all Churches : that it is alwayes visible : hath alwayes Pastors,* and the like: And of another principle, which may be tryed by our sense and experience, as that the foresayd properties agree neither to the Protes-

1. Eth. 1.

* 4   stants

tants nor to the Anabaptiſts , nor to any hereticall company . And therfore theſe kind of demonſtrations moue euen the moſt obſtinate
heretiques, and are euident euen to the moſt ignorant and vnlearned perſons .

3 . And hence ariſeth a fift cauſe of handling
rather queſtions of Fact thenof doctrin, becauſe
the fruit of debating thoſe queſtions is reaped
with more facility and of far more .For wheras
few but diuines do themſelues perceaue the true
meaning of the teſtimonyes of Scripture wherwith the queſtions of doctrin are debated; as the
true meaning of the law, few but lawyers thēſelues do ſee; all perceaue the meaning of thoſe
teſtimonyes wherwith the queſtions of fact are
Epiſt. de- diſputed, who will affoard an attētiue eye to ſee,
dicat.exer- or eare to heare.And heerupō Caſaubon wrote,
cit. cont.
Baron. *that for to inſinuate into the mind of the Reader any*
opinion now in controuerſie, Baronius hiſteryes are of
D. Flaui- *greater force, then Bellarmines diſputes* . And ſayd
gnie . alſo ſometyme, as one moſt worthy of credit ,
who heard him, told me , that whiles he read
Bellarmines diſputations, he began to doubt of
all Religion , but whiles he peruſed Baronius
Annales, he felt himſelfe by little & little drawn
towards Papiſtry: which thing might wel haue
befallen him and ſuch others, not becauſe Cardinall Bellarmine proueth leſſe ſoundly, for the
nature of the matter, the truth of Catholik Religion

ligion in queſtions of doctrine, then Cardinall
Baronius doth the ſame in queſtions of Fact, but
becauſe ſuch is the nature of the teſtimonyes ,
wherewith the truth of Catholike fayth in queſtions of doctrine is proued , that they are leſſe
euident then the teſtimonyes wherewith the
Catholike truth in matters of Fact is proued ,
and alſo haue many thinges which ſeeme to be
contrary and repugnant to them . Whereupon
it falleth out that ſome hearing or reading controuerſies of doctrine diſputed between Catholikes and Heretikes, and not being able of thēſelues to diſcern betwixt truth & ſhew of truth,
either follow neither party, but become vncertaine or Atheiſtes, or content with any ſhew of
truth take that part to which any affection of
their will doth draw them . Whereas none by
hearing or reading controuerſies of Fact, becommeth not more confirmed in the Catholik faith
or more auerted from hereſy . And therefore
Tertullian counſaileth vs, not to diſpute with *Præſcrip.*
Heretikes out of Scripture , by which que- *cap.* 19 .
ſtions of doctrine are diſputed, but aduiſeth vs
to appeale to antiquity, ſucceſſion, and ſuch like
which concerne queſtions of fact .

4. Laſtly, though the fruit of diſputing
both thoſe kind of queſtions were equall , yet
ſith the Author, by order of nature, goeth before
the thing whereof he is Authour , according to

* 5   the

The preface to the Reader.

the order of Nature we ought to intreate of the Author of Proteftancy before we difpute of Proteftancy it felfe. For (as well fayth Tertullian) *nothing but God alone is without beginning which how much it goeth before in the state of all thinges, so much ought it to go before in the handling of them, that the state may be knowne.* And other where: *Nothing is knowne before the beginning is knowne.* Wherfore I will begin my firft difpute concerning the Proteftant Religion of the Authour thereof : Yet before I do that, I muft fet downe and determine what a Proteftant, or the Proteftant Church and Religion is, and what is neceffary for one to be a Proteftant, and difcouer the vncertainty of Proteftants . And this much touching the matter which I haue made choice of to handle in this little worke and the caufes thereof .

Lib 5. cont Mar.

Lib 3 cont Mar.

5.   As for the manner wherwith I vndertake to difcuffe this queftion of Fact , whether Luther was the firft Author & beginner of the Proteftant Church , and Religion, I purpofe to proue it only out of the confeffions of Luther himfelfe, and of the three forts of Proteftants, to wit, Lutherans, who profeffe to follow Luther in all points of doctrine ; Sacramentaries , who notorioufly diffent from him touching the reall prefence of Chrifts body in the Sacrament; and our Englifh Proteftants , who differ from both

VVhy proued only out of Proteftants,

The preface to the Reader.

both the former at least in discipline & gouerment of their Church : because this kind of proofe out of their owne wordes I find to be both necessary and most effectuall with Protestants . Necessary , because of this question of Fact , neither the Scripture , or the Fathers Necessary. say any thing , as also ; because , seeing Protestants deny part of the scripture , and interprete the rest as they please , and will not stand to the sentence of the Church , Councels , or Fathers , account reason Sophistrie , & contemme the testimonies of Catholique writers , they haue left nothing but their own cōfessiōs , by which we may dispute with them . And I pray God they do giue place to their own most frequent and most plaine confessions , and not delude them by voluntary and friuolous interpretations ; for then hope may be , that there wilbe some end of these controuersies . At least we shall reape this profit by this labour , that by it shall be manifest to all , that either Protestants will beare no testimony , admit no iudgement , no not their owne , which is a most euident argument of a most desperat cause ; or that they shall be condemned by their owne verdict & sentence ; or lastly that there can be no forme of speech so plaine , no words so cleare , no sentence so manifest , which they with their faigned figures & deuises will not wrest , frustrate ,
and

and delude; which is in effect to difanull al kind
of proofe which is taken out of words or teſtimonies whatſoeuer . For I will bring ſo plaine
teſtimonies of theirs, as plaine can ſcarce or not
at all be deuiſed; I will bring ſo many, as themſelues will require no more ; I will bring ſo
weighty , as themſelues will demaund none
more weighty; I wil bring them alſo moſt freely
and often iterated and repeated; laſtly I will
bring not only thoſe which indirectly and by
conſequence proue that which I would , but
thoſe alſo, & that eſpecially & ofteneſt, which
directly teſtify that which they are brought
to confirme . Wherfore either they will not
delude theſe words of theirs , or they wil delude
all wordes whatſoeuer ; And either they will
not refuſe theſe their owne teſtimonies and confeſſions, or they will reiect all teſtimonies and
iudgements whatſoeuer , which is in effect to
confeſſe that their cauſe is moſt deſperate and
moſt worthy to be reiected and condemned of
all .

    Moſt ef-
fectuall .   This maner alſo of proofe is moſt effectuall , for what can be of greater force to conuince a man , then his owne iudgement and
acknowledgement of the truth? Surely vnleſſe a
By reaſō . man will profeſſe himſelfe to be en enemy of
truth, and of the number of them who ſee good
and follow bad , he muſt needs imbrace that
                        truth

The preface to the Reader.

truth which himselfe confesseth. Experience also sheweth the same. For when our Sauiour could neither by infinite miracles nor euident scriptures stop the mouthes of the Iewes, he so conuinced them out of their owne words, that (as the Euangelist writeth) *they answeared him not a word nor from that day any durst aske him a question.* And the Donatists, when they made answeare to the Catholikes arguments taken out of scripture, were so intangled in their owne fact touching the Maximinists, as (sayth S. (d) Augustine (*they euer more stood dumbe at that.* And now we see, that Protestants are tonguetied at no sort of bookes so much, as at those, which are composed of their owne testimonies. This manner of dealing vsed the holy Fathers against the Pagans, as is to bee seen in Clement, Tertullian, Origen, Cyprian, Arnobius, Lactantius, Augustin, and others; and against heretiques also, as appeareth in the sayd S. Augustin. S. Hierome, and others, most often, and the same they most highly commend. For thus writeth (e) S. Denis of Alexandria: *It helpeth me much, that I can disproue them out of their owne wordes.* S. (f) Gregorie Nazianzen: *It is the greatest cunning and wisdome of speach to bind* (the Aduersary) *with his owne wordes.* And (g) Tertullian, or Nouatian: *It is a strong kind of proofe, which is taken of the ad-*

uersary

(marginal notes:)

By experience.

Matt. 22.

(d) In collat. 3. diei c.11.

By the Fathers.

(e) In Euseb. l 7. c. 6.

(f) Orat. de S. Basil.

(g) De Trini. c. 13.

uerſary, that truth may be proued euē by the enemyes of truth. S. (^h) Ireneus: *We often diſgrace them by their owne doctrine.* And (ⁱ) S. Auguſtine: *Neither will I bring againſt thee any other ſentences for to ſhew the errour of Manichee, then out of thyne owne epiſtle*: Which worke of his he (^k) preferreth before al the other which he wrote againſt that hereſy. Nay, the ſame holy Fathers account this manner of dealing with heretiks neceſſary, and preferre it before all others. For thus ſayth S. Ireneus (^l) *It is needfull to diſproue the Valentinians by their Mothers, Fathers and Anceſtours.* And in another (^m) place: *That is a true and vnanſwerable proofe which bringeth atteſtation frō the aduerſaryes themſelues.* And (ⁿ) Tertullian: *The aduerſaryes teſtimony is eftſoones neceſſary.* Againe: *I muſt ſtrike them with their own weapons.* And (^o) S. Athanaſius, who was moſt tryed in combates with heretikes: *Againſt wranglers we muſt oppoſe their owne arguments, in which (ſayth he) I haue the greateſt hope of victory.* S. Chryſoſtome (^p) alſo: *We muſt conuince them by this, when we turne their owne ill ſayings againſt themſelues, as often as we make thoſe who were the famouſeſt amongſt them, their accuſers.* And laſtly (^q) S. Auguſtine the moſt fortunate champion of the Church againſt heretiks ſeeing that the Donatiſts could be euidently conuinced by their owne dealing with the Maximiniſts, exhorteth

(h) *Lib. 2. cap. 53.*
(i) *Lib. cont. Seūd. c. 3.*
(k) *Lib. 2. Retract. c. 50.*

(l) *Lib. 1. cap. 35.*
(m) *Lib. 4. c. 14.*
(n) *Lib. de anima c. 3.*

(o) *Atha. l. de carne Chriſti.*

(p) *Hom. 3. in epiſt. ad Tit.*

(q) *Lib. 1. cont. Petil. c. 27.*

horteth Catholikes to let alone all other kind of arguments, and still to vrge this only: *Remember (sayth he) this only fact of the Maximinists, cast this in their faces, answere to al obiections by the Maximinists alone.* And (r) againe: *I will not leaue this only fact which God hath put before their eyes to stop their mouthes, and to amend them if they be wise, or to confound them if they remayne obstinate.* And in like manner, when he saw, that the Donatists cause was quite ouerthrowne by that saying of theirs: *Neither one cause doth preiudice another, nor one person another*, he thus speaketh vnto Catholiques: (s)*I request you, I beseech you for Christs sake, that you remember it, speake it, and haue it euer in your mouthes. There could not be pronounced on our behalfe, a briefer, surer, and plainer sentence.* Thus you see how greatly the Fathers esteeme of this kind of dealing with herétikes, and how earnestly they vrge vs for to vse it.

(r) Ibid. cap. 18.

(s) Serm: 22. de verb. Apostol.

7. And Protestants ought the more to allow this kind of proceeding with them, because they much commend it, and preferre it before all others. Luther: *There (t) is no stronger proofe, then his owne confession, who is accused, and his testimony against himselfe.* And againe: *No (v) man can conuince a lyer better then by his own words.* Hethusius: *The (x) shortest way of al to conuince an aduersary is that which is taken out of his owne con-*
fession.

(t) De ser. arbit. fol. 442.

(u) Inc. 1. 1. Pet. fol. 449.

(x) Lib. de Cœna.

(y) Epist. Enchar .

session , wherwith he openly acknowledgeth that which is obiected. Lucas (y) Oſiander: *The confeſſion and teſtimōy of the aduerſary is of greateſt authority .* Peter (z) Martyr ; *Surely amongſt other teſtimonyes that is of greateſt weight, which is giuen by the enemies .* D Bancroft : *Let* (a) *vs take hold of that which they haue graunted You may be bold to build vpon it for a truth , that they are ſo cōſtrayned to yield vnto .* D (b) Whitaker : *It muſt needs be a ſtrong argument, which is taken out of the confeſſion of the Aduerſaryes . For the teſtimony of the aduerſaryes is of force againſt themſelues .* And (c) againe : *It is a notable matter and encreaſeth much the triumph for to be proued by the teſtimony of the aduerſaries.* And D. Morton in the Epiſtle dedicatory of his anſwere to the Proteſtants Apology : *VVhich kind of aſſiſtance of learned aduerſaryes the Apologiſts thēſelues haue layd down for the greateſt reaſon of ſatisfaction, & we do accordingly admit .* Nay, they begin to vſe this kind of arguing againſt vs, and vaunt much therof : *VVho may not* (ſayth the ſayd . D . (d) Morton) *iuſtly congratulate the Proteſtants happines , whome truth it ſelfe proceeding out of their aduerſaries mouths doth patroniz ?*

(z) Loc. tit. de ludæis fol. 390.

(a) Suruey c. 8. pag. 147.

(b) Cont. 292. c. 14.

(c) Præf. in Cant .

(d) Apol. l. 1 cap. 25. Differences betwixt Proteſt. manner of dealing & ours.

8   But , by their leaue , there are many and great differences betweene their and our kind of proceeding in this matter . Firſt many of the Catholikes, whome they produce againſt vs,

wrote

wrote before their Religion was risen, & therfore we answere that of them, which S. Hierom answered of the ancient Fathers, who liued before Arius appeared: *Before Arius* (sayth he) *arose in Alexandria like a noon-tide Diuell, they spake some things innocently and not so warily, which cannot escape the obloquie of certaine peruerse men.* And which S. Augustin answered of S. Chrysostom when the Pelagians alleadged his testimony. *Discoursing* (sayth he) *in the Catholike Church, he thought not that he was otherwise vnderstood. None was yet troubled with such a question; you not yet iangling, he spake more securely.* But the Protestāts which we produce liued al afterthat protestancy was both bred and hatched, & after the Catholike fayth had for many ages shined through out the world, and therfore could not be ignorant what wordes of theirs might make for the Catholike fayth, and preiudice their owne cause. Another difference is, that none of the Catholikes whose testimonyes Protestants alleage against vs, is accounted of vs for a man sent extraordinarily of God, and much lesse for a Prophet, Euangelist, or Apostle. Nay, many of them are obscure writers, and of small or no reckoning among vs, some of them are not held for Catholikes of vs, and some of them euen by the iudgments of Protestants themselues are our open enemyes. But the confessions of fayth

Lib. 2. contr. Rufin.

Lib. 2. cont Iul. c. 6.

Cassander Erasmus. Cornelius Agrippa. Marsil of Padua.

Beatus Rhenanus Faber Stapulensis, Orthuinus Gratius.

**   which

which we cite against Protestāts containe their faith, so that they cannot be reiected of them, vnles they will renounce their fayth. And of the men whose testimonyes we produce, one is accounted of them a (e) God, another a Prophet an (f) Euangelist, an Apostle, a third Elias, an Angell. His writings are held for inspired from heauen, for a rule of fayth, and equall to the writinges of the Apostles. Another is called a (g) great and admirable Prophet, others are esteemed for lights, lampes, bright starres, props, founders, parents, renewers of the Protestants church and religion. Others are men extraordinarily sent and diuinely raised to lighten the world; most of them for very learned, famous & well deseruing of the Protestant religion; & finally all for sincere Protestants. The holy Fathers were wont to refute both the (h) Pagans superstition and the (i) heretikes errours out of the Diuels confessions. Of which kind of proof (k) Tertullian, vsing it, maketh this account: *What more manifest then this fact? what more sure then this proofe? Belieue them, they speake true of themselues, who vse to credit them when they lye. No man lyeth to his owne disgrace.* And S. (l) Cyprian: *Who so sayest that thou worshipest the Gods belieue euen them whom thou worshippest.* And likewise Minutius in Octauio: *Neither do they lye to their owne shame, especially if some of you be by.* Be-

lieue

(e) *Humf. ad Rat. 4. Camp.*
(f) *Colloq. Aldebnr. Schusseib. Catal. 13.*
Hunius præfat. de liber.arbit.
(g) *Danæ. lib. 4. de Eccles.c.9. Beza ep. 6.*
(h) *iustin. dial. cum Tryphon. Augu∫t.l. de ciuit. Chrysost. hom. 26.in 2. Cor. Cyril. l. 6. in Iulian.*
(i) *Hier cont. Vigilant. Ambros. serm. 5. de Sanctis. Hilar. l. 1, & 6. de Trinit.*
(k) *Apol. cap. 22.*
(l) *Lib. ad Demetr.*

ßene themselues witnessing that they are Diuels, and confessing the truth of themselues. But our proofe taken out of the Protestants confessions of faith & out of Luther & such like famous Protestants testimony against Protestancy, is much more euident and stronger; both becaufe it is more likely that man will confesse the truth, though against themselues, then the Diuell the father of lyes and sworne enemy of truth; as also becaufe the confessions of the Diuel were extorted from him by force, as the Fathers themselues doe acknowledge, but these of Luther and his mates come most freely from them. Belieue therefore (O Protestants) your chiefe leaders, your founders, Instructors Prophets, Euágelists, & Apost. les, in that which they freely & of their own accord côfeffe of themselues & of their doctrine. Euen by the testimony of your own Prophets & teachers belieue, that Protestacy is newly risen, first founded by Luther, & before knowne to none. No man willingly lyeth to his owne shame; no man freely confesseth that which ouerthroweth his owne cause, but which he cannot deny. No man knew protestancy better then they, no man fauoured it more then they. *Who (sayth Caluin) is to be credited touching Popery, more then the Pope himselfe?* And whom shal we belieue touching the author and hatching of protestancy amongst the Lutherans, rather then

Note.

De ver Ecclesiæ form.

**2   Luther

Luther himselfe , Melancthon , the Century-
writers, Kemnice, Schuffelburg, and the like?
Or amongst the Sacramentaryes , rather then
Zuinglius, Bullinger, Bucer, Peter Martyr, Caluin, Beza, Pleffie, and such others ? or amongst
English Protestants rather then Iewell , Fox ,
Whitaker, Fulke , Humfrey , Perkins, and the
like, whose frequent and plaine confeffions we
heerin produce. A third difference between our
and the Protestants manner of proceeding in
this kind of proofe is, that Proteftantes oftentymes alleadge Catholikes teftimonyes corrupted, mangled, and falfifyed ; and fometymes also the obiections which they make againft thé-
felues, infteed of their anfweres , as Cardinall
conferen- Peron not long fince fhewed Pleffie to haue don
rence at before the French King , euen by the iudgment
fountaine of Protestant themfelues . And it were eafy to
Bel-eaue . demonftrate that D.(m) Morton hath done the
like in his Apology . But I produce the teftimo-
(m) *Apol.* nyes of Protestants certaine and entiere, at leaft
part.1.l. 1. for that fenfe for which I alleadge them . For I
c.23. l.2.c. haue cited none in this worke which either I
41.part.2. haue not feene with myne owne eyes, and for
l. c. 35. l.2. the moft part haue quoted not only the bookes
c. 41. and cháp ters but alfo the leaues and pages, or if
I haue wanted the booke, I haue cited them out
of fome good Author . The fourth difference &
that of great moment is, that the Catholiques ,
whose

whose testimonyes Protestants alleadge against
is (if so be they were true Catholikes) were alwayes ready to reuoke and recall whatsoeuer
they had written contrary to the catholik fayth,
& to submit all their wordes or writings to the
censure of the catholike Church , which to be
the mind & disposition of all Catholiks, Protestants themselues confesse . For thus writeth D.
(n) Whitaker : *This is the condition, this the con-* (n) *Contr.*
sent of the Popish Church, that all hang their salua- 2. *q.*5. *c.*8.
tion vpon one man , and submit themselues to one
mans iudgment. And D . (o) Morton : *Is there a-* (o) *Apol.*
ny Papist that thinkes any decree of the Pope can be *part.* 1'. *l.*
contemned or broken without cryme or heresy ? 1. *cap.* 31.
Which sith it is so, in vaine do they obiect any
Catholikes words against the Catholike fayth.
For either they are not contrary thereto, or if
they be, they are already reuoked , recalled and
disanulled by himselfe . But the mind and proceeding of Protestāts is far otherwise, who subiect not their opinions to the iudgment of the
Church, but as they thinke that she may erre,
so will they hold their opinions notwithstanding her sentence to the contrary ; and therfore
iustly may we produce their testimonies against
their owne Church .

9. The fift difference, & which is much to be
noted , is, that Protestants alleadge Catholik
witnesses in matters of doctrin , in which some

* * 3   tymes

The preface to the Reader.

August.l. *11. cont.* *Faust. c. 5.* tymes by reason of the obſcurity of the matter a man may chance to erre & ſlip; or els in ſuch matters of fact, as were in times or places far diſtant from them, ſo that themſelues could not ſearch the truth, but belieued the reports of others. Such a queſtion is that of Pope *Ioane*, in which Proteſtants cite no Catholike author which liued not ſome ages after that time, wherin Pope *Ioan* is ſayd to haue beene. Or if they produce any Catholike Author in any matter of fact, the truth wherof he might haue tried, either he is of no credit, or the matter is ſuch, as it turneth to no preiudice of the Catholike faith. But we heer produce Proteſtants in a matter of fact, & ſuch a matter as they could moſt eaſily know. For what was more eaſy, then for Luther and his felloweſto try either then or euer ſince, whether, when he firſt began, there was in the world any Proteſtant company, whether it were viſible, whether it had Paſtours, and the like? For who can thinke, that only the Proteſtant company could lye ſo cloſe hid, that neither in all Luthers time or euer ſince, either the being, or the eſtate or condition, or place or Paſtours, or any thing at all therof could be eſpied out of ſo many Arguſes, which now in one whole age haue ſifted all corners of the world to find it out? And beſides, this is ſuch a queſtion of Fact, as vpon the deciſion therof

an

an end may be made of all cōtrouerſies betweene Catholikes and Proteſtants. For (as I ſayd
before) if Luther be the Author and beginner
of the Proteſtant Church , it is certaine, that
it is not the Church of Chriſt , nor to be followed of Chriſtians, but to be forſaken & dete-
ſted. To which I ad now, that if Luther himſelf
& ſuch & ſo many learned & famous Proteſtāts
as I haue cited, do by many wayes, & ſo plainly confeſſe , that Luther was the Author therof,
it cānnot be doubted , but that he was in truth
the Author of it. For I alleadge not men of
ſmall credit among Proteſtants , but ſuch as are
of greateſt authority with them ; nor a few ,
but many ; nor of one nation alone, but of
diuers , to wit , Germans , Italians , French ,
Engliſh , Scottes , Flemings and others ; not
Proteſtants of one ſort or ſect , but of all three
namely Lutherans, Sacramétaries and Engliſh
Proteſtants. So that they could not beare falſe
witneſſe in this matter either for wāt of knowledge , becauſe they were many and learned &
of different countries , and moſt diligent in
ſearching the matter, and the matter it ſelfe
moſt eaſy ; nor for want of good will towards
the cauſe, becauſe they were all moſt earneſt
Proteſtants. And to refuſe the teſtimonies of
ſuch witneſſes in a matter of faƈt, in their owne
time , ſo eaſy to be knowne , and ſo diligently

* * 4   ſearched

searched of them, what other thing is it, then obstinately to refuse to know the truth of this matter so important to be knowne, and wherby may be made an end of all contentions in Religion? Wherfore let Protestants say as they **Note.** please, that in questions of doctrine they will not depend vpon Luther, Caluin, or any one, or all their doctours together, but vpon the scripture alone: Neuertheles in matter of fact, wherof the scripture saith nothing, (such as this is (for the Scripture telleth not what was the state and condition of the Protestant Church when Luther began, in what place it was, what Pastours it had, who saw it, and the like) either they must confesse, that they refuse all triall & knowledge of so important a truth, or they must giue credit to the deposition of sufficient witnesses. And if euer men were or can be sufficiet witnesses of any matter of Fact, Luther and those Protestants which here I produce, are sufficient witnesses of that which I bring them for to testify. And thus much touching the cause why I proue Luther to haue been the founder of Protestant Religio only by the testimonies of Protestants.

Why so many Protestãts testimonyes are alleaged. 10. As for the reason why I alleadge so many Protestants, that is, that it many appeare, that it is not the priuate testimony of some one or few, but the generall consent of them all, or

a£

at leaſt the common ſentence of many of them.
And if I ſeeme to any Catholike ouer tedious in
heaping vp ſo many teſtimonies of Proteſtants,
I pray him to cōſider, that I write not this book
to Catholikes to confirme them in the Catholike faith, who I know to that end doe not need
the teſtimonies of Proteſtants; but that I write
it partly to Catholikes, for to furniſh them
with ſtore of Proteſtants teſtimonies to ſtopp
their mouthes, and to ſhew them that they are
right Heretikes, that is, condemned (as the
Apoſtle ſpeaketh) by their owne iudgement,
to which end a few teſtimonies of theirs would
not ſuffice. And therfore to ſuch as intend this
end the multitude of teſtimonies will not be
troubleſome . For who, that indeauoureth to
vāquiſh moſt obſtinate enemies, will complain
of the abundance of good ſoldiers wherof he
may make choice ? And if I had rehearſed only
ſome few teſtimonies, and named the places
where the reſt may be found, ſome would haue
cauilled, as M . Iewel did againſt D . Harding,
that I had cited dumbe witneſſes. Beſides, ſeing
the iudgments of men are diuers, it may fall out,
that what kind of teſtimonyes ſeem ſtrong &
forcible to ſome, others acount but weake and
litle to the purpoſe; and therfore it was behofull,
that there ſhould be as it were a ſtore-houſe of
Proteſtants teſtimonies, that euery one might

** ⸫

take

take what weapon he thinketh fitteſt for him , & vſe it againſt them . But eſpecially I gathered theſe teſtimonies of Proteſtants for the Proteſtants themſelues, that by their owne mens iudgement I might withdraw them from their errour . And therfore I was not ſo fearfull to bring too many for Catholikes , as carefull to prouide inough for Proteſtants . In which I could hardly offend by multitude . For as S (p) Vigil ſaith, *Mans mind poſſeſſed with the errour of a falſe opinion , is hard and ſlow to perceiue truth , with how many witneſſes ſo euer it be vrged therto* . Or as (q) Tertullian writeth *much talke in matter of edification is not foule if at any time it be foule* . And (r) S. Hierom: *delay is no loſſe, when by delay the victory is more aſſured.* Wherupon S. Auguſtin counſaileth vs, not to regard and delay whatſoeuer , ſo we bring good proofe of what we ſay. Beſides, (t) Proteſtants deny that we ought to iudge of them by one or few; though they be Paſtors , and (u) write that M. Brierly in his Proteſtants Apologie , although it be ſtuffed with all kind of Proteſtant teſtimonies, hath brought but a few teſtimonies . And as S. (x) Auguſtin ſaith of the Donatiſts , they *are ready to deny vvhat they can* . Or as S (y) Hierome ſpeaketh : *Shutting their eyes deny vvhat they vvould vvere not* . For what could be more impudently denyed, then that which D . (z) Field denyeth

(p) *Lib.* 1 .

(q) *Lib. de Patient .*

(r) *Lib.* 1. *cont . Iou.*

(ſ) *De geſtis cum Emerit .*

(t) *VVbi. cont.* 295. *c.* 17. *l.* 1. *de ſcript. c.* 11. *ſect .* Sadeel . in Refut . Poſnan . *c.* 11.

(u) White in defence of his way . *c.* 7.

(x) *Lib* 3. *cont. Creſ. c.* 6.

(y) *Epiſt. ad Cteſiph* .

(z) *Lib.* 3. *de Eccleſ* . 6. 6. 8. 49.

denieth that when Luther began , the publique
and generall face of Religion in the Westerne
Church was Papisticall? These men need haue
their mouthes shut , and their eares stopt with
multitude of testimonies . For as (a) Caluin
saith *) it is the part of wicked & furious obstinacie,* (a) *Instit.*
to discredit so many and so authenticall testimonies . 3. *c.* 25. §. 3.
Or as an (b) other sayth : *sin a matter of great*
importance one only witnes were alleadged, what place (b) *Præfa.*
would his testimony find? But vnder so many and so *Synt. conf.*
great witnesses as are heere produced all pretext of
not receauing the truth is taken away. In so great
certainty of so many witnesses how is there so great
loue of darknes, that they open not their eyes to see
the light? So which I add that saying of Varius
in (c) Cicero : *Either these witnesses will suffice,* (c) *Lib.* 2.
or nothing will suffice Neuerthelesse, that I might *de finibus.*
both somewhat ease the wearines of Catholikes
in reading so many testimonyes, and better set
before the eyes of Protestants the force of their
testimonyes, I doe for the most part marke in
the margent those testimonyes which are most
forcible, & after I haue recited them all, I gather
the force and summe of them togeather which
he may read, who loatheth to runne ouer so
many.

11. I bring also diuers testimonies of the Why ma-
same Protestants , especially of Luther , that it ny testi-
may appeare, that that confession slipt not from same m̄.
of the same m̄.

him

him vnawares and vnaduiſedly, but that it was
his conſtant iudgement, if there can be any

conſtancy in heretikes. For I remember that (d)
Beza, for to couer Caluins foule contradictiõs
of himſelfe, wrote; *As if of that vvhich one hath*

vvrittenbriefly in ſome pl.ce, t vvere to be gathe-
red vvhat he thought of euery point of doctrine . I
graunt notwithſtanding, that I haue brought
ſome teſtimonies which are not ſo cleare, as of
themſelues they would conuince the matter;
Yet ſuch they are as ſtrengthen thoſe that are
cleare, and of them receiue light. For as in
gathering an armie not only ſtout men but alſo
ſome other are choſen, who may increaſe the
ſtrength of thoſe that are ſtout, and likewiſe
may be encouraged by them; ſo it fareth alſo in
gathering teſtimonies. Neither yet did I gather
all that occurred:but only ſuch as ſeemed more
to the purpoſe. It will alſo delight the reader to
ſee how ſome Proteſtants plainly and roundly
confeſſe the truth, others deale more craftily &
cloſely, and in them he ſhal eſpy that difference

which S. Auſtin (e) noted between Celeſtius,
and Pelagius, of whome he writeth, *that he was*
more opẽ this more cloſe, he more obſtinate, this more
falſe, he more free, this more wily . If any aske how
it fell out, that Proteſtãts ſhould giue ſuch plain
teſtimonies againſt their own cauſe; I anſwere,
that there were many cauſes heerof. Firſt the e-
uidence

uidéce of truth, which maketh its enemies, yea the deuils themselues sometimes to confesse it : *The very coyners of lyes (sayth (f) S. Basil) oftentyms catcht with the euidence of truth, as with a snare, euen against their wills do witnes it.* Againe, *It is the nature of lyes to bewray themselues,* like (g) as Tertullian writeth : *Theeues commonly leaue some thing behind them, which bewrayeth them.* For as S. Augustine (h) sayth : *It is incredible, that he should not be taken by lyes, who lyeth to take others.* Or as S. Basil (i) hath : *So it is, that euill is not only contrary to good but also to it selfe.* And Luther (k) himselfe : *There is no heretike, who is not found of spirituall men to speak against himself in his lyes.* And els where : *This happeneth to the wicked, that by lying they cannot beware not to bewray thē-selues by their wordes. They lye some while an some-tymes, but continually they cannot. At last lyes be-wray themselues especially with them who marie and obserue. For there escapeth some word from them with which they are taken.* The same confesse (l) Caluin, (m) Beza, (n) Whitaker, and others. Another cause is, because Protestants (as here-tiques are wont to do, and (o) themselues con-fesse that they practise it) accommodate their sayings and doctrine to time, place, and occa-sions, & therfore vtter those sayings which we here alleadge, before whome and when they thinck they will make to their purpose ; but

where

(f) *Lib. 2. cont. Eun.*

(g) *Lib. 5. cont. Mar.*

(h) *In senc. Prof.*
(i) *Lib. 1. cont. Eun.*
(k) *In cap. 12. Mat. in cap. 4. & 37. Genes.*
(l) *Resp. ad Nebul. & admon. vlt.*
(m) *Cont. Castel. p. 421.*
(n) *Cont. 1. q. 2. c. 3. & q. 5. c. 8.*
(o) *Zuin. 1. de relig. c. de Euch. Hospin. part. 2. fol 90. colloq. Aldeb fol 154. Schuslelb. som. 7. catal p. 126.*

The preface to the Reader.

where they see they will hurt their cause, either they deny them, or seeke by friuolous and fond expositions to auoyd and delude them. So the Donatists (as (p) Augustin noteth) would not confesse that, which would haue confounded them, when the Catholikes vrged it, *but after when an other point was in handling*. A fourth cause may be giuen, that as the Scorpion affordeth a remedy for her sting, and of the vipers flesh is made the counterpoyson; so God hath ordayned, that heretiques affoard sufficient meanes to refute their errors: *Neither yet therfore (as S. (q) Augustin writeth) giue we any thanks to them, but to God alone. For that they should for our cause produce & discouer all these things by speaking or writing, truth enforced them, not charity inuited them.* And (r) Luther himselfe : *So must the enemies of truth confound and mock themselues for a reward of their blasphemies.* And (s) againe: *Since God ordayneth that folly is alwayes ioyned with malice, Cain betrayeth himselfe. And for this cause the defence of truth is easy against the aduersaries therof.* Wherupon (t) Holpinian thus writeth of the Lutherans : *They are become grieuous enemyes and aduersaryes, not so much of others, as of themselues; surely by a most euident testimony of Gods iudgment, and a worthy punishment and confusion for these kind of ambitious and contentious men.* Which I would God Protestants would obserue,

(p) Lib. ad Donat. past collat.

(q) Supr. c.33.

(r) Cont. R. Angl. fol. 345.

(s) In cap. 4. Genes.

(t) Hospi. part. 2. histor. fol. 39.

obſerue, not in Lutherans only, but alſo in other Proteſtants. For they ſhould find, that they haue no heauier aduerſaries then themſelues, & that Proteſtants (as (ⁿ) Lactantius wrote of Cice-ro) cannot be more ſorely confuted, then they are by Proteſtants themſelues.

(u) *Lib.* 3. c. 9.

Faultes

Faults escaped in the printing.

Page	Line	Fault	Correction
81.	11.	himelf	himselfe
82.	27.	vnles he	vnles he be
96.	6.	numb. 66.	numb. 96.
107.	19.	The	There
109.	23.	light of	*dele* of
120.	4.	credible	incredible
127.	7.	the	these
131.	6.	*dele*	haue bin
137.	2.	be	be by
140.	6.	fourth	third
147.	33.	waye	waxe
154.	7.	in	is
168.	23.	sonde	sponge
169.	3.	one	our
170.	33.	1525.	1535.
181.	14.	should only	should only say
184.	27.	predigious	prodigious
205.	31.	boasteth	boasteth that
219.	vlt.	Taye	Faye
221.	33.	of fayth	faith of
222.	21.	first	fifth.

If any other faults haue escaped, it is desired of the Gentle
Reader, to correct them of his courtesy, the Author being
far absent from the Print.

THE

THE FIRST BOOKE.

*Of the substance of the Protestants Church
and Religion, and of their vncertainty therein.*

CHAP. I.

BECAVSE, as after Plato and A-ristotle, Tully sayth very truly: *VVhosoeuer will according to the order of reason treat of any thing, must first define or explicate the nature thereof, that it may be knowne what it is whereof he speaketh;* and Protestants agree, that the definition is *the very ground of all disputation;* before I do shew, who was the first author of the Protestant Church and Religion (which I will do in the second booke) I will in this first define and determine what is a Protestant, and what is the Protestant Church and Religion. And because Protestants in this matter (as in all others) are variable and inconstant, sometymes requiring many things to the making and constitution of a Protestant, & sometymes being content with very

Lib. 1. offic

Caluin. 3. Institut. cap. 4. §. 1. Sadeel. in Refut. Thes. Posnan. cap. 2.

A   few

few things, sometyms stretching the bounds of their
Church most largly, otherwhiles drawing the very
strait, according as it serueth to their present purpose; I will first discouer this their vncertainty a-
bout so weighty a matter, & afterward out of their
owne principles and confessions of fayth, set downe
what is indeed necessary to the very substance and
being of a Protestant, and of their Church and Religion. And in this Chapter I will shew, how few
they sometymes do admit to be of the Church, and
how many things they require to the making of a
Protestant; and in some chapters following, how
many they at other tymes do graunt to be of their
Church, and how few things they account necessary for to be a member thereof. That done I will
make manifest, what is indeed necessary thereto.

They ex-
clude Pa-
pists.

2.   First of all therefore they sometymes exclude Catholiques, (whome they terme Papists)
out of the Church, as is manifest by all their writings, in so much that the French Protestants in the
28. article of their confession say: *VVe openly affirme
that where the word of God is not receiued, nor there is any
profession of obedience due thereto, nor any vse of Sacraments,
there, properly speaking, we cannot iudge to be any Church.
VVherfore we condemne the Popish Conuenticles.* And D.
Whitaker in his second booke against Dureus & 2.
section, is so earnest that he sayth: *I will not allow the very name of a lawfull Church vnto the Roman Church, because
it hath nothing, which a true Church ought to haue* And both
he in his 2. Controuersy 6. question 3. Chapter, D.
Sutliue in his first booke of the Church 3. *cap.* and *lib.*
2. *cap.* 9. M. *Perkins* in his reformed Catholique towards the end, *Caluin* in his book against the Chaunter of Lions, *Beza* in his of the notes of the Church,

the

the Confession of Saxony in the Chapter of the Church, and many others do reckon diuers articles, for euery one whereof they pronounce Papists to be out of the Church. And becaufe their opinion herein is well inough knowne, and hereafter alfo we fhall haue occafio to fhew how haynoufly they condemne the Popedome or Papiftry, I will heere rehearfe no more of their fayings touching this point. The like fentence they fometymes pronounce of the Anabaptifts and Arians. For thus fpeaketh the confeffion of Aufpurg Cap. 9. *They condemne the Anabaptifts, who difallow the baptifme of infants, and think them to be faued without baptifme.* And the Confession of Switzerland cap. 20. *VVe condemne the Anabaptifts, who deny that infants ought to be baptized.* The fame is manifeft by the Englifh Confeffion c. 38. & by the Confeffion of Bafle c. 24 & others. Of Arians they giue this verdict in the forfayd Confeffion of Aufpurg in the firft article: *They condemne all herefies rifen againft this article (of the Trinity) as the Manichees, Arians, Eunomians &c.* And in like fort the French Confeffion art. 6. the Englifh art. 1. the confent of Poland, and others; in fomuch as in England the Proteftants haue burnt fome Arians.

3. Sometymes alfo they thruft out all heretickes. For thus writeth *Luther* in his explication of the Creed. *Neither Gentile, Iew, Heretike, or any finner is faued, vnleffe he make attonement with the Church, and in all things, thinke, do, and teach the fame.* And the Magdeburgians in the preface of their 6. Century: *Neither Heretikes, nor deuifers or patrons of fanaticall opinions, are of Chrift, but they are of Antichrift, and of the diuell, and appertaine to Antichrift and the diuell: they are the impoftume and the plague of the people of God.* The minifters of the Prince

A 2 Elector

Marginal notes: Anabaptifts. Arians. Heretiks Lutherãs.

Elector of Saxony in the Conference held at Aldburg, in the 3. writ, cast out of the Church all, *Who*
(say they) *wittingly and willingly defend such corruptions of*
doctrine, as haue byn condemned by the lawfull iudgment and
consent of the Catholike Church. And the Ministers of the
Duke of Saxony in the 4. writ of the sayd Conference, pronounce this sentence: *Whosoeuer they are,*
that do cloak and defend corruptions of the word of God, that
is, of the articles of fayth, after they haue byn admonished; we
iudge not to be true members of Christ, vnlesse they repent. And
Vrbanus Regius, one of the first and cheifest scho-
lers of *Luther*, in his Catechisme sayth: *All Heretikes*
are out of the Church. The same teacheth Schusselburg,
a principall superintendent amongst the *Lutherans* in
his Catalogue of heresies, and many others. As for
Sacra-   the Sacramentaries, thus professeth the French Con-
mētaries . fession in the 6. article: *We detest all Sects and heresies*
which haue byn reiected by the holy Fathers as S. Hilary, S. A-
thanase, S. Ambrose, S. Cyrill. Whereupon Sadeel in his
preface of his answere to the abiured articles, sayth:
Our Confession of fayth condemneth all Heretikes. Likewise
the Confession of Basle in 24. article writeth in this
sort: *We driue away all, whosoeuer dissenting from the so-*
ciety of the holy Church, do either bring in, or follow strange &
wicked doctrines. And Peter Martyr in his Common
places, in the title of heretiks: *This in summe I will say,*
heretikes are not otherwise to be dealt with all, then Infidells &
Iewes. Caluin also in his 2. booke of Institutions
cap. 15. number. 1. *Rightly Augustin denyeth Heretikes to*
haue the same foundation with the godly, albeit they preach the
name of Christ. And in his instruction against the Li-
bertines: *That we may speake properly, Heretikes are not on-*
ly like to wolues or theeues, but much worse. Beza in his book
of punishing Heretiks: *If one terme Heretikes faithlesse*
apostata,

apostatas , he shall giue them their due title. And againe:
Heretikes affirme Christ in word, and deny him indeed. Danæus in his 5.Controuersy and 691. pag. *An heretike,
condemned by lawfull iudgement , and actually cast out of the
Church, is not of the visible Church, nor of the inuisible neither,
actually or apparently , so long as he remaineth in that state .*
Polanus in his 7. booke which he termeth Syntag-
ma, cap.5. *Heretikes, whiles they remayne such are not members of the Catholique Church.* And Vorstius in his Anti-bellarmin pag.79. *The Ghospellers do esteem Antichrist
in common to be euery heretike who opposeth himselfe eyther
openly and plainly,or closely and indirectly to Christ and his doctrine.* And in the 121. pag. *There is no controuersy betweene vs and our aduersaries touching heretikes, Schismatikes
and Apostatas properly and truly so called , that they are altogether out of the Church of Christ .* Thus forraine Protestants. In England, his Maiesty in his epistle to Car-
dinal Peron written by Casaubon: *The King dam-
neth and detesteth those , who either haue departed from the
fayth of the Catholike Church, and are become heretikes,or from
the Communion , and are become Schismatikes.* The Apology of the Church of England part.3.diuis.3. *VVe condemne all sortes of the old heretiks , as the Arians, the Eutichians
&c. and shortly, all them that haue a wicked opinion either of
God the Father, or of Christ, or of the holy Ghost , or of any other
point of Christian Religion : for so much as they be confuted by
the Ghospell of Christ we plainly pronounce them for damnable
and detestable persons, and defy them euen to the diuell.* D. Whitaker in the preface of his Controuersies : *If we be heretikes , it is reason they should warne all theirs to fly from vs .*
And Controuer.2. question. 1. cap. 4. *That he proueth
heretikes and Apostatas and Schismatikes not to be members of
the true Church maketh nothing against vs. None of our men
euer taught that .* The like he hath question 5.cap. 1.

English Prote-stants.

A 3   and

and 18. D. Sutliue in his firt booke of the Church cap. 1. *Heretikes are not of the Church* . D. Morton in his Apology 1.part. 1. booke cap. 3. affirmeth, that *Heretikes are not to be accounted of the Church in truth but in name, not indeed but equiuocally.* Finally D. White in his way to the Church pag 110 . *All heretickes teach the truth in some things, and yet we deny them to be the Church of God.* And in the defence of the same way cap.8. sect. 1. *There is little or no difference betweene the Diuell and an Apostata, or Heretike* .

They exclude Schismatikes.

4. The same censure they sometymes giue of Schismatikes, as appeareth by the words of his Maiesty, D. Whitaker, and Vorstius already rehearsed. Besides , Luther in his great Catechisme tom. 5. pag.628. affirmeth the sense of that article , *The Communion of Saints* , to be this : *I belieue that there is on earth a litle Congregation of Saints, agreeing in all things without sectes or Schismes.* And Melancthon in his book against

Lutherãs.

Swenfeild tom. 2. pag. 201. *Neither is there more then one Church, the Spouse of Christ, neither doth this company consist of diuers Sectes.* Salomon Gesnerus in his Common places the 24.place of the Church : *Catholiks are opposite to Schismatikes & heretiks.* The same teacheth Schusselburg in his 8. tome of the Catalogue of heretikes, pag. 726 . 727 . Amongst the Sacramentaries , the

Sacramētaries.

Switzers in their Confession, article 17. do thus professe: *VVe so much esteeme the Communion with the true Church of Christ, as that we teach, that those cannot liue before God ; who communicate not with his true Church.* And the French Protestants in theirs , article 26. *VVe belieue, that none can lawfully withdraw themselues from the assemblies.* Bullinger in his Epitome or Compendium of fayth 6.booke, 11. cap: *They be out of this Church, who vpon enuy or contention separate themselues from her, & without*

cause

cause will haue some thing peculiar to themselues . Musculus
also in his common places, in the title of the church:
The vnity of Heretiks and Schismatikes is bastard and diuided.
True, entier , and Catholike vnity is not among Schismatikes.
And in the title of Schismatikes : *A Schismatike putteth*
himselfe in daunger of losse of his saluation , in departing from
the Communion of the flock of the Lord. For by that departure ,
he is not only separated and diuided from that Ecclesiasticall and
externall society of the faythfull , but also from participation of
the bloud and spirit of Christ . Caluin likewise in his treatise of the necessity of reforming the Church : *VVe do*
professe the vnity of the Church, such as is described by S. Paul,
to be most deare vnto vs ; and we accurse all them, that shall any
way violate it. And in his fourth booke of Institutions
chap. 1. numb. 2 : *Vnlesse vnder Christ our head, we be vnited*
to all the rest of his members , there is no hope for vs of the euerla-
sting inheritance. For we cannot haue two or three (Churches)
vnlesse Christ be torne in pieces. And num. 4. *Out of the lap*
the Church there is no saluation : departure from thence is al-
wayes pernicious. Againe num. 10 : *God maketh so great ac-*
count of the Communion with his Church as he holdeth him for a
renagate and fugitiue, whosoeuer obstinatly separateth himselfe
from any Christian society , which retaineth the true vse of the
word and Sacraments. And he addeth, that the forsaking
of the Church , *Is the deniall of God and Christ.* The like
doctrine he deliuereth in his Catechisme , vpon the
1. Cor. cap. 1. and other where Polanus in his Theses
part. 2. sayth : *Schismaticall Churches are to be forsaken.* And
Bucanus in his places, loc . 41. of the Church, quest.
33. auouchcth Schismatiks to be out of the Church,
and quest. 5. that *they are not vniuocally a Church,* that is,
they haue not the true nature of a Church. The same
sayth Danæus in his treatise of Antichrist cap. 17.
And in his 3. booke of the Church cap. 5. writeth
thus:

thus: *Schismatikes actually excommunicated and cast out of the Church by lawfull sentence, are no more of the visible Church. For (sayth he) the marke that you be of the visible Church, is this, that you outwardly professe the fayth, and communicate in Sacraments with the rest of the Church.* And he addeth, that such are neither *actually of the inuisible Church, but only in possibility, and that the holy Fathers liken such to Heathens, Pagans, and Infidells.* And in his Apology for the Switzers Churches he defineth Schisme to be *a separation from the rest of the body of the Catholike Church.* Zanchius also in his treatise of the Church cap. 7. teacheth, that Schismatikes are not in the Church. And Iunius in his 3. booke of the Church c. 5. approueth the same of such Schismatikes, as separate themselues from the whole Church. The strangers in England writing to Beza in the 24. epistle haue these words in their 13. article: *VVhosoeuer is lawfully excommunicated of a particuler Church, or cutteth himselfe of vpon vnlawfull causes, and with scandall, in that doth loose all priuiledge of the Catholike Church.* And Beza answereth them in the name of the Church of Geneua in this manner: *Your thirteenth article we wholy receiue as most orthodoxall.* Casaubon in his 15. exercitation against Baronius num. 6. *It is an vndoubted truth, that how often soeuer a pious flock is ioyned to a true Bishop, there is a Church of God; in so much that if any forsake that Church, it cannot be doubted, but that he is out of the Church.* Finally, Chamier in his epistle to Armand, excludeth Schismatikes out of the Church, because (sayth he) *they want the sincerity of the Sacraments.* Amongst our English Protestants, his Maiesty in his foresayd epistle to Cardinall Peron. *All those testimonies of Augustin, proue only this, that there is no hope of saluation for those, who leaue the Communion of the Catholike Church; which the King willingly graunteth.* D. WhitakeR

English
Protestāts

ker in his 2. controuer. 5. queſt. 6. cap. ſayth : *It ſ*
falſe, that hereticall and Schiſmaticall Churches be true Chur-
ches. Againe: *The Catholike Church conſiſteth not of diuided,*
but of vnited members. And cap. 2 : *The true and Catholike*
Church is that, which conſiſteth of Catholiks. D. Fulke in his
booke of the ſucceſſion of the Church : *VVhat auailed it*
them to eternall ſaluation, to haue byn ſound in Religion and do-
ctrine, ſeing they were cut off from the Communion of the true
Church, in which alone ſaluation is, and from her true head?
VVhat skilleth it whether one, being drawne by hereſy or Schiſme,
from the body of Chriſt, be ſubiect to euerlaſting damnation? D.
Humfrey in his anſwere to the 3. reaſon of F. Campian: *VVe confeſſe, that he is vndone, who is ſeparated from*
the followſhip of the Church. And D. Feild in his firſt
booke of the Church, cap. 7 : *The name of the Catholike*
Church is applyed to diſtinguiſh men holding the fayth in vnity,
from Schiſmatiks. And in his 2. booke c. 2. he ſayth, that
Schiſmatikes are not Catholike Chriſtians. Thus
we ſee how Proteſtants ſometymes do teach, that
the true Church conſiſteth of Catholiks, & of members vnited not deuided, that it hath no Schiſmes or
Sects : That Schiſmatiks are not Catholiks, that
their vnity is not true, nor Catholike, that their
Churches ought to be forſaken, that they are not
vniuocally Churches, nor true Churches, that they
are not members of the true Church, but out of the
Church, altogeather out of the Church, and actually
neither of the viſible nor inuiſible Church, and that
this is an vndoubted truth: which cōfeſſion of theirs
muſt be well noted and kept in mind, for thereby is
ouerthrowne (as we ſhall ſee in the 2. booke) their
only argument wherwith they endeauour to proue,
that their Church was before Luther, and alſo is de-
faced their only eſſentiall mark of finding the true
A 5 Church,

Church, by the truth of doctrine. For Schiſmatikes (as we ſhall heare them confeſſe in the 2. booke) hold true doctrine, and neuertheles (as here they acknowledge) are not of the true Church .

They exclude thoſe that deny any fundamétal article.

5. In like manner they do commonly debarre from their Church, all ſuch as deny any principall or fundamentall point of fayth; Melancthon in his booke of common places in the title of the Church: *They are not members of the Church who pertinaciouſly maintaine errours oppoſite to the foundation.* And in his anſwere to the Bauarian articles : *Saints may haue errours, but not ſuch as ouerthrow the foundation .* In his examen of thoſe that are to take orders: *Agreement in the*

Lutherãs. *foundation, is a thing neceſſary to the vnity of the Church.* And vpon the 3. cap. of the 1. epiſtle to Timothy: *The foundation is held in the Church, otherwiſe there ſhould be no Church at all.* And in his 79. propoſition, tom. 4 : *It is moſt certaine, that thoſe companies are not the Church of God, who either are altogeather ignorant of the Ghoſpell, or impugne ſome article of the foundation, that is, ſome article of fayth or doctrine of the decalogue, or maintaine open idols.* Chemnitius in his common places pa. 3. title of the Church : *Neither can theſe be acknowledged for the true Church, who imbrace fundamentall errours.* And the Lutherans in the conference at Ratisbon, Seſ. 14. Hutter in his Analyſis of the Confeſſion of Auſpurg, Geſner in his 24. place, Adam Francis in his 11. place, and other Lutherans commonly agree, that the Church *cannot erre Fundamentally, or in the Foundation.* And the Confeſſion of Saxony giueth this note, to know who are in the

Sacramé- Church : *Thoſe who hold the Foundation.* As for Sacra-
taries. mentaries, Caluin in his 4. booke of Inſtitutions cap. 2. num 1 : *So ſoone as a lye hath broken into the caſtle of Religion, the ſumme of neceſſary doctrine is inuerted, the vſe of*
SACRA-

Sacraments is fallen, certainly the destruction of the Church ensueth, euen as a mans life is lost, when his throat is cut, or his vitall parts deadly wounded. And soone after: *It is certaine, that there is no Church, where lyes and errour haue gotten to the toppe.* And cap. 19. num. 17 : *VVithout doubt the Church of the faythfull must agree in all the heads of our Religion.* Sadeel in his answere to the Theses held at Posna cap. 12 : *I thinke the matter is thus to be defined by the word of God, that if any in what Church soeuer dissent in the foundation of fayth, and be obstinate in their errours : such appertaine not to the vnity of the Church.* The like he hath in his answere to Artbure, cap. 12. Vesinus in his Catechisme quest. 54. cap. 4 : *The whole Church erreth not, nor wholly, nor in the foundation.* Polanus in his Thesis of the Church sayth : *The Church erreth not in the foundation.* The same teacheth Zanchius in his treatise of the Church c. 7. Lubbertus in his 2. booke of the Church c. 3. Vorstius in his Anti-bellarmin pag 139. Bucanus in his 41. place, and other Sacramentaries commonly. And with them herein agree our English Protestants. For thus sayth his Maiesty in his epistle to Cardinall Peron : *The Churches are vnited in vnity of fayth and doctrine, in those heads which are necessary to saluation.* And D. Whitaker in the preface of his Controuersies : *The foundations of fayth are of that nature, that one being shaken, nothing in all religion remaineth sound.* And Contr. 2. quest. 4. cap. 1 : *We say, that the Church cannot erre in things simply necessary.* Which he often repeateth in the 2. cap. And quest. 5. cap. 17 : *If any fundamentall doctrine be takenaway, the Church straight way falleth.* And cap. 18 : *The fundamentall articles are those; on which our fayth relyeth, as the house vpon the foundation.* Againe : *If any fundamentall and essentiall principle of fayth be ouerturned or shaken, it cannot be truly called a Church.*

English Protestāts

And

And quest. 6. cap. 3 : *That is no true Church which taketh away one only foundation.* The same he teacheth in his 1. booke of the scripture cap. 7. sect. 8. and cap. 12. sect. 3. M. Perkins in his explication of the Creed : *If any man or Church, retaine, or defend, obstinatly, or of willfull ignorance, a fundamentall errour, we must not account them any more Christians or Churches.* D. Sutliue in his first booke of the Church cap. 1 : *Those blemishes take away the name of the true Church, which are against the grounds of fayth.* D. Feild in his 2. booke of the Church cap. 3 : *Purity free from fundamentall and essentiall errour, is necessarily required in the Church.* D. Morton in the 1. part of his Apology, booke 2. cap 38 : *Purity of doctrine in fundamentall principles of fayth, is required to the being and constitution of the Church.* And in his answere to the Protestants Apology l. 4. c. 3. Sect. 5 : *The deniall of fundamentall doctrines, doth exclude men from saluation, and disannulleth the name of the Church in the gainsayers.* D. White in his way to the Church pag. 110 : *VVe do not thinke euery company to be the true Church, that holdeth only some points of the true fayth : but it is requisite that the foundation be holden.* And in his defence of the way cap. 17 : *A fundamentall point is that which belongs to the substance of fayth, and is so necessary that there can be no saluation without the knowledge and explicite fayth thereof.* And surely they all, and at all tymes, ought to affirme this, seeing they deliuer truth of doctrine, as an essentiall marke of the Church, which they must needs vnderstand (and so Vorstius in his Anti-bellarmin pag. 148. expresseth it) of true doctrine in fundamentall points. And this their doctrine touching this matter, I earnestly commend to the memory of the Reader, because it is necessary to find out, what a Protestant is, and also is one of the grounds, whereby it may appeare,

that

that there was no Proteſtant Church before *Luther*,
becauſe before him there was no company which
held all the ſame fundamentall points of doctrine
which Proteſtants do hold.

6. Finally; they ſometyms ſhut out of their
Church all thoſe, who deny any one point of fayth,
be it fundamentall or other. For thus writeth the A-
pology of the Confeſſion of Auſpurge : *The Church of
Chriſt is not among them, who defend naughty opinions, contrary
to the Ghoſpell.* And *Luther* in his epiſtle to Gount Al-
bert : *It is not inough, if in other things he confeſſe Chriſt and
his Ghoſpell. For who denieth Chriſt in one article or word, denieth him, who is denied in all, becauſe there is but one Chriſt,
the ſame in all his words.* And vpon the 17.cap. of Deu-
teronomy : *Faith ſuffereth nothing, and the word tolerateth
nothing, but the word muſt be perfectly pure, and the doctrine
alwayes ſound throughout.* And vpon the 17. cap. of S.
Matthew : *Fayth muſt be round, that is, belieuing all articles,
though ſmall ones. For who belieueth not one article rightly, belieueth nothing rightly, as Iames ſayth, VVho offendeth in one, is
guilty of all : and ſo who in one article doubteth or belieueth not
(at leaſt obſtinatly) diſſolueth the roundnes of the graine, and ſo
can do no good.* And vpon the 5. cap. to the Galathians :
*In diuinity a ſmall errour ouerthroweth all the doctrine. Doctrine
is like to a Mathematicall point, it cannot be deuided, that is, it
cannot ſuffer either addition or detraction.* And when Zuinglius and his followers deſired of the Lutherans to
be eſteemed as their brethren, Melancthon (as Hoſpinian reporteth in his Sacramentarian hiſtory fol.
81.) roughly ſayd vnto them : *VVe meruaile with what conſcience they can account vs for brethren, whome they iudge to
erre in doctrine.* And againe fol. 82. *Luther grauely ſpake
vnto them, ſaying : he greatly merueiled how they could hold him
for a brother, if they thought his doctrine to be vntrue.* And the

They ex-
clude all
that deny
any arti-
cle of
fayth.

Lutheräs.

same

same Melancthon togeather with Brentius writeth thus to the Lantgraue : *Perhaps Christians, who are entangled in some errour, which they do not obstinatly defend, may be tolerated as brethren, but they which not only bring false doctrine into the Church, but also maintaine it, are not to be acknowledged for brethren.* And againe Melancthon in his examen of those who are to take orders, tom. 3. *There are in that company (of the Church) many who are not Saints, but yet agreeing in doctrine.* The Deuines of Wittemberg in their refutation of the orthodoxall consent pag. 73 : *Like as he who keepeth the whole law and offendeth in one (as Iames the Apostle witnesseth) is guilty of all : so who beleeueth not one word of Christ, albeit he seeme to beleiue the other articles of the Creed, yet beleeueth nothing, and is to be damned as incredulous.* For euery heretike did not impugne euery article of fayth, but commonly each of them of purpose impugned some one or other, whome neuertheles the Church iustly condemned as heretikes, if they pertinaciously stood in their errours. Schussel-burg also in his 3. tom. of the Catalogue of Heretiks, pag. 85. *Christian fayth is one copulatiue, and who denieth one article of fayth, calleth in doubt the whole body of the heauenly doctrine.* Which he repeateth againe in the next pag. And tome 8. pag. 361 : *The Lutherans do fly him, who depraueth the doctrine of truth in any article whatsoeuer.* And in his 2. booke of Caluinisticall diuinity, article 1 : *VVe are certaine by the testimony of Gods word, that an errour in one false doctrine, obstinatly defended, maketh an heretike.* For S. Chrysostome vpon the epistle to the Galathians sayd most truly, that he corrupteth the whole doctrine who ouerthroweth it in the least article. And Ambrose wrote rightly to the Virgin Demetrias, That he is out of the number of the faythfull, and hath no part in the inheritance of Saints, who disagreeth in any thing from the Catholike truth. Thus the Lutherans. Peter Martyr in his epistle to the straungers in England

tom.

tom.2.loc.col.136 : *VVe answere, all the words of God, as farre forth as they proceeded from him, are of equall waight and authority, and therefore none may receiue this, and reiect that as false.* Iames sayth boldly, *who sinneth in one, becommeth guilty of all.* That, if it haue place in keeping of the commandements, is also true in points of fayth. Sadeel in his index of Turriās Repetitions pag. 806 : *I sayd, that it was no true Church, which teacheth doctrine repugnant to the written word of God.* And his Maiesty in his Monitory epistle pag. 97. in Latin : *I call God to witnes, that I hold him not for a Christian who in this learned age belieueth that.* (to wit, that Enoch and Elias are to come.) And D. Morton in his answere to the Protestants Apology lib. 4. c. 2. sect. 3. after he had sayd, that in a Church, albeit corrupted with errour and superstition, yet if it do not ruinate the foundation, the erroneous & superstitious professors may be saued, adddeth : *VVhich notwithstanding we must so vnderstand, as that the errour and superstition do not proceed from knowledge but from ignorance, which ignorance is not affected but simple.* Thus we see that Protestants somtymes confesse that true fayth is like a graine, or Mathematicall point, which cannot be parted ; that the articles of fayth are one copulatiue, and cannot be deuided, that who so obstinatly denieth one article, belieueth, truly, none ; that the obstinate deniall of any one poynt of fayth is sufficient to damne, or to make an heretik, and no brother of the faythfull, or member of the Church. And finally, that she is no true Church, who willfully maintaineth any one thing repugnant to the Ghospell or word of God. Which indeed is most true, and is the doctrine of the holy Fathers and Catholiks, and I would to God Protestants would constantly stand vnto it.

English Protestāts

7.   By all, which hath byn rehearsed in this

chapter out of Protestants, it appeareth how many sortes of Christians, Protestants do sometymes exclude out of the Church, namely Papists, Anabaptists, Arians, al Heretiks, all Schismatiks, all those, who deny any fundamentall point of fayth, and finally al who obstinatly deny any point whatsoeuer of fayth, or of the word of God. And how many things they sometymes require to the making and being of a Protestant, to wit, that he belieue all and euery point of their fayth, and obstinatly dissent in none. To which their doctrine, if they would (as I haue sayd) alwayes constantly stand, it would easily appeare, first how small a company the Protestants Church is, and how little it is spread through the world, and much lesse Catholike or vniuersal, seeing there is no Prouince, nor scarse any citty, in which all Protestants agree amongst themselues in al points of their doctrine. Secondly it would easily appeare that the Protestant Church was neuer before *Luther*, seeing there is no apparence, that before him there was any company of Christians who in all points of doctrine agreed with Protestants. But Protestäts (as I sayd in the Preface) accommodate their doctrine and opinions to tymes and occasions. And the tymes, when they deny Papists to be of the Church, are when they exhort them to leaue the Roman Church, or excuse their owne reuolting from her, or when they dehort others from returning to her. For at all these tymes, it serueth to their purpose to deny that Papists are of the Church, or in the way of saluation; which at other tymes, as we shall see in the next chapter, they are content to graunt. And the tymes when they exclude Anabaptists, Arians, Heretiks, Schismatiks, and all that deny either fundamentall

damentall or other articles of fayth , out of the
Church , are, when either the euidence of truth en-
forceth them thereto , or when they are ashamed to
acknowledge such vgly monsters for brethren and
members of their Church , or would exhort such as
haue left their company to returne vnto them , and
keep others from forsaking them : or finally would
brag of the agreement and purity in doctrine of
their company . For at those tymes it serueth their
turne to renoùce all the foresayd kind of men, whom
at other tymes , especially when we demaund of
them , who were of their Church before Luther ,
they are most willing to receiue , as their kind brethren ; diligently scraping & gathering such shreeds
and clouts, when they perceiue their owne nakednes
and beggary, which themselues, when they thought
they were rich and had no need thereof , most dis-
dainfully cast on the dunghills , as shall appeare in
the chapters following.

CHAP. II.

That Protestants sometymes account Papists for members of their Church.

IN the former chapter we haue seene how sparing
Protestants sometyms be in admitting others into
their Church, now we shall see how liberall they be
at other tymes, in so much that they graunt, not only
all those, whome in the former chapter they reiected,
but also their professed enemies, idolaters, Infidells,
Atheists, Antichrist himselfe , and all , whosoeuer
vnder the name of Christians, impugne the deeds or

B   doctrine

doctrine of the Pope, to be their brethren, their fellowes, and members of their Church. This we will
shew concerning the Papists in this chapter, and of
the others afterward.

1.   That Protestants sometymes do acknowledge Papists to be in the Church is manifest. First
by their open confession thereof. For in the preface
of their Confession of Auspurg, speaking of themselues and Papists, they say: *VVe are all soldiers vnder one*
Christ. And Luther in his epistle against the Anabaptists (as Caluin in his booke against the Chaunter of
Lions, and D. Whitaker in the place hereafter cited
do confesse) writeth : *That in Popery is true Christianity,*
yea the kernell of Christianity, and many pious and great Saints.
Againe: *If Christianity be vnder the Pope, then it must be the*
body and member of Christ. And vpon the 28 chapter of
Genesis: *VVe confesse, that there is a Church among the Pa-*
pists, because they haue Baptisme, absolution, the text of the
Ghospell, and many godly men are among them. Caluin in his
140.epistle to Sozin: *I think I haue sufficiently proued, that*
in Popery there remayneth some Church, albeit halfe destroyed,
and if you will, broken and deformed. And vpon the 2.
chap. of the 2. epistle to the Thessalonians : *I confesse*
it is the temple of God, in which the Pope ruleth; and he calleth
it the very sanctuary of God. And, de vera reform. pag.
332.sayth, *that S Paul affirmeth that Antichrist (whom he*
will haue to be the Pope) *shall sit in the temple of God.*
And lib. de scandalis pag. 103: *In the midest of Gods tem-*
ple. And lib. cont. Precentorem pag. 372 : *In the very*
sanctuary of God, And Responf. ad Sadolet : *In the midest*
of Gods sanctuary. Surely this is to graunt, that the Romane Church, in which the Pope sitteth, is the very
temple and very sanctuary of God. And in his answeare to Sadolet: *VVe deny not those to be Churches of*
                                                     Christ,

Lutheras.

Papists
serue vn-
der christ.

The ker-
nel of
Christia-
nity in
Popery.

The Body
of Christ.

Sacramé-
earies.

Chrift, *which you gouerne*. In his 4. booke of Inftitutions, chap. 2. num. 11. he fayth, that among Papifts
Gods couenant remayned inuiolable. And num. 12 *VVe deny* — Not yet
not, that there are Churches among them. Neither deny we, killed.
but there remaine Churches vnder his (the Pope he meaneth)
tyranny, but which he hath almoft killed. Iunius in his booke
of the Church, cap. 17. writeth that the Popifh
Church, *as farre as it hath that which belongeth to the defini-*
tion of a Church, is a Church; that it hath not giuen vp the
ghoft, that it hath all diuine things, and of Gods part is yet the — Not yet
Church. Zanchius in the preface of his booke of the dead.
nature of God : *Satan euen in the very Roman Church could*
not bring all thing to that paffe, that it should no more haue the
forme of a Chriftian Church. And foone after : *VVhere-*
fore the Roman Church is yet the Church of Chrift. Pleffy — Yet the
in his booke of the Church 2. chap. auoucheth, that Church
the Roman Church is the Spoufe of Chrift, is not of Chrift.
yet forfaken of him, that as a Mother, fhe beareth
children to God (which he repeateth againe in the — Spoufe of
30. chap.) that fhe retaineth life, and that the name Chrift.
of the Church ought no more to be denied to her,
then the name of a man vnto a liuing man. Bucan
in his 41. place of the Church, queft. 5: *The affemblies of*
Papifts are Churches, as a man infected with leprofy or befides his
wittes, doth not leaue to be a man. Polanus in his firft part
and Thefis of the Church : *The Roman Church truly is a*
Church; becaufe Antichrift fitteth in the Church. And in his
Syntagme of diuinity lib. 7. c. 8 : *The prefent Roman*
Church is yet the Church of Chrift. Serauia in his defence
of the degrees of minifters, pag. 30: *The Roman Church,*
is a Church, and mark what I fay more, fhe is our mother, in
whome and by whom, God did regenerate vs. And pag. 31:
The couenant of God remayneth this day in the Latin Church.
Boyffeul in his confutation of Spondé pag. 6 : I ex-
clude

clude not the Roman Church out of the vniuerſall Church. I
acknowledge her to be yet in the couenant of God; which he
repeateth oftentymes. And pag. 12: *The Roman Church,*
is the Church of God. Pag 19 : *It is a member of the vniuerſall*

Yet the
Church
Spouſe &
temple of
God.

Church. p. 283 : *It is yet the Church, Spouſe and temple of God.*
And pag. 822 : *VVe deny not, that the Roman Church is the*
Church of Ieſus Chriſt, redeemed by him. Vorſtius in his
Anti-bellarmin p. 188: *The vulgar Roman church hath not*
yet loſt all ſpirituall life, is not yet openly deuorced from Chriſt.

Yet aliue.

And Peter Martyr in his epiſtle to Bullinger, writeth, that he gaue counſaile, that the Papiſts & they
ſhould not call one the other Heretiks, but account
themſelues for brethren. As for Engliſh Proteſtants,
his Maieſty in his ſpeach to the Parlament, anno

Engliſh
Proteſtãts

1605. 9. of Nouember, and put forth in print, ſpeaketh thus : *VVe do iuſtly confeſſe, that many Papiſts, eſpecially*
our foreſathers, laying their only truſt vpon Chriſt and his me-
rits, may be, and oftentymes are ſaued; deteſting in that point,

Papiſts
may be
ſaued.

and thinking the cruelty of Puritans worthy of fire, that will ad-
mit no ſaluation to any Papiſt. And in his epiſtle to Cardinall Peron : *The Roman, the Greek &c Churches, are mem-*
bers of the Catholike Church. And D. Andrews in his

Members
of the Ca-
tholike
Church.

Tortura Torti towards the end, ſpeaketh thus to the
Papiſts : *VVe are content to call you members of the Catholike*
Church, though not ſound members. Hooker in his 3. book
of Eccleſiaſticall policy pag. 128 : *VVe gladly acknow-*

Of the
family of
Chriſt.

ledge them to be of the family of Ieſus Chriſt And lib. 5. pag.
188 : *They ſhould acknowledge ſo much neuertheleſ ſtill due to*
the ſame Church (of Rome) as to be held and reputed a part
of the houſe of God, a limme of the viſible Church of Chriſt. D.

May be
ſaued.
Note.

Couel in his defence of Hooker pag. 68, ſayth : *VVe*
affirme them of the Church of Rome, to be parts of the Church
of Chriſt, and that thoſe that liue and dye in that Church, may
notwithſtanding be ſaued. D. **Barlow** in his 3. ſermon ad
Clerum :

Clerum : *The learneder writers do acknowledge the Church of Rome, to be the Church of God.* M. Bunny in his treatise of Pacification, sect. 18 : *Neither of vs (Papists & Protestants) may iustly account the other to be none of the Church of God. VVe are no seuerall Church from them , nor they from vs.* D. Some againt Penry in diuers places auoucth, *That Papists are not altogeather aliens from Gods couenant. That in the iudgement of all learned men , and all reformed Churches , there is in Popery a Church , a Ministery . a true Christ : If you think that all the Popish sect which dyed in the Popish Church , are damned, you think absurdly, and dissent from the iudgement of the learned Protestants.* D. Whitaker in his fourth controuersy quest. 5.cap. 3 calleth the Papists Church, *the temple of God, more then halfe dead , and almost decayed.* And that temple, wherein the Apostle sayth, that Antichrist shall sit , and which he affirmeth to be the Roman Church , he termeth *the very Church of God, the true Church of God, the society of the faythfull, the liuely temple composed of liuely stones; such as are the faythfull & the elect.* And he addeth : *There is among them* (Papists) *some Ministery and some preaching of the word , which doubtlesse affordeth saluation vnto some. And as the giftes of God are without repentance ; so the couenant which God made with Christian people, is not quite broken.* And cont. 2. quest. 5. cap.15. after he had confessed , that Luther had sayd, that in Popery are all the goods belonging to Christians, the keyes , the office of preaching , true Christianity, and the very kernell of Christianity; he addeth : *These things are indeed among them.* M. Powell in his 2. booke of Antichrist, cap. 2. graunteth the Roman Church to be the true Church , albeit with a new kind of distinction he deny the Popish church. And D Rainolds in his 5. Thesis, albeit he say that the Roman Church be more then sickly and weak,

Gods couenant with Papists.

yet he dares not say that she is quite dead. And D. White in his way, p. 352. sayth, *That Popery in as much as it differeth from vs, is not to be imagined by vs to be another Church distinct in place and countries from the true Church of Christ : but we affirme it to be a contagion, raging in the midst of the Church of Christ it selfe.* And in his defence c. 37. pag. 355 : *I neuer denied the Church of Rome to be the visible Church of God, wherein our auncestors professed the truth, and were saued.* And cap. 41. pag. 408 : *Professing the Church of Rome it selfe in all ages, to haue byn the visible Church of God.* Lastly D. Hall in his Rome Irreconciliable sect. 1. sayth, that the Roman Church *is a true visible Church, but not sound,* and that it differeth from the Protestant Church, *As the sick from the whole.* Heereto I adde, that oftentymes they call the Roman Church their Mother, which hath borne them to Christ, as we shall rehearse hereafter, & that before Luthers tyme they seeke their Church in Popery, and amongst the Papists.

2.   Secondly I prooue this same out of that which diuers tymes they graunt, that the Roman Church holdeth all the fundamentall articles of fayth, which themselues commonly teach (as hereafter shall be shewed) to suffice to make a Church. Their Confession of Auspurg in the 21. chapter hath these wodrs: *This is almost the summe of doctrine among vs, in which as it may seeme, there is nothing which differeth from scripture, or from the Catholike Church, or from the Roman Church, so farre as it appeareth by writers. All the dissention is about some few abuses, which haue crept into Churches without certaine authority.* Whereby we see that the first and auncientest Protestants, publikly professed, that they differed not from the Roman Church in the summe of doctrine ; but that all their

[margin: That Papists hold the foundation of fayth.]

[margin: Lutherās.]

[margin: The sume of faith in Popery.]

their difagreement was about fome few abufes. And
albeit the wordes be fomewhat altered in the printed copies ; yet that they were in the originall copie
which was prefented to Charles 5. Emperour, is
manifeft by Fabritius, who repeateth them fo out
of that copie ; by Pappus, in his 3. defence againft
Sturmius, who fo alfo reporteth them ; by Zanchius
in his difpute between two Deuines, where he repeateth thefe wordes out of the faid Confeffion :
There is nothing in our doctrine which differeth from the church
of Rome, as far as it is knowne by writers : and finally by
Hieremias Patriarch of Conftantinople in his cenfure vpon the faid Confeffion , it being fent vnto
him by the Proteftants, where he thus writeth to
them : *Yee say, yee agree in all things with the Latins* , and Cocleus
that the difference betwixt you and them, is only touching some anno 1528
abufes : likwife Luther in his forefaid epift.cont. Ana- Vleberg.
bap : *VVe confesse that in Popery is much good belonging to* cauta 17.
Christians, yea all Christian good, to wit , that in Popery is All Chri-
the true Scripture, true baptisme, the true Sacrament of the ftiā good.
altar , the true keyes for remission of sinnes, the true office of
preaching , the true Catechisme , as the Lords prayer , the ten
commaundements , and the articles of faith. Whereupon
Schuffelburg in his 8 . tome of the Catalogue of
heretikes pag. 439. faith : *VVe deny not but that Luther*
sayd that all Christian goods are in Popery , and came from What
thence vnto vs Iohn Regius in his confideration of the was need-
cenfure &c : *Albeit the Ministery of Papists be corrupted with* full to fal-
many traditions and inuentions of men , yet it had that which uation.
was necessary to saluation , to wit the Canonicall scripture, the
Creed &c. Leonard Crentzen : *The bishop of Rome holdeth*
the same foundation of the Catholike faith 1. Cor. 3. *which* The foū-
I *and the Catholik apostolik Church do acknowledge , although* dation of
there be some difference of opinions in certaine circumstances. Fayth.

B 4   **Thus**

Thus the Lutherans. Of the Sacramentaries, Iunius

Sacramē- in his 5. controuerſy lib. 3. cap. 19. writeth thus of
taries. Papiſts, Lutherans, and Caluiniſts: *VVe agree in the*
eſſentiall foundation. Zanchius in his foreſayd preface :

Eſſentiall *In deſpite of the Diuell that Church (of Rome) hath kept the*
foundati- *principall grounds of fayth.* Boyſſeul alſo in his forenamed
on. confutation pag. 79 : *VVe acknowledge that it is pure in the*
cheiſe articles of Chriſtian Religion . And Vorſtius in his

Principall Anti-bellarmin pag. 188. *It is manifeſt that there are ma-*
grounds *ny in that company (of Papiſts) who rightly hold the ſunda-*
of fayth *mentall poin s of our Religion .* And of the Engliſh Proteſtants, his Maieſty in his monitory epiſtle pag. 148.

The fun- plainly intimateth that Papiſts *do ſtick vnto the auncient*
damentall *foundations of the old true Catholike and Apoſtolike fayth.* M.
points. Hooker in his 3. booke of Eccleſiaſticall policy pag.
128.ſayth : *Touching thoſe maine points of Chriſtian truth,*

Engliſh *wherein they conſtantly ſtill perſiſt, we gladly acknowledge them*
Proteſtāts *to be of the family of Ieſus Chriſt.* D. Whitaker in his 2.
cont.queſt.5.cap.14 : *Papiſts haue the Scripture, Baptiſme,*
Catechiſme, the articles of fayth, the ten commandments, the

The main *Lords prayer ; and thoſe things came to vs from them.* D. Whit-
points. gift in his anſwere to the admonition pag. 40: *Papiſtry*
confeſſeth the ſame articles of fayth that we do, although not ſin-
cerely. And pag. 62 : *Papiſts belieue the ſame articles of fayth*
that we do. M. Perkins in the preface of his reformed
Catholike: *By a reformed Catholike I vnderſtand any one*
that holds the ſame neceſſary heads of Religion , with the Roman

The ne- *Church, yet ſo as he pares of, and reiects all errours in doctrine,*
ceſſary *whereby the ſayd religion is corrupted.* D. Morton in his an-
heads. ſwere to the Proteſtants Apology lib. 3. cap. 18. ſect.
1 : *VVe may graunt, that God may cooperate with them to the*

The ghoſ- *conuerſion of Infidels, ſo far as the Ghoſpell of Chriſt, which is*
pell of *the power of God to ſaluation, is preached by them.* D. White
ſaluation. in defence of his way cap. 38 : *In the ſubſtantiall articles*

of

of fayth, we agree with them. Laftly D. Hall in his forefayd booke fayth, that the Romane Church is one
touching the common principles of fayth. Thofe things which she
holdeth together with vs, make a Church. As farre as she holdeth
the foundation, she is a church.

The fub-
ftantiall
articles.

3. Thirdly, the fame point is proued, by that
they graunt fome to be faints, whom they acknowledge alfo to haue liued and died Papifts. For of S.
Bernards holines thus writeth Luther vpon the 4. cap.
to the Galathians: *Bernard a man so holy, pious, chast, &c.*
The Apology of the Confeffion of Aufpurg in the
chapter of anfwere to the Argumēts : *Antony, Bernard,*
Francis, Dominicke, and other holy Fathers. Brentius in his
Apology for the Confeffion of Wirtenberg pag. 297:
I iudge Bernard to haue byn a man indued with great piety, and
to liue now happily with Chriſt. Caluin in his 4. booke of
inftitutions c. 7. num. 22: *Gregory and Bernard holy men.*
Vorftius in Anti-bellarmin pag. 181: *VVe graunt Ber-*
nard indeed to haue byn pious. Lubbert in his 6. booke of
the church c. 7: *VVe think Bernard to haue byn truly holy.*
D. Whitaker cont. 2. queft. 5. c. 14: *I take Bernard to haue*
byn holy indeed. And D. Morton in his Apology part. 2.
lib. 2. c. 23: *I confeffe Bernard was a Saint.* And as plainly
do they confeffe that he was a Papift. For thus Luther in the place now cited: *Let vs imagine that Religion*
and discipline of the ancient Popery to flourish now, and to be ob-
serued with that rigour, with which the Eremits, Hierome,
Auguſtin, Bernard, Francis, and many others obserued it. And
in his booke of abrogating Maffe: *Bernard, Bonauenture,*
Francis, Dominicke, with their followers, not knowing the Pope,
did honour his Kingdome; belieuing all things thereof to be good
and iuſt, and of God. The Magdeburgians in their 12.
Century col. 1637. fpeake thus of him: *He worshipped*
the God of Maozim (they meane the maffe) till the laſt mo-

The arti-
cles which
make a
Church.

That they
say some
Papists be
faints.

ment of his life. And in the next columne : *He was a most eager defender of the seat of Antichrist.* Melancthon in his booke of the Church, and vpon the 14. cap. to the Romanes : *He yelded to many errours, as to the Abuses of the Masse, to the Popes power, to vowes, to the worship of Saints.* Danæus in his controuersies, pag. 313. sayth : *He approued the Popery.* M. Iewell in his defence of the Apology 21. art. diuis. 8. pag. 450: *Bernard was a monck. and liuing in a tyme of such corruption, and being caryed with the tempest and violence of the same, must &c.* Bale in his 2. century of writers pag. 177: *He increased the authority of the bishop of Rome, as much as he could.* D. Feild vpon the 14. ot S. Matthew : *Bernard was deceiued with the errour of Peters superiority.* And D. Whitaker in his answere to the 7. reason of Father Campian: *Bernard, whome alone your church in many yeares hath brought forth a holy man.* And in his 4. controuersy quest. 2. c. 17. he affirmeth that he endeauoureth to confirme the Popes superiority. Seing therefore by the confession of Protestants, he was both an earnest Papist vnto his dying day, for all his life tyme he honoured masse, belciued the Popes superiority (in which two points Protestants say the essence and soule of a Papist doth consist) and briefly belieued all things belonging to the Pope to come from God : and also was a very holy man, in his life tyme, and now a blessed Saint in heauen; they must needs confesse, that euen the most vehemét Papist may be of the church; because neither true sanctity, nor saluatió can be found out of the church. Whereunto the Protestants in the late Conference at Ratisbon Sess. 13. say: *If they were truly saints, then their errour was not of that kind which ouerturneth the foundation. For it implieth contradiction, that one should be a true Saint, and yet soster errour which ouerturneth the ground of saluation, nation.* In like sort they graunt diuers others to be true saints, and yet withall Papists, but for breuities sake I will content my selfe with this example of S. Bernard. But I will not omit to say, that they confesse our Christian forefathers before Luthers tyme to haue byn Papists, from the top to the toe, from the first to the last, as shall be shewed in the 2. booke cap. 3. and notwithstanding dare not say, that they be damned, yea confesse them to be saued. Luther in his booke of priuate masse enquireth, what is to be thought of our auncestors who haue founded innumerable Masses; and answereth: *I cannot tell certainly.* But vpon the 41. cap. of Genesis, he sayth: *Doubtlesse many haue byn saued vnder Popery.* And vpon the 5. of S. Matthew: *Neither do we condemne the Christians who liued* Our Papish forevnder *the Pope.* Brentius in the preface of his Recognition: *VVe doubt not, but that many haue obtayned true saluation in Popery.* Osiander in his Manual englished: *VVe do not condemne our godly ancestors who liued in tyme of Popery.* Zuinglius in his actes of disputation fol. 638: *It is impious to pronounce our ancestors to be damned.* D. Morton in his Apology part. 1. l. 1. c. 90: *Be this impiety far from vs, to adiudge our ancestours, to damnation.* And D. White in his defence pag. 356: *I neuer denyed the church of Rome to be the visible church of God, wherein our ancestors possessed the true faith and were saued.* But how could our Popish ancestors be not damned, how could they be saued, vnles they were in the true church, out of which euen Protestants themselues confesse, that there is no saluation, but only damnation.

fathers saued.

4. Fourthly I prooue that Protestants cannot deny Papists to be of the true Church, because they oftentymes both by word and deed acknowledge the vocation and Mission of Popish Pastors, to

That they confesse true mission and Pastors in Popery.

be

be lawfull and sufficient to make a true Pastour of the Church .Luther vpon the 5. cap.of S. Matthew: *VVe confesse that amongst Papists are pulpits, Baptisme, Sacraments, and all other things belonging to Apostolicall vocation and function .* And in his booke of priuate masse : *There remaineth in Popery,Vocation, Ordination, Ministery of the word, and keyes to bind and loose.* Againe : *Christ hath conserued his Ministery vnder Popery.* And as is before cited : *There is all Christian good in Popery,the keyes, the charge of preaching &c.* Iohn Regius in considerat. Censuræ pag. 93 : *Although it be true that the Popish ministery was depraued with sundry traditions and deuises of men, yet had it those things which were necessary to saluation.* Bucer in Rom. 8. pag. 427. telling vs by what authority and right he preached Protestantisme, sayth : *I had by lawfull meanes already attayned the charge to preach Christ ; and to teach those things which he commanded.* Iunius lib. singulari de eccles.cap. 17 : *God calleth the church wherein Popery raigneth , by his spirit, by his word , by the publike instrument of that holy marriage by the ministery, by sacred affaires & actions. On Gods part these things are apparantly in that church.* Plessy lib. de Ecclef. cap. 11. p. 361. *The vocation (of our men) is the same that they (the Papists) boast of.* Pag. 362 : *Our aduersaries and our first ministers had the same Ecclesiasticall calling.* Boysseul in confutat. Spondæi pag. 486 : *It is no reproach for our Pastors to haue issued out of yours ; or, as you say, to haue had their vocation from yours.* Moulins lib. 1. de vocat. cap. 5. pag. 20. endeauouring to vphold the calling of their first Reformers , sayth : *They haue that calling which is ordinary in the church of Rome* Pa. 21 : *They had their calling of the Pope.* cap. 9.pag. 36 : *They haue the same ordinary calling which our aduersaries haue.* And lib. 2. tract. 1. cap. 1. pag. 172 : *The calling they had in the church of Rome , sufficed to bind them to preach.* And pag. 173: *Their commission was no other, then the*
ordinary

ordinary charge. Serauia in deten. Grad. minist. cap. 2.
pag. 31. VVe ought not to thinke, that in the church of Rome
ecclesiasticall ministery is decayed. And pag. 33: I like not their
frowardnes, who acknowledge no ministery in the church of
Rome, but deeme all that is there, diuelish. Ibid : *Beza doth ex-*
agitate Popish orders ouer much, wherein I feare least he pre-
iudice a good cause. D. Whitaker contr. 4. quest. 5. cap. 3.
pag. 682 : *The Papists haue some sort of ministery, and some*
preaching of the word, which doubtles auaileth many to salua-
tion. And other where (as is before cited) *Among the Pa-*
pists there are the keyes, the office of preaching, &c. M. Bell in
his first booke of the Popes funerall cap. 5. affirmeth
that he had reiected only the accidents of his Popish
orders, but retayned the substance still. M. Mason in
his 5. booke of the ordination of ministers, cap. 12.
say h, that Popish ordination consistes of two
parts, to wit, of power to offer sacrifice, & of power
to administer the word and Sacraments, and albeit
he reiecteth the former, yet the later he approues, as
that wherein true ministery consisteth. Sadeel respon. ad
artic. abiurat. 61. And Vorstius in Anti-bellarmin
pag 177. teach the same; and so must all others do,
who hold the mission of Luther and their first ministers to haue byn ordinary, and receiued from the
Papists: which opinion most Protestants do now
follow, retracting, vpon better aduise their former
assertion, & confessing that the mission of their new
Reformers, was not in substance extraordinary. And
their deeds and actions do no lesse declare their ap-
probation and esteeme of the mission and Pastorall
charge which is in the church of Rome. For as
Turrian reporteth lib. 2. de Eccles. cap. 3. and Luther
intimateth tom. 2. epist. ad Bohemos, when the Catholike Bishops giue orders, the Hussites of Bohemia
steale

steale in priuily among the rest. The Lutherans also made sute to the estats of the Empire, that their ministers might receiue orders from the bishops of Misnia and Numburg. And in artic. 10. Smalcald. they professe thus : *If the bishops (of the church of Rome) would truly execute their office, and looke carefully to the church and word of God, it might be permitted them to giue orders vnto vs and our preachers.* You may adde hereunto, that neither Luther nor any Reformer else euer sought other ordination, then what they had receiued of Papists; and that in the beginning of Queene Elizabeths raigne, the supposed Prelates earnestly besought a Catholike Bishop to consecrate them. And euen to this day, if any renegate Priest ioyne himselfe to the Protestants, they order him not anew, but deeme him fit for their ministeriall function, by vertue of the orders he receiued of Papists. Now if Papists haue true Mission, true pastorall charge, and true Pastors, surely they haue also the true church; it being impossible, that the church should be seuered frō the true Pastours; or that the keyes of heauen which are in the true Pastours hands, should be out of the church, or that the power to remit sinnes, the prerogatiue of true Pastours, shold be where the church is not. Nay, the Protestants themselues confesse as much. Luther tom. 4. in cap. 4. Oseæ fol. 295: *True it is, that the Ministery is only in the Church.* Melancthon tom. 1. Lutheri disput. de Ecclef. Polit. fol. 483: *The ordination of Ministers is one of the peculiar gistes of the Church.* Caluin lib. de neces. reform. Ecclef. pag. 57 : *This one reason is as good as thousands, that who so hath shewed himselfe an enemy to true doctrine, hath lost all authority in the Church.* D. Whitaker ad demonstrat. 18. Sanderi : *Out of the Church there is no other seate but the seat of errour, of pestilence,*
and

True mission and Pastors insepara- ble frō the Church.

and euerlaſting deſtruction. The ſame teacheth Sadeel ad
Sophiſm. Turrian loc. 10. D. Feild in his 1. booke of
the church cap. 14. and others.

5. Fittly it is euident by the doctrine of the
Sacramentaries, who hold that the children of Papiſts are in the couenant of God, and eſtate of ſaluation, through the fayth of their parents; and may
therefore be baptiſed: much more then muſt they
teach, that the parents themſelues are for their owne
fayth in the couenant of God and eſtate of ſaluation;
which could not be, were they not in the Church.
The antecedent is manifeſt by the ſaying of many
Proteſtants. For thus writeth Luther lib. de capt.
Babylon. tom. 2. fol. 77: *Here I ſay that which all ſay, that
infants are holpen by the fayth of them which offer them.* Caluin
in his Catechiſme cap. de lege: *God extendeth his bounty
ſo ſarte vnto the faythfull, that for their ſake he is good to their
children, not only bleſſing their affaires in this world, but alſo
ſanctiſying their ſoules, that they may be accounted of his flock.*
Contr. Seruetum. pag. 601: *We think, that there will be
no vſe of Baptiſme vntill this promiſe, I will be thy God and of thy
ſeed, be apprehended by fayth; but euery one apprehendeth it not
only to himſelfe, but alſo to his iſſue.* Beza part. 2. Reſpon. ad
acta Montisbel. pag. 118: *Parents through Gods grace do
apprehend grace by true fayth, according to the forme of the Couenant, as well to their poſterity as to themſelues.* Which he
oftentymes repeateth. And likewiſe in Confeſ. cap.
4. ſect. 48. and cap. 5. ſect. 9. and pag. 126 M. Perkins
de Sacramento Baptiſmi tom. 1. col. 846: *Others ſay,
that the fayth of the Parents is alſo the fayth of their children, all
the tyme of their infancy or childhood, and that becauſe parents
do by their fayth apprehend the promiſe both for themſelues and
for their children: Which opinion ſeemeth to me the fitteſt of all.*
The like he ſayth in cap. 3. Galat. The ſequele likewiſe

Papiſts
children
ſaued by
the fayth
of their
parents.

wise is vndoubted. For if the fayth of Popish parents
be of force to establish their very children in the Couenant of God and estate of saluation, though it re-
side not in them, nor be their act; much more doth
it establish the parents themselues, who haue that
fayth in them, and whose act it is. Nor do the in-
stances D. Morton brings against it in his answere
to the Protestants Apology, lib. 4. cap. 6. make any
thing to the purpose; as that in case of necessity an
hereticall Priest or Schismatike may absolue from
sinnes; and an Infidell administer Baptisme. Againe:
That if such as were free of a citty and are araigned
of treason, should haue issue after their condemnation, their children neuertheles shall enioy the title
and right of cittizens, whereof their parents were
destitute. These examples (I say) are not to the purpose; because he, who is eyther baptized by an Infidell, or absolued by an hereticall Priest, enters not
into the couenant of God and estate of saluation for
ought that is in the person which baptizeth or ab-
solueth him, but for the Sacrament of Baptisme or
Pennance, which he recciueth indeed by the others
administration, but hath it in himselfe. And the
sonne of a traytor is not made a Cittizen, in regard
of any thing that is in the father alone, but for his
owne birth which appertaines to himselfe, though
his Father be author thereof. But the Sacramentaries
teach, that the child of a Papist is in the couenant of
God and estate of saluation, not for his owne fayth
(for they say he hath none) but for the beliefe of his
father; which is no way possible, if the same fayth
be not of force to worke the like effect in the father
himselfe; seeing it belongs farre more to him, then
to his child, and therefore must sooner giue him in-
terest

terest in the couenant, then the child that is descended of him. For how can the fathers beliefe lay hold on the promises and couenant of God for his children, and cannot do it for himselfe?

6.　These allegations demonstrate, that by the Confession of the Protestants, the starkest Papists (such as are of beliefe that the masse, the Popes primacy, and all things else of his are good, vpright and of God) *are soldiers vnder Christ, may attaine to saluation, may be Saints ; yea that there are among them both many and great Saints. That there is in the Church of Rome what so is necessary to saluation, the summe of fayth, the ground-works the essentiall ground-worke, the principall grounds of fayth, the cheife articles, the fundamentall heads, the necessary heads, the cheife parts, the Ghospell of saluation, the kernell of Christianity, and all Christian good.* Lastly that the Church of Rome, *Is a limme and member of the vniuersall church, of the Catholike Church, a member of the true Church, and is of the family of Iesus Christ ; that it is mother to the children of God, that it is the Church of God, the temple of God, the body of Christ, the Spouse of Christ, that it abides yet in the couenant, is not yet cast of, or put away, is not yet killed, but is yet aliue.* Which words plainly import that the Roman or Popish Church is a true Church in the sight of God.

7.　But is it credible, that such as make profession of Christian religion, should mount to that height of impiety, as dare to reiect & diuorce themselues, from that Church which they confesse remaynes yet in the couenant of God, & which Christ hath not yet reiected? Is it credible, that they feare not to impugne, to make bitter inuectiues, to disgorge curses and execrations against her, whom they acknowledge to be their Mother, which bore them to Christ, to be the Church of God, to be the body

C　　　　and

and Eſpouſe of Chriſt? What can be more lewd and impious, then to rage and raile againſt their owne mother, againſt the Church of God, againſt the very body and Eſpouſe of Chriſt? What ſtrang and mon-ſtrous blindnes is it, not to perceiue, that whiles they confeſſe the church of Rome to be the church of God & Eſpouſe of Chriſt, they acknowledge their owne to be the Synagogue of Antichriſt and ſtrum-pet of the Duell? For Chriſt cannot haue two E-ſpouſes, repugnant each to other · Now the Prote-ſtant church and church of Rome are parts ſo op-poſite, as can neuer make one. For they iarre and diſ-agree mainely in diuers weighty points, as namely touching the canon and expoſition of the Scripture, touching ſacrifice and the Sacraments, touching the worſhip of God, & his Saints; touching the m-anes to obtaine remiſſion of ſinnes, and many the like. Whereupon Beza in Confeſ.cap.7. pag.56: *VVe diſſent (ſayth he) from the Papiſts, about the very ſumme of ſaluatiō.* And others ſay no leſſe, as ſhall be ſhewed hereafter in the 2. booke and 6. cap: *If ours be true Religion (ſayth*

Lib.2. cōt. Gaud.c.11.
S. Auguſtin to the Donatiſts which yet came nearer to Catholiks then Proteſtants do) *yours is ſuperſtition.*
Againe: *If our communion be the Church of Chriſt, yours is not*
Lib.1. de Bapt. c.11.
Chriſts Church; for that is but one, which ſo euer it be. And in anoth-r place: *VVhen they approue that Church, which (as is manifeſt) we communicate with all, and they do not; by that*
Lib ad Do-nat. poſt collat.
their teſtimony they acknowledge themſelues conuinced, and giue you plaine not ce (if you be wiſe) what you ought to forgoe, and what it beloues you to cleaue to and retaine. And S. Cy-prian epiſtle 76: *If the Church were on Nouatus ſide, it was not with Cornelius.*

Num. 4.
　　　　8.　The Proteſtants now and then perceiue as much, when they acertaine vs (as hath byn ſhewed
　　　　　　　　　　　　　　　　　　　　　　　　　　　　in

in the first chapter) that who so seuereth himselfe
from any particuler congregation, which is a true
Church, excludes himselfe wholy from the church.
Caluin saw it, when 4. Insti. c. 2. §. 10. he wrote thus:
VVe cannot graunt them (Papists) that they are the church, but the
necessity of subiection & obediece will befall vs. If they be churches,
the power of the keyes is in their possession. If they be churches, that
promise of Christ: VVhatsoeuer ye bind on earth shall be boūd in
heauen, takes effect in them. M. Perkins perceiued it to,
when in his explicatiō of the Creed col. 794. he sayd:
As long as any church forsakes not Christ, we may not withdraw
our selues from it. The reason is apparant, because in so
doing we should depart from Christ, or Christ shold
be parted, euen as we are rent and disioynted from
the church wherein he is. And in his Reformed Catholike tract. 22. col. 470. Where he sayth: *VVe ought*
not to deuide our selues from any nation or people, which hath not
before cut it selfe of from Christ. D. Feild likewise saw it
in his 3. booke of the Church c. 47. Where he makes
this acknowledgement: *Surely if he can proue that we con-*
fesse it (the Church of Rome) to be the true Church, he nee-
deth not vse any other argument. But we haue clearely
prooued it by sundry plaine confessions of many famous Protestants. And hitherto we haue discouered
how they sometyme harbour and receiue Papists into their church: now we will shew that they vse the
like curtesy towards the rest.

Zanchius
lib. 1. de
Eccl. c. 7.

C 2   CHAP.

CHAP. III.

That Protestants acknowledge for members of their Church, sometyme those that deny as well funda-mentall as other articles of their fayth; some-tymes Heretiks, Schismatiks, yea their profest and sworne enemies.

THAT they esteeme all such to be members of their Church, as swarue from the Christian fayth only in points not fundamentall, themselues in the preface of the Switzers Confession declare in these words: *Mutuall consent and agreement in the principall points of doctrine, in orthodoxe sense, and brotherly charity, was of religious antiquity thought abundantly sufficient.* And D. Whitaker cont. 4. quest. 1. c. 2. pag. 527: *God forbid that they should be no longer of the number of the faythfull, who are in some points of a contrary opinion, so they assent in the cheise and principall and necessary matters.* And for as much as the Protestants opinion herein is well knowne (for whē it is obiected vnto them, that their churches disagree in points of fayth, this serues them for excuse) I think it needlesse to alleage any more of their sayings. He that will may looke the Confession of Saxony cap. de Eccles. Luther tom. 7. lib. de not. Eccles. fol. 149. Melancthon tom. 4. in ca. 3. 1. Cor. Kemnitius 1. part. Examinis tit. de bonis operibus pag. 332. Zuinglius tom. 1. in Prefat. lib. de Prouident. Caluin. 4. Institut. cap 1. §. 12. and cap. 2. §. 1. Beza epist. 2. Zanchius in prefat. lib. de natura Dei. Hospin. part. 1. Histor. lib. z. cap. 2. Vorstius in Anti-bellarmin. pag. 116. and others moe. And as their iudgements are different
touching

touching the fundamentall articles of fayth, ſo in
determining, who are to be accounted members of
their Church their opinions are vnlike. Some of thē
ſay, that the ſumme, the cheife and principall heads
of fayth, and all things neceſſary to be belieued are
comprized in the Apoſtles Creed. *The principall heads of*
fayth (ſayth Caluin 2. Inſtitut. c. 16. §. 8) *are ſet downe in* The A-
the Creed. And it is (as D. Whitaker ſayth lib. 3. de poſtles
Scriptura cap. 3. ſect. 1.) *a liſt of the cheife heads of fayth. It* Creed.
containes (ſayth M. Perkins in his Reformed Catholik
col. 476.) *all points of Religion which we are neceſſarily to be-*
lieue. Hemingius in Syntagmate pag. 196: *It containes*
the ground-work of the whole frame of Religion. Vrſinus in
Cathecheſi : *The ſumme of thoſe things which the Ghoſpell*
propoſeth vnto vs to belieue, that we may be partakers of Gods co-
uenant, is comprehended in the Apoſtles Creed. Pareus lib. 1.
de Iuſtificat. cap 9. hath theſe words: *In the Creed is*
layd open the ſumme of that doctrine, which we muſt belieue to
ſaluation. The ſame teacheth Luther tom. 7. in 3 ſymbol. fol. 138. Confeſſio Palatina in initio, preſat. Syn-
tagmat. Confeſ. the French Catechiſme, Brentius in
Prolegomenis, pag. 244. The Catechiſme of Heidle-
berg part. 2. Bullinger in compendio fidei lib. 6. cap.
2. and tom. 1. decad. 5. ſerm. 2. Polanus in Analyſi.
Catechiſmi Baſle. Boyſſeul in confutat. Spondei p.
10. Raynolds in Apol. Theſ. pag. 241. Carleton in
Conſenſu tract. de Eccleſ. c. 9. The ſame is intimated
by Zanchius lib. 1. epiſt. pag. 219. and by Muſculus in
locis tit. de Eccleſ. pag. 309. Theſe men then, if the ſequele of their doctrine be correſpondent to the pre-
miſes, muſt needs acknowledge, that the profeſſion
of the Apoſtles Creed, though ioyned with the denyall of whatſoeuer other articles of fayth, ſufficeth
to make a Proteſtant, and a limme of their Church.
C 3   And

And some of them there be who confeſſe it. For Bullinger lib.cit.cap.11.fol.83.ſayth: *All that we compriſe in the 12. articles, is the true and Chriſtian fayth, vnto which whoſoeuer cleaueth, he belieueth right, is approued of God, is iuſtified, and made partner of euerlaſting life.* Caluin conf. Gentil.pag.659: *The confeſſion of fayth contayned in the Apoſtles Creed, ought to be inough for all modeſt Chriſtians.* And Muſculus in the place laſt quoted. *They are wonderfull vnreaſonable and vnaduiſed, who not content with this belieſe, exact of the faythfull, that they belieue yet other things which are neither mentioned in the Apoſtles Creed, nor in baptiſme.* Aretius in locis part 3.fol.67: *The articles neceſſary to ſaluation are thoſe, which the Creed hath ſet vs downe. As for the reſt, ſince the matter cannot be decided, variety of iudgements muſt be borne with all.* Polanus alſo in the place before cited: *Theſe articles (of the Creed) if they be vnfaynedly belieued ſuffice to purchaſe ſaluation; nor is it required we ſhould belieue ought beſides.* And Hall in ſuis Roma irreconcil.ſect.1: *VVe are all one and the ſame Church, as many as in any part of the earth worſhip Ieſus Chriſt the only Sonne of God and Sauiour of the world, and profeſſe the ſame common belieſe compriſed in the Creed.*

2.   Some of them will haue the grounds of fayth to be contained in the Creed; as Pleſſy lib. de Eccleſ.c.5. Hereupon Marke Antony de Dominis in confil.ſuæ profect. pag. 18. & 20. ſayth: *Reſtore peace and charity to all Chriſtian Churches, which profeſſe Chriſt by the eſſentiall cogniſances of belieſe.* Others ad to the Creeds the 4. generall Councels or at leaſt one of them, as D. Andrews in Reſponf. ad Apol. Bellarmin.cap.1.pag. 52: *That which is ſet downe in the Creeds and 4. generall councells, is to vs a ſufficient obiect of fayth.* And in Tortura Torti pag.127: *Nor do we lightly diſcerne and try hereſy by other touch-ſtone, then by examining whether it be repugnant to*

any

any of the three ancient Creeds, or 4.anciem generall councels.
And Melancthon tom. 3. l. de iudicijs Synodorum
fol. 389. sayth of himself, that he is not without the
Gnuich, because *he saythfully imbraceth all the articles of the*
Apostles and Nycen Creed . Musculus also in the place a-
boue quoted puts downe this conclusion : *As many as*
belieue the Apostles and Athanasius Creed, hold all the Catholike
fayth, and are not heretikes but Catholiks. Some of them are
of opinion, that al the fundamental points of beliefe
are contayned in the Creed and decalogue; as Melancthon tom.1. in cap. 7. Matth. pag.402.tom.2. in
respons.ad artic.Bauar. fol. 363. Vrsinus in Miscella-
neis Thes.8.pag.114. M. Perkins in his exposition of
the Creed col.789. Some of them say, they are in the
Creed, the decalogue, and Lords prayer ; as Luther
tom.7. in Enchirid.fol 118. Beza lib.de notis Ecclef.
pag. 52. Keckerman lib. 1. System. Theol. 201. D.
White in the preface of his way, and in his defence
of the same cap.8.pag.54. Others reckon the 10. commandements, the Creed, the Lords prayer,& the Sacraments; as D. Whitaker cont.1. quest.4.cap.4. pag.
342. (howbeit quest. 5. cap. 9. pag. 362. he omitteth
Sacraments,& putteth in Catechisme in exchaunge.)
Vorstius in Antibellarm.pag.24. vnto which Ieslerus
lib.de bello Euchar.pag.40. adioyneth the ministry.
And these men according to their seuerall decisions
concerning the fundamentall points of beliefe, must
with like diuersity require in a limme of the Protestant Church either the beliefe of the Creed alone,
and decalogue ; or must adde besides (as each think it
needfull) the Lords prayer, the Sacraments, the Catechisme, and the Ministery.

3. But sometymes they giue larger scope, &
demaund farre lesse, to wit, Baptisme only, or faith

C 4 *in*

The creed and Deca-logue.

The creed Decalo-gue, and Lords prayer.

The creed Decalogue, Lords prayer, & Sacra-ments. And the Ministry.

Baptisme and wor-ship of Christ.

in Christ. *Let him let Christianity stad* (saith D. Andrews in respont. cit. cap. 5. pag. 126) *in baptisme and worship of Christ.* M. Morton in his booke of the Kingdome of Israel and the Church pag. 91 : *In what place soeuer any society of men adore true God in Christ, they professe the substance of Christian Religion :* Ierlachius disput. 22. de Ecclel. pag. 662 : *VVheresoeuer baptisme remaines entier in regard of its substance, thither reacheth the territory of the Catholike Church :* Againe : *If they acknowledge true baptisme both in ours and in other congregations, they must yeld, that in the same there is likewise the Catholike Church.* And Hutterus in his Analysis of the Confession of Ausburge pag. 525 : *As many as are enrolled for Christs soldiers by sacred baptisme, or at least wise are ioyned to him, by profession of fayth, are euery one of them members of the Church simply taken, as it signifieth the company of them that are called.* Serauia defens. contra Bezam cap. 2. pag. 31 : *As long as there remaines amongst them the new and old testament, together with the Sacrament of baptisme, and beliefe in God the Father, and in the Sonne, and holy Ghost ; and they trust to be saued by the Sonne of God and his death ; albeit they adioyne a number of their owne wicked forgeries, they are notwithstanding parts and members of the vniuersall Church.* The ministers of the scattered Church of the Netherlands in sua narrat. pag. 71 : *No man can, nor ought to giue sentence in the Church of an others condemnation, of whome it is not publikely knowne, that he is fallen away from the foundation of the Apostolicall Confession, vttered by the mouth of Peter.* Oecolampadius epist. ad Bucerum apud Hospin. part. 2. Histor. fol. 112 : *VVe are gladly at peace withall those that confesse with vs and teach Iesus Christ true God and true man in vnity of person.* And Bucerus apud eundem fol. 84: *VVho so preach the same Christ with vs, we account them ours, what estimate soeuer they make of vs.* Beza de lib. notis Eccles. pag. 30 : *VVe say it is a true definition*

[margin:]
Baptisme alone.

Luther de Notis Eccl. fol. 150.

Professio of Christ.

Professio of Christ God and man.

definition of the true Church, whether generally conſidered or in particuler, wherein it is ſayd to be a company which acknowledgeth one Sauiour. For (ſayth he) this alone is the only groundwork of that ſpirituall houſe of God; Chriſt Ieſus is the ſoule of that myſticall body, the only rule and ſquare of that building. And the Conteſſion of Bohemia artic. 8. defines the Catholike Church to be all Chriſtians, That are aſſociated in one beliefe concerning Chriſt and the holy Trinity. The Conteſſion of Baſle artic. 5. hath this aſſertion: VVe belieue the holy Chriſtian Church &c. VVherein all thoſe are Cittizens, that confeſſe Ieſu to be Chriſt, the lambe of God which taketh away the ſinnes of the world, and ſhew openly the ſame beliefe by works of charity. Acontius l. 3. Stratagem. Satanæ pag. 119 concludes that nothing elſe is neceſſarily to be belieued, but That there is one God and Chriſt his Sonne, made man and raiſed from the dead; and that ſaluation is purchaſed by his name, and not by any other name, nor by the works of the law. And Luther vpon the 7. of Math. fol. 86. cloſeth vpall with this epilogue: The head and ſumme of Chriſtian doctrine is this: that God ſent and gaue his Sonne, by whome alone he pardoneth our offences, and doth iuſtiſy and ſaue vs. This (ſayth he) and nothing elſe, it behoues thee firmely to belieue. Sometyme to belieue their article of iuſtification by only fayth is as much as they require in a limme of their Church, or think needfull to ſaluation. Luther tom. 7. tract. in 3. ſymbol. fol. 140: I haue found by experience, that who ſo haue truly and ſincerly belieued that principall article of Chriſtian fayth concerning Ieſu Chriſt, though they had their errours and faults, haue at laſt notwithſtanding byn ſaued. And tom. 4. in cap. 42. Iſaiæ fol. 178: If we abide in this article, we are ſecure from hereſies, and retaine remiſſion of ſinnes; which pardoneth our weaknes in ciuill dueties and beliefe. And in cap. 43. fol. 200: VVho ſo belieueth this article, is out of danger for euer falling into

C 5 *error,*

To acknow-ledge one Sauiour.

The faith of Chriſt and the Trinity.

Beliefe of one God & Chriſt.

That God ſaueth by Chriſt.

The only article of iuſtification ſuffiæeth.

Pareus in 1. Galat. lect. 8. Iezler. de bello Euch. fol. 77.

error, and the holy Ghost must needs assist him. And Brocard vpon the 2. cap. of the Apocalips fol. 45 : *The former Ministers who were before the first councell of Trent, determined, that we ought not to contend, but that their Supper should be common, which had receiued one doctrine touching iustification.* Caluin de vera Eccles. reform. pag. 316. writeth thus: *I know it is the common saying of a great many, that so the doctrine of vndeserued Iustification continue sound, we should not be so stifly contentious about the rest.* And the Author of the Preface in Syntagma Confess. after he had affirmed that the article of iustification is the ground work, the forme and soule of Christian religion, makes this demaund: *How can they then but haue peace one with another, who soeuer are fellow-partners of so great good?* And he saith, it is, *An vnseemly and h tinous thing, that betweene such there should be enmity and debate.* And indeed all Protestants should teach so, since they make this article the definition, the summe, and very soule of Protestantisme, as shall be herrafter shewed in the 6. chapter. Sometymes in a member of their Church, they require only some one point of Christianity, or but the profession of Christs name. For Sturmius apud Hospin. in Corcord. discord. c. 24. testifieth that Bucer sayd: *He would neuer condemne any one, in whome he saw any point of Christianity.* And Plessy lib de Eccles. cap. 2. affirmeth that the Church may be infected with heresy from top to toe, & yet be a part of the vniuersall Church, *as long as it professeth the name of Christ* And Moulins in his buckler of tayth pag. 42. *The vniuersall visible Church is the company of all them who professe themselues to be Christians.* Thus we see, that to *a member of the visible Church, yea to fayth, to Christianity, to a member of the true and Catholike Church, to eternall saluation* (as Protestants sometyme iudge and determine) litle or nothing sufficeth.

Any point of Christianity.

Do

Do not these men go about to expose the Church &
meanes of saluation vnto scorne and mockery? What
Iew or Turke did euer make his Synagogue so common?

4. Albeit the former allegations do sufficiently conuince, that when Protestants calculate
the limmes and members of their Church, they take,
to make vp the number, such as renounce the very
fundamentall articles of their beliefe; yet to make it
more euident, and to preuent all colour of doubt, I
will adde other proofes besides. And first we haue in
this behalfe their owne Confessions. For Beza lib. de
Notis Eccles. pag. 45. teacheth plainly, that *some er-*
rours euen in some fundamentall heads of fayth, may creep into
the Catholike Church. And D. Whitaker cont. 2. quest. 4.
cap. 3. pag. 490 : *It is manifest, that the true Church may erre*
for a tyme euen in necessary points. The like hath Hutterus
in Analysi Confessionis Augustanæ pag. 453. and Iunius doth intimate as much lib. 3. de Eccles. cap. 17.
D. Whitaker againe cont 2. quest. 5 cap. 17: *VVe gather,*
that the Church may for a tyme swarue from the truth euen in
some fundamentall points, and be notwithstanding safe. And
Zanchius lib. 1. epist. pag. 221. will not haue vs forsake any cōpany on occasion of false opinions, *which*
swarue from the groundwork of fayth. D. Hall likewise in
sua Roma irreconc. sect. 1. sayth, that the true Church
may foster such errours, *As by deduction and consequence*
destroy the foundations of beliefe. D. Fulke in his serm. vpō
the Apocalips, hauing made this obiection to himselfe, that seing the Church is the Espouse of Christ,
it cannot be, that he suffered it to be possessed so many ages with damnable errors; answeares it in this
manner: *VVhat? Christ himselfe hath sayd: that the errors*
of false Prophets should be exceeding great, in as much as the very
                                                    elect,

Protestāts
challenge
those that
deny euē
fundamē-
tall arti-
cles.

elect, if it might be, should be led into errour. And lib. de Succes. Eccles. pag. 122. he sayth : *It seemes not fitting to take from the Grecians the name of a Church ;* whome notwithstanding he confesseth to be ensnared with grieuous errors. Now a grieuous errour (according to D. Whitaker cont. 2. quest 4 cap. 1.) *dissolues the foundation, and may therfore be termed fundamentall.* M. Perkins in his exposition of the Creed, col. 790 : *VVhen an errour is repugnant to the foundation, either directly or by necessary consequence if it proceed of weaknes, he in whome it is, ought to be reputed a member of the vniuersall Church.* And vpon 1. Galat. v. 2: *If a Church through frailty fall into errour, although it concerne the foundation, notwithstanding it remaynes yet a Church, as is certaine by the example of the Galathians :* And vpon the epistle of Iude v. 19 : *The Church of Galatia through weaknesse remoued it selfe vnto another Ghospell, and erred in the foundation, yet Paul writeth to it as to the Church of God.* D. Willet affirmeth the same in his Synopsis cont. 2. q. 3. pag. 104. And Melancthon tom. 2. lib. de Eccl. pag. 123. toucheth the same string when he sayth : *The true Church it selfe may haue errours which obscure and darken the articles of fayth.* And tom. 4. in cap. 9. Rom : *God gathereth alwayes some company, in which the foundation is kept, sometymes lesse pure, sometymes more.* D. White in his way pag. 111 : *Some articles lying in the very foundation may be belieued not so clearly .* Nay sometymes they dare auouch, that those very Corinthians that denyed the resurrection, and those Galatians also that changed the Ghospell of Christ into another Ghospell, were of the Church. For thus the Switzers Confession c. 17. *VVe are not ignorant, what manner of Churches those of the Corinthians and Galathians were in the Apostles tyme : which the Apostle accuseth of many and grieuous crimes, and yet termeth them the holy Churches of Christ.* And Caluin 4. Institut. cap. 1.

*Luther. in *
r. cap. Galat. fol. 215.
Perkins loc. cit.

cap. 1. 4. 27 : *Most greiuou* sinnes possesse sometymes whole Churches. The Apostasy of the Galathians was no small offence ; the Corinthians were lesse excusable then they ; howbeit neither of them are excluded from the Lords mercy. Sadeel in his an-Iwere ad Thes. Posnan. cap. 12. pag. 866 : *The Gala-thians and Corinthians, though corrupted with errour, and disagreeing each from other about the cheise groundwork of be-liefe, and that not concerning the manner but touching the mat-ter it selfe, retained notwithstanding the name of a true Church.* And hence he gathereth, that the debate and disagrement betweene the Lutherans and Caluinists concerning the Eucharist, doth not let either of them from being of the true Church.

5. The deeds of the Lutherans and Sacramen-taries yeld vs a second kind of proofe. For the Electo-rall or milde Lutherans in colloq. Aldeburg. scripto 8 call themselues, *Fellowes and companions of the same Mi-nistery. fellow-cittizent and fellow-soldiers* of those of Saxo-ny or rigorous Lutherans : of whome notwithstan-ding scripto 6. pag. 111. they giue this censure : *They haue shewed themselues to dissent from our Churches in the foun-dation.* Againe : *VVe will make it euident, that they impugne the fundamentall doctrine.* And scripto 4. pag. 4: *Our opi-nion is, that we disagree not about impertiment matters only; or things of no consequence ; but about the maine and cheisest mat-ters.* And scripto 7 : *This one thing they ayme at, and bend all their endeauours to vndermine and ouerturne the groundwork of sauing doctrine.* And pag. 374. they complaine that those of Saxony *do often cry out of them, that they are worse then any idolaters.* And the Sacramentaries in Præfat. Apologet. Orthodoxi consensus, write thus of the Lutherans : *They haue hitherto suffered among them, such as call in question the doctrine of iustification, of originall sinne, of free will, of the Ghospell, of the law and vse thereof, of Christs*
descent

Lutherãs professe that thẽ-selues dif-fer funda-mentally.

deſcent into hell, of his perſon, of the election of Gods children, and many other articles of no ſmall moment; which things they eaſily put vp, becauſe all theſe go vnder the name of Lutherans. Now that the Sacramentaries likewiſe acknowledg the Lutherans for their brethren, is apparent by the Apology of the Church of England, by the conſent of Poland, by the preface of the Syntagme of Confeſ-

Sacramē- ſions, by the Conferences of Marſpurg and Mont-
taries belgard, and other publike writings and regiſtred
challenge acts: and yet they ſee and openly exclaime againſt
Lutherās. their errours in fundamental points of fayth. Of Luther thus writeth Zuinglius tom. 2. Reſp. ad Luther.
And yet fol. 401: *VVe iudge thee a worſe ſeductour, impoſtour, and de-*
ſay they *nyer of Chriſt, then was Marcion himſelfe.* And fol. 430. *Lu-*
differ fun- *ther as yet, is entangled and ſticks faſt in two errours exceeding*
damētally *grieuous, and in moſt foule ignorance.* Of Melancthon thus
from thē. ſayth Caluin epiſt. 183: *Either he openly impugneth true doctrine in the cheifeſt heads, or elſe hideth his meaning craftily or not very honeſtly.* And epiſt. 179. he complaineth that Melancthon endeauoureth to ouerthrow his doctrine of predeſtination: *VVithout which (ſayth he) the knowledge of Gods free and vndeſerued mercy is vtterly loſt.* The like he ſayth, epiſt. 141. Sturmius lib. de Ratione ineundæ Concordiæ, ſayth plainly, that the Lutherans *do pluck vp the foundation of Chriſtian Religion.* And Bullinger in fundamento firmo writeth, that *the very infidelity of the Iewes and Gentils is by the Lutherans brought into the Churches.* Cureus in Exegeſi Sacramentaria pag. 91: *Surely the controueſy (between the Lutherans and Sacramentaries) is concerning the foundation.* The Sacramentaries in the Preface of the Conference at Mulbrun ſay, that the Lutherans. *Teare in preces and adulterate the articles of the incarnation, of the true humane nature &c. VVhich articles (ſay they) no Chriſtian man can doubt*

doubt but are the *groundwork of saluation.* And in the foresayd preface: *They are at variance, not about the Lords supper only, but touching the person of Christ, touching the vnion of
his diuine and humane nature, touching the vbiquity of his body
and corporall manducation thereof common both to good and bad,
touching his ascending vp to heauen, and his sitting at the right
hand of his Father: of all these points they contend, and that with
such exceeding heat of disputation, as that old heresies not a few,
long since abolished and condemned, begin againe to lift vp their
head, as if they were recalled from hell.* The like they haue
ibidem in Prolegomenis. Of the controuersy which
is betweene the Lutherans & Sacramentaries about
the reall presence of Christs body in the Eucharist,
Martyr in locis tom. 2. p. 156. giues this iudgement:
*The contention and difference therein concernes the cheefe heads
of Religion.* Caluin epist. 292. sayth, that the opinion of
the Lutherans doth, *By mischeiuous iuglings and legierde-
mains ouerturne the principles of fayth.* Beza in his 5. epist.
that it *destroyeth the verity of Christs body.* And epist. 81.
that it *recalleth from hell the folly and doting errours of Marcion and Eutiches.* Bucer cited by Hospin. part. 2. Hist.
fol. 84: *It followeth thereupon, that Christ is not true man.*
Paraeus in cap 3 Galat. lecstion. 37: *There is nothing more
directly opposite to Christian Religion, then to think that the body
of Christ doth indeed lye hid really vnder the bread, and that the
same is truly eaten with the mouth.* Sadeel. in tract. de Con-
iunctione &c. pag. 369. *that it ouerthroweth the true nature of the true body and bloud of Christ. Which thing (sayth
he) we still lay to their charge.* And tract. de Sacramen-
tali manducatione pag. 26. *that it is a word of euils.* pag.
267: *That it traines after it idolatry.* And pag. 268: *that it
cannot stand with the verity of Christs body.* Hospin. part 2.
citat. fol. 2. *that it is the foundation of Papistry.* And fol.
381: *The base and pillar which sustaineth all the whole blended
and*

and *disordered heape of abuses, and all the bread-worship which hath vnder the Popedome byn deuised and brought in*. Lauaterus lib. de dissid. Euchar. fol. 7. that it is the *Foundation of the Popedome*. Curcus in Spongia, that *it is the foundation, the strength, the throne of the God Maozim, and of the Popish state*. And Vrsinus in Catechism. quest. 78. cap. 3.

Caluin de Cœna p. 8. & in Cõf pag. 754. Beza in fo. 6. v. 23. 61. & ad 4. Demonstr. Illyri i Zanchius in Confess c. 16. sect. 12.

sayth : *As long as the opinion of the corporall presence is maintained, Popish adoration, and oblation, and the whole Popish masse is kept on foot*. And there is not one Sacramentary, but thinks the verity of Christs body, and his ascention, & sitting at the right hand of the Father cleane taken away, if he should say he were substantially in the Eucharist. Whereupon Zanchius tom. 1. Miscell. in iudicio de dissidio Cœnæ pag. 553. sayth : *There are two maine reasons why the one party* (to wit the Sacramentaries) *renounce the presence of the body : The one, that the article of Christs ascension into heauen may be kept entire : the other that the nature and verity of his humane body be not destroyed*. Nay some of the Sacramentaries in their Confessions of faith condemne the opinion of the Lutherans as mad and blasphemous. For Confess. Crengerina cap. de cœna Domini, sayth : *VVe condemne their madnes, who auouch and maintaine flesh-eating, that is, who hold, that Christs naturall and very body, raw and bloudy without any change or transubstantiation at all, is receiued with the very mouth*. And the Scots in their Confess. pag. 159. say they, *Detest that blasphemous opinion, which auoucheth Christs reall presence in the bread & wine, and that he is receiued by the wicked or taken into the belly*. This and much more of the like is sometymes the Sacramentaries plea against the reall presence of Christs body in the Eucharist ; and yet at other tymes they professe that this controuersy is not of so great weight and moment, as that it should dissolue Ecclesiasticall Communion and
fel-

fellowſhip. For ſo teacheth Martir apud Simlerum in vita eius, the author of the orthodoxe Conſent. Preſat. Apologet. Hoſpinian part. 2. Hiſtor. fol. 78. Caluin de ſcandalis pag. 95. In Conſent. p. 764. Beza lib. de cœna cont. Weſtphalium. pag. 258. M. Perkins in his expoſition of the Creed, col. 792. and others. Nay (as we ſayd before) theſe men beſought the Lutherans, who ſtedfaſtly maintaine the reall preſence, to hold them for brethren and members of their Church. They can then find in their conſcience to haue fellowſhip and Communion with thoſe men, whoſe doctrine they condemne, *As Frantike & blaſphemous; whoſe doctrine (they ſay) deſtroyeth Chriſts aſcenſion, and the verity of his humane nature; ſubuerteth the principles or kind of ſayth and cheifeſt points of religion; recalleth the doting ſoules of men. So Marcion and Eutyches, eſtabliſheth the Kingdome of Antichriſt traines after it idolatry and a world of euills.* Fy on theſe mē beliefe, who think the maintenance of an opinion, which (as themſelues profeſſe) ouerthroweth the principall articles of Chriſtian ſayth, drawes after it idolatry, and moſt foule hereſies, layeth the foundation whereon Antichriſtianity is raiſed; of ſo ſleight conſequence as it ought not to diſſolue fraternity and Communion. What regard of ſayth or ſaluation may we think theſe men haue? There is yet another point of Luteraniſme touching the vbiquity, or preſence of Chriſts body euery where reproued of the Sacramentaries, and held in extreme diſlike; of which they likewiſe exclaime: *that it is* (a) *forged and compoſed of Eutychianiſme and Neſtorianiſme: that the hereſies of* (b) *Marcion and Eutyches, yea well nigh* (c) *all old hereſies are by it raiſed againe from hell; that it ſubuerteth the whole* (d) *Creed; that it takes away the* (e) *cheife heads of Chriſtian Religion; & that there is ſcant any one article of Chriſtian beliefe*

What ſacramentaries chalenge for brethren.

(a) *Beza reſ. onſ. ad act. i montisb. l. pag. 252.*
(b) *Caluin 4 inſtit. c. 17 p. 17.*
(c) *Huſp. pref. par. 2.*
(d) *Perkins expoſ. Symb. c. ll. 792.*
(e) *Sideal. de veru hum. nat.*

D

beliefe which it doth not vtterly abolish. And yet these selfe
same Sacramentaries stile them who defend this opinion (f) *Most flourishing Churches*; and made earnest sute
to be held for (g) brethren of those very men, who
vpheld this doctrine against them, and maintayned
it to their face. Nay the particuler Churches of Sacramentaries themselues consist of parts mainly dis-
ioyned in matters of beliefe. Examples hereof we
need not seeke abroad. Our owne Protestants tell vs,
how the Puritans their brethren allow not of the
booke of common prayer, but *hold it to be full of* (a) *corruptions and all abominations*, and teach that Protestants
(b) *wickedly mangle and wrest the Scriptures, that they haue no*
(c) *Pastours, that they haue not a true Church, yea not so much
as the outward face of a Church; and that they exhort the Court
of Parlament with perfect* (d) *hatred to detest the present state
of the Church; that no* (e) *Iew, no Turke, no Papist, could pos-
sibly haue spoken more spitefully of their Church and state, and
that they seeke to shake, nay to ouerthrow the* (f) *foundations,
grounds, and pillars of their Church.* Finally, that the Puritans *will not account the Protestants their* (g) *brethren*, and
yet the Protestants neuertheleste acknowledge Puritans for *their* (h) *brethren and fellow-labourers in the Lords
haruest.* In Scotland likewise (as his Maiesty witnesseth) *That which was Catechisticall doctrine in one assembly,
was hardly admitted for sound and orthodoxe in another*; and
yet these assemblies excluded not one another from
the Church. What can be therefore more cleare and
euident, then that both the Lutherans and Sacramentaries acknowledge (when they list) those to be
members of their Church, who deny fundamentall
articles of their fayth?

     6.   A third proofe may be drawne from the
Protestants demeanour and carriage towards the
                                    Fathers,

(f) Sadeel.
Iup.
(g) Beza in
colloq. mō-
tisbel. pag.
462.

Sacramē-
taries say
there is
fundamē-
tall diffe-
rēce amōg
them.
(a) Whit-
gift. resp.
ad Admo-
nit. p. 149.
357.
(b) Ib. resp.
ad schedas.
(c) Resp.
Purit. pag. 6.
(d) Pag. 31.
(e) Pag. 33
(f) Pag. 6.
(g) Resp.
ad schedas.
Bancrofts
Suruey c. 33
(h) Resp.
ad schedas
Oxon. resp.
ad Millen.
Confer. ad
Hampton
Court. p.
44.

Fathers, whome they claime and challenge for their
fellow-cittizens, and yet confesse plainly (to omit
what they acknowledge concerning other points)
that they were of a contrary beliefe in the article of
Iustification by sole fayth; wherein (as shall be hereafter shewed) they say the soule, the summe, and definition of Protestantisme consisteth. Luther tom. 1.
colloq. German. apud Coccium tom. 1. pag. 131 : *In
which errour (that works ioyned with fayth do iustify) were many of the Fathers.* And tom. 5. in cap. 3. Galat.
fol. 358. he sayth, that of the difference, which he
espied betwcen the law and the Ghospell, as that the
law taught iustification by works, the Ghospell by
sole beliefe, *There is nothing to be found in the works of the
old Fathers. Augustin held it in part, Hierome and the rest knew
it not.* Melancthon tom. 1. in Dominicam Trinitatis
pag. 89 : *It is meruaile, that the cheife Doctours had no knowledge of the iustice of fayth.* Tom. 2. lib. de Ecclef. pag. 134 :
*Chrysostome reckons vp many wayes and meanes to obtaine re-
mission of sinnes, as almes deeds, teares and other works.* The
Centuriatours of Magdeburg. cent. 3. cap. 4. col. 79.
& seqq. say, that the Doctours of the third age *Make
workes the cause of our iustice in Gods sight.* Cent. 4. c. 4. col.
293 : *In this article of iustification this age reuolted wholly
from the doctrine of the Apostles.* And Cent. 5. in Prefat.
they say of the Fathers of that age : Chrysostome and
the residue *attribute iustice vnto works, they make works the
meanes of saluation, and ascribe iustification either in part, or
formally, or wholly vnto works.* Gerlachius tom. 2. disput.
13 : *The ancient Fathers would haue the iustice, life, and saluation of a Christian man consist in obseruing Gods commaundements, as Hilary, Origen, Tertullian, Eusebius, Chrysostome,
Augustine, &c.* Kemnitius in locis part. 1. tit. de Iustificat. pag. 242. sayth that the Fathers Intermingled some-
D 2

tymes

Protestāts
say the fa-
thers dif-
fert fun-
damētally
from the.

In the art.
of iustifi-
cation by
onlyfaith.

tymes and entwyned the doctrine of good workes with the articles of iustification, sometymes plied and bended the article of iustification to good workes. And part. 2. tit. de lege pag. 106: *If the Fathers disputes be all layd together, the summe of them is this in effect, that sinne and infirmity of nature is manifested by the law, to the end we may search out a Phisitian, by whose grace it may be so healed, as it be able to satisfy and fullfill the law, and so we be saued.* And ibidem in orat. de lectione Patrum

The summe of the fathers doctrine is iustification by workes.

pag. 3. he sayth of S. Cyprian, *He had a fundamentall errour*. And pag. 4. of S. Hilary: *He held an erroneous opinion touching the foundation.* Caluin also lib. cont. Versipellem pag. 353: *Three maine points of our fayth, to wit, the corruption of our nature, free and vndeserued iustification, and Christs Priesthood, are so darkly and obscurely touched in the ancientest writers, that no certainty can be drawne thence.* Againe: *VVe shall neuer learne by the Fathers, how we may be reconciled to God, how the obedieuce of Christ is freely and vndeseruedly reputed ours.* Martyr in locis cit. de scriptura col. 1432: *Other Fathers think good works much auaileable to iustification.* Hospin. in epist. dedicat. part. 1. Histor: *All the Fathers well nigh do now and then sprinkle and cast on with all the leauen of good works, and attribute iustification to them, either in part, or formally or wholy.* Pareus lib. 4, de Iustificat. c. 12: *The Fathers both Greek and Latin especially those that wrote before the Pelagian bickerings, fancied ouer much, and tooke too great a liking to the Philosophers doctrine, concerning the iustification of worcks.* Finally M·Perkins in Problem. cap. de Iustificat. sayth, that the *old writers confound the law with the Ghospell, and do not distinguish the iustice of the law from the iustice of the Ghospell.*

7.   To them, who in this manner ioyne friend-ship and Communion as well with such as renounce fundamentall articles of fayth, as with those whose beliefe is contrary in articles not fundamental, what

                                        meruaile

meruaile is it, it all heretiks and Schiſmatiks ſeeme fit companions, and worthy to be accounted their brethren and fellow-cittizens? But let vs heare their owne words, wherein they acquaint vs, what ranke hereticks & Schiſmatiks hold amongſt them. Luther tom. 7. ſerm. de Dominica 20. poſt Trinit. fol. 262. ſayth: *They are frantique and beſide themſelues who go about to ſeuer the Church corporally from heretikes.* Hemingius in Syntag. Inſtitut. pag. 192: *In the outward ſociety of the Church, are many heretiks and Schiſmatiks.* Salomon Geſner in locis loc. 24: *Are heretiks then in the Church? By any meanes.* Brentius in Præfat. Recognit: *Chriſt giues not ouer the conſeruation of his ſheep in the middeſt of hereſies, but they muſt be ſuch, as do not quite take away the foundation and Miniſtery.* Reineccius tom. 4. Armatur. cap. 6. pag. 35: *VVe affirme there are heretiques euen in the true Church.* Huttelus in Analyſi Confeſſ. Auguſt. pag. 435: *Neither were hereſies without the territory and limits of the true Church.* Pleſſy in his booke of the Church cap. 2. affirmeth plainly, that *all hereticall and Schiſinaticall congregations are truly the Church.* And ibid. pag. 25. he ſayth: *Although particuler Churches be inſected with hereſies, from top to toe, neuertheleſſe they are parts of the vniuerſall Church as long as they profeſſe the name of Chriſt.* Moulins in his Bukler of fayth part. 1. ſect. 89: *An hereticall Church may be ſayd to be a true Church, euen as man blemiſhed with a canker or infected with the plague is notwithſtanding a true man.* Sonis Reſponſ. ad Spondeum c. 10. pag. 365. *Heretiks are within the Church.* Lubbert lib. 2. de Eccleſ. cap. 3: *It is manifeſt, that heretikes are, ſome as yet in the viſible Church, ſome alſo in the church of the elect.* Iunius lib. 3. de Eccleſ. cap. 4: *Heretiks abſolutely are of the Church, vnleſſe they be ſuch as ouerthrow fundamentall articles of religion.* Bullinger teacheth the same Decad. 2. ſerm. 8. and it is the common doctrine of

Cap. 3: next

D 3   the

the Proteſtants, who (as is before proued) exclude none from being members of their Church, that deny only ſuch articles as are not fundamẽtall. How beit ſome of them *vpon hereticall priuiledge* (as Tertullian ſpeaketh) will not haue ſuch called heretiks; being indeed more aſhamed of the name then of the thing it ſelfe. Zanchius likewiſe lib. 1. epiſt. ad Dudit. pag. 150. ſayth, that *hereticall and Schiſmaticall ſects are within the Church.* Tilenus in Syntag. diſput. 14: *Heretiks, euen thoſe that ſubuert the foundation, and Schiſmatiks in regard of outward Communion, are in the Church, till either of themſelues they go to the enemies ſide, or are caſt out by the lawfull iudgement of the Church.* And D. Feild in his firſt booke of the Church cap. 14: *Seing God gaue the power of the keyes and the diſpenſation of his word and Sacraments only to his Church, if Heretiks be not of the Church, they do not then baptize.* And cap. 7: *They that are partakers of the heauenly calling, and ſanctified by the profeſſion of diuine truth, and the vſe of the meanes of ſaluation, are of very diuers ſortes; as heretikes, Schiſmatiks, hypocrites, and thoſe that profeſſe the whole ſauing truth in vnity and ſinceritẏ of a good and ſanctified heart. All theſe are partakers of the heauenly calling, and ſanctified by the profeſsion of truth, and conſequently are all in ſome degree and ſort of that ſociety of men, whome God calleth out vnto himſelfe, & ſeparateth from Infidels, which is rightly named the Church* D. Whitaker contr. 4: queſt. 5. c. 3. pag. 679: *All heretiks are within the Church.* Hooker in his 3. booke of Eccleſiaſticall policy pag. 128: *VVe muſt acknowledge euen heretikes themſelues to be, though a maymed part, yet a part of a viſible Church: Againe: If an Infidell ſhould purſue to death an heretike profeſſing Chriſtianity only for Chriſtian Profeſſion ſake, could we deny vnto him the honour of Martyrdome?* By which words it is plaine, that they admit heretiks not only into the viſible

Church,

Lib. de car-li̅ne Coriſti, cap. 15.

Church, but into the inuisible also, or company of
the elect and predestinate to saluation. And D. Andrews in his answere to Bellarmines Apology cap.
5.pag.121.denyeth that the words, *Catholik* and *Heretike* are opposite; wherefore vnlesse he will debarre
and shut out some Catholiks from the Church, he
must needs giue admittance to heretiks, seing by his
owne verdict they may be Catholiks. D.White in
defence of his way cap. 38. pag. 367: *The second sort of
the militant Church are hypocrites and vnsound members, that
are not called effectually, but disobey the truth whereof they make
profession such are heretiks, schismatiks &c.* Touching their
acceptations of Schismatiks, besides what hath byn
already alleaged, D. Feild in his first booke of the
Church cap.13.writeth thus: *The departure of Schisma- They
tiks is not such, but that, notwithstanding their schisme, they are* challenge
and remaine parts of the Church of God. Iunius in the place Schisma-
before quoted layeth clayme to those Schismatikes, tiks.
*Who (sayth he) seuer not themselues from the whole Church
but only from a part thereof.* But D. Morton in the 1.part
of his Apology lib.1.cap.2.sayth absolutely without
any acception or restraint at all: *Schismatiks are of the
Church.* And lib.2.cap.10.pag.288: *Variances (sayth he)
and schismes do not betoken the false Church.* And D. Willet
in his Synopsis cont.2. quest. 3. pag. 104: *We say that
Schismatiks, though they hold some false points of doctrine, yet if
their errours be not fundamentall, and if they retaine the purity of
doctrine in all points necessary to saluation, and the administration of the Sacraments, may make a particuler Church by themselues.* These are their acknowledgements touching
Heretikes and Schismatikes in generall. Let vs now They ac-
descend to particularities, and see the courteous ad- know-
mission they giue to some of them by name. ledge the
　　8. The Grecians and other Easterne Schis- Grecians.
　　　　　　　　　D 4　　　　　　　matiks,

matiks, yea heretiks to, for the moſt part, find that
fauour at their hands, as they vouchſafe to account
them members of their Church. His Maieſty epiſt.
ad Card. Peron pa. 13 hath thus: *The Churches of Rome,*
Greece, Antioch *, Aegipt , Aethiopia , Muſcouy, and others more*
are members of the Catholike church. D. White in defence
of his way c. 37. pag. 355 : *The viſible churches of Greece,*
Aethiope, Armenia, and Rome, with the nations contayned ther-
in, haue in them the true church of God, wherin men may be
ſaued. D. Morton in his anſwere to the Proteſtants
Apology lib. 4. cap. 2. ſect. 7. ſayth, that the Aſſyrian
Churches keep the true foundation of Chriſtian
fayth . The ſame, (eſpecially of the Grecians) teacheth Luther. tom. 2. lib. de captiu. Babylon. fol. 65.
& in Aſſert. art. 37. fol. 114. Iunius cont. 4 lib. 4. cap.
6. Sadeel. Reſponſ. ad Theſ. Poſnan. cap. 12. D. Whitaker lib. 7. cont. Duræum ſect. 3. Bucanus loco 41.
queſt. 5. D. Feild lib. 3. de Eccleſ. cap. 5. & 28. D. Fulke
de Succeſſ. pag. 120. Burhill pro Tortura Torti c. 15.
and others .

    9.   And ſometymes they are not leſſe free-har-
ted towards weſterne heretiks. Melancthon in locis

They
challenge
the Ana-
baptiſts.

à Manlio editis tit. de Eccleſ. pag. 491. writeth, that
two girles, who were burnt (as he ſayth) for Anabaptiſme, *held the foundation of fayth, and dyed in a good Con-*
feſſion. And Zuinglius tom. 2. lib. de Author. ſedit.
fol. 134. & ſeq. exhorting his fellowers, not to reuolt
from his doctrine, for the debates and quarels between the Proteſtants and the Anabaptiſts, calleth
both parts *moſt learned and ſonnes of the ſame Father.* Neither
muſt thou (ſayth he) *giue any man way to ſhake and weaken*
thy fayth, although thou ſee that men of the greateſt learning
moue diſputes, and fall by the eares, with much eagerneſſe of con-
tention ; touching externall matters (he meanes baptiſme)

but

but let this be *rather thy stedfast persuasion, that by the Sonne of God we are all made sonnes of the same Father.* Againe: *Neither am I wont to speake these things, for that I am so greatly moued with the baptisme of children.* And ibidem lib. de Baptismo tol.96. he layth, that *baptisme is a matter of ceremony, which the church may omit or take quite away.* Oecolampadius in his 2 booke of epistles p. 363. fayth, *baptisme is an externall thing, which by the law of charity may be dispensed withall.* And Musculus in locis tit. de hæresi pag.605. reckons the Anabaptists amongst those, *who* (fayth he) *keeping the foundations of fayth, about secondary matters haue fallen into misbeliese.* And Bucanus loc.41.de Ecclef. queft. 5. auoucheth plainly, that Anabaptists are a Church, *Like as a man attainted with leprosy or out of his wits, is a man.* His Maiesty epist. ad Card. Peron pag. 25. fayth : *Some reckon baptisme among those things, which whether we haue or want, the matter is not great.* And D. Whitaker cont. 4. queft. 7. cap.2. pag. 716. fayth we may abstaine from baptisme, so there be no contempt and scandall in the fact. Finally D. Morton in his answere to the Proteftants Apology lib. 4. albeit in the 6.chapter he make a doubt whether Anabaptists retaine and hold the foundation, yet in the 2.cap. fect.10.speaketh thus : *The Anabaptists exclude Proteftants and all different professions from the hope of spirituall life, yet do not Proteftants iudge the state of euery Anabaptist to be so vtterly desperate.* We fee how they teach that Anabaptists hold the foundation, and deny but an externall, secondary, and ceremoniall matter, and such as may be omitted, so it be don without scandall; that Anabaptists and themselues are sonnes of the same Father, that they are in the state of saluation, and that they are a church as a man tainted with leprosy is a man. Now concerning the Arrians of these tymes, M. Morton in his booke of the Kingdome of Israel, and the Church

And the
Arrians.

Danæus in
c.53. Aug.
de hæres .
VVhitak.
ad Rat. 10.
pag.241.
Parentius
in Instruct
Gall.p.27.

pag. 94. auoucheth plainly, that their Churches are
to be accounted the Churches of God, *Because* (sayth
he) *they hold the foundation of the Ghospell.* Hooker in his
4.booke of Ecclesiasticall policy pag. 181. writeth
thus : *The Arians in the reformed churches of Poland &c.* Nay
some of the Protestants lay clayme to that old heretike Aërius, for that he agreed with them in denyall
of prayer for the dead, and some other points; yet
that he was stained with Arianisme, S. Epiphanius,
who liued in those tymes hær. 75. and S. Augustin
53. (witnesses whose credit herein can no way be
impeached) do plainly testify .

They lay
claime to
their pro-
fessed eni-
mies.

In Concil.
Trid. In
Censura
Orient .

10.   Lastly they forbeare not sometymes to
challenge for their owne, such as were their profest
enemies, as is certaine by their clayme to the Papists
and Grecians, who condemned and branded their
doctrine with the marck of heresy. And the Sacramentaries pretend a right to Luther and the Lutherans, howbeit it is well known, that both the Master
and the sect haue diuers tymes censured and condemned their doctrine by name, as in the Confessions of
Auspurg, Mansfeld, Antwerpe, & that of Sueueland
set forth anno 1563. in the booke of Concord, in the
visitation of Saxony, and else where it appeareth.
And that in the Conference of Marpurge and Montbelgard they gaue them the repulse and flatly refused
to admit them for brethren. Nay, as Lauatherus
writeth lib. de dissid. Euchar. anno 1556 : *There haue*
byn many Synodes held (by the Lutherans) *wherein they con-*
sulted what way they might take to quell and make an end of the
Sacramentaries. And they shew the same encroaching
desire in personall Claimes. For Illyricus in his Catalogue lib.19. col. 1917, entolleth amongst his witnesses Clicthouæus, an earnest and vehement aduersary

sary both of Luther and Oecolampadius. D. Humfrey in vita Iuelli claymeth Erasmus, for a main-
tayner and Champion of the truth. M. Fox vouch-
safes him a place in his kalender of Protestant Saints, *Rainolds l. 1. de Idolat. cap. 2.*
and Verheiden sets his pourtraiture amongst the
Worthies and Pairs of their religion. Vorstius in Ap-
pend. Respons. ad Sladum pag. 136. accounteth him
one of his owne, *that is (sayth he) one of the reformed.*
D. Whitaker Contr. 4. quest. 5. cap. 3. pag. 693 sayth:
*It is most apparent that Erasmus thought the same of religion that
we do.* And yet Erasmus himselfe lib. 16. epist. 11. professeth, that he acknowledgeth not Luther, and impugneth openly both him and his doctrine. And (as
Amiderfius writeth in epist. apud Lutherum tom. 2.
fol. 487.): *The summe of Erasmus doctrine is this, that Luthers
doctrine is heresy.* Otho Brunsfelsius in his answere to
Erasmus spunge, layth these things to his charge:
*Thou makest protestation neuer to haue conuersation or fellow-
ship with those men, who imbrace the ghospell vnder Luthers
name.* Againe: *It is well knowne and confest, that of so many
enemies of the (Protestant) ghospell, no one euer did it more
harme then thou.* Hutterus in Expostulat. Hospin. part.
2. Histor. fol. 72. Iames Andrew lib. cont. Hosium p.
110 D. Iames l. de corrupt. scripturæ & Patrum pag.
66. and others, say the like of him. D. Hun phrey ad
Rat. 3. Campiani will haue King Henry 8. to haue
byn a member of their Church. D. Fulke lib. cont.
Heskins. & Sander. sect. 82. sayth, *he was a member of
the Catholike church of Christ.* And D. Andrews in Resp.
ad Apoll. Bellarm. cap. 1. sayth: *He was a true defender of
the true fayth.* Bucer epist. dedicat. Comment. ad Rom:
*He imbraced the pure Ghospell of Christ reiecting those forgeries
of men which are repugnant to it.* And yet, it is most certaine, that he sharply persecuted and pursued Protes-
stants

stants euen vnto death. And as Melancthon writeth to him in epist. tom. 4: *He oppressed the truth then appearing and shewing it selfe.* And as Cambden sayth in Apparatu Annalium Anglic. *Protestants he burnt for heretikes.* Of Charles 5. Scultetus in Conc. secular. pag. 10. writeth thus: *It is knowne by vndoubted demonstration, that Charles 5. departed this life trusting to the same comfort and the same sayth, which Luther drew from the sacred welsprings, and breached to the people,* (Iames Andrews lib.cont.Hosium pag. 2 3 3. hath the like) and yet in the same sermon p. 2 7. he sayth: *To this alone he bent his whole endeauours, that he might pluck vp the Lutheran religion by the rootes.* M Doue in his booke of Recusancy will needs persuade vs, that Bellarmine himselfe is a Protestant, or at least no right Papist. What meruaile is it, if these men be so hardy as to challenge the ancient Fathers, seing they are not ashamed to claime in this manner their professed enemies, such as are knowne to all the world, and are yet aliue.

That Protestants sometymes acknowledge Idolaters,
Infidels, Antichrist himselfe, and Atheists
to be members of their Church.

C H A P. I V.

Protestāts challenge Idolaters.

1. THAT they sometymes confesse idolaters are members of their Church, is euident. First for that they refuse not to receiue Papists, (as we haue heard before) in exclamations and outcries against whose idolatry, their tongues and pennes are set most a worke, for to their worship of the Eucharist, of Saincts, of images, of reliques, they afford no

mildes

milder name. And secondly it appeareth by their
owne words. For M. Hooker in his 3. booke of Ecclesiasticall Policy pag. 126. sayth: *Christians by externall*
profession they are all, whose marke of recogniscance hath in it
those things which we haue mentioned; yea although they be im-
pious idolaters, wicked heretikes, persons excommunicable.
Againe: *Those whose knees were bowed vnto Baal, euen they*
were also of the visible Church of God. Boysseul in Confut.
p. 822 answering to the place where Spondeus obiected that if the Church of Rome be an Idolatresse,
(as Boysseul had auouched) it is not the Church of
Christ; makes this reply: *And why not as well as Israel?*
And D. Whitaker Cont. 2. quest. 3. cap. 3. pag. 475.
saith: *Although this errour* (Idolatry in adoring the calfe)
were most grieuous, yet it destroyed not the whole nature of the
Church.

2. That they sometymes comprize also Infidels in the Church, is manifest, first because they affirme that such may be saued; For M. Fox in his Martyrologe pag. 495. reporteth that a certaine Protestant Martyr whose learning piety & zeale he greatly commendeth, taught *that a Turke, Saracen, or any*
Mahumetan whatsoeuer may be saued; if he trust in one God and
keep his law. M. Bale in his 6 Century pag. 464. bids vs
beware *that we condemne not rashly any Turke.* And Zuinglius tom. 1. lib. de prouid. fol. 370. sayth: *It is not vni-*
uersally true, that who so hath no fayth is damned. Againe: *As*
for the damnation of vnbeleiuers it is meant only of those, who
heard and did not beleiue. And tom. 2. declarat. de peccat.
orig. fol. 118: *This saying* (who so doth not beleiue shall
be condemned) *must in no wise be absolutely vnderstood, but*
it is to be vnderstood of those, who hauing heard the ghospell
would not beleiue. And ibidem in exposit. fidei fol. 559.
he sayth, that in heauen Christians shall meet many
heathens,

And
Infidells?

See Homil.
in Specim.
Contr. art.
27.

heathens, whose names he there sets downe, and a-
mongst the rest that cruel Theseus, and Magician
Numa, the founder of heathenish superstitions a-
mongst the Romans. Which opinion of his those of
Zurich in Apolog. Gualter.in prefat. tom. 1. Zuinglij, Simler.in vita Bullengeri, and others seeke to
patronize and make good. Now it were folly and
madnes, to auouch that these men were of the number of the faythfull. They belieue then that infidels
may be saued. But S. Augustin was of a farre different beliefe lib 4. cont. Iul. cap. 3. where he writes
thus: *VVhat one of those, who would be accounted Chri-*
stians, will say an Infidell is iust, be it euen Fabritius.

3.   Secondly their doctrine touching the predestinate carrieth with it a necessary acknovledge-
ment of their Communion with Infidels. For they
teach, that who so is predestinate is alwayes a member of the Church. Hus his first article condemned
by the Councel of Constance was this: *The predestinate*
remayneth euer a member of the Church. And Luther tom.
2. in Assert.art.30: *I say the opinions of Iohn Hus are all E-*
uangelicall and Christian. Againe: *I admit all the condemned*
articles of Iohn Hus. And tom. 1. in disput. Lypsic. fol.
254. he maintaineth openly this article of Hus: *The*
Church is the whole multitude of the predestinate. Vorstius in
Anti-bellarmine page 125: *VVe affirme that the Councell*
of Constance, which condemned the doctrine of Hus (that who
so is predestinate is alwayes a mēber of the Church)
was surely in this respect Antichristian. Danæus in Resp. ad
Bellarm. Contr. 4. lib. 3. cap.2. sayth: *The first opinion*
(which was the opinion of Hus) is true, and is ours. A-
gaine: *our opinion is that the Church is the whole company of*
men, whome God hath predestinated to saluation. And cap. 7:
It must be answered that Paul was alwayes (but not always ap-
                                                parently

parently in regard of men) of *Gods true Church.* Againe: *Such Turkes and Iewes as God hath predestinated to saluation, are of the Church, euen now at this tyme in regard they are predestinate and in respect of God ; but they are not yet of Gods Church apparently, and in respect of vs, for as much as they lack yet those marks, whereby God doth heere shew vs men who are of the church.* And Cont. 4. lib. 3. cap. 12 : *The true definition of the true church is this: The company and multitude of those, whome God hath chosen to saluation.* And Iunius lib. 3. de Ecclef. cap. 7 : *Paul was alwayes of the church according to predestination; from which (sayth he) the church taketh her being, or formal definition; but not according to the outward forme of the church.* What can be more apparent, then that these men teach, that the predestinate are members of the church according to the true being therof and in the sight of God, euen during the tyme of their infidelity.

4. Thirdly this followeth necessarily vpon that which they teach concerning infants (especially such as are descended from faythfull parents) departing this life vnbaptized. For they affirme, that the children of the faythfull are actually in the Church, as the French Confession article 35 : *Togeather with the parents God accounteth also their offspring in the church.* And the Zuitzers cap. 20 : *VVhy should not they (the children of the faythfull) be ingrafted by sacred baptisme, who are Gods proper possession and within his church?* Caluin in Instruct. cont. Anabap. art. 1 : *Vnspotted infants are in the Communion of the church before they come forth of their Mothers wombe.* And Pareus lib. 3. de Iustificat. cap. 4. pag. 884: *Caluin on good reason determineth, that the children of the church, are borne cittizens of the church.* Their doctrine also hath the same issue, who teach that infants (at leastwise the children of the faythfull) are saued

without

without baptisme; as the Protestants in the colloq. Ratisbon. And Zuinglius tom. 2. Declarat. de peccat. orig. fol. 119: *Concerning Christians children we are assured, that they are not damned for originall sinn; of others we haue not the like assurance: howbeit, to confesse ingenuously, the opinion we taught heretofore; to wit, that we ought not to iudge rashly of heathens children, seemes to vs the more probable* Vorstius in Anti-bellarmine pag. 542: *Zuinglius and some other ghospellers auouch, that all children whatsoeuer are by the grace of Christ saued, others for the most part hold, that at leastwise all the elect, whether extract from faythfull or other parents do euen vnbaptized attaine to saluation.* Whereof he sayth: *The opinion of these later is surely the safest; and yet the first opinion is probable inough and ought not to be rashly condemned.* Now as D. Whitaker sayth Cont. 2. quest. 1. cap. 5. & 6: *All that are saued are really and actually in the church.* And D. Morton part. 1. Apol. lib. 1. cap. 4: *To be of the church in possibility, sufficeth not to saluation.* Lubbertus lib. 2. de Eccles. cap. 2: *Neither can any one be saued except he be actually and really in the church.* Whence Martyr in 1. Cor. 7. fol. 177. sayth: *Infants must of necessity appertaine vnto the church, seing there is no saluation without it.* They teach moreouer, that

Infants without all faith according to Protestants.

Infants haue no fayth, and consequently that they are infidels, whence it ensueth that they account some infidels to be actually of the church. Caluin 4. Institut. cap. 16. §. 19: *I will not lightly affirme, that they* (infants) *are endued with the same fayth we find in our selues.* And §. seq. he sayth: *Infants are baptized for future repentance and fayth. Now if they dye before they are of yeares, God reneweth them by the vertue of his spirit, which we do not comprehend, in such manner as himselfe alone knoweth how to bring to passe.* Lib. cont. Seruet. pag. 647. he sayth, that that sentence of the Scripture: *VVhosoeuer belieueth not in the Sonne of God abideth in death, and the wrath of God remayneth*

vpon

vpon him, belongeth not to infants, but only to such as are obstinate. And in cap.5. Rom. v.17 : *That you may be partaker of iustice, it is needfull that you be faythfull, because it is receiued by fayth. To infants it is communicated by a speciall manner.*
Bucer in cap.19. Matthæi pag.404 : *Paul fayth that fayth commeth by hearing the word preached, and in the same sort all the Scripture speaketh of fayth. Seing therefore infants heare not the word preached, they cannot haue this kind of fayth. But out of that, that infants want fayth, nothing lesse can be concluded, then (which some thinke) that therefore they cannot please God. Infants are blessed by the grace of God and merits of Christ. But if they be taken hence in their infancy, they shall know God and reape felicity by some other knowledge then fayth.* Musculus in locis tit. de baptismo : *Infants haue yet no fayth.* Againe : *Infants are saued by Gods election, though they be taken out of this life not only vnbaptized, but euen before they haue fayth.*
Beza in Confess. cap.4. sect.48 : *It doth not appeare to vs that infants are endowed with that habit of fayth, which we sayd was required to the receiuing of the matter and effect of the Sacraments, nor is it likely that they are.* And in colloq. Montisbel.pag.407 : *VVherefore, though the children of the faythfull want fayth, yet is not baptisme vnprofitable to them.* And part.2. Respons.ad acta Montisbel. pag.124 : *All beit infants haue no fayth of their owne, especially actuall; yet rightly are they baptized according to the forme of the Couenant, I will be thy God, and of thy seed, which is apprehended by the parents to themselues and their children.* And pag.129 : *I confesse that fayth is required, that infants comprehended in the Couenant may please God; but I deny, that they can or ought to be endowed with their owne fayth inherent in them.* Dancus l.4. de baptismo cap.10. pag.268. proposeth to himselfe this question : *VVhat is the fayth which in baptisme we require in infants?* and answereth : *None.* Vrsinus in defens. argument. Beza. *God receiueth infants into the Church with-*

Infants haue not so much as the habit of fayth.

E   *out* eut ſayth. Peter Martyr in 1. Cor. 7. pag. 94 : *Seing the holy Scripture doth not tell me, that infants belieue, or thoſe miracles are wrought in them, neither ſee I that it is neceſſary for their ſaluation, I think it is inough that they be thought to be ſaued, becauſe by election and predeſtination they belong to the people of God, & are endued with the holy Ghoſt, who is the author of ſayth, hope, and Charity.* Perhaps they will anſweare out of Auguſtins opinion, that they are ſaued by the ſayth of others, to wit of their parents. But the Prophet ſayth that euery one is ſaued by his owne ſayth, not by other mens ſayth. VVherefore we anſwere more eaſily, who exact expreſſe and actuall ſayth in thoſe that are of yeares, but in the children of Chriſtians, who are brought to be Chriſtened, we ſay ſayth is begun in its principle & root, becauſe they haue the holy Ghoſt from whence all both ſayth and other vertues do flow. D. Whitaker Cont. 2. queſt. 6. c. 3. pag. 566: *Baptiſme doth not infuſe any ſayth or grace into infants.* And he ſayth plainly, that infants haue no ſayth. And lib. 8. cont. Duræum ſect. 77 : *albeit in the Sacraments ſayth which receiueth the word of promiſe, be neceſſary, yet that ſayth is not needfull in infants, albeit it be not to be doubted but the holy Ghoſt effectually worketh in them after a ſecret and wonderfull manner.* M. Perkins de prædeſtinat. tom. 1. col. 149 : *Infants which dye in the Couenant, we belieue to be ſaued by tenour of that Couenant, but they were not choſen for ſayth or according to ſayth, which yet they had not.* And in ſerie caular. cap. 35 : *Elected infants dying in the wombe or ſoone after they be borne, are ſaued after a hidden and vnſpeakeable manner ingraſted in Chriſt by the ſpirit of God.* Luther tom. 6. in cap. 25. Gen. ſol. 322 : *Vnbaptized infants haue no ſayth.* Melancthon in locis tit. de baptiſmo to 3. fol. 238: It is moſt true, that ſayth is required in all that are of years. But concerning infants (ſayth he) the matter is other wiſe. Kemnitius part. 2. Exam. tit. de baptiſm. pag. 89. telleth vs that ſome Proteſtants are of opinion, that infants are in-

deed

Infants ſaued without ſayth.

seed saued by the grace of God, but without fayth. Nor doth
their saying that the seed or root of fayth, or else an
inclination or disposition to fayth (which some of
them affirme infants to haue) help them any thing
at all, both because Scharpe cont. 1. de Iustifi. graunteth that this seed *can neither haue the knowledge nor apply-
ing of the promises,* and therefore is not Protestant faith,
and because Musculus in locis tit. de fide art. 7. confesseth, that they *distinguish and put a difference betweene
fayth and this hidden seed.* Now if it be no fayth, it maketh not him faythfull in whome it is. And lastly because (as themselues acknowledge) they are not assured, whither infants haue any such seed or no. For
Caluin lib. 4. cap. 16. § 9. cit: *VVhether they haue at all any
knowledge like vnto fayth, I choose rather to leaue it vndetermi-
ned.* And he addeth, that the manner of their renewing *is knowne to God alone.* To these allegations you
may adde, that M. Perkins in his Reformed Catholike cont. 16. fayth, a man may be saued *by a desire to
haue fayth :* And neuerthelesse confesseth that this desire *is not indeed fayth.* And in 2. Galat. col. 91 : *God accep-
teth the will and desire to belieue, for beliefe it selfe.* Now as
long as a man hath not fayth but only a desire thereof, he is an infidel.

5. You might think, that hauing made this
graunt of saluation to infidels, their liberality wold
rest here, and not passe these bounds ; but they go yet
further, and bestow it sometymes euen vpon him,
whome they sweare, yea belieue as an article of their
fayth (and that with as great certainty and assurance
as they belieue God is in heauen, or Christ is the
Messias) to be that notable Antichrist foretold in
Scripture. For thus writeth M. Powell lib. de Antichristo cap. 33. pag. 338 : *I will in no wise say, that all the*

*Protestãts
challenge
Antichrist.*

Popes from the tyme wherein Papistry was first reuealed to be Antichristianity, are damned. Howbeit in the beginning of his booke he makes this protestation : *I solemnely take God to record, that I as certainly know the Bishop of Rome to be that great Antichrist, and the Popish church to be the Synagogue of Antichrist, as I know God to be in the heauens, or Iesus Christ to be the true Messias promised to the Fathers.* D. Whitaker likewise cont. 4. q.5. cap. 3. pag. 694. sayth : *Let vs cry aloud and swere by him who liues for euer, that the Bishop of Rome is Antichrist.* And to D. Sanders last demonstration that the Pope is not Antichrist pag. 799 : *VVe may take that most sacred and most true oath, and sweare by him who liues for euer, that the Bishoppe of Rome is the very Antichrist.* And neuerthelesse in his answere to the first demonstration he sayth with M. Powell: *I will not say, that from the tyme that Papistry began to be Antichristianity, the Popes themselues haue byn all damned.* And both he cap. cit. pag. 679. & 682. & other Protestants ordinarily affirme that Antichrists Sea shalbe *in the true Church, among the company of the faythfull,* and that he shall be *a cittizen, and inhabitant, and Pastour of the Church.* To whom I pray will these men deny saluation, or a place in their Church, who graunt it vnto Antichrist the sworne enemy of Christ, whome the scripture it self styleth: *Christs aduersary, the man of sin, the sonne of perdition?* I see not why they should henceforward vpbrayd vs with Antichrist, since they themselues clayme him for a member of their Church.

6.   It is also certaine, that they challenge Atheists. For Illyricus in Catal. lib. 9. col. 1916. D. Humfrey responf. ad Rat. 3. Camp. M. Fox in his Acts printed anno 1596. pag. 646. allot that Atheist Machiauel an honorable roome among the witnesses and maintayners of the truth. And Luther apud

That they challenge Atheists.

Manlium

Manlium in loc.tit.de Eccl.pag.486.fayth of Valla, *that he gaue place to none but Epicure himselfe, and professed openly, that he held opinions repugnant to the foundation of fayth.* Neuerthelesse the same Luther respons. ad Louan.& Colen.tom.2.fol.38. writeth thus of him: *Valla in my iudgement was either a remanent sparke, or some iewell of the primitiue Church, whose like in constancy and vn-fayned zeale of Christian fayth Italy or the whole Church had not for many ages.* One Epicure then in Luthers iudge-ment was the remanent sparke, and iewell of the Church.

That sometymes Protestants account all those their brethren, who vnder the name of Christians oppose themselues any way against the Pope.

C H A P. V.

1.   T H A T Protestants sometymes acknowledge all those for members of their Church, who vnder the name of Christians do any way oppose themselues against the Pope, I proue: First because some of them do openly so professe. For (as Kemnice reporteth in locis tit.de Eccles.pag.122.) *Some faine the Church to be a rable of all Sects, of Anabaptists, Sacramenta-ries, Swincfeldians, and others, so they be not Papists.* And Ca-pito in Caluin.epist.6. *Some haue brought in a liberty as if all were of the Ghospells side, whosoeuer haue cast of the Popes yoke.* Musculus also in locis tit.de cœna pag.522.sayth: *I imbrace all for brethren in the Lord, howsoeuer they disagree from me or among themselues, as long as they mayntaine not the Popish impiety.* Secondly, because they professe, that

E 3   the

the end of their preaching was to leſſen the authority of the Pope, and Biſhops, and to be contrary to
them. For thus Luther writeth of himſelfe epiſt. ad
Frederic. Elect. tom. 2. fol. 330: *The Eccleſiaſticall tyranny*
is now weakned and broaken, which only I purpoſed in writing.
Or as Sleidan lib. 3. reporteth, *He ſaieth, that the Ec-*
cleſiaſticall tyranny is now weakned, & that, that alone was his
deſigne at the firſt. And epiſt. ad Waldenſes in Hoſpin.
part 2. fol. 8. he ſayth, that *he impugned tranſubſtantiation*
only for enuy of the Papiſts. And in parua Confeſſ. apud
eundem fol. 13. that he impugned the Eleuation *only*
to ſpite the Papiſts. Caluin 4. Inſtitut. cap. 10. §. 1. ſayth:
The end of our contention is, to bridle that infinite and barbarous
Dominion, which thoſe, who would be accounted Paſtors, haue
vſurped ouer ſoules. Zuinglius lib. de Auctor. Sedit. tom.
2. fol. 125. affirmeth, that there is a ſort of Proteſtãts,
which for no other cauſe do beare the doctrine of the Ghoſpell then
becauſe they extremely hate the Popedome, and enuy Papiſts their
felicity and glory. Bucer lib. de regno Chriſti cap. 4:
The greateſt part of men ſeeme to haue ſought only theſe things of
the ghoſpell. Firſt that they might ſhake of the tyranny of the Ro-
mane Antichriſt, and of the falſe Biſhops &c. Luther alſo
tom. 2. German. fol. 22. telleth what was the end of
the Sacramentaries & Anabaptiſts: *I heare (ſayth he)*
that ſome imbrace Anabaptiſme for this only end, that ſo they may
ſpite the Biſhop of Rome, euen as the Sacramentaries do only in
hatred of the Romiſh Biſhop, deny that there is any thing in the
ſacrament beſide bread and wine. Of the new Arians end
thus writeth Zanchius lib. 1. epiſt. pag. 154: *Our*
Arians haue determined to ouerturne from the foundation what-
ſoeuer is in the Church of Rome. And what end Illyricus
had, thus telleth D. Whitaker ad Rat. 8. Campiani:
Illyricus went further then he ſhould, as I think to be the further
of from you, whome he hated.

                           2. Third-

(marginal note:) For what end Lu-ther and his fel-lowes preached.

2. Thirdly, because they call the departure from the Pope and Popish doctrine, *the foundation, a good part, and the summe of the Protestant building,* S. deel Respons. ad Arthu. cap. 12 : *Protestants agree in this foundation, that the Church ought to be reformed out of the word of God, and that Popish errours must be remoued out of the Church.* Serarua epist. dedicat ad Episc. Angliæ: *It is to be wondered, how much almost all the Reformers please themselues in this point, that they will haue nothing common with the church of Rome.* Grotius apud Homium in Specimine &c: *Neither can I forebeare to shew the fountaine and offspring of this and other calamities ; VVe think that we are so much the purer, the farther we go from points of Romish doctrine without any difference.* Vergerius dial. 1. pag. 20 : *VVe hope, that shortly all matters will be composed. VVe could do, by Gods helpe, that which seemed the cheifest of all, and the hardest and well nigh impossible, that is, pull our selues and ridde vs of the Papists tyranny. VVherefore nothing is to be doubted, but we shall compasse other matters of lesse moment. For a good feundation is layd, yea a good part of the building is set vp.* And Zuinglius Respons. ad Billi. tom. 2. fol. 261. When one obiected vnto him the dissention amongst the Sacramentaries in expouding Chrisis words of the supper, answereth: *No man ought to be offended with this diuersity, more then with the difference among many captaines, who go about to conquer a castle, whiles one would haue it battered, another vndermined, and a third would haue it scaled. For all agree to destroy the castle, the difference is only about the way, not about the summe of the matter.* And so concludeth, that if any Sacramētaries haue erred, *They erred* (sayth hc) *in the letter not in spirit, in the summe they agree all*. The summe therefore wherein all Protestants agree, is to ouerthrow the Popish castle, and Catholike fayth, (in which also the ancient heretikes agreed amongst themselues as

Tertull. præf. c. 41. Athanas. orat.t.cōc. Arian. Hieron.ad Ctesiphont: August.in Psal. 80. Beda l.1.in Iob.c.7.

E 4   the

the holy Fathers do testify) and who attempteth that by what meanes soeuer, erreth not in spirit, but in letter only, not in the summe but in some circumstance only of Protestacy. But with what spirit they are led herein, let them heare of their owne Prophet Luther, defens. verb. cœnæ tom. 7. f. 411: *VVhat a kind of spirit is that (sayth he) which hath no other end, but to weaken the aduerse party? without all doubt it is no other spirit then the Diuell.*

3. Fourthly, because they describe, paint, & name a Protestant by departure from the Pope and Popish doctrine. The Confession of Wittenberg in Prefat. describeth Protestants to be such, *as haue changed in their Churches a kind of (Popish) doctrine, which had byn vsed for many yeares, and some other ancient ceremonies.* M. Perkins in the Preface of his Reformed Catholik, sayth: *By a Reformed Catholike (so he termeth a Protestant) I vnderstand any one, that holds the same necessary heads of Religion with the Roman Church, yet so as he pares of and reiects all errors in doctrine, whereby the sayd religion is corrupted.* D. Willet in the Preface of his Synopsis: *A Protestant is he that professeth the ghospell of Iesus Christ, and hath renounced the iurisdiction of the Sea of Rome, and the forced and vnnaturall obedience to the Pope.* Schusselburg tom. 13. Catal. Hæret. pag. 22: *A Lutheran or true Christian is he, who hath seuered himselfe from Papists &c.* And tom. 8. pag. 363: *True Lutherans are they who imbrace the doctrine of the ghospell, amending Popish abuses.* You see how in all these descriptions of a Protestant, the denyall of the Pope and Popish doctrine is put as a certaine difference, which concurreth to the making and distinguishing of a Protestant from all others. Hereupon D. Andrews Apol. Cont Bellarm. cap. 1. sayth: *Sauing this Protestation (that they will not suffer certaine Popish*

errors

errors and abuses) *our fayth is no other then yours is* , or *ought to be*. And he addeth, that they call their religion reformed , *only because it is purged from certaine deuises and corruptions, which had crept into it*. And sayth, that Bucer and Peter Martyr *did only pluck vp certaine cockle, which Papists had sowed*. In like sort Boysseul in his Confutation of Spondé pag. 724. sayth: *Take away your Popery & that which dependeth thereof , and you and we shall be but one church* , *because we shall haue but one Confession of fayth*. Moreouer Plessy in the forefront of his mystery of iniquity , painteth a Protestant with a torch in his hand, setting fire to the tower of Babylon , by which he vnderstandeth the Popedome . And finally Luther in exempl. Theol. Papist. tom.2 .fol. 401. calleth himselfe an *Anti-papist* , as of his principall end or office, and sayth, that he was called by diuine reuelation to destroy the Popes Kingdom. D. Humfrey also termeth Ochinus *a stout Anti-papist* , as if to be a Protestant and an Anti-papist were all one.

4. Fiftly , because the same opinions which in Papists they detest , in other who are opposite to the Pope, they dissemble or extenuate. Lubbert. lib. 1. Replicat. cap. 4. sayth : *The Lutherans dispute not with vs about the Canon of Scriptures, nor we with them*. And lib. 4. de Concil. cap. vlt : *VVe contend not with the Churches of Saxony, which keep images in the Churches* . And yet they dispute most eagerly against Catholiks about the Canon of scriptures, and images. The Scots in their generall Confession professe to detest Popery, for maintayning the reall presence of Christs body in the Eucharist, for making the signe of the Crosse, for denying infants without baptisme to be saued. And in their other Confession c.22. they say they shunne the

Commu-

Conf. Augustana & Confest. Saxon. Liturgia. Anglica. Conference at Hampt. Court.

(a) *Lasko & Erastus in Schuffel. l. 4. Theol. Calvin p. 816. Feild l. 3. of the Church cap. 24.*

(b) *Apol. Anglic.*

(c) *Whit. Cont. 2 q. 5. cap. 8.*

(d) *Bucer in Schuffel. lib. cit. Calvin de rat. concord. p. 862.*

(e) *Epist. Monitor.*

(f) *Mart. in loc. tit. de Euchar. §. 65. Hosp part. 2 fol. 234. 163. 209. Brutsfeld. resp. ad Erasm.*

Communion of the Popish Church, because her ministers are not Ministers of Christ, because she permitteth women to christen in case of necessity; and yet dissemble, that the Lutheran Protestants allow all these points; and that the English Protestants admit Popish Priests for sufficient ministers, command the making of the crosse in baptisme, & allow womens baptisme in case of necessity; but because they are against the Pope, as well as the Scots, their opposition to the Pope, like sole fayth couereth all, and maketh that the Scots impute not these matters to them. And if at any tyme the Catholiks do set before their eyes the errors or dissentions amongst them, either they impudently (a) deny them or greatly extenuate them, saying, that *they are not about the* (b) *foundation, not of* (c) *weighty matters, of light matters, not of the* (d) *matter but of the manner, of* (e) *things indifferent, of I know not what titles, and finally only of* (f) *words.* Surely I imagine, as they say, that all sinnes in the elect faythfull are veniall, but in others all are mortall: so they deeme, that all errors in those that are opposite to the Pope are veniall and light; but in Papists all are haynous and mortall. So much the alteration of the person changeth the case with them. Hereupon Q. Elizabeth enacted, not that it should be treason for any one to dissuade frō that religion which she had established, vnlesse it were done with intention to induce him who was dissuaded, to the obedience of the Bishop of Rome. And hereupon also some of them openly professe, that they more esteeme Turks then Papists; forsooth because the Turke agreeth with them in hatred of the Pope and Popery, in respect whereof they little regard the consent in the mysteries of the Trinity, and Incarnation and Passion,

sion, and other articles of Christian fayth. Sixtly they make the forsaking of Popery an euident argument of true religion, and oppose their consent therin, as a sufficient cloake to couer all their dissentions in other matters. Zuinglius Prefat. Ecclesiast. tom. 1. fol. 39 : *It is an euident argument of true Religion among you, that you cast out all the filth of (Popish) idolatry and bridle the sloathfull company of Priests and put them from the Church.* And when Cardinall Hosius obiected to Protestants their disagreement about the Eucharist, Iames Andrews in his answere pag. 367. sayth : *VVhat is this dissention to you Papists? Be it we truly disagree in this point, yet in that we especially agree, that with one mind we impugne your Popery as true Antichristianisme.* And Brentius in the Preface of the same booke : *Otherwise with one consent they fight against Popery.* And to the same obicction Caluin in Confutat. Holland. pag. 576 sayth thus : *True; yet with one consent we all teach, that (Popish) idolatry is to be detested.* In like manner Beza in Hospin. part. 2. Hist. fol. 300 : *I confesse ; yet in this we all agree with vnited winds to impugne your transubstantiation.* Sadeel also Respons, ad Sophism. Turriani pag. 562: *Yet neuerthelesse this my litle booke will be witnesse with how conioyned strength all our Churches do set vpon the Popish errors.* And in indice Repet. pag. 808 : *It is well that all they who conioyned themselues to the reformed Church, with one consent reiect the Popes Primacy.* And D. Whitaker Contr. 2. quest 5. cap. 8. pag. 521 : *Yet in the meane tyme we all agree against the Pope.* And in this vnity of theirs to be against the Pope, they greatly triumph. His maiesty in his monitory epistle p. 174: *Almost the halfe part of the Christian world is gon out of Babylon.* And D. Andrews respons. ad Apol. Bellarm. cap. 14: *Almost halfe of the Christian world is so farre vnited in one profession, as that they are gon out of Babylon.* And when Beccanus

In what Protestãts especially agree.

nus had found fault with him, because he sayd, *The King of great Britany and the Kings of Denmarck and Sweden with the Princes of Germany who are of one beliefe with him, are a part of the Lords flock*; because the Kings of Denmarck and Sweden be Lutherans, and therefore are not of one beliefe, with the King of great Britany; Burhill in defence of him cap. 15. answereth: *That, who are of one beliefe with King Iames, is put in steed of who with him refuse to be vnder the Pope.* They meane then, that all those are of one beliefe with them, and be part of the Lords flock, who refuse to be vnder the Pope. Which kind of vnity is that, which his Maiesty in his declaration against Vorstius noted Heretiques to keep, saying pag. 49: *There are in Hungary and Bohemia innumerable Heretiks, who agree together only in hatred of the Pope.* But not only Heretiks, but also Iewes, Turcks and Infidells agree with Protestants in this point. An excellent vnity surely, & worthy of Christians, wherein they shall haue such partners and fellowes. Seauenthly I proue it, because when they be asked, who were Protestants before Luther, they produce no other then such as were aduersaries to the Pope. Illyricus being to make a role of witnesses, dares not call them Protestants or witnesses of the Protestant truth, but simply *witnesses of the truth, or witnesses who reclaymed against the Pope and Popish errors.* And in the Preface professeth, that he gathereth, as farre as he cold, all those, who in any sort did before Luther *giue testimony to the truth of Christ against the errors and furies of Antichrist.* And l. 20. col. 1951. after he had brought forth all his witnesses, he sayth of them thus: *They desired a fuller manifestation of the truth, which at last (sayth he) we in this sixteenth age haue obtained.* That is, his witnesses attayned not to the knowledge of Protestant truth,

Editio Lugdun.

which

which was reuealed but in the sixteenth age. Neuerthelesse they seemed witnesses good inough for Illyricus, because in some sort they were opposite to the doctrine and deeds of the Pope. Beza also lib. de notis Eccles. pag. 80. when he had obiected to himself, that in former tymes their Church was not visible, answereth : *I say , that from the Apostles tyme there was scarce any age, in which as soone as this Antichrist* (the Pope) *began to put out his head , God did not raise some , who opposed themselues against his tyranny* . And to the same question thus answeareth Sadeel in Refutat. art. 6 1. Posnan. pag. 851: *VVe are ready to shew , that there was no age, in which there were not some , who reproued your false Church* . Surely these men imagine Protestancy to consist in opposition to the Pope and Popery, or they say nothing to the question proposed . Likewise D. Whitaker Cont. 2. quest. 3. cap. 2. pag. 474. proueth, that the Protestant Church hath alwayes byn in Popery, because therein haue byn some, who *though they communicated with Papists, yet before death reiected their opinions* ; which kind of proofe supposeth , that it sufficeth to a Protestant to reiect Popish opinions.

5. You see then, that the cheife ringleaders of the Protestants confesse , that theirs and their followers end was to abate the authority of the Pope; that they deeme the forsaking of the Pope to be the foundation, a good part , and summe of the Protestant building; that they account the leauing of Popery an euident argument of true religion; that they define, describe, paint, and name a Protestant by opposition to the Pope ; that they say their faith differeth not from ours, but in denyall of some of our articles ; that they deny , dissemble , and extenuate whatsoeuer they dislike in those, who are aduersaries

to

to the Pope; that they oppose their consent in opposition against the Pope as a buckler against all obiections about their dissentions in other articles; &
finally that being bidden to produce Protestants before Luther, they name such as any way opposed
themselues against the Pope. What do all these things
declare, but that which some of them say in plaine
words, that the Protestant Church is a rable of all
sects which are not Papists.

    6. But out of all things which haue byn sayd
in this and the former chapters. First we see, what
great power Protestants take to themselues, that according as they please they include, or exclude the
same men out of the Church. *VVho will not* (to vse S.
Augustins words) *feare these men, who haue receiued such
wonderfull power ouer men.* Secondly we see, that they
imitate the old heretiks, who (as Tertullian sayth)
make *peace generally with all, and with whome diuision is their
very vnity.* For (as S. Augustin noteth) *the diuell hath stir-
red vp heretikes, as if they might be indifferently permitted in the
citty of God without amendment, as the citty of confusion indifferently had Philosophers of different, yea of contrary opinions.*
Thirdly we see, how infamous a society Protestan-
cy is, into which all heretikes and Schismatikes,
likewise Idolaters, Infidels, Antichrist, Atheists, are
admitted. What sinke euer did receiue such filth? Surely such a rable deserueth better the name of hell,
then of the holy Church. Fourthly we see, how
monstruous a company it is which consisteth of so
different and opposite members. Fiftly, we may gather, what Protestants meane, when they say Protestants haue byn alwayes, or before Luther. For
they meane not, that there haue byn alwayes some,
who belieued at least all their fundamentall articles,

                                 but

Marginal notes:

1.
What
followeth
of all hi-
therto
sayd.

2.
*lib. 3. cont.
Crescon. c.
20.
Præscript.
c. 41. 42.
L. 18. de
Ciuit. c. 50.*

3.

4.

5.
What
they
meane by
a Prote-
stant in
tymes past.

but that there were alwayes some, *who(as they speake) opposed themselues against the Pope or his errors,* whether they were otherwise Schismatiks, Heretiks, infidels, or Atheists. Of which kind of men I deny not but there haue byn alwayes some rable, but none but a mad man will say, that it was the holy Church & spouse of Christ. Sixtly we see how litle Protestants account of their Church, fayth, and religion; and belieue nothing lesse then that it is the church of God, or fayth of Christ. For who doubteth, but Schisme, heresy, infidelity, Atheisme, are most pestilent plagues and internall darknesse directly opposite to ecclesiasticall Communion and fayth, which are the forme, life, & soule of the Church ? And who can imagin, that he can associate and vnite together formes so contrary as are light and darknesse, life and death, truth and lies ? or that the society in darknesse, lies, and death, as are the societies in Schisme, Heresy, and infidelity, can become one with the society in light, life, & truth, as the Church is ? If therfore seriously they belieued their Church to be the church of Christ, they would neuer thinke, that she could become one with the society in Schisme, heresy, and infidelity. And this sometymes Protestants themselues perceiue. For Brentius in Appendice Recognit. thus speaketh to the Sacramentaries, when they desired to be held for brethren of the Lutherans, whome yet they condemned of heresy : *If they iudge our opinion to be impious, with what face do they desire to ioyne themselues with that Church which maintayneth impious doctrine, and to be held of her for brethren? VVhat fellowship (sayth Paul) is there of iustice with iniustice ? or what Communion of light with darknesse, or what agreement of Christ with Belial ? or what for the faythfull with the infidell ? VVherefore if they desire this sincerely, and*

in

6.

Note.

in earnest, they manifestly shew, that they make mockery of religion, as if it skilled not which one follow, so he may passe his life peaceably and quietly. In like manner those of Wittenberge in their Refutation of the orthodoxall consent pag. 636. say : *VVe cannot wounder inough, that seing they not only accuse the doctours of our Church of horrible and damned heresies, but also haue long since condemned them, to wit, of Arianisme, Nestorianisme, Eutichianisme, Marcionisme, Manicheisme, and the Monothelites heresies ; neuerthelesse they dare account vs for brethren and desire our brotherhood. VVho that is carefull of piety and truth can persuade himselfe, that these Sectmasters do in earnest handle religion? For if we be such as we are indged of them, our friendship and fraternity is to be detested, not desired.* Thus speake the Lutherans to the Sacramentaries, which no whit lesse falleth vpon théselues, because they also challenge the Hussites and other old heretiks, whome they cannot excuse from holding vile heresies. Finally we see, how vncertaine Protestants be in determing what a Protestant is, and what is necessary to the essence & making of a Protestant ; & consequently how vncertaine they must be, whome to hold for one of their houshould, whome for a stranger, whome for a brother, whom for an enemy ; which church or company they must imbrace, which they must fly, which they must account the spouse of Christ, which the Synagogue of Satan. Then the which vncertainty nothing can be more miserable in matter of religion. Wherefore sith they are so vncertaine in this matter, we must therin setle some certainty, and that according to their own principles.

7.

C H A P.

That it is necessary for a Protestant to belieue
with only speciall fayth that himselfe
is iustified.

CHAP. VI.

1. ABOVE all things it is most necessary to an inuisible or true Protestant in the sight of God (as they terme him) that with only speciall or peculiar fayth he belieue some thing belonging to himselfe, to wit, that he is iustified in Christ, or (as they vse to speake) that with fayth he apprehend Christs iustice, and apply it vnto him elf in particuler. And to a visible Protestant in sight of men it is in like sort necessary, that he professe himself to belieue with such a fayth that he is iustified in Christ. For example; For Luther to haue byn a true Protestant before God, it is needfull that he haue truly belieued himselfe to be iustified by only the foresayd speciall fayth, which he had of his own iustice; which faith they call speciall or particuler, because it was particuler to Luther, no man being bound to belieue Luther to be iustified besides himselfe. And for Luther to haue byn a visible Protestant in the sight of men, it was needful in like manner to haue professed himself to haue belieued that he was iustified by only the sayd fayth. The same I say of Caluin and of euery Protestant in particuler. That according to their doctrine it is most necessary to a Protestant that he belieue himselfe to be iustified by only speciall fayth is manifest. First because they teach, that a man is iustified by only speciall fayth, wherwith he belieueth

F   some-

something belonging to himselfe alone, not by an vniuersall or Catholike fayth whereby he beleiueth the mysteryes of Christian religion common to all, and which euery one must belieue, for this fayth they call historicall, and say it may be in such as are not iust, yea in hipocrites and Deuills. Seing therefore in their opinion no man is a true Protestant in the sight of God, but only he that is iust, nor any iust but who hath a speciall or peculiar fayth wherewith he apprehendeth Christs iustice to himselfe, it is manifest, that according to their principles, none can be a true Protestant before God, vnlesse he haue the foresayd speciall fayth; and in like manner that none can be a visible Protestant before men, vnlesse he professe to belieue iustification by only speciall fayth; because none can be accounted to be of any religion, vnlesse he professe to belieue those meanes of obtayning iustification and remission of sins, which that religion teacheth. Caluin 3. Instit.cap.2.§.16: *None is a true faythfull man, but he, who with a solid persuasio, that God loueth him, assureth himselfe of all things from his goodnes &c.* And §.39. he sayth: *VVithout this, Christianity standeth not.* And in Rom. 1.v.7: *Hence we gather, that none do rightly account themselues faythfull, vnlesse they certainly assure themselues that God loueth them.* M. Perkins in his exposition of the Creed col. 780: *No man can belieue himselfe to be a member of the Church, vnlesse he firmely and certainly persuaded that he is predestinated to eternall life.* Besides Caluin in his litle Catechisme cap. de fide defineth iustifying fayth, to be *a certaine and stedfast knowledge of our heauenly Fathers goodwill towards vs.* The like definition he hath 3.Instit.cap 2.§.2, Luther in cap. 4.Ioelis tom.4. and generally all Lutherans and Sacramentaries, except that where some define it to be

a know-

None
faythfull
without
speciall
fayth.

What
fayth is
according
to Prote-
stants.

*Pareus l.1.
de Iustif.
cap 11.*

a knowledge, others ſay it is an aſſurance or confidence of Gods fauour. Hence it is manifeſt, that they account none a iuſt or faythfull man, vnleſſe he haue a ſpeciall fayth of his iuſtification and Gods fauour towards him.

2. Secondly I proue the ſame out of diuers commendations of Proteſtants touching the neceſſity and excellency of this article. For Luther tom. 1. in diſp. fol. 410. ſayth: *In vaine he belieueth other articles, who denieth that we are iuſtified by only fayth.* And tom. 2. lib. cont. Miſſam fol. 390. he ſayth, that this article **The** *is the ſumme of his doctrine and Ghoſpell.* And lib. de votis **Summe.** fol. 278. *that this is the definition of a Chriſtian, who belieueth to be iuſtified by the only works of Christ alone, without his* **The De-** *owne.* Tom 3. in Pſalm. Grad. fol. 573: *That the only* **finition.** knowledge of this article *conſerueth the Church.* And fol. 576. that it is *the ſumme of Christian doctrine, the ſunne* **The Sun.** *which lightneth the Church, which falling the Church falleth.* Tom. 4. in cap. 53. Iſaiæ fol. 200. he writeth, that it is *as it were the foundation on which the Goſpell relyeth, and which alone diſtinguiſheth his religion from all others.* Fol. 201. that *it is like the liuely fountaine whence all treaſares of diuine wiſedome do flow, and the foundation of all the Church and Chri-* **The foun-** *ſtianity.* And Prefat. in Ionam, that it is *the cheiſe of* **dation.** *Christian doctrine, and the ſumme of all the ſcripture.* Tom. 5. Prefat. in Galat. fol. 269. he affirmeth, that it is *the only rock of the Church.* And 273: *Who holdeth not this arti-* **The rock** *cle, are* (ſayth he) *either Iewes, or Turks, or Papiſts, or Heretiques.* And fol. 274. that *in this doctrine alone the Church is made and conſiſteth.* And fol. 333. he plainly confeſſeth, that *it is his only defence, without which* (as he ſpeaketh) *both we and heretiks togeather with vs, had long ſince* **defence.** *periſhed.* Tom. 6. in cap. 21. Geneſ. fol. 265. he termeth it *the cheiſeſt article of fayth.* And tom. 7. epiſt. ad Liuones

fol.499. auoucheth, that *it is the only way to heauen, and*
The only *the summe of Christian life.* And finally in the first article
way. concluded at Smalcald: *In this article are and consist all*
which in our life we teach, witnesse, and do against the Pope, the
Diuell, and all the world. This and much more writeth
Luther in commendation of the necessity and excellency of the article touching iustification by only
fayth. And of the contrary beliefe concerning iustification by works tom.5. in cap.3. Galat. fol.357. he
sayth : *It is the sinck of all euills.* And in cap. 4. fol. 402:
That it *taketh away the truth of the Ghospell, faith, & Christ*
himselfe.

     3.   With Luther herein agree the Lutherans.
For the Confession of Auspurg cap. de discrimine ci-
borum, sayth, that this article *is the proper doctrine of the*
ghospell. And the Apology therof cap. de iustificat. that
it is *the principall place of Christian doctrine.* And cap. de
poenit: *the cheifest place and principallest article about which*
they fight with their aduersaries; and the knowledge wherof they
account most necessary to all. The Confession of Saxony,
that *this article being extinguished, there is no difference be-*
twixt the Church and other men. The Contession of Bo-
The fume hemia, that *this article is held of them for the cheifest of all, as*
of all *which is the summe of all Christianity and piety.* The vniuer-
Christia- sity of Wittemberg. tom.2. Lutheri. fol. 248 : *It is the*
nity and *cheifest article of the ghospell.* The Ministers of the Prince
piety. Electour in Colloq. Aldeburg. pag. 1. say, that this
article is *as it were the summe and last end, to which all the*
other articles do look vnto. And those of the D. of Saxony
pag. 132. affirme, that *as long as this doctrine standeth, Lu-*
ther standeth, yea Paul, yea God. Th is doctrine falling, Luther
This fal- *falleth, Paul falleth, God falleth; and all men are necessarily*
ling, God *damned.* Those of Magdeburg in Sleidan lib. 21. call
falleth. this article *the stay of saluation.* Melancthon tom. 2.
                                         Lutheri

Lutheri fol. 506. termeth it *the cheifest article.* Kemnice part. 1. Examen. tit. de Iustificat. pag. 231: *The cheifest place.* And in locis part. 1. tit. de Iustificat. pag. 216. writeth, that *it is like the castle and principall bulwarck of all Christian doctrine and religion.* Lobechius disput. 22. pag. 515. addeth, that *it is one of the cheifest points of our fayth, because the prore and poupe of Christianity is contayned therein, and on it hangeth the hinges of our saluation.* Schusselburg. tom 8. Catal. hæret. affirmeth, it to be *the cheifest article, wherein consisteth our saluation, and which is the head of our religion.* Finally (to omit other Lutherans) Brentius in Apolog. Wittemberg. part. 3. pag. 703. sayth, that *the essentiall difference betwixt a Protestant and a Papist is, that of the Protestant religion these are the first principles: The scriptur, Christ the Sonne of God, & fayth or assurance of Gods fauour towards vs for Christs sake.*

The Bulwarck.

The essentiall differéce.

4   Neither do Sacramentaries dissent herein from the Lutherans, For the Confession of Basle auoucheth it to be *the first and cheifest point in Euangelicall doctrine.* The French Confess. art. 18. calleth it *the foundation.* Zuinglius in Isagoge fol. 268. sayth it is *the summe of the Ghospell.* Bucer Respons. ad Abrincens. pag. 613. And Gualter Præfat. in Ioan. write, that *about this article is almost all the whole substance of dispute with them and Papists.* Bullinger in Compend. lib. 5. cap. 1. termeth it the *cheifest point of holy, Euangelicall, and Apostolicall doctrine.* And lib. 8. cap. 8 : *The highest and cheifest head of Christian doctrine and of fayth.* Peter Martyr in locis tit. de Iustif. col. 939. sayth, *it is the head, fountaine, and stay of all piety.* Tom. 2. epist. ad Peregrin. col. 136 : *It is the summe of summes, and cheifest head.* Caluin 4. Institut. cap. 11. §. 1. that it is *the cheifest proppe of religion.* lib. 11. §. 17: *The summe of all piety.* And Respons. and Sadolet. pag. 125. that *the knowledge thereof being gone, Christs glory is extinct,*

The summe of Summes.

tinct, religion abolished, and hope of saluation wholy ouerturned.
And lib. de Necess. Reform. fol. 47. that the safety of the
Church dependeth vpon this doctrine no lesse then mans life dependeth of his soule, Parcus in Procem. lib. de Iustificat: *On
this alone the hinges of our comfort and saluation do hang.* And
lib. 2. cap. 2. affirmeth that *it was the cheifest cause of the
separation of the Protestant Church from Popery.* And lib. 4.
cap. 2. sayth: *The only doctrine of obtayning iustice and saluation by only fayth and of loosing them by incredulity, is the sincere
and proper ghospell; all other doctrine in the scripture belongeth
to the law.* And those of Geneua Prefat. Syntag. Confess. auouch, that this article *is the groundworke, forme,*
The soule. *and soule of Christian religion; the summe of Euangelicall doctrine, of which men are called faythfull and true Christians,
without which the knowledge of other articles hath no holesome
fruit. For it is the substantiall, inward, and formall
cause of saluation; of which all Sacraments instituted by God
are and were pledges and seales, vnto which article all the
other do tend as to their center, and in which mans felicity consisteth.*

     5.   Neither do our English Protestants make
lesse account of this their article of iustification by
only fayth. For D. Whitaker Cont. 2. quest. 6. cap. 3.
pag. 562. sayth: *It seemes to be the cheifest of all, and most
The Prore fundamentall, as in which the Prore and puppe of our saluation
& Puppe. consisteth; and who faine any other meanes of Iustification, do
ouerthrow the foundation and most necessary heads of Christian
religion, and are fallen from saluation and euerlasting life.* And
Respons. ad Rat. r. Camp. he writeth thus of their
doctrine of Iustification by only fayth: *If Iames, or a
heauenly Angell disallow it, he is impure, wicked, and to be detested to hell.* D. Humfrey in his oration de vitando fer-
mento calleth this article, *The cheifest point and hinges of
fayth.* D. Fulke de Success. pag. 4. *The principall head of the
ghospell.*

ghospell. M. Fox in his acts pag. 440 : *The foundation of all*
Christianity. And pag. 770 : *The only principall origen of our* The foun-
saluation. And finally M. Powell lib. 2. de Antichristo dation.
cap. 5 : *The summe of the doctrine of fayth.* Neither is it to
be marueiled, that Protestants so highly esteeme this
their article, both because it is the cheifest bait wherwith they draw men vnto them, as also because (as
Luther confessed) it is their cheife defence, without
which they had long since perished ; and finally because Iustification being one principall end of religion, if speciall fayth be the only meanes to attaine
to iustification, vndoubtedly it ought highly to be
esteemed of that religion, which belieueth it to be
such a meanes. Thus we see that according to the Protestāts
common opinion of Protestants, to belieue himselfe esteeme
to be iustified by only fayth, *is the cheifest article, the* of only
foundation, the stay, the head, the fountaine, the summe, the last faith.
end, the prore and puppe, the hinges, the proppe, the castle, the
bulwarck, the essentiall difference, the definition, the soule, the
forme, the formall cause, the only rocke, the only safegard of
Protestancy, & the only way to heauen, which failing the church,
yea God himselfe falleth. But none can be a Protestant
without the foundation, head, soule, forme, summe,
definition &c. of a Protestant. Therefore none can
be held for a Protestant, vnlesse he professe to belieue
to be iustified by only speciall fayth. Whomesoeuer
therefore Protestants cannot proue to haue held this
article, they cannot with any reason and coulour
challenge for Protestants. And because (as it shall
hereafter appeare) they cannot proue that any one
before Luther held this article, nay on the contrary
we will proue that Luther first deuised it, they cannot with any apparence of truth auouch, that there
was any Protestant before him. And in like sort,

F 4 whome

whome we can proue not to haue belieued this article, we may euidently conclude, that they were no
Proteſtants.

That it is neceſſary for a Proteſtant *to belieue
all the fundamentall articles of
Proteſtancy.*

CHAP. VII.

1. BESIDE the foreſayd article of Iuſtification
by only fayth, it is alſo neceſſary to the making of a Proteſtant or a member of the Proteſtant
Church, that he belieue at leaſt all the fundamentall
Feild. l. 3. de points of Proteſtancy, either explicitly or implicit-
Eccleſ. c. 2. ly, ſo that he obſtinatly deny no one of them. This
is manifeſt. Firſt becauſe (as I ſhewed before cap. 1)
it is the common opinion of Proteſtants, that all
thoſe are out of the Church, whoſoeuer deny one
Num. 3. fundamentall article. Againe, becauſe themſelues
ſay, that the name of a fundamentall article doth inſinuate, that it ſuſtaineth the Church as the foundation ſuſtaineth the houſe. Beſides, all Proteſtants aſ-
ſigne truth or purity in doctrine for the mark of the
Church, As the Confeſſion of Auſpurg cap. 7. The
Engliſh Confeſſion cap. 19. The Suitzers cap. de Eccleſ. and other Proteſtants commonly; and their
Truth   meaning is, that it is the eſſentiall marck. Wherupon
eſſentiall D. Whitaker Controuerſ. 2. queſt. 5. cap. 17. pag. 541.
to the   ſayth, that it *is abſolutely neceſſary and the eſſentiall marck.*
Church.   And at Rat. 3. Campiani, that *it is the ſubſtantiall note.*
His Maieſty in his epiſtle to Cardinall Peron, that
it is the ſubſtantiall forme of the Church. Caluin. epiſt. 190.
                                                        The

The purity of doctrine is the ſoule of the Church. And the ſame
ſay Sadeel ad Sophiſm. Turriani loc. 1. Author de
Ecclef.in Danæo pag.1029.Vorſtius in Antibellarm.
pag. 145. D. Willet. cont.2.queſt. 3. pag. 102. Yea D.
Morton part. 1. Apol. lib. 1. cap. 6. affirmeth, that
*Proteſtants account the truth of Euangelicall doctrin the cheſſeſt
and almoſt only eſſentiall inſeparable and perpetuall marck of the
Church.* And hence it proceedeth, that they put the
truth or purity of doctrine in their definition of the
Church as an eſſentiall part thereof; as the French
Confeſſion cap. 27. The Magdeburgians Cent. 1. lib.
1. cap. 4 col. 140. Melanchthon tom. 1 in cap. 16. Matthæi. D. Whitaker Cont. 2. queſt. 5. cap. 20. pag. 552.
Sadeel ad Sophiſm. Turriani loc. 21. and others
commonly. But this purity of doctrine if it muſt be
in any articles, eſpecially it muſt be in thoſe which
are fundamentall, as is manifeſt, and the Proteſtants
do graunt. For thus writeth D. Morton part.1.Apol.
lib.2.cap.38. *Purity in the fundamentall principles of fayth is
neceſſary to the being and making of the Church.* And D. Fcild

Purity in
fundamē-
tal points
eſſentiall
to the
Church.

lib.2.de Eccleſ.cap.3: *Purity from fundamentall errour, is
neceſſarily required to a Church.* And the like hath Vorſtius lib. cit. pag. 148. Nay the Engliſh Confeſſion art.
19. defineth *the viſible Church of Chriſt to be a congregation
of faytl full men in which the pure word of God is preached and
the Sacraments duely miniſtred according to Chriſts ordinance in
al thoſe things that of neceſſity are requiſite to the ſame.* And his
maieſty ep. cit: *It is needfull that the churches be vnited amōg
themſelues in vnity of faith and doctrine in thoſe points, which are
neceſſary to ſaluation.* And hereupon diuers Proteſtants
deny thoſe Corinthians who denyed the Reſurrection, and thoſe Galathians, who ouerturned the
Ghoſpell of Chriſt, to haue byn members of the
Church; becauſe they denyed a fundamentall point

Whitak.
Cont.2 q.5
c.18. Suile
l.1.de Eccl.
c.1. Mort.
Apol.42.
cap.39.

F 5 point

point of Christian fayth. Wherefore vnlesse Protestants will deny their common doctrine in this matter, reiect their owne definition of the Church, cast away their only marke of the Church, and leaue no marke of her at all, they cannot auouch any one to haue byn a Protestant, who dissented from them in any fundamentall point of doctrine.

2. If any one say, that although he, who denyeth any fundamentall point of Protestancy, cannot be of the visible Protestant Church, yet may he be of their inuisible Church: I answeare, that (as shall be shewed hereafter) there can be no Church which is inuisible in profession of fayth, howsoeuer it be inuisible in iustice and predestination; and therefore none can be of the inuisible Church, who is not also of the visible. Againe Protestants will haue none to be of the inuisible Church, but such as are iust. But how is he iust, who denieth Gods faith, and maketh him a lyer, and that in a principall point of religion? Besides, Protestants say, that none can be a member of the inuisible Church, vnlesse he be also a member of the visible Church, if so conueniently he may.

3. Moreouer the holy Fathers most frequently, and sometymes also Protestants themselues, do teach, that it is necessary to a faythful and belieuing man, that he deny no one article of fayth, and much lesse a fundamentall or principall article. Finally, Protestants are wont to laugh at Catholiks if they proue any Father to haue byn a Papist, because he held some fundamentall point of Papistry. For thus writeth Pareus lib. 1. de amiss. gratiae cap. 1: *It is ridiculous for him to conclude S. Augustin to haue byn a Papist, because in this errour he agreed with them; no lesse them if you inferre,*

Leo. serm. 4. de Nat. Mier. lib. 3. cōt. Ruffi. Aug. l. de bar. & q 11. in Mat. & 18. de ciuit. c. 51. Basilius in Theodor. lib. 4. c. 19.

ſerre, that we are *Papiſts, becauſe we agree with Papiſts in some*
truth. And D. White in defence of his Way cap. 45.
p. g. 432 : *His holding of some things superſtitiously which the*
Church of Rome hath entertayned, proues not that he profeſſed
the ſame fayth the Church of Rome now doth, becauſe the fayth
of the ſayd Church comprehends much more then be held ; and
what be held is now otherwiſe expounded and applyed then by
him it was. And in his Way pag. 298 : *If he would deale*
fayrhfully and to the point, he should not ſay Bernard profeſſed the
Roman fayth and was a monke ; but he should haue shewed, that
he profeſſed the preſent Roman fayth, as the Councell of Trent
and the Ieſuits haue ſet it downe, at leaſt in the fundamentall
points thereof. Let them then abide the law which
themſelues haue made, and let not them conclude
any one to haue byn a Proteſtant, becauſe he agreed
with them in one or more points, vnleſſe he agreed
with them at leaſt in all fundamétall points of their
doctrine. I adde alſo, that againſt Proteſtants we do
rightly conclude, that the holy Fathers were Papiſts, if we do shew that they diſſented from Proteſtants in one or more fundamentall points. For they
will not deny, but that the Fathers were either Papiſts or Proteſtants : But Proteſtants they were not,
if they denyed their doctrine in any fundamentall
point thereof : therfore they muſt needs be Papiſts.
And the like is not of others, whome Proteſtants
cannot cóclude to haue byn theirs, if they can proue
that they were none of ours. Becauſe neither we wil
graunt, nor they can auouch, that such were either
ours or theirs, as they graunt of the holy Fathers. Be
it therefore certaine and aſſured, that to a Proteſtant
is neceſſarily required, that either explicitly, or at
leaſt implicitly and vertually he belicue all the fundamentall points of Proteſtancy, and willfully deny

What is
neceſſari-
ly requi-
red to a
Proteſtāt

no one

no one of them. And that therefore Protestants can no way challenge any, who reiected any one of their fundamentall and principall articles. It remayneth *lib.de vnic. baptism.c. 34.* that we set downe the fundamentall articles of Protestancy, because Protestants themselues agree not herein, but as S. Augustin sayd, that the Donatists did, concerning sinnes which they would haue to exclude men out of the Church; so Protestants, in a strange fashion distinguish the fundamentall points of their fayth, deuising rules of distinction amongst them, not out of the scriptures but out of their owne heads.

Which be the fundamentall heads of Protestancy.

CHAP. VIII.

1. THAT we may determine which be the fundamentall articles of Protestant religion, we must first shew, that all Protestants professe to receiue the Confession of Auspurge, at least in the principall and fundamentall articles thereof. Of the Lutheran Protestants this is manifest. For in their conference at Aldeburg both parties of them agreed to admit it for a rule of their disputation. And ibidem pag. 404. those of the Electors side do say: *VVe referre our selues and do looke vnto the Confession of Auspurg, as to the foundation of religion next after the word of God.* And other Lutherans in Zanchius in Supplicat. ad Senat. Argentinens. pag. 70. do appoint, that *it be taught according to the Confession of Auspurge, presented to Charles the 5. anno 1530, and the Apology thereof subscribed at Numberg, and that*

How much Protestāts esteeme the Conf. of Ausp.

The foūdation of Religion.

that it be the square and rule of all religion in all articles. Heshusius lib. de present. corp. Christi in cælo affirmeth,
that amongst the Lutherans *all that are promoted to de-*
grees and cure of soules, do sweare to the Confession of Auspurg
and the Apology thereof. The same testifyeth Lobechius
disp. 1. pag. 12. and as Lauatherus addeth anno 1530:
The lawes of the vniuersity of VVittemberg do streightly forbid
to defend any opinions which are contrary to this Confession.
Heshusius also lib. cit. writeth, that the *authority thereof*
ought to be most holy amongst all godly men. Westphalus cont.
Laskum affimeth, that it *containeth the summe of doctrine*
founded in the word of God. Ernestus Regius in vita Vr-
bani, *that it is the square and rule of controuersies in the*
Church. Lobechius lib. cit. *that it is the rule of fayth and*
doctrine distinguishing the orthodoxall Church from the hetero-
doxall. Reineccius in armatura tom. 1. cap. 28. affirmeth, that *it was inspired from heauen, and written by instinct*
of the holy ghost. Nay some Lutherans, (as testifieth Las-
kus epist. ad Regem Poloniæ) fayd, *that they would ra-*
ther doubt of the doctrine of Paul, then of the Confession of Aus-
purg. And with the Lutherans herein conspire the
Sacramentaries. For as Bucer confessed in the Conference of Ratisbon: *The Protestants condemne all writings,*
which are repugnant to the Confession of Auspurge and the Apolo-
gy thereof. Caluin admonit. vlt. ad Westphalum pag.
797. sayth: *Touching the Confession of Auspurg I answere*
thus, that as it was published at Ratisbon, there is not one word
in it contrary to our doctrine. And epist. 236. sayth, that
he wittingly and willingly subscribed to it. Beza epist. 1. writeth in this sort: *I define those to be our Churches, which hold*
the Confession of Auspurg, the French Confession &c. And
Apol. 1. cont. Saintem pag. 297: *Neither is the Confession*
of Auspurg such, as any pious man may reiect it. Zanchius loc.
cit. recciued the Confession of Auspurge *as the square*
and

The square of religion.

They sweare to it.

The authority thereof most holy.

Cōtaineth the sūme of do-ctrine.

The Rule of fayth.

Inspired frō heauē.

Surius anno 1546.

and rule of all doctrine. And as Vorſtius writeth Reſponſ.
ad epiſt. Parei pag. 91 : *In the vniuerſity of Heddelberg they
vſed to ſweare to no Confeſſion, but to that of Auſpurg.* Or as
D. Whitaker affirmeth Cont. 2. queſt. 5. cap. 5. pag.
505 : *The Confeſſion of Auſpurg is receiued of all Proteſtants,
vnleſſe perhapps it be in one word or two, rather then in any opinion.* And in truth ſeing all Sacramentaries profeſſe to
hold the Lutherans, (who follow the Confeſſion of
Auſpurg) for their brethren in Chriſt, and beſides,
when we obiect vnto them their diſſention in matters of fayth, they appeale vnto their harmony or
ſyntagme of Confeſſions, amongſt which the Confeſſion of Auſpurg is placed, as do thoſe of Geneua
Prefat. Syntagmatis, the Switzers Prefat. ſuæ Confeſſ. Beza epiſt. 1. Sadeel Indice Repetit. Turrian pag.
808. and reſponſ. ad Theſes Poſnan. c. 11. Vorſtius in
Antibellarm. pag. 168. D. Feild lib. 3. de Eccleſ. cap.
12. & 42. D. Whitaker Cont. 2. queſt. 5. cap. 8. pag. 521.
D. Andrews Reſponſ. ad Apol. Bellarm. c. 1. D. Fulke
de Succeſſ. pag. 287. & 304. D. White in his way to
the Church pag. 138. and others commonly. When
as (I ſay) the Sacrametaries do thus, they muſt needs
approue the Confeſſion of Auſpurg, at leaſt in all the
principall and fundamentall points thereof. For (I
hope) they will not hold thē for brethren in Chriſt,
whome they ſee to diſſent from them in fundamentall points of Chriſtian fayth; nor ſay, that thoſe
Confeſſions agree, which are repugnant in the very
foundation of beliefe.

Which
the cōfeſſ.
of Auſp.
accoūteth
fundamē-
tal articles   2. But this Confeſſion of Auſpurg ſo generally
receiued, and of ſo high account with Proteſtants,
as we haue rehearſed, hath ſet downe and declared
which be the fundamentall points of Proteſtancy.
For in the beginning thereof is ſet this title: *The prin-*
cipall

sipall articles; and after that many Protestanticall opinions are rehearsed, thus it sayth of them. cap. 2 1. *This* The summe
is the summe of the doctrine which is deliuered in our Churches. of Protest.
And etterward naming certaine controuersies of In- doctrine.
dulgences, Pilgrimages, & the like, it sayth of them:
These kind of matters we haue let passe, that those things which
are the cheifest in this cause might be easierly knowne. Againe: Cheifest
those things only are rehearsed, which were necessary to be told. points.
And finally; *VVe would present these articles before written,*
in which our Confession might be extant, and the summe of their Only ne-
doctrine who teach vs, might be seene. And in another edi- cessary.
tion of this Confession in Melancthon. tom. 3. thus
is written in the end thereof: *VVe haue comprised the*
summe of Euangelicall doctrine necessary to Churches. Where- Summe of
fore, vnlesse Protestants will reiect their first and doctrine
most maiesticall Confession of Auspurg, they must necessary.
needs confesse that the articles thereof are the summe
of Protestant doctrine, the principal articles of their
fayth, are they only, which are necessary to be told,
and the summe of Euangelicall doctrine necessary to
Churches. But surely such are fundamentall articles.

3. Neither doth the sayd Confession alone,
but also many other great Protestants acknowledge
the articles of it to be fundamentall. For thus hath
the Apology of that Confession in Melancthon tom.
3. fol. 9 1 : *VVe haue comprised in the Confession of Auspurg al-* Truth
most the summe of all Christian doctrine. And Melancthon necessary
himselfe in the preface of that Apology writeth, that to the
that Confession *is truth necessary to the Church.* And like- Church.
wise in the preface of his 3. tome : *I gathered together the*
heads of confession, comprising almost the summe of the doctrine
of our Churches. The whole forme of the Confession was after
sent to Luther, who wrote back that he had read and allowed this
Con-

Confession. And tom. 4. Responf. ad Staphylum pag. 817.fayth, that *the Confeſſion (of Aufpurg) contayneth the whole body of doctrine*. And in Prefat. 2. tom. Lutheri: *The ſumme of doctrine which our Church preached is publikely*

The whole body of doctrine. *comprehended in the Confeſſion of Aufpurg*. Likewiſe the D. of Wittemberg in the preface of his Confeſſion ſpeaking of the Confeſſion of Aufpurg ſayth thus: *VVe commanded our preachers to write the ſumme of their doctrine*. And the Miniſters of the Elector in colloq. Aldeburg ſcrip. 3. pag. 21. ſay: *VVe doubt not but the ſumme of doctrine reuealed from heauen is dextrouſly, plainly, and moſt ſweetly contayned in the Confeſſion of Aufpurg*. And pag. ſeq: *VVith the Confeſſion of Aufpurg we comprehended the ſumme of doctrine*. Kemnice Præfat. lib. de cœna: *The ſumme of holeſome doctrine is comprehended in the Confeſſion of Aufpurg out of the word of God*. Weſtphalus defenſ. altera cont. Laſkum ſayth; *It containeth in brieſe the ſumme of Chriſtian doctrine*. Iames Andrews lib. cont. Hoſium pag. 22: *The ſumme of pious doctrine is contained in the Confeſſion of Aufpurg*. Finally the Lutherans (as the Sacramentaries of

Note. Newſtad write in Admonit. de lib. Concord. cap. 4. pag. 116) *do place in the role of heretiks, as erring in the foundation of ſayth and ſaluation, all thoſe who find any fault with the Confeſſion of Aufpurg, or diſſent from it in any article*. And as touching the Sacramentaries themſelues, the Palatin Confeſſion pag. 198. ſayth thus: *That Confeſſion of ſayth which was preſented at Aufpurg, and the Apology annexed thereto, it as taken out of the doctrine of the Apoſtles & Prophets, and the foreſayd Creed, as a certaine litle ſumme*. Caluin. lib. 1. de Lib. arbit. pag. 142: *VVhen at Aufpurg*

Doctrine neceſſary to ſaluation. *there was to be exhibited a forme of Confeſſion (Melanċton the Author thereof) would not make any ſtay, but only in that doctrine, which alone is proper to the Church and neceſſary to ſaluation to be knowne.*

4. Accor-

4. According therefore to the verdict, both of Lutherans and Sacramentary Proteſtants, their Confeſſion of Auſpurg contayneth *the ſumme & whole body of Proteſtant doctrine, and only thoſe things which are neceſſary to be told, and that only doctrine which is proper to the church, and is neceſſary to be knowne for ſaluation.* Whoſoeuer therfore diſſenteth from the Confeſſion of Auſpurg, diſſenteth from Proteſtants in the ſumme and body of Proteſtancy, in things that are neceſſary, in doctrine neceſſary to the Church, and neceſſary to ſalnation. But vndoubtedly who diſſenteth in ſuch things diſſenteth in fundamentall points. And this manner of examining who is a Proteſtant, cannot be diſliked of Proteſtants, becauſe themſelues vſed it againſt the Anabaptiſts in their Conference at Frankentall, wherein they proue, that the Anabaptiſts were not before the yeare of Chriſt 1522 : *For (ſay they) if you read ouer all hiſtories, you ſhall not find any people from the beginning of the world, who had a Confeſſion of ſayth like to yours.* They are therefore of opinion, that it is neceſſary for an Anabaptiſt, that he hold their Confeſſion. Why then may not we ſay the like is neceſſary to a Proteſtant. Beſides, Sadeel in Refutat. Theſ. Poſnan. pag. 866. ſayth, that we ought to iudge of the fayth of the reformed Churches by the Confeſſions of their fayth; which rule we now follow.

5. And if any Proteſtant do not thinke, that the articles of the Confeſſion of Auſpurg be fundamentall, let him take the Confeſſion of Saxony, to which many principall Proteſtants ſubſcribed, and which they compoſed with mind to preſent it to the Councell of Trent . For this Confeſſion affirmeth her articles to be fundamentall ſaying cap. 23 : *This is the ſumme of doctrine, which with one mouth we preach in our Churches.*

Fundam. articles according to the Cōfeſſ.of Saxony.

G

Churches. And foone after : *It is true doctrine and necessary to the Church*. And Hospin part. 2. Hist. fol. 215. fayth, that the composers of this Confession auouch this in summe, *that that writing contayneth clearly and fundamentally the principall articles of Christian fayth, and doctrine of Sacraments instituted of Christ*. Or if he please let him take the

According to the Confession of Strasburg

Confession of Strasburg, which in the end thus writeth of the articles thereof : *These are the cheise points, in which our men haue somewhat gone from the common doctrine of the Clergy*. Or else the Scottish general Confessiō, wherin thus speake the Scots : *VVe belieue, confesse, and subscribe, and affirme before God and the whole world, that this only is the true Christian fayth, which pleaseth God, and bringeth saluation to men, which is now layd open to the world and receiued of diuers Churches and Kingdoms, especially of the Scottish Church*. For these Confessions do affirme, that their

According to the Confession of Scotland.

articles *are principall necessary to the Church*, and their doctrine the only true Christian doctrine which bringeth saluation. But surely such articles be fundamentall. Therefore the articles of these Confessions be fundamentall articles in Proteltancy. And consequently, that a man be accounted a Protestant according to the iudgement of these Confessions, it is necessary, that he professe their articles. Or finally let him make choice of

According to the Confession of Bohemia.

the Bohemian Confession, in the Preface whereof it is written thus : *VVe imbrace and hold all things which belong to the true Church, and without which she can be no where on earth*. For without doubt such things are fundamentall.

　　6.　But if any will not admit either the articles of the Confession of Auspurg or of Saxony (which are Confessions of Lutherans) nor the articles of the Confessions of Strasburg or Scotland (which are Confessions of Sacramentaries) nor finally

finally the articles of the Bohemian Confession
(which is fayd to be the Confession of the Waldenfes) to be the fundamentall articles of Protestancy;
Firft he shall shew, that touching which are fundamentall articles, he agreeth neither which Lutherás
nor Sacramentaries, nor Waldenses. Againe, besides
that which we haue repeated out of Protestants concerning their account of the Confession of Aufpurg
he shall herein reiect thofe Confessions to which
Protestants (as themfelues fay) *yeld almoft as much as Pa-*
pifts do to the Councell of Trent, which they hold for authenticall
writings, and which they fay haue byn fealed with the blud of
many martyrs, and approued of Kings, Princes, and common
wealthes, moft excellent Deuines, & great feruants of God. Af-
furedly if there be any certainty or worth in Proteftant doctrine, it is in their Confession of fayth.
Moreouer, he can name no other articles which Proteftants by publike and common iudgement haue
agreed to be fundamentall, and therefore either they
haue not by publike confent determined which articles they hold for fundamentall, or certainly no iudgement or decree of theirs is to be more esteemed of
them, then that which we find in their Confessions
of fayth. Wherefore either they are to be held for fundamental articles, or elfe Protestants are not certaine
which are fundamentall articles of their fayth. And
if they be not certaine herof, they cannot be certaine
what is the essence or substance of a Proteftant, or
who is a Proteftant, who not, feing (as I shewed before) the only essentiall forme and substance of a
Proteftant they put in the beliefe of their fundamentall articles. Either therefore they haue not yet determined which are their fundamentall articles, and
consequently they haue not determined what is the

Vorstius in Præfat. Antibell. Præfat. Syntagm. Confessio- num.

If Prote- stants be not cer- taine which are fundam. articles they are not cer- taine of their Church.

G 2   substance

substance of a Protestant, or who is a Protestant, who not, who is a member of their Church, who an alien; or that which they haue determined in their forsayd Confessions, is to be taken for their decree and determination in this matter. Finally, I regard not, what articles this or that Protestant iudgeth to be fundamentall, for I might set downe which Luther tom. 1. in Præfat. Disput. fol. 419. or which Zuinglius Prefat. Conf. fidei, or which Beza in fine breuis Confess. or which Bullinger Præfat. Compend. haue reckoned for fundamentall articles; but I would determine this matter out of their publike Confessions of fayth, because they cannot deny them, but in denying their fayth; as also because they are of more authority amongst Protestants, and finally because themselues require vs so to do.

Sadeel ad Thes. Pos-
nan c. 11.
Beza epist.
1, Rainold.
prælect. 4.

7.   Let it be therefore assured and stedfast, that according to the iudgement generally of all Protestants it is necessarily and before all matters required to a Protestant that he belieue Iustification by only speciall or particuler fayth, because this is the soule, life, definition and all in a Protestant; and moreouer (according to the iudgements of the foresayd Confessions) that he belieue at least virtually and implicitly all their articles, and wittingly deny none of them, because as we see they are fundamentall articles of Protestancy, without which one cannot haue the whole essence or substance of a Protestant, nor be an entire and absolute Protestant, but only in part and in some sort. And we (as hath byn often sayd) treat here only of an entire and absolute Protestant, such as at least hath all the substantiall parts of a Protestant, and endeauour to proue that Luther was the author of such a company and of such a faith and

What ne-
cessary to
a Prote-
stant.

We speak
of any
who are
Protestāts
only in
part.

and religion, and regard not whither that before his tyme there were any, who were Proteſtants only in part and in ſome ſort, and held only ſome part of Proteſtant religion, but not the whole ſubſtance thereof. And hereupon we frame an inuincible argument, to proue that there was no true Proteſtant or Proteſtant church before Luther. Euery true Proteſtant belieueth Iuſtification by only ſpeciall faith, and at leaſt virtually and implicitly belieueth the articles of the Confeſsion of Auſpurg, or of Saxony, Scotland, Strasburg, or Bohemia. But there was no man, no Church before Luther who thus belieued. Therefore no true Proteſtant or Proteſtant church. The Maior is the very definition of a true Proteſtant, gathered partly out of the common doctrine of all Proteſtants, partly out of the foreſayd Confeſsions of their fayth. The Minor being negatiue is ſufficiently manifeſt, by that neither Luther, nor any in his tyme, or to this day could produce any one man or company who before Luthers preaching had belieued in that ſort. This foundation therefore touching the eſſence and ſubſtance of a Proteſtant and Proteſtant Church being layd, to wit, that he only is a true abſolute Proteſtant, who belieueth Iuſtification by only ſpeciall fayth, and the foreſayd other fundamentall points of Proteſtancy, and that the Proteſtant Church is a company of ſuch belieuers, and the Proteſtant religion ſuch a beliefe and worſhip of God; I will endeauour in this next book out of Proteſtants teſtimonies and Confeſsions to proue, that Luther was the firſt beginner of their Church and Religion.

The deſinition of a true Proteſtāt.

The end of the firſt Booke.

G 3

THE SECOND

BOOKE.

Of the Author, or Beginner of the Protestant Church and Religion.

CHAP. I.

*That Protestants confesse, that the substance
of their Church and Religion was perished when Luther began.*

Protestáts
confesse
their reli-
gion was
perished.

HE first demonstration, wherewith we will proue, that Luther
was the author and first beginner
of the Protestant Church and religion we will take out of Protestants Confessions of the substantiall destruction of their Church,
religion & principall article of Iustification by only
fayth,

fayth, before Luther arose. For of the destruction of
their fayth and religion thus writeth Luther himself
tom.1. Proposit. 62. fol.375 : *Certaine it is that our Apo-*
stolicall Bishops raigning, Gods fayth perished. And lib. de Perished.
Captiu. Babylon. tom. 2. fol.77 : *The Popes tyranny hath*
many ages agone extinguished the fayth. And lib. de abrog. Extingui-
Miss. fol.249. he sayth to the Catholikes : *Ye haue ex-* shed.
tinguished the Ghospell. And lib. de pijs ceremonijs fol.
387 : aliàs 393 : *The doctrine of the ghospell lay destroyed by* Destroyed
humane traditions. Tom.3. in psalm. 1. fol. 126 : *VVhat*
thinkest thou was in the Church, but a whirle-wind of Gods
wrath, by which we were thrust into so many, so different, so in-
constant, so vncertaine, and those infinite, glasses of Laiwyers, and Christ al-
opinions of Deuines, & in the meane tyme Christ being altogea- togeather
ther vnknowne, stumbling into many quicke sands, gulfes, and vnknown
snares of conscience were knockt together. And in psalm. 22.
fol.345 : *Christ together with fayth is now extinguished.* And christ and
fol.348 : *Fayth lyeth extinct.* And in psalm. 51. fol. 460 : fayth ex-
The former age could neither vnderstand nor soundly teach the tingui-
greatest and weightiest points. Præfat. in psalm. Grad. fol. shed.
509 : *God punisheth contempt so as he plainly taketh away his*
word, whereof Popery is a notable example, in which we see it A lknow-
hath so fallen out. And fol. 568 : *Fayth it selfe was plainly ex-* ledge of
tinct. Tom.4. Præfat. Eccl. fol. 1 : *The schooles of Deuines* Christ
haue wholy extinguished most assured fayth in Christ, togeather wholy ex-
with all the knowledge of Christ. Tom. 5. in cap. 2. Galat. tinct.
fol. 306 : *The Papists with their impious and blasphemous do-* Not only
ctrine haue not only obscured, but simply haue taken away the obserued
Ghospell, and ouerwhelmed Christ. And fol. 222 : *Christs ghos-* but sim-
pell being obscured, yea truly ouerwhelmed, the Pope &c. In c. ply taken
4. fol. 376 : *This most common and most receiued opinion of the* away.
vncertainty (of the remission of sinnes) was surely an ar- christ shut
ticle of fayth in all Popery, wherewith truly they ouerwhelmed out of the
the doctrine of fayth, destroyed fayth, and shut Christ out of the Church.

Church-Fol. 400 : *The Pope hath vtterly extinguished Chri-*
ſtian liberty. In cap. 1. Petri : *The ſincere knowledge of fayth*
was extinct. In cap. 15. 1. Cor. fol. 134 : *VVithout our helpe*

Without *they had neuer learnt one word of the Ghoſpell.* Anc fol. 141 :
Luther *They had not knowne one iote of the Goſpell vnleſſe by our labour*
not one *and ſtudy it had byn brought forth into the worla.* Tom. 6. in
word or cap. 3. Geneſ. fol. 43 : *Holeſome doctrine was by little and*
iot of the *litle extinct.* In cap. 4. fol. 57 : *The light of the word was ex-*
Ghoſpell. *tinguiſhed by wicked Popes.* In cap. 17. fol. 199 : *That I may*
ſay all in one word the Pope hath truly buryed Chriſt. in cap. 48.
fol. 643 : *The Pope hath obſcured , nay deſtroyed the doctrine of*
fayth. In cap. 49. fol. 660 : *The Pope hath truly obſcured the*
Chriſt tru *doctrine and taken away the Promiſes , that we knew not what*
ly buried. *Chriſt was.* Fol. 666 : *He hath extinguiſhed the Goſpell.* Tom.
7. lib. de Miſſa fol. 230 : *The knowledge of Chriſt was truly*
aboliſhed and deſtroyed This ye Papiſts ye cannot deny , the mat-
ter it ſelfe proclaimeth it. And fol. 231 : *All true VVorſhip of*
Know- *God being extinct from the bottom &c* Epiſt. ad Fredericum
ledge of Electorem fol. 506 : *The Pope of Rome hath moſt plainly roo-*
Chriſt *ted out the Ghoſpell truly oppreſſed and ouerthrowne.* lib. cont.
truly de- Papatum fol. 469 : *Fayth was weakened , choaked , and ex-*
ſtroyed. *tinguiſhed, and Chriſtian liberty loſt.* Thus plainly ſpeaketh
Luther almoſt in all his Latin tomes of the ſubſtan-
Ghoſpell tiall deſtruction of his fayth and Ghoſpell before
moſt that (as he ſayth) he brought it againe into the
plainly world. To which he addeth in his 7. Dutch tome in
rooted his admonition to the Germans : *This abomination was*
out. *increaſed ſo , that they blotted out and ſuppreſt the words of this*
Sacrament and fayth, ſo that neither a letter nor point of them
remayned in all Popery , in all maſſes , and bookes. Thus Luther.

    2.   In like manner the Proteſtants in Sleidan
lib. 1. fol. 258 : *The Pope made lawes, by which true knowledg*
was vtterly oppreſſed. Melancthon tom. 2. Lutheri fol.
192 :

192: *Scholasticall diuinity being receiued, sayth was destroyed, the doctrine of works being admitted.* The Magdeburgians Præfat. Centur. 5: *There was an extreme abolition of true Religion and the word of God vnder Popery.* Caluin Præfat. Inftitut: *In former ages men had extinguished the light of God.* And 1. Inftitut. cap. 11. §. 9 : *Many ages since true religion was drowned and ouerthrowne.* 4. Inftitut. cap. 2. §. 2 : *Vnder Popery that doctrine without which Christianity cannot consift was all buryed and shut out.* Refponf. ad Sadolet. pag. 128. he fayth, that the necefsity to leaue the Roman Church was, *That the light of diuine truth was extinct, the word of God buryed &c.* And p. 130. maketh this fpeach vnto God in defence of his forfaking the Roman Church: *There were not a few profane opinions, which euen by the ground ouerthrow the cheifest points of that doctrine, which thou diddest deliuer vnto vs by word.* Lib. de necefl. Refor. pa. 49: *VVhen the word of God was choaked with these so many & so thick darknesses, Luther stept forth &c.* pag. 62: *None prayed to God with assured fayth, that is in earnest, neither could they, for Christ being buryed in that manner as he was &c.* Refponf. ad Verfipell. pag. 358: *They haue extinguished the doctrine of faluation.* In Pfycopan. pag. 388: *The word of God being ended by peruerse vse and sloth now returneth to light.* In Rom. 11. verf. 22: *The truth was taken away.* S. decl. de vocat. Minift. pag. 552: *God suffered that light to be put out which should perpetually haue lightned vs in gouerning our life.* Crifpin Præfat. operum Oecolampadij: *Both the doctrine of faluation and piety were taken away, they banished out of the Church all pure worship of God.* Celius fecundus Cario de amplitudine regni Dei lib. 1. pag. 32: *And so by litle and litle true Christ was taken out of the world, and Antichrist put in his steed.* And Hofpin. part. 1. Hiftor. lib. 4. pag. 291. writeth, that *after 800. yeares after Christ the light of the holesome and true doctrine began to be darkned, till*

G 5   *it was*

Marginal notes:

Extreme abolitiõ of religion.

The fubftance of Christianity buried.

Cheifest points of doctrine ouerthrowne from the root.

Word of God ended.

The light put out.

Pure worfhips banished.

True Christ taken out of the world.

it was vtterly put out. Thus forraine Protestants, both Lutherans and Sacramentaries.

3.   Amongst English Protestants thus writeth M. Bale Cent.4.c. 6 : *Holesome truth perished from the earth.* Cent.1.pag.69: *From this tyme (anno 607) purity of heauenly doctrine vanished out of the Church.* In his Apology against Priesthood and vowes fol. 3 : *Two things haue cheifly byn the cause of the vtter decay and full destruction of Christian religion &c.* M. Powell in Itinerarium Cambriæ lib.2. cap.7. sayth, that about the yeare 1189: *There was the cheife raigne of darknesse, in so much that not only preaching of the true word, but also the true religion was banished, and scarce the name of Christianity remayned.* M. Fox in the Protestation before his Acts, affirmeth that about the yeare 1215. and 1080 : *Christian fayth was extinguished.* And pag. 840. that *Christian Religion was wholy changed into Idolatry.* D. Fulke ad Cauillat. Stapletoni : *Scarce could he fiue hundred yeares after banish the true doctrine of saluation out of the Churches of Europe.* And finally the Apology of the English Church part.5. cap.13.diuis.1.sayth, that *Papists haue broken in peeces all the pipes and conduicts, haue stopped vp all the springs and choaked the fountaine of liuing waters, and by damning vp all the fountains of Gods word, haue brought the people into a pittifull thirst.* Item: *With great distresse went they scattering about seeking some sparck of heauenly light to refresh their consciences withall, but that light was already throughly quenched out, so that they could find none. This was a rufull state, this was a lamentable forme of Gods Church. It was a misery to liue therein without the Ghospell, without light, without all comfort.* Thus write these learned Protestants both English and strangers of the destruction of their doctrine, their fayth, their religion, and Ghospell before Luther arose; which do so plainly testify the substantiall destruction therof, as

The truth perished frō earth.

Vanished out of the Church.

Vtter decay & full destructiō of religiō.

Scarse name of Christianity remayned.

Not a sparck of diuine light found.

Protestāts light thoroughly quenched out,

of, as I may well vse S. Augustins words in the like
occasion : *If I should speake thus, they would resist and cry,
that I speake not truly, thought not truly. For in these words, if
they were spoken by others, they would imagin no other meaning, then that, which in the foresayd (Protestants) they will
not vnderstand.*

Lib 1. de
pec. mer. c.
9.

4. Neither write they otherwise of the destruction of their principall and most fundamentall
article of Iustification by only fayth. For thus the
Confession of Ansburg cap. 20: *VVhen the doctrine of
fayth, which ought to be principall in the Church, lay so long vnknowne, as all must needs confesse that there was a most profound
silence of the iustice of fayth, that in sermons only the iustice of
works was spoken of in Churches &c.* And tit. de bonis operibus pag. 25 : *In tymes past certaine absurd opinions horribly ouerwhelmed this doctrine, in which the vnlearned faigned
that men did satisfy the law of God. in the meane tyme there was
great silence how Christ is to be apprehended by fayth.* And pag.
27 : *The was no word of fayth which is necessary for remission of
sinnes.* And pag. 19 : *In tymes past there was great silence in
Churches of the exercises of fayth.* And Præfat. Apol. Confess. August. in Melancthon tom. 3. fol. 27 : *All Churches, Monasteries, schooles, briefly all bookes of late diuines, were
before mute of the iustice of fayth: No man taught sinnes to be forgiuen by fayth in Christ, Sacraments were impiously profaned,
after that opinion, that they iustify by the work wrought, was
receiued. And this opinion did wholy oppresse the doctrine of faith.*
Præfat. Conf. Saxoniæ: *All this comfort, which is necessary to euery one, how a man conuerted to God is iustified, was vnknown.* The Protestant Princes and Cities in Sleidan
lib. 11. fol. 240: *The contention is about the doctrine of fayth,
and of the true knowledge of God, which is the cheifest head of
Christian life and of pure religion. And it cannot (say they) be
denyed, that this doctrine was vterly extinct, and a new doctrine
brought*

Protestāts
cō fesse
their fun-
dam. art.
perished.

Sole faith
vnknown

Horribly
ouerwhel
med.

No man
taught &c
All Prot.
cōfort
vnknown

Vtterly
extinct.

brought in. And lib.13.fol. 304 : *It cannot be denyed, that there was no word taught of receiuing grace by Chriſt of remiſſion of ſinnes.* Luther in Catechiſmo Maiori tom.5.fol.

No mā be-
lieued iu-
ſtification
without
works.

627 : *Popery raigning, ſayth wholy neglected and obſerued was in pitifull plight . No man belieued Chriſt to be a Lord, who had reconciled vs to the Father without our workes.* Tom. 7. in c. 5.Matthæi.fol.23 : *The Popiſh company ſaying nothing of the cheifeſt article of iuſtification by ſayth in Chriſt &c.* And in 3. Symbol. fol. 140. *I haue obſerued, that all errours, hereſies, and all impiety came into the church principally, becauſe this article, or this part of Chriſtian ſayth in Ieſus Chriſt was deſpiſed and neglected, or vtterly loſt .* And in the Epitaphe grauen vpon Luthers tombe is this verſe : *He reſtored to the world the difference loſt before,* which is meant of the difference which Luther taught to be between the law and the ghoſpell, that the law teacheth iuſtification by good works, the ghoſpell by only fayth, without which difference Luther profeſſeth that Chriſtianity cannot ſtand. And in his table talkes cap. de morte he thus ſpeaketh : *Shew me one place of iuſtification of ſayth in the decrees, in the decretals, in the Clementines, in all the*

Coccius to·
1.pag.1217

ſummes and ſentences, in all the ſermons of Monks, in the ſtatutes of Synods, in all the Poſtilles, in all Hierome, Gregorie &c. Thus aſſured Luther was, that before he preached, of this principall article of iuſtification by only ſayth, there was no news in the whole world.

5.   The ſame confeſſeth his Copemate Melan-&thon, who tom.2. Reſponſ.ad Clerum Colon. pag. 96.hath theſe words : *The doctrine of pennance was ouerwhelmed, there was no word of fayth by which remiſſion of ſinnes is to be receiued*: and pag. 97 : *The doctrine of true inuocation and of the exerciſes of fayth lay dead. If any* (ſayth he) *denie, that ſuch was the ſtate of the Church he may be diſproued not only by teſtimonies of honeſt men, but alſo by the bookes of Monkes.* And

And pag. 99: *There was no speach of the hope of free mercy.*
And lib. de vsu integri Sacramenti pag. 188: *The Popes
haue deſtroyed the true doctrine of fayth.* And the ſame Melancthon or Carion in Chronico lib. 4. pag. 418. &
ſeq: *Theſe errours being ſetled and eſtablished by publike authority, drew after them a great ruine, wherewith they wholy deſtroyed the doctrine of iuſtice before God, and free remiſſion of
ſinnes.* And pag. 439: *Schoole diuinity qu te trampled and*
extinguished the leaſt ſparkles of pure doctrine, touching the law,
the gnoſpell fayth and iuſtification before God. And pag 483:
They haue quite taken away the difference betweene the law and
the ghoſpell. Vigand. lib. de bonis & malis Germaniæ:
The difference betwixt the law and the ghoſpell was quite blotted
out after the Apoſtles tym. The Magdeburgi ins Pref. Centur. 12. *The doctrine of fayth without works was extinct. The*
matter it ſelfe ſheued, that pure doctrine was vtterly ſuppreſt.
Kemnice in locis part. 2. tit. de Iuſtificat. pag. 246: *In*
all ages the light of holeſome doctrine touching iuſtification first
decayed, after more and more obſcured, and laſt it was plainly loſt
and extinguished. And pag. 244: *In our tyme God hath reſto-*
red the doctrine of iuſtification out of moſt thick darkneſſe. And
Huonius Præfat. lib. de libero arbit: *The article of Iuſti-*
fication was by Luther brought into light of out of the more then
Chymerian darkneſſe of former ages. Thus the Lutherans.

    6.   The like Confeſſion make the Sacramen-
taries. For thus writeth Caluin Reſponſ. ad Sadolet.
pag. 125: *VVe ſay, that doctrine (of Iuſtification by only*
fayth) was by you blotted out of the memory of men. Lib. de
Neceſſ. Reform. pag. 46: *The vertue of fayth was vtterly ex-*
tinct, the benefit of Chriſt deſtroyed, mans ſaluation ouerthrown.
And lib. de vera Reform. pag. 322: *By theſe, the Apoſtoli-*
call doctrine was corrupted, nay deſtroyed and abolished. Iezle-
gus de bello Euchar. fol. 24: *The doctrine of iuſtification* deſtroyed

was

The leaſt
ſparkles
extingui-
ſhed.

Quite
blotted
out.

Plainly
loſt.

Blotted
out of
memory.

Corrup-
ted, nay
deſtroyed

was moſt fowly darkned & corrupted. Pareus lib. 5 de Iuſtificat. cap. 3: *The doctrine of grace began to be obſcured, and at*
laſt to be vtterly oppreſſed in Popery . Finally M. Fox in his
Acts printed 1610. pag. 391. ſayth: *In theſe later dayes the*
only name of Chriſt remayned among Chriſtians. As touching
ſayth, the end, and the vſe of the law, of grace and iuſtification by
ſayth, of liberty of a Chriſtian man , there was no mention nor
any word almoſt ſpoken of. Thus both Lutheran and Sacramentary Proteſtants confeſſe, their doctrine of
iuſtification (in which as we haue ſeene they affirme
the definition, life, ſoule, and all points of a Proteſtant to conſiſt) to haue periſhed, byn extinguiſhed,
horribly ouerwhelmed, vaniſhed out of the church,
no ſpark thereof to be found, the light therof cleane
put out, and vtterly extinct, before Luther ſtart
vp. And conſequently they muſt needs alſo confeſſe,
that the ſubſtance of their Church and religion was
periſhed, which could not be without the ſoule, life,
definition and ſumme thereof.

Only nam
of Chriſt
remained

7. Neither do they leſſe openly confeſſe that
their Church was periſhed. For thus ſayth Luther
lib. de Captiu. Babylon, tom. 2. fol 76: *But now ſayth*
being not ſtoken of, the Church is extinguished by infinite laws of
works and ceremonies . Reſponſ. ad Catharin. fol. 140.
after he had ſayd that the Church is *conceiued, formed,*
borne, nouriſhed and conſerned only by the vocall word , he addeth : *By the Pope and Papiſts the vocall ghoſpell being choaked*
and extinct, was ſilent through all the world . Tom. 3. in pſal.
17. fol. 285 : *And now that common ſort of preachers reprobate*
what propoſeth it to vs in the Church of the deeds of Saints , but
ſome ſmall works , vntill faith being extinguished there become
nothing but heatheniſh ſuperſtition where once the Church of God
was, the name only of the Church left , the ſubſtance quite loſt.
In pſalm. 22. fol. 332 : *This day vnder the Popes dominion*
there

Proteſtãts
confeſſe
that their
church
periſhed.

Extingui-
ſhed.

Name on-
ly of the
Church
left.

there is not left one trace of the Church which appeares. And to 6.in cap.49.Genef.fol. 666: *The Pope hath extinguished & swallowed vp the Church.* Caluin Refponf. ad Sadolet. pag.132 : *The matter came to that passe, that it was manifest and euident to the learned and vnlearned, that the true order of the Church then perished, the Kingdome of Christ was throwne downe, when this dominion (of the Pope) was erected.* 4. Inftitut.cap.3. § 4. after he fayd that Apoftles, Euangelifts, Prophets were inftituted only for that tyme when Churches were to be fet vp, or to be drawne from Moyfes to Chrift, he addeth : *In our tyme God raifeth apostles, or at least Euangelists . For there was need of such to reduce the Church from the reuolt of Antichrist.* The Frech Confeffion art 31: *In our dayes the state of the Curch being interrupted, God raised vp some extraordinarily which might restore the decayed ruines of the Church.* Or as it is in the French copy : *In our dayes when the state of the Church was interrupted, God raised vp some after an extraordinary manner, that they might set vp the church a new which was in ruine and desolation.* But furely that church, which was in ruine and defolation, & fo as it needed to be fet vp a new, was fubftantially fallen. Danæus in lib. Auguftini de hærefibus cap.95 : *About the yeare after Christs passion 574: This slaughter, plague and tyranny of the whole Church began, which afterward vtterly destroyed the Kingdome of Christ.* And lib.3.de Ecclef. cap. 8: *The Church was in banishment 250. yeares.* Aretius in locis part.3.fol.25.hauing fayd that Luther was immediatly fent of God, addeth : *God then vseth immediat vocation, when there is no Church founded, or hauing byn founded is so degenerated, that the only shadow of her remayneth.* Chaffan. in locis lib.2. de Ecclef. pag. 151: *It is false that the Church shall neuer be broken of.* Sadeel. lib.de vocat. oftentyms fayth, that the Church was corrupted, decayed, ouerthrowne, and her foundation shaken and

The order of the Church perifhed.

Chrifts Kingdom throwne downe.

State of the church interrupted.

Church to be fet vp a new.

Slaughter of the whole Church.

Kingdom of Chrift vtterly deftroyed

No church or only .ha- dow ther- of.

ouer-

ouerturned. And p. 555, that to restore her we must do, as men vse to do in renewing that building which is quite fallen. And in Refutat. Thes. Posnan. cap. 8: *VVhen Popish errours had possessed almost the whole world, nor there appeared openly true fruits of the Church, nay not true lea-*

The Church was in one or two.

nes; we say the Church was in one or two. Boysseul in Confutat. Spondæi pag. 742: *It is true that all the Church was corrupted, all adulteresse, all Idolatresse.* Sohinus in Methodo Theol. pag. 212: *About the tyme of Gregory the great the Church degenerated more and more, vntill at last it lost all purity and plainly fell to dotage, yea to madnes, and in the VVest ended in Popery, and in the East in Mahometisme.* D. Whitaker Controuers. 2. quest. 5. cap 6. pag. 512: *As men do in a building fallen, that who will renew it buildeth not in the old foundation because it is loosed and not sound, but layeth some new foundation; so it was done in the renewing of the Church* (by Lu-

A new foundatio of the Church layd.

ther). Behold the old foundation of the Church put away, and a new layd. And pag. 510. he sayth, that before Luther the state of the Church was *fallen and quite ouerthrowne, and the church decayed & ouerturned.* And quæst. 5. cit. pag. 528: *Luther tooke vpon him to restore religion corrupted.* And Controuers. 4. quest. 5. cap. 12. pag. 683: *So at last the Curch was oppressed & extinguished.* D. Fulke in his answere to a false Catholike pag. 35. *The true Church failed immediatly after the Apostles tyme.* D. Morton. Apol. part. 1. lib. 2. cap. 25, *Protestant mini-*

Nothing in the Church but pitiful ruines.

sters were raised to set vp againe the Church being pitifully fallen. The Apology of the English Church part. 4. cap. 9. diuis. 3: *For these men now after they haue left nothing remayning in the church of God that hath any liknesse of his church, yet will &c* Ibidem cap. 14. diuis. 1. & 2: *Long agoe hath the Bishop of Rome willed to haue the whole church depend vpon himselfe alone; wherefore it is no meruaile though it be cleane fallen downe long agoe.* And part. 6. cap. 17. diuis. 1. & 2.

VVhen

VVhen we likewise saw, that all things were quite trodden vnder foot by these men, and that nothing remayned in the temple of God but pitifull spoiles and decayes, we reckoned it &c. M. Fox *loc.* cit : *The Church being degenerated from the Apostolike institution aboue all measure, reseruing only the name of the Apostolike Church but farre from the truth thereof in very deed, did fal into al kind of extreme tyranny &c.* And M. Cartwright in D. Whitgifts defens. pag. 217 : *VVhen Antichrist had rooted out the Church euen from the ground.* Lastly Orhinus one of the foure false Apostles of England hath these words : *Considering how Christ by his wisedome power, goodnes, had founded, builded, setled, his Church, with his bloud washed it, with his holy spirit enriched it, and at last seing it quite ouerthrowne, I could not but meruaile.*

The only name of the Apostolike Church rooted out from the groud

Coccius to. 1 pag. 983.

Quite ouerthrowne.

8. To these their plaine Confessions of the entire destruction of their Church we may add that commonly they say, that Elias the Prophet did think, that the Church had sayled in his tyme, and that besides himselfe there was no faythfull man or member of the Church. Luther lib. de Missa tom. 7. fol. 237 : *Elias thought the whole church of God to haue byn extinct, that himselfe was left alone, and the only Christian.* Beurlin in Refutat. Soti cap: 53 : *Elias complaineth before God, that besides himselfe there was neuer a Godly man remayning.* Lobechius disput. Theol. 10 : *Elias thought the Church had holy perished.* Zuinglius lib. de vera & falsa relig. cap. de Euchar : *Elias thought that he was alone.* Peter Martyr in Rom. 11 : *Elias thought that piety was perished, and that all Saincts were cut of in Israel.* Caluin in Antid. art. 18. Paris: *Elias thought himselfe alone to remaine of the Church.* And in Rom. cap. 11. v. 2 : *He thought that in his nation religion and worship of God had perished. He condemned the whole nation besides himselfe of impiety. He imagined that he had byn left alone.* Keckerman lib. 3. System Theol. pag.

Protestãts say that Elias thought thechurch was perished.

H 389:

389 : *Elias belieued that he alone remayned of the people of Israel, who could be sayd to be actually a member of the true Church.* Lubbert lib.6.cap.3. *Elias thought that besid himselfe there remayned none who was truly turned to God.* Riuet. in Epitome Controuerf. tract. 1. sect.37 : *Elias thought that he had remayned alone.* Vorstius in Antibellarm. pag. 134 : *Elias thought that of the true worshippers of God he alone remayned.* Boysseul in Confutat. Spondæi pag. 247 : *Elias thought that he was the whole Church of God* Nay Polanus part. 3. Thes. de Eccles. sayth plainly in his owne person, that *the church failed in Elias his tyme.* The Apology of the English Church part.4.cap.12. diuis. 1.&.2. sayth : *VVher was that Church then when Ely the Prophet so lamentably and bitterly made his mone, that only himselfe was left of all the whole world, who did duely and truly worship God?* And M. Iewel in Defe. Apol. part.4.c.4. diuis.2. *Elias thought all the godly in Israel had byn slaine and not one left aliue.* D. Fulke ad Cauillat. Stapletoni : *It fell to Elias, that he seemed to be left alone of all the number of the Godly, which sincerely worshipped God.* M. Hooker in his 3.booke of Eccles. policy pag. 126 : *He tooke it as though there had not byn remayning in the world any besides himselfe, that caryed a true ana an vpright hart towards God, with care to serue him according vnto his holy will.* D. Sutclife lib.1. de Eccl. cap. 6.pag.95 : *The church in Elias his dayes did seeme to him so destroyed, that he thought he had byn left alone.* D. Whitaker Cont.2.quest.3. cap.3. pag.476 : *Elias thought the whole Church of the faythfull was perished in his tyme. Elias belieued that none remayned besides himselfe. Elias thought that he alone was left a true worshipper of God.* And pag. 475 : *Elias sayd that he was alone left the true seruant of God.* I dispute not now, how falsly they impose vpon Elias this blasphemous opinion of the church perishing or destruction, only I note, how vnder the name and authority

rity of that great Prophet, they teach that the church
may perish, which sometymes they are ashamed to
auouch in their owne names.

9. Moreouer they teach, that the Church may
consist of one or two, which is in effect and in other
words to say, that it may perish. Luther lib. de notis
Eccles. tom. 7. fol. 148: *This is called the Christian socie-*
ty, & it is necessary that there be alwayes such men in the world,
albeit of them there be only two or three, or children alone. Aretius in locis part. 3. tol. 50: *Any number, though neuer so*
small, sufficeth to the Church for externall matters. Iunius
cont. 4. lib. 3. cap. 16: *Two men ordered towards God are*
a Church. D. Whitaker cont. 2. quest. 3. cap. 3. pag. 474:
It is false, which he sayth, that two men cannot make a Church.
And pag. seq he graunteth that Protestants teach that
ech man is a seuerall Church. And pag. 478: *If in the most*
forlorne tymes of the Church there be one or another faythfull
seruant of God, it is inough. Which also Bucanus saith l. c.
41. de Eccles. sect. 14. Nay Luther in cap. 7. Gen. tom.
7. fol. 107. sayth: *If I were the only man in the whole world*
who did hold the word, I alone should be the church. And
Riuet. in Epitom. Cont. tract. 1. sect. 27. *The Church*
subsisteth in euery one of her members. Finally they think,
that their Church and religion shall not alwayes
endure. For thus Luther writeth in cap. 2. Matthæi
tom. 4. fol. 438: *VVe cannot comfort our selues so as the Pa-*
pists do, with that consolation, that the Church shall not perish.
For wheresoeuer we cast our eyes we are diuersly terrified, the fu-
ry of Satan and the world is extreme, wherewith he endeauou-
reth to extinguish this doctrine. But the Popes boast, and that with
full mouth, that the Church shall not perish. In cap. 55. Isaiæ
fol. 226: *There is danger least it short ly fall out, that the word*
be againe taken from vs. Tom. 3. in psalm. grad. fol. 489.
alias 508: *The Pope obstinatly keepeth those promises, with*

which

H 2

Protestãts
Church
may cõsist
of only
children.

Of any
number,

Of two
only.

Of one
alone.

Protestãts
belieue
not the
cõtinuãce
of their
Church.

which Christ *did comfort his followers, that he would be with them to the end of the world. That* S. Peters *boat althought it be in danger, shall neuer be drowned. But the true* (Proteſtãt) *Church to which alone that was ſayd, doth not ſo belieue that, nor ſo cheare vp her ſelfe with the truſt of thoſe promiſes.* Kemnice in locis part. 1. tit. de Iuſtificat. pag. 216 : *I often tremble that* Luther *oftentymes (I know not with what abode) repeateth thoſe words, Thus doctrine after my death shall be darkened againe.* The Confeſſion of Mansfeld : *It is euident what shall follow at length, to wit, a horrible deſtruction of pure doctrine, which ſuddenly we shall leeſe beyond all expectation.* The Magdeburgians Prætat. Cent. 5 : *The reuealed truth is already periſhed, and that vpon the ſuddaine, what remayneth but vtter abolition of true religion?* Caluin in his Catechiſm: *I am ſo doubtfull touching poſterity, that I ſcarce dare thinke thereof.* Author Præfat. in Syntag. Confeſſ. *VVe haue cauſe to ſcare, that matters will returne to the darkeneſſe of former tymes.* And Paræus in Miſcellanea Vrſini pag. 39. ſayth, *that all good and wiſe men do eaſily perceiue, that there hangeth ouer their heads ſome dreadfull night and darckneſſe.* M. Iewell in his ſermon in cap. 1. Aggæi : *This Ghoſpell which ye now loath, shall be taken from you.* D. Whitaker cont 2 queſt. 5. cap. 4. pag. 503 : *That which he ſayth that neither Lutherans nor Zuinglians nor Caluiniſts shall laſt euer, is vncertaine.* And laſtly D. Morton part. 1. Apol. lib. 1. cap. 31. ſayth : *Proteſtants ſay not, that their Church cannot faile :* Thus ye ſee that Proteſtants cannot comfort themſelues that their Church shall not periſh, that they do not belieue that they shall not be drowned, that a horrible deſtruction and vtter abolition of their doctrine is to follow, that they dare ſcarce thinke of poſterity, that it is vncertaine whether they are to laſt for euer, and that they belieue not that their Church cannot faile.

Con-

Consider now diligently (good reader) First how not few but very many Protestant writers haue confessed that their Church and religion was then perished when Luther began. Secondly, that not obscure writers, but the most famous amongst them. Thirdly, that they haue not seldome confessed it, but oftentymes. Fourthly, that not in obscure or generall termes only, but in plaine and most particuler words. Lastly, that not only in their contentious writings against their aduersaries, or in their sermons to the people (in which speaches some vse to speake hyperbolicaly) but also in their most sober and temperate writings, as in those wherin they deliuer their doctrine or relate histories, in their commentaries vpon the scripture, in their Confessions of fayth, and in their speaches vnto God himself. Be it so, that one or two, or some few in heat of contention should haue hyperbolically sayd, that their church and religion was perished without meaning so. But that so many, and so great maisters, so often, and in so many kinds of writings, so plainly and so patticulerly, should say that their Church and religion was perished, and yet not meane so; cannot be sayd, vnlesse we will graunt that so many & so great Maisters of Protestants in so great a matter haue deceiued their Readers, and haue written one thinge and meant another, and that their meaning is not to be gathered out of their owne most frequent and most plaine words, vttered in all kinds of writings, but out of our fancie and pleasure. VVhat (as Tertullian sayth) *meane they otherwise then they write, masters of decett not of truth?* *Scorp c.12.*

10. If any demaund, how it came to passe, that Protestants should so often and so plainly say,

H 3 that

that their Church and religion was periſhed before
Luther appeared, I anſweare, that there were many
causes thereof. Firſt becauſe it was ſo euident, that
their Church and religion was not at all when Luther began, that (as themſelues haue confeſſed) *they
cannot deny it. It cannot be denyed. If any deny it he may be conuinced. All men muſt confeſſe it. The matter it ſelfe proclaimeth
and proueth it. And finally that it is manifeſt both to learned and
vnlearned.* Secondly, they ſayd ſo for to moue men to
hate the Pope and Papiſts, whome they affirmed to
haue deſtroyed the fayth and Church. Thirdly, for
to purchaſe the loue of the people, as who had reſtored to them againe the Church and Religion.
Fourthly, they ſayd ſo for to excuſe their preaching
and playing the Paſtours without ordinary calling,
as if forſooth when they began, there had byn no
church which could giue them comiſſion. Finally,
as phrantike men ſo Proteſtants ſometymes are in
good fittes, in which they ſee and confeſſe the truth.
But at other tymes when Catholiks out of this peri-
ſhing and deſtruction of their Church and religion
do inferre, that it is not the Church or religion of
Chriſt, againſt which (as he hath promiſed) the gats
of hell ſhall not preuaile, but ſome other Church &
religion either firſt began by Luther, or elſe reſtored
and renowed by him after that it was ſubſtantially
periſhed and deſtroyed; then they mollify and gloſe
their former ſayings, deuiſe ſtrange & violent ſenſes
of their words, and euery way ſeeke out ſhiftes and
ſleights whereby they may auoyd the force of their
owne teſtimonies, which we ſhall rehearſe and refute in the next chapter.

Wherfor
Proteſtāts
ſay their
Church
was peri-
ſhed.
1.
Num. 14.
5.7.
2.
3.

4.

5.

Matth. 16.

The

The Protestants shiftes for to delude their foresayd
Confessions touching the substantiall decay of
their Church and Religion refuted.

C H A P. I I.

1. A L b e i t the foresayd confessions of the Protestants touching the substantiall decay of
their Church and religion before Luther arose, be so
plaine and euident, as we may well say with Tertul-
lian: *VVho will not acknowledge these rather then expound the?* *De Resur.*
Yet because the obstinacy of heretiks is so great, as it *c.21.*
may be sooner ouercome then persuaded, & is wont
to seek out all shifts to auoyd the force euen of their
owne words, I will heare set downe their shifts and
confute them.

2. Their first shift is, that the forenamed Pro- *Their first*
testants by the words of *fayth*, *religion*, and the like, *shift.*
when they say that they perished, did not meane the
inward fayth of the heart, as if no man in his heart
had held the Protestant fayth or religion, but only
the outward profession thereof, and so meane only,
that the outward profession of Protestancy was perished, or that none professed it. I graunt indeed, that
somtyme they speake of outward profession of faith,
but this commeth all to one purpose. Because the *That they*
profession of faith can no more perish in the church, *say in-*
then the fayth it selfe, as hereafter we shall proue by *ward faith*
the confessions of Protestants themselues. But that *perished.*
they speake not also of the inward fayth, or of fayth
it selfe, is most false. First, because they say so with- *1.*
out all proofe, neither can they proue it otherwise
then

H 4

then because perhaps the same Protestants haue o-
ther where sayd the contrary, which kind of proofe
we hereafter shew to be nothing worth. Againe it is
credible, vnlesse one will belieue what he list, that
by so many words of *light, clarity, religion, worship of God,*
truth of God, fayth, true knowledge, knowledge of fayth, Chri-
stian fayth, knowledge of Christ, as they haue vied and we
repeated, they meant not fayth it selfe, but only the
outward profession of faith. Besides, they sayd plainly, *That none belieued to be iustified without workes. That the*
doctrine of Iustification by fayth, was blotted out of the memory
of men, that holesome truth perished from earth, and that it was
taken from men, that Christ was buryed and taken out of the
world and the Church, that all (Protestant) consolation was
vnknowne, that without Luther one iot had not byn knowne, that
the knowledge of Christ, the knowledge of fayth, fayled, and last-
ly that Christ was not vnderstood but vtterly vnknowne. Which
words are manifestly spoken & meant of true or inward fayth. I adde also, that it is a rule of ciuil law
approued by Luther and Protestants, that who cold
speak clearely, and yet spake obscurely, should haue
his words expounded against him. Seeing therefore
Protestants could haue spoken farre more clearly, if
they had meant only that outward profession of faith
had perished, we may lawfully expound their words
against themselues.

3. To this shift is another like, wherewith
they say that the foresayd testimonies of Protestants
touching the destruction or decay of their Church
are not to be vnderstood of their inuisible Church,
which they say is the company of only true faythfull and predestinate men, but of the decay of their
visible Church, which they say is the company of al
those that professe true doctrine, and is the Church
not in

(marginal notes, left margin:)

Lib. 2. c. vl.
2.

Ca. 1. n. 2. 3.

3.

Cap. 1. nu.
1. 2. 3. 4. 5. 6

Luther de
abrog mis.
& epist. ad
Amsd.
Schusselb.
tom. 4. Ca-
tal. hæret.

The secód
shift.

not in the sight of God, but only in the eyes of men.
I do not deny, that sometymes they speake of the visible Church, notwithstanding (as before I sayd) it
comes all to one purpose, because (as shall be proued
hereafter) there can be no inuisible Church without
a visible, nor a company of faythfull and predestinate men, but they must professe their fayth. But
most false it is, that they speake not also of the true
Church, which they will haue to be inuisible to any
but to God alone. For first (as before I argued) this
cannot be proued otherwise, then that perhaps the
same men haue at other tymes sayd the contrary,
which will proue, that they like lyers haue contradicted themselues, not, that they haue not sayd this,
which they haue as clearly sayd, as euer they sayd a-
ny thing else. Besides, in saying (according to their
meaning) that the Church hath not perished or cannot perish, they do not indeed contradict themselues,
when they say that it hath or can perish. For when
they say, that the Church cannot perish, by the name
of the *Church*, they vnderstand not the Catholike
Church, that is, the Church spread throughout the
world: for (as we saw) they teach that the Church
may consist or be reduced to one or two, and that
Elias thought there was none of the Church but
himselfe. Whereupon D. Whitaker Cont. 2. quest. 2.
pag. 608: findeth fault with Cardinall Bellarmine,
*when he sayth that there is alwayes a visible Church, by the name
of the Church he vnderstandeth not one or two, but a multitude.*
Neither also do they by the name of the *Church*, when
then say it cannot perish, vnderstand any true particuler Church consisting of a Pastour and flock, as is
euident; both because they say the Church may be
reduced to one or two, as also because (as shall hereafter

The Pro-
testãts say
the true
Church
hath peri,
shed.

1.

2.

Cap. 1. n. 9.

H 5

after appeare) they thinke that all Paſtors may periſh ; and laſtly becauſe D. Whitaker loc. cit. repre-
hendeth Bellarmine for that by the *name of the Church
which cannot faile, he vnderſtandeth a multitude gathered together, in which are Prelates and ſubiects.* They are therefore
of opinion , that both the Catholike Church ſpred
through out the world , and euery particuler church
conſiſting of Preiates and ſubiects, may faile and periſh; and when they ſay the Church cannot faile, by
the name of the Church, they vnderſtand fayth; and
meane, that there ſhall alwayes be fayth in ſome one
or other , as clearly appeareth by their former
words, and alſo by theſe of D. Whitaker loc. cit. pag.

What
Proteſtāts
meane by
the church
whē they
ſay it can-
not periſh.

469 : *Hence he gathereth, not as our aduerſaries do, that the viſible Church ſhall neuer faile , but that fayth ſhall neuer faile in
the whole, but that to the end of the world Chriſtian religion ſhal
remayne in ſome. This* (ſayth he) *is the very thing which we
ſay & maintaine.* Ye ſee plainly, that when they ſay the
church cannot faile, they only meane that fayth cannot vtterly faile, but that it ſhall be alwayes in ſome.
Wherein there is no contradiction to that which o-
therwiſe they teach, that the Church can faile, becauſe fayth and the Church are different things; neither doth fayth in whome ſoeuer, and in how few
ſoeuer, make the Church. Wherefore if they be mad
men and no Chriſtians, who ſay that the Catholike
Church may faile, or that the Church is not to dure
for euer (as D. Whitaker himſelfe ſayth cap. 1. & 2.
cit.) certainly theſe Proteſtants are ſuch. For whiles
they ſay, that the Church may be brought to one or
two, and that all Paſtors may periſh ; they manifeſtly ſay indeed and effect, that both the Catholike and
all kind of true Churches may faile . Moreouer I
3.   proue, that they meane that the true Church was
                                                    periſhed,

perished, because they think that she is made by inward fayth; but this they affirme to haue perished, as euen now appeared. Besides, the very name of the Church properly signifieth the true Church, and only improperly that which is not the true Church. And therefore when it is simply and absolutely put, it ought to be taken for the true Church; which thing also themselues do teach. For thus writeth Sadeel in Refutat. Thes. Posnan. cap. 4. pag. 827 : *VVhen the Church is simply put, or when it is sayd the Church of Christ, it properly signifieth only the elect.* Hereupon also Kemnice in loc. tit. de Ecclef. cap. 3. defineth the Church *to be the Catholike company.* But the Catholike company is the true Church, as is euident by the Creed, where we professe to belieue the Catholike Church, and is confessed by D. Whitaker Contr. 2. quest. 1. cap. 2. & 5. by D. Morton Apol. part. 1. l. 1. cap. 13. by Lubbert lib. 1. de Eccl. cap. 4. by the French Catechisme Domin. 15. and others. And therefore most rightly saith S. Augustin, that *it is a wicked, impudent, detestable, and abominable speach to say the Church hath perished*; which yet would not be, vnlesse by the name of the Church were vnderstood the true Church. For what offence were it to say, that the false Church had perished? Furthermore, when heretikes as the Donatists, Seruetus, and the like, do say that *the Church was perished or banished,* the Protestants themselues vnderstand the of the true Church; why then ought not Protestants to be vnderstood in the same manner, when they vse the same words? Againe, because sometymes they say, that *the Kingdome of Christ, the temple of God hath perished.* But what can be the Kingdome of Christ and temple of God, but the true Church, for the false is rather the Kingdome and temple of Satan? Whereupon

4.i

De vnic. Bapt. c. 14. Conc. 2. in Psal. 101.

Calu. cont. Seruet. pa. 657. Whitak. Cont. 2. q. 3. c. 2. & 3.

Cap. 1. n. 7.

upon D. Whitaker Controuerſ.2. queſt.3.cap.1.pag, 466.ſayth : *The ſcriptures moſt plainly teach , that there will be no end of the Kingdome of Chriſt*. And ad Demonſtrat. 17. Sanderi: *VVhat other thing is the temple of God, but the Church of Chriſt , which is built with liuely ſtones?* And M. Powell lib.1. de Antichriſto cap.2 : *The Church is defined 1.Tim.3. to be the temple of God*. Hereto we may add, that Ochim ſayth, that that Church *which Chriſt foun-ded , waſhed with his bloud, & enriched with his holy ſpirit,* (which vndoubtedly is the true Church) *was vtterly deſtroyed.* Finally becauſe they ſay, that Elias thought that there was not remayning one pious man beſides himſelfe , that he was the only Chriſtian, the only true worſhipper of God, which was left aliue, and actuall member of the true Church. Seing therfore they will make Elias to thinke ſo of the true church, of the ſame alſo ought themſelues to be vnderſtood, who vſe to draw arguments out of Elias his words ; eſpecially when as they ſay, that it ſufficeth if there be one or two faythfull men in the moſt forlorne tymes of the Church, which they muſt needs meane of the true Church which they will haue to conſiſt only of the faythfull ſeruants of God.

Num. 8.

That they meane of the vni-uerſall Church.

4. Their third ſhift may be , that when they ſpeake of the deſtruction of the Church, they meane not of the vniuerſall or whole Church, but of ſome particuler, or part of the Church. But this is eaſily refuted. Firſt becauſe (as we haue rehearſed) they ſay *there was a ſlaughter of the whole Church , that all the Church was corrupted , all became idolatrous , that ſcarce the name of Chriſtianity was left , that none belieued , that not one iot of the ghoſpell had byn knowne without Luther , that the whole know-ledge of Chriſt, all pure worſhip, all true religion was aboliſhed.* Secōdly becauſe vnder the name of Elias they plain-ly ſay,

ly say, that *the whole Church was extinct, the whole Church*
failed, he alone was a faythfull man, and actuall member of the
true Church. Wherefore either they thinke it not blasphemy to say the whole Church hath perished, or
this horrible blasphemy which calleth in question
all religion, they most impiously attribute to that
holy Prophet. Thirdly, because they say that their
Church *was brought to one or two, and that it is inough to the*
Church, if there be one or two faythfull persons. But what
man well in his wittes will say, that one or two are
inough to make the Catholike or vniuersall church.
Finally, this shall yet more appeare out of the chapter following, where we shall see, that they teach that
the whole world did fall from the fayth.

5. Their fourth shift is, that by the words
Destruction, decaying, failing, ouerthrowing, and such o-
thers, they meane not a substantiall perishing of the
fayth or Church, but only an accidentall corruption
or becomming worse. But this shift also is soone refuted. First because Luther sayth of his fayth, doctrine or ghospell, that it *dyed, was neglected, ouerwhel-*
med, extinct, blotted out, taken away, ouerthrowne, lost, aboli-
shed, forgotten, and rooted out. And that he might put it
out of all doubt, that by these words he meant a true
and substantiall destruction or perishing, he added
vnto them most significant aduerbes, saying that *it*
was truly ouerwhelmed, wholy extinct, vtterly extinct, extinct
from the bottome, plainly extinct, plainly taken away, simply
taken away, quite taken away, vtterly buryed, vtterly lost, wholy
abolished, and blotted out, and most plainly rooted out. And
least any one might also cauill that these words are
not meant of a true and substantiall destruction, he
sayd further, that *the Pope hath obscured, nay extinguished*
the doctrine of fayth: They haue darckned, nay wholy ouerwhel-
                                                    med

med Christs Ghospell: *They haue not only obscured, but absolutely taken away the ghospell.* Surely (as S. Augustin sayth) *such kind of words needs no Expositor but only a reader.* In like sort other Protestants say of their fayth or ghospell, that it *was banished, cast out, extinct, ended, choaked, buryed, obscured: till it was vtterly extinguished, that it perished from the earth, and vanished out of the Church.* They add also, that it was *wholy ouerturned, vtterly extinct, quite changed into idolatries, ouerturned from the root, and that there was an vtter abolition, an extreme falling away, and full destruction of it, so that not so much as one litle sparke could be found, but it was quite extinct, & scarce the name of Christianity was left.*

Lib. 1 de peccat. mer. c. 4.

Num. 2. 3.

6.   Besides of their principall and most fundamentall article of Iustification by only fayth they say, that *lay long vnknowne, that there was profound silence of it, that no man taught it, that it was neglected, lost, blotted out, extinct and horribly opprest, that it was corrupted, nay extinct and abolished, that no man belieued it, that it was vtterly extinct, plainly lost, quite lost, wholy suppressed, wholy oppressed, wholy trampled, wholy dasht out, vtterly blotted out, quite extinct, quite taken away, quite neglected and blotted out of the memory of men, and not only obscured but quite extinguished.* But if this doctrine were so extinct as no man belieued it, and blotted out of mens memory, surely not only the Profession of their fayth but also their fayth it selfe was vtterly perished; and consequently also their Church, whereof this article is the life, soule, summe, definition, and all.

C.1. n. 4. 5. 6.

7.   Of the Church also they say, that it *was banished, fayled, was oppressed, extinct, ouerturned, fallen, wholy fallen, that it fell to Antichrist, that the old foundation thereof was remoued, and a new layd, that the order of the Church perished, that there was a slaughter of the whole Church, that Christs Kingdome was throwne downe & razed to the ground,*
that

Num. 7.

that in the temple of God there was nought but pittifull ruines, that the Church was from the foundation rooted out and ouer-throwne by the ground, and that where it once was there remayned only the name, the substance being quite lost. Surely either by these manner of speaches is signified a substantiall destruction, or that cannot be plainly signifyed by any manner of words. Besides the formes of speach do more clearly signify a substantial destruction, thē those which Protestants condemne in some heretiks. For Caluin lib. cont. Seruetum pag. 657. condemneth Seruet for saying, that *there had byn a long banishment of the Church from the earth*, *and that she had byn driuen out of the world*. And yet as we see Danæus sayth, *that the Church was banished*. Powell, that *all true religion was banished*. D. Fulke, that *the true doctrine of saluation was driuen out*. And Crispin, *that all true worship of God was driuen out*. D. Whitaker Cont. 2. quest. 3. cap. 3. pag. 471. and otherwhere, condemneth the Donatists and other Heretikes for saying, that *the Church perished*; and yet Bale sayth that *holesome truth perished from the earth*. And Lobechius vnder Elias his name, that *the Church quite perished*. Moreouer they say, that the Church may be reduced to one or two, which is indeed to say that the Church may substantially perish, for the Church is defined to be a company or multitude in the English Confession article 19. in the French art. 27. in the Suitzers art. 17. and in the Flemish art. 27. But one or two are not a company. Whereupon Danæus lib. 3. de Eccles. cap. 16. sayth: *It is written of Vlpian the Lawyer in the ciuill law, that at least three persons are required to make a Colledge*; and if to a Colledge much more to the Church. And Lubbert lib. 2. Replicat. cap. 3. sayth plainly, *that one man makes not a Church*. And Polanus in Syntag. lib. 7. cap. 1: *One man, though neuer so holy,*

Num. 8.

That the Church cannot consist of one.

holy, cannot be a church. Beurlin also in Refut. Soti: *Neither do we call the solitude of one man, which worshippeth God, the Church.* And D. Whitaker. lib. 1 de Scriptura cap. 11. Sect. 4. *How can the Church be in one, seeing the very name of the Church doth signify a company or multitude? If therefore there be but one, there is no Church. For the Church cannot be imagined to be but in many.* And much lesse can one or

Iuel. Defes. Ap. part. 1. c. 1. Fulk. de Succes. p. 89. Beza in Catech. c: 5. Brent. in Prolog. q. 4.

two be the Catholike Church, that is (as the Protestants themselues expound it) the Church spred throughout the whole world, because one or two cannot be spred throughout the world. Whereupon the Scots in their Confession cap. 18. say, that *two or three make not the vniuersall Church.* And Zuinglius lib. de vera & falsa relig. tom. 2. tol. 192: *VVho sayes that the Church signifieth some few, erreth, like to him who sayth that people signifieth the King.* Surely it should be a notable flock which consisted of one or two sheep, a worthy Kingdome which had but one or two subiects, and a strange Catholike or vniuersall Church which contayned but one or two faythfull persons. What? can the gates of hell preuaile so farre against the Church, as they can reduce her to one or two Christians? What other thing is this, then to say that the Church can perish? For seing the Church cannot be imagined but in company or multitude, who sayth that the Church can be brought to one or two, doth indeed say the Church can be destroyed.

8. If any reply, that S. Augustin vpon the 128. psalme sayth that the Church *was once in Abel alone,* and Tertullian. lib. de pœnit. cap. 10. *the Church is in one or two* ; I answere, that S. Augustin there by the Church vnderstandeth those only, whome the scripture by name hath canonized, as it hath Abel; for otherwise it is manifest, that in Abels tyme, there were

were others that were of the Church besides himselfe, to wit Adam and Eue. And Tertullian by the
Church vnderstandeth, not the Catholike or vniuersall Church as we do, but any number of Christians, such as were those domesticall Churches,
which S. Paul sometymes saluted.

9. The last refuge may be, that what Protestants haue sayd of the destruction of the Church and
fayth, they meant not of their owne Church and
fayth, but of some others. But this is a fond shift. For
first, as I haue shewed, they meant the destruction of
the true Church and fayth. Eyther therefore their
Church and fayth is not the true but false, or else
they meane of their owne. For the true Church and
fayth is but one, as the Apostle sayth Ephes. 4: *One*
God, one fayth. And the Nycen Creed: *I belieue one church.*
S. Cyprian lib. de vnit: *One God, one Christ, one Church,*
and one fayth. S. Hilary ad Constant: *VVhatsoeuer is be-*
sides one fayth, is not fayth but treachery. And S. Leo serm. 4.
de Natiuit: *Vnlesse it be one it is no fayth.* Nay Luther lib.
cont. Papatum tom. 7. fol. 461: *Christ knoweth not two*
kinds of vnlike Churches, but one only Church. Caluin 4. Inst.
cap. 1. §. 2: *VVe cannot find two or three churches vnlesse Christ*
be pluckt in peeces. And in his Catechisme: *As there is one*
head of the faythfull, so they must all be vnited in one body, that
there be not many Churches, but one only. And hereupon inferreth Sadeel in Refutat. Thes. Posnan. art. 61. that
what is sayd of the true Church, is sayd of theirs. Seeing (sayth
he) *the true Church is one and not many, as often as the truth of*
doctrine shineth openly, so often we say the true Church and ther-
fore our Church was visible. Secondly because (as we haue
seene) they speake of the destruction of their most
principall article of iustificatiõ by only fayth, which
they affirme to be the life, soule, and summe of their

I   Church.

Church. Thirdly becauſe they eftſoones ſpeake of the deſtruction of the Ghoſpell : but by the name of the Ghoſpell they meane their owne doctrine , as by the name of Goſpellers they vnderſtand themſelues, as hereafter ſhall appeare. Finally, becauſe they profeſſe that by the name of a Proteſtant , Lutheran, or Caluiniſt they vnderſtand a true Chriſtian. Sadeel lib. de peccat.remiſſ. cap. 1 : *Ours, that is the true Chriſtian Catholikes opinion.* D. Fulke lib. de Succeſſ. pag. 186 : *I will neuer deny that Iewell was a noble Proteſtant , that is a Chriſtian.* And ad Cauillat. Stapiet: *The communitṭy of Chriſtians, whome ye call Proteſtants.* Hutten in Expoſtul. cum Eraſmo : *Againſt Lutherans , that is maintayners of the truth.* Schuſſelburg. tom 7. Catal. hæret. Pap·73: *A Lutheran or true Chriſtian, &c.* And lib. 2. Theol. Caluin. fol. 131: *Lutherans that is true ſeruants of Chriſt.* Beza cont. Illyricum pag.168: *VVe perceiue no difference betweene Sacramentaries and Chriſtians.* Hoſpinian part. 2. Hiſtor. fol. 384 : *The Sacramentaries, that is the orthodoxall.* And Dinæus cont. Bellarm. pag. 311 : *The Caluiniſts , that is Chriſtians.* pag. 169: *A Caluiniſt, that is a godly man.*

　　10.　　Wherefore out of all whch hath byn ſayd in this and the former Chapter , I thus make my firſt demonſtration to proue that Luther was the Author and firſt beginner of the Proteſtant Church and religion. *If the Proteſtant Church were not at all when Luther began, he was the author thereof : But it was not at all : Therefore he was the author of it.* The Maior or firſt propoſition is euident. For if it were not at all when Luther began, he was the beginner of it. The minor is manifeſt by the foreſayd Cófeſſions of Proteſtants, wherein they plainly ſay, that it was ſubſtantially periſhed.

That

That euery man followed a Church and religion
different from the Protestant before
Luther arose.

CHAP. III.

1. THE second demonstration wherewith we
will proue Luther to haue byn haue byn the
Author of the Protestant Church and religion we
will take from the Protestants confessions, that whē
Luther first began a l the world and euery man imbraced a different religion. Luther in the Pieface of
his first tome : *Here see euen by my case , how hard it is to get* The whole
out of errours which are confirmed by the example of the whole world.
world, and by long custome as it were changed into nature. And
to. 2. this is written in his Epitaph : *O Christ, he shewed* Long
thee when all the world was ouerwhelmed with darkenesse. And custome.
lib. 1. de captiuit. Babylon. fol. 72 being to write a-
gainst Masse , he sayth : *Neither let it moue thee , that the*
whole world hath the contrary opinion and custome. And fol.
68 : *There is almost this day nothing more receiued or more set-*
led in the Church, then that Masse is a sacrifice. Againe : I set So many
vpon a thing , which being approued by the custome of so many ages.
ages and consent of all , is so ingrafted as it is needfull to change
almost the whole face of the Church. And dub. de abrog. Consent
Miss. fol. 244 : *How often did my trembling hart quake , and* of all.
reprehending me obiected that their strongest and only argument:
Art thou only wise , what did all erre , were so many ages igno- Only Lu-
rant? Behold how Luthers heart or conscience did ther wise.
tell him that he alone knew Protestancy, and that
for many ages all were ignorant of it. And in his table talkes , fol. 19: *These cogitations were very troublesome*

to me : Thou only haſt the pure word of God , all others want it.
And lib.cit. de Miſſa fol. 247: *The common people without
doubt are moſt fully perſuaded, that all men are holpen by Maſſes,
for it ſeemeth incredible , that all the world ſhould be ſo forſaken
of God.* And fol. 256: *It ſeemes incredible to them , that Luther alone ſhould be wiſe.* Contra Cochiæum tol. 408: *The
Sophiſters and Monks haue ſeduced the whole world to truſt in*

The whole world vn-der the Pope. *works.* Tom. 3. in pſal. 82. fol. 481: *In tymes paſt the whole
world was vnder the Popes Dominion.* Tom. 5. in 4. Galat.
fol. 388 : *In former ages Paul was vnknown to the whole world.*
Tom. 6. in cap. 11. Genel. fol. 130 : *The wicked impoſtour
(ſo he termeth the Pope) hath deceiued all the word.* In c.
37. fol. 506: *The whole world was horribly brought into madnes
and folly by Papiſts.* In cap. 19 fol. 238 : *In the former age all
things lay in darkneſſe.* Tom. 7. epiſt. ad D. Sabaudiæ tol.
433: *VVe conſeſſe that the world was by the Pope moſt miſerably
ſeduced & enſnared in thoſe traditions of men, but rather ſnares
of the deuill, whiles all were perſuaded that in keeping them they
obtayned ſaluation , in omitting them fell into damnation.* And
ſerm. de Simulacris fol. 277 : *All the world was filled with
the other abuſe of images: For who would (haue put images
in Churches) if thereby he had not thought that he did ſeruice
to God.* Thus much Luther.

    2.   And in like manner ſpeake the Lutherans.
The Confeſſion of Auſpurg. cap. 20: *No man admoniſhed of the difference betwixt humane traditions and Gods law,
no man taught how good works did pleaſe.* The Magdeburgians Præfat. Centur. 5: *All alike were drowned in the im-*

All alike. *pieties and Aegiptian darkneſſe of Antichriſt.* And Præfat.
Centur. 8: *Antichriſt had brought vnder his yok all Europe that*

All Europe. *we may (ſay they) ſpeake nothing of other parts of the earth.*
Melancthon tom. 4. Prefat. in Act. Rarisbon. pag.
730: *Only Luther durſt touch the errours of the Popes & ſchooles.
Our Churches follow him rather then the conſent of ſo many ages,*
                                      Popes

Popes and schooles. Lobechius disput. 29 : *The Roman ty-*
ranny hath ouerwhelmed the Church and held the Christian The
world in thraldome. Huber. in Antibellarm. lib. 4. cap. Christian
3. *Our Church hath a new forme not vsed at that tyme when* world.
the Pope possessed all. Morgestern tract. de Eccles. pag. 145:
The whole Christian world knoweth that before Luther all chur-
ches were ouerwhelmed with more then Cymmerian darknesse. All
Hitherto the Lutherans. churches.

3. Amongst the Sacramentaries Caluin 2.
Instut. cap. 2. §. 4: *All, euen to the commonpeople are em-* All euē to
bued with this principle that man hath free will. Lib. 4. cap. the com-
18. §. 18 : *The Abomination of Masse profered in a golden* monpeo-
cuppe hath made so drunke all Kings and people of the earth from ple.
the highest to the lowest that they put the whole hope of their sal-
uation in it alone. Which very words are repeated by on earth
Lobechius disput. 26. and by Hospin. epist. dedicat. from the
1, part: Histor. and part. 2. fol. 25. And the sayd Cal- highest to
uin lib. 4. cit. cap. 10. §. 5 : *The whole world was couered* the lowest
with a most thick mist of ignorance. And lib. de Cœn. pag.
10: *VVith how thick a mist of darknes was the world beseiged.*
Againe: *VVhen Luther began to teach he so handled the m..tter*
of the supper, as that, what belongeth to the corporall presence, he
seemed to leaue such as all then receiued. And lib. de Necess.
Reform. pag. 46: *It is manifest that the whole world was* Thewhole
bewitched with these wicked opinions before Luther appeared. world.
And Respons. ad Sadolet. pag. 130 : *All things were stuft*
with pernicious errours. There was none which truly esteemed
that only sacrifice (of Christ) *none which so much as dreamed* Nomā so
of his eternall Priesthood and the intercession which dependeth much as
thereupon, none rested in his only iustice. But now whereas all dreamed
did put their trust in good works when they went about by good of &c.
words to purchase thy (God he speaketh to) *grace, to ob-*
taine iustice, to purge their sinnes, to satisfy thee. All which
(sayth he) *do dash out and annihilate the vertue of the crosse of*
Christ.

All the westerne Church.

Chrisst. Responf. ad Verspel. pag. 354 : *Seeing the whole Westerne Church as he calles it defendeth obstinatly all the impiety which we iustly detest &c.* And epist. 141 : *We are compelled to make a separation from the whole world.* Bucer lib. de vi & vsu Ministerij pag. 602 : *It is plaine, that for many ages past God reueated to no nation the doctrine of our saluation, and all things belonging to his Kingdome so farre as he hath don in our age :* Lib. de Concord. pag. 660 : *This error of the reall presence preuailed with all Nations of the whole world.* Danæus lib. de Antichristo cap. 26 : *At length Antichrist and his doctrine ouercame, all men holding their peace & shamefully and basely submitting themselues vnto him vntill Iohn Vuiclef arose who stoutly opposed himselfe against him.* Sleidan epist. dedicat. Histor. : *The beginning (of Protestancy) was slender and almost contemptible, and one only bare the hatred and brunt of the whole world.* Bibliander Orat. ad

One only man.

Principes Germ : *We put it as a thing knowne by it selfe most cleare and out of all doubt, that after Gregory the great his death the Pope of Rome was Antichrist, who with his abominations blasphemies and idolatries did so besot all Kings and people from the first to the last, that they became more blockish then brute beasts* Zuinglius lib. de vera & falsa relig. cap. de Euchar : *I think no man will deny this that we all ran to masse as to a sacred refuge.* Daniel Camier. epist. 49 : *Errour possessed not one or two small parcels, but Apostasy turned the very whole body away from Christ.* Hospin. Præfat. part. 2. Histor : *From Gregories tyme no man stroue against superstition, but all added and put to what strength each one could.* And ep. dedicat part. 1 : *This most grosse and more then Cymmerian darknesse endured in the whole Christian world these 6. hundred years last past.* Viretus in Hospin. part. 2. fol. 224 : *The whole Christian Nation vtterly bewitched as it were with sorceries and alienated from God and true religion &c.* Præfat. Syntag. Confess : *When all was couered with most grosse darknesse*

Al people from the first to the last.

The whole body of Christendome.

None stroue against.

The whole Christian Nation.

darkneſſe of ignorance and idolatry. Gualter.Præfat.Comment. Edit. ad Rom : *In the point of the reall preſence the whole Chriſtian world was greatly deceined.* And Præfat. in tom. 2. Zuinglij : *The whole world was before bewitched with truſt in outward ſignes.* Iezler de bello.Euchar. fol. 24: *The former age was euery where drowned in moſt thick darkneſſe which no man in his witts can deny.*Brocard in c.2. Apocal. fol. 41 : *VVhen the preaching of the ghoſpell was allowed in Luther and his firſt onſet againſt the Papacy , the knowledge of Chriſt was found miſſing in all and euery of his members .*

Al & euery mēber of Chriſt.

4. Amongſt our Engliſh Proteſtants thus ſpeaketh the Author of the Apology of the Engliſh Church pag.28: *VVe are indeed departed from him, who we ſaw had blinded the world for many ages.* His Maieſty in his Monitory epiſtle pag.37 : *In thoſe ages a thicker and more blind ignorance of truth poſſeſſed the world.* Pag. 100: *How many ages was the Chriſtian people held in ſo great blindnes and ignorance of holeſome doctrine .* And pag.160: *A darck night of Popiſh doctrine poſſeſſed the world.* D. Whitaker Cont.2. q. 3.pag.467: *the plague (of Popery) at laſt went through the whole world.* Pag. 468: *That Antichriſtians plague raged through all parts of the world, and through all viſible Churches.* And Cont.4.quæſt.5.cap.3.pag.684:*In tymes paſt no religion had place in Churches but Papiſticall .* D. Humfrey ad Rat.3. Campiani : *At length all left the fellowſhip of the Church.* M. Perkins in Expoſit. Symboli: *During the ſpace of 900. yeares the Popiſh hereſy ſpred it ſelfe ouer the whole world* And D. White in his way pag.352.compareth Popery before Luthers tyme to a leproſy, which (ſayth he) *poſſeſſeth euery part of man .* And in his defence cap. 37 he ſayth : *I affirme Papacy to be a leproſy breeding in the Church ſo vniuerſally , that there was no viſible company of people appearing to the world free from it.* And whe-

ther

ther any company at all, knowne or vnknowne were free from it wholy or not, I neither determine, nor greatly care. M. Iewel ſerm. in cap. 11. Lucæ pag. 208 : VVhen all the world the people Prieſts and Princes were ouerwhelmed with ignorance, when the word of God was put out of ſight : when all ſchooles, Prieſts, Biſhops, & Kings of the world were ſworne to him (the Pope) that whatſoeuer he tooke in hand they ſhould vphold it : VVhen whoſoeuer had muttered against him, muſt ſtraight way haue byn excommunicate & put to moſt cruel death as Gods enemy. M. Fox in his Acts p. 391 : All the whole world was filled and ouerwhelmed with errors and darkneſſe. And finally D. Bancroft in his ſuruey c. 4. pag. 60. hath theſe words:

Al people from the toppe to the toe. *Both the Prieſts of all ſortes and likewiſe the people became in tyme to be ſo drowned in the puddles of Popery, all of them together from the toppe to the toe, forgetting &c.*

　　5.　By theſe confeſſions of Proteſtants we ſee plainly, that *all the weſterne Church, all Europe, all Chriſtian Churches, the whole Chriſtian nation, the whole body of the Church, the whole world, all, all without exception, all alike, all euen to the laſt, all euen to the common people, all Kings and people from the firſt to the laſt, all Prieſts and people from top to toe, all and euery one were ouerwhelmed with Popiſh and more then Cymmerian darkneſſe.* Secondly we ſee, that *no man ſtroue againſt Popery, no man admoniſhed, no man taught, no man beleeued, no man ſo much as dreamed of that which is the cheifeſt and moſt principall point of Proteſtancy, but one only, and Luther alone was wiſe.* Thirdly that the caſe was ſuch for ſo many ages, for 600, yea for 900. years laſt paſt. Fourthly that it is ſo manifeſt, that as themſelues confeſſe *the whole Chriſtian world knoweth it, it is confeſſed, manifeſt by it ſelfe, moſt cleare, and out of all doubt, and no man in his wittes can deny it.* To all which if you add, that very many, and moſt famous Proteſtants, oftentymes, moſt plainly, moſt freely, and in all kind

of

of writings haue confessed this, ye shall most euidently perceiue, that vnlesse it be hereticall licence (as
Tertullian speaketh) *or by some diuelish priuiledge* (as S.
Augustins word is) their confessions can be vnderstood in no other sense, then that when Luther began, there was not one Protestant in the whole
world. Lastly we see hereby, that Protestant herein
imitate the phrases of old heretiks: for Manichee as
S. Augustin writeth sayd: *Almost all nations are ignorant
how the truth is.* And the Donatists: *The Church is perished
from the whole world.* The Luciferians in S. Hieronie:
The whole world is become Diuels. Whose damned speach
sayth he, *doth frustrate the Passion of Christ.* Nestorius in
Vincent. Lyrin. auouched. *That the whole Church had
erred.* And other heretiks there say, *Learne true fayth
which besides vs none vnderstandeth, which lay hid for many ages
and now of late is reuealed and shewed.* Marcion also and
Valentinian in Tertullian auouch, that all had erred, at whome he pleasantly iesteth in these words:
*Forsooth truth which was to be freed expected some Marcionists
or Valentinians* (Lutherans or Caluinists.) *In the meane
tyme men preached amisse, belieued amisse, so many thousands
we wrongly Christened, so many works of fayth wrongly done, so
many miracles so many graces done amisse, so many Priesthoods
so many functions wrongly executed.*

    6.   If any say that the scripture sometyme
speaketh vniuersally when notwithstanding it is
not to be vnderstood vniuersally, as when it sayth:
All seeke their owne: There is not one that doth good, no not one,
and the like, and therefore though the foresayd speaches of Protestants be vniuersall, yet they are not
to be vnderstood vniuersally: I answeare, that it is
found to affirme, that the foresayd speaches of Protestants ought to be vnderstood according to certaine

speaches

Lib. 1. *cont
marc. ca.* 3.
*de carne
Chri. li.*
22 *cont.
Faust.* c.15

*Cont epist.
funa.* c. 4.

Heres. 69.

*Dial. cont.
Lucifer.*

Cap. 26.

Præf. c. 18.

speaches of the scripture, and those spoken of other matters, rather then according to their own plaine and manifest signification. Who made this law of expounding Protestants words? Or do they keep it in expounding Catholiks or other mens wordes? God may speake in scripture as he thinkes best, Protestants ought according to custome, (which as is sayd is the law and rule of speach) both to speak and to be vnderstood. Besides, sith we know, that the scripture cannot lye or gainsay it selfe, and in other places it sayth the contrary, we iustly limitate its vniuersall speaches in this or that place. And therfore vnlesse Protestants can shew that they haue the like priuiledge that they cannot contradict themselues as the Scripture hath, there is no reason to expound them according as we do the holy Scripture.

      7.   If any reply that also Saint Hierome Dial. cont. Lucifer. sayd that the *whole world meruayled how it was become Arian*, and yet meant not that the whole world was Arian? I answeare, that Saint Hieromes example doth nothing auaile Protestants. First because Saint Hierome sayd once so, Protestants very often. Againe, he sayd so only in heat of dispute with his aduersary; Protestants haue written so when they disputed with none. Besides, Saint Hierome in the very same place expoundeth himselfe, that he meant not that indeed the whole world was become Arian: For he sayth, that it *was euident that the Bishops vvere no Arians, but belieued a right and abode in the agreement of fayth*, but only speaketh so because all the Bishops assembled at Arimini yelded to the Arians, that the word Consubstantiall should not be vsed. But Protestants say not that all the world yelded to the Pope about the suppressing of
one

one only word, but that all from the firſt to the laſt, from the top to the toe were drowned in Popiſh errours, and none belieued or ſo much as dreamed of that which is moſt fundamentall and neceſſary in Proteſtant religion : Which kind of ſpeaches S. Hierome neuer vſed. Againe, Saint Hierome vſed only this phraſe : *The whole world*, but Proteſtants vſe both that and many more and more plaine. Laſtly albeit Saint Hierome had ſpoken altogether as Pro- teſtants do, yet there were no reaſon that they ſhould be vnderſtood rather according to Saint Hieromes meaning, then according to their owne moſt pro- per, moſt plaine, and moſt frequent words, eſpecial- ly when as Luther ſayth tom. 1. fol. 414 : *Many thinges are borne withall in the Fathers, who were knowne to be ortho- doxe, which we may not imitate.*

8.   Wherefore out of all which hath byn re- hearſed in this chapter I thus frame my ſecond de- monſtration : *If ſo be that before Luther aroſe there were not one only Proteſtant in the whole world, but that all & euery man followed a different Religion, Luther was the Author and begin- ner of the Proteſtant Church and Religion. But that is true, as manifeſtly appeareth by the manyfold and open confeſſions of Luther and many and moſt famous Proteſtants. Therefore &c.*

That

That Protestants confesse their Church and re-
ligion to haue byn altogeather inuisible
before Luther appeared.

CHAP. IV.

1. THE fourth demonstration, wherewith we
will proue Luther to haue byn the Author
of the Protestant church and religion we will draw
out of that which they confesse of the inuisibility
thereof before Luther brake out. And by the way I
must aduertise the Reader of two things. The one
is, that by the name of the Church is not to be vnderstood only the men who are of the Church, but
their society in religiō wherby they make a church.
wherefore these Protestants speake not to the purpose, who to excuse the absurdity of their doctrine
touching the inuisibility of the Church, say they
meane not, that the men, whereof it consisted, were
inuisible men; for it sufficeth, that they confesse, that
they were inuisible worshippers of God, according
to the Protestant manner; or that their society in this
kind of worship of God was inuisible. The other
point is, that in these kind of questions: *VVhether be-*
fore Luther the Protestant Church were? VVhether it were visi-
ble? VVhither it had Pastors? and the like: the Catholiks
hold the negatiue part, and Protestants the affirmatiue, and that it belongeth to the affirmer, to proue
what he affirmeth: wherein if he faile, he is ouercome: and it is not needfull for the denyer to proue
his denyall, but is sufficient reasonably to answere
the proofes of the affirmer: which if he performe, he

hath

Note.

Colloq. Ba-
tisbon. Sef.
1.6. 10.17.
Iuel. Def.
Apol. par.
5.c. 15. d. 1.

hath wonne the caule. As if one like Anaxagoras
would say, that there were many worlds besides
this: or that such and such things haue byn done in
tymes past; he were bound to proue what he sayth,
& he that should deny such matters, were not bound
to proue his denyall, but only reasonably to answere
his aduersaries arguments. And the reason is manifest, because for to affirme or belieue any thinge, we
must haue reason or proofe thereof : but for the not
belieuing of it, we need no other reason, then to
shew that there is no sufficient reason why it should
be belieued. Hereupon Luther in his booke against
Henry 8. King of England tom.2.fol.240 sayd: *He
must be taught the principles of disputation, who hauing to proue
his affirmation, vrgeth his aduersary to proue his denyall* And
Voetius in his Antibellarm. pag.464: *It is inough for
the denyer, probably to deny*. Wherefore in these kind of
questions Protestants ought to be vrged to performe
their part, that is, to proue what they affirme, to
wit, that before Luthers tyme their Church was,
had Pastors, and the like : which if they cannot do,
they must needs confesse, that in this debate they
haue lost their cause. And they ought not to presse vs
to proue, that before Luther their Church was not,
had not Pastors &c. Because (as I sayd) herein we
are only the defenders and denyers, and therefore it
sufficeth for vs to shew, that no reasons, which the
Protestants alledge conuince a reasonable man to belieue that there was any such Church before Luther
appeared: which if we do, we haue wonne the cause.
Neuerthelesse, (that I may vse Luthers words in the
booke before cited) *albeit it belong not to vs to proue the negatiue, let vs do it.*

2. First therefore, touching the inuisibility of

Tom.1.fo 389.473.

That the Protestãt Church was inuisible to strangers,

of the Protestant Church before Luthers tyme, Protestants confesse, that it was inuisible to Papists, to enemies, to the world, and to all that were not of it. For thus sayth Sadeel in his Refutation of the 61. article pag. 538: *VVe deny not that the Godly men lurcked vnder Popish darknesse ; and we giue God thanks, that such persons, families, and companies, were for a tyme inuisible and vnknowne*

Inuisible to Papists.

to the Pope and all his Catchpoles seing they were for a long tyme like sparckles couered with much ashes. The same he sayth in his answere to Arthur cap. 8. and to the Sophismes of Turrian loco 10. and to the Repetition of them pag. 706. Danæus in his booke of Antichrist cap. 38. writeth : *That there were very few Protestants and those dwelling*

vnknown to others.

in wildernesses, and also vnknowne to others. Iunius in his 4. booke of the Church cap. 5. speaketh thus of Protestants before Luther : *They professed their fayth amongst themselues, but not before dogges & wild beasts who would runne vpon them.* D. Whitaker Cont. 2. quæst. 2. cap. 2. pag. 458. *VVas it (the Protestant Church) manifest to all? No: but to those only who had eyes.* And pag. 468 : *There was no true Church on earth, which appeared to all.* And quest. 6.

Knowne only to Protestãts

cap. 2. pag 359: *VVe care not for their obiecting solitude vnto vs. For we are not ashamed to haue recalled our Church out of this kind of solitude.* D. Fulke to the Cauillations of Stapleton : *The whole forme of the Church was for some ages vnknowne to the vngratefull world.* And in his booke of succession pag. 118 : *They confessed Christ, but not alwayes before heretiks ; but before then elues and the Church.* And in his notes vpon the 11. cap. of the Acts : *If by visible you vnderstand that which is seene and knowne to the whole world ; it is not true, that the Church was alwayes visible.* D. Morton in the 1. part of his Apology booke 1. cap. 16. sayth : *They professed secretly not publikely.* D. White in his way to the Church pag. 95 : *That they professed among*
them-

themselues. Osiander in his Manuel pag.59 : *In the visible Church of Rome there was the inuisible company of beleeuers hidden to the eye of the world.* Cælius secundus Curio in his booke of the largenes of the Kingdome of God, pag. 212 : *It came to passe that for many yeares the Church lay hid; and that the Citizens of this Kingdome could scarce, or not at all be discerned from others.* And the Scots in their generall confession : *VVe say, that this is the only true Christian fayth, which is now reuealed to the world.* Thus they acknowledg that before Luthers tym Protestants were vnknown to the Pope and his officers, to their enemies, to the world, to all others besides themselues, could not be discerned from others, lurcked in desertes, in darknesses, like sparkles vnder much ashes, professed not their fayth before the world, or their aduersaries, but at most before themselues, and were known only to those that had eyes, that is, to themselues.

3. The same also they meane, when they teach that the church of God may be inuisible to the world, and all that are out of it. Iunius in his 2. book of the church cap.13 : *VVe conclude that the outward forme and visible shape of the Church, may so in common vanish, that it cannot be pointed at, or perceiued of the world.* And againe: *The Church is oftentymes couered and inuisible to the world.* And cap.16: *The visible fashion of the Church may be hid and faile from the vngratefull world* And in his Theologicall Theses cap.43 : *Sometymes the church appeareth to the faithfull alone; sometymes it is knowne to some godly persons, not to euery one.* Besnage in his booke of the state of the visible and innisible Church, cap. 4: *The Church is not alwayes knowne to the world.* Sonis in his answere to Spondé cap. 2. pag. 32 : *God sometymes taketh away the face of the Church from men.* Lubbertus in his 3. booke of the Church cap.4: *VVe affirme that the Church may be*

driuen

They teach that the church may be inuisible to the world.

Often inuisible to the worlde.

driuen to those straights, that it may lye hid from the world and persecutors. And cap. 6 : VVe deny that she is alwayes visible to the world; which he repeateth againe cap. 7. Riuet in his Epitome of Controuersies treatise 1. sect. 37 : *It happeneth sometymes that the Church hath byn inuisible, or rather hidden sometymes from the eyes of persecutors, sometymes from the eyes of the faythfull themselues, to wit of some and the most of them*. D. Whitaker Controuers. 2. quest. 3. cap. 3. pag. 474: VVe say, that the Church may be conserued in so few, that it appeare not to the world. And quæst. 5. cap. 6. pag. 508 : *It is most false, that the Church shall alwayes be knowne, and manifest to the world*. D. Fulke to Stapletons Cauillat. *Bullinger, Alphonse, Chytrew, Marlorate and all the rest, do acknowledge that the Church by the defence of Christ shalbe protected in the desert, that is in places remote from the sight and accesse of the wicked*. Againe: *The Church is not alwayes apparent to the multitude of the wicked*. And in his booke of Succession pag. 19: *It is not doubted, whether the Ecclesiasticall succession of persons and places ought sometymes to be visible to the world, but whether at all tymes*. And pag. 21: *Sometyms the Church is vnknowne to the world*. Pag. 42: *God would sometymes prouide for the Church in this sort, in striking her enemies with blindnes, that they could not find her*. And pag. 129. *The externall policy of the Church is vnknowne to the world, that is, to the enemies of the Church*. And pag. 366: *I affirme that the Church is sometymes vnknowne to the world*. D. White in his way to the Church pag 86: *The question is only of the outward state of the Church, whether it be alway visible to the world or not, that in euery age those congregations may be discerned and pointed to, which are the true Church; For we say not*. Pag. 87 : *This number may be very small, and their profession so secret amongst themselues, that the world, and such as loue not the truth shall not see them, they remayning so hidden, as if they were not at all*. And pag. 97. *The Church may*

*may be hid or become inuisible sometyme, so that the world can-
not see it.* D. Morton in the 1. part of his Apology, lib.
1. cap. 16 : *Protestants say the Church is not alwayes knowne* Protestāts
to all the faythfull, nor to her enemies. And this he termeth proper the proper defence of Protestants. And cap. 13 : *VVhen Prote-* defence.
*stant say, the Church is sometymes ecclipsed like the moone they
meane that she is brought sometymes to so few, that it is not
seene but of these, which are in her, but not openly knowne by
her visibility, rites, or visible Succession, or to all the faythfull* D.
Willet in his Synopsis Cont. 2 quest. 1. pag. 67 : *A number of faythfull people hath byn always in the world, but not alwayes visible to the world.* Againe ; *If by visible they vnderstand
that which is actually visible, we say it is not so alwayes visible to
the world.* Thus we see that for to maintaine the inuisibility of their Church, they teach that the visible
forme of the Church of God may vanish, may ly hid,
may faile from the world, is often taken away from
men by God, is vnknowne to the world. That the
Church sometymes is vnknowne or appeares not visible to the world, sometyme knowne only to the
faythfull, & yet not to all them neither, but to some
and the fewer of them, and that neither, by any visible rites, nor by visible succession, and that this kind
of doctrine they terme the proper defence of Protestants, to wit, for to defend the inuisibility of their
Church before Luther. Which kind of defence hath
neither truth nor probability, and though it had,
yet would it not suffice to defend the inuisibility of
their Church before Luthers tyme, when it was inuisible not only to the world, to enemies, to straungers, to some or most of the faythfull ; but to all and
euery one, as shall manifestly appeare hereafter.

4. If any say, that it is no meruayle if Protestants teach that their Church was inuisible to the
K   world,

world, because the true Church cannot be seene but
by fayth: I answeare, first that this supposeth their
Church to be the true Church, which ought not to
be supposed, but proued. Secondly that they teach,
that the Church may be vnknowne, not only to the
world, but also to some or most of the faythfull.
Lastly that the true Church may be knowne two
wayes, one way to be the true Church of God, an

**The true
Church
discerned
from all
other
Churches
euen by
Infidels.**
other to be knowne distinctly from all other Churches; as Christ was knowne to be the Messias only
by his disciples, but yet he was knowne distinctly
from all other men by the Iewes. And the scripture is
knowne to be the word of God only by Christi. ns,
but is knowne distinctly from other writings by Infidels. And in Christstyme his company was knowwn
to be the true Church of God, only by the faythfull,
but knowne distinctly from all other companies or
Churches euen by Infidels. And the same we say of
his Church from his tyme vnto our dayes, that it is
and euer was knowne to be the true Church of God,
only of the faythfull, but known and seene distinctly from all other Churches euen by the world & Infidels. And of his kind of knowledge and visibility,
wherewith the true Church is knowne and visible
not only to the faythfull, but euen to Infidels, and of
the opposite ignorance or inuisibility we speake in
this matter, and Protestants also, as appeareth by
their testimonies already rehearsed, & shall yet more
by those which we shall repeat hereafter.

**That they
say their
Church
was sim-
ply inuisi-
ble.**
5.   Furthermore therefore Protestants do not
only teach that their Church may and hath byn inuisible respectiuely, that is, to this or that kind of
men, (as we haue already heard,) but also they
graunt, that it may be simply and absolutely inuisible.

fible. Luther vpon the 90. pfalm. tom. 3 fol. 493 : *The Church was and abode in Popery, but truly fo hidden, as to one that would iudge by the appearance, she feemed to be no where* Seemed *at all.* And vpon the pfalm. 22. fol. 344 : *The Church is* to be no *brought into the duft of death, fo that no where there appeareth* where. *any shew or trace of her.* And vpon the firft chap. of Micheas tom. 4. fol. 434: *In the former ages there was no true* No trace *forme of religion extant.* The Magdeburgians in the pre- of church face of their 10. Century: *It is very hard to find, where &* appeared. *which the Church was in this age.* Likewife in the Preface of the 11. Century: *Euery where was darknes, neither durft* No forme *the Church mutter any thing.* Gerlachius in his 22. difput. extant. of the Church pag. 927. writeth, that before Luther: *The true Church withdrew it felfe from the eyes & fight of men, into lurking holes, and hid her felfe in darkneffe.* Zuinglius in his fupplication to the Bifhop of Conftance, tom. 1. fol. 120 : *The heauenly doctrine lay a long tyme hid.* Hofpinian in the epiftle dedicatory of the firft part of his Hiftory : *From the yeare* 1200. *vntill the yeare* 1575. *the Church lay miferably ouerwhelmed, as it were, with a moft deep and moft ftrong deluge.* Caluin in the Preface of his Inftitutions : *God permitted that in former ages there should be no face of the true Church extant.* And addeth of his owne No face of doctrine : *It lay a long tyme vnknowne and buryed.* Againe: the church *For fome ages all things were drowned in deep darknes.* And extant. vpon the 23. chapter of the Acts verf. 6. he fayth : *The Church was hidden from the eyes of men.* And in his Preface vpon Ifaias : *Touching the outward shew of the church, nothing for many ages appeared, but defolate and confufed waft on all fides.* Beza in his book of the notes of the church pag. 99: *The Church lurked in the wildernes.* Pareus in his 4. booke of grace and freewill cap. 6: *In Conftantines tyme the church began to way fick to death; notwithftanding the Catholike Church remayned.* But where? In the defert, as in the

world

world withdrawne from the eyes of men. Sadeel in his treatiſe of the vocation of Miniſters pag. 533 : *After the Church had a long tyme lurked , the Lord called her at this tyme*

Could
not be
diſcerned.

into light. Voyen in his Preface of Catalog. Doct : *The true viſible Church could not be diſcerned : no tract of Gods grace appeared in his Church .* The Apology of the Engliſh Church part.4.cap.4.diuiſ 2.ſayth, that 40. yeares agoe *truth firſt began to ſpring , vnknowne at that tyme and vnheard*

Vnheard
of.

of. D. Humfrey vnto the 3.reaſon of F. Campian pag. 286 : *VVhy the picture of the Church in theſe later tymes cannot be ſeene of our aduerſaries,or drawne of vs &c.* And pag. 288: *If the only names of our Fathers were extant, who eyther by tea-*

Not ſo
much as
their
names ex-
tant,

ching, or moniſhing , or writing , did help the Church of Chriſt, we ſhould ſee another ranck and progreſſe of the Church , another ſucceſſion of Biſhops , another picture of Proteſtants . And pag. 29 ɴ : *And yet they will obiect that our Church was hidden , which they no where ſuffered aliue.* D. Whitaker Controu. 2.queſt.3.pag.479 : *VVhen they aske of vs , where was our Church in tymes paſt ſor ſo many ages , we anſwere , that it was in a cloſe wilderneſſe, that is, that it was hidden , lay ſecret, fled the ſight of men.* And queſt.5.c.3.pag.499: *Luther brought the ſayth out of darkneſſe, wherein before it lay drowned.* And cap.4.pag.502 : *Our Church was then, but you will ſay , it was not viſible. VVhat then? therefore was it not ? No . For it*

Not
viſible.

lay hid in the wilderneſſe. M. Perkins in his expoſition of the Creed colum. 788 : *VVe ſay that many ages paſt before this our age, that vniuerſall defection ouerwhelmed almoſt all the world , and that our Church was not viſible at that tyme .* M.

Not
viſible.

Bale , in his 1.Century of the writers of Britanny cap.4 : *From Phocas vntill the renewing of the Ghoſpell, the doctrine of Chriſt lay ſo long in lurking holes.* M. Downham in his 2.booke of Antichriſt cap 2: *The generall defection of the viſible Church began to worke in the Apoſtles tyme .* M. Powell in his 1. book of Antichriſt c. 23: *Our religion*

lay

lay long tyme vnknowne and buryed. And M. Cox Chancell-our of Oxford in King Edward 6. tyme exhorting the Vniuersity men to Protestantisme, biddeth them *pluck out truth lying long tyme lurking in Trophonius denne.* Thus clearely and thus many wayes they simply and absolutely graunt, that their Church was inuisible vnknowne and buryed before Luther arose.

6. The same also they intend, when they say, that the Church either was, or can be inuisible. For they would neuer say so, vnlesse they knew that such was the condition of their Church before Lu-ther began. Luther vpon the 90. psalm. tom. 3. fol. 495 : *Sometymes the Church was most weake and so dispersed as it appeared no where.* Hutter in his Analysis of the Confession of Auspurg pag. 448: *It is certaine that it may fall out, that the true Church may ly hidden, and her visible forme not at all tymes appeare to the eyes.*

Herbrand in his Compend. of diuinity, place of the Church, pag. 502. writeth: *That the faythfull sometymes appeare not to the eyes, euen of the Godly.*

Kemnitius in his common places tit. the epistles of the Apostles pag. 78 : *Sometymes the true Church (another bastard company preuailing and ouertop-ping) doth so as it were ly hid, that Elias may say, I am lest alone.* Gerlachius in his 22. dispute of the Church, pag. 946: *No surely, if at some tyme the Church be not seene with corporall eyes, therefore she is not.* Caluin in the Pre-face of his Institutions: *Sometyme God taketh away the outward knowledge of his Church from the sight of men. Some-tyme the Church hath no apparent forme.* And in his treatise of the true Reformation of the Church pag. 232 : *The Church sometyme lyeth hid, and flieth the sight of men.* And in his Antidote of the 18. article of the Vniuersity of Paris. *We gather, that the Church is not at all tymes subiect to the eyes of men, as the experience of many ages witnesseth.*

K 3 Againe

Againe : *Elias thought himselfe only left of the Church ; falsly indeed , but that is a proofe , that she may lye so hidden.* And in his 4. booke of Institutions cap. 1 §. 3. he affirmeth, that it is not needfull to see or to feele the Church , and that she may passe our knowledge. Beza in his Confession cap. 5.§.9 : *Diuers tymes the Church seemeth to haue perished vtterly.* Iunius in his 3. book of the church cap. 16 : *The Church shall neuer end , but shall lye hidden , according to her visible forme.* Chassanio in his common places loc. 2. of the Church pag. 148 : *The Church is not alwayes visible.* Danæus in his 3. booke of the Church cap. 2. *Bellarmine will haue that only to be the Church which is visible which is most false.* Cap. 12 : *God oftentymes will haue*

Oftétymes no visible Church on earth.

some visible Church on earth, and often tymes none. VVhen there is no visible Church, then this precept (of adioyning himself to the Church) ceaseth. And cap. 13 : *Bellarmine laboureth to proue the true Church of God on earth : o be alwayes visible. That being most false &c.* And cap. 16 : *VVe say, we affirme, we anouch that the Church may so faile on earth, not that there is none at all, but that there is none in respect of vs, that is , of men, that there be none visible to vs on earth.* Againe : S. Paul inferreth generally that the whole Church may haue to be visible. And lib. 4. cap. 8 : *The true Church may sometymes faile to be visible.* Sonis in his answere to Spondé cap. 2. pag. 33 : *God maketh that the Church is not alwayes visible.*

The whole Church may haue to be visible.

Plessy Mornay in his booke of the Church cap. 1 : *Oftentymes the good corne is hidden vnder the chaffe without any appearance of the Church.* Polanus in his Antibellarm. Colledge disput. 14 : *The visible Church may faile.* Bucanus in his common places loc. 41. sect. 9 : *It oftentymes happeneth that there is no company of men extant which publikely and visibly worshippeth God purely.* And sect. 12 : *There is*

The visible church may faile.

alwayes on earth some number which worshippeth Christ piously, but this number is not alwayes visible. Trelcatius in his 2. booke

booke of Theologicall Institutions maketh this title
of one Chapter : : *That the visible church may fayle against*
Bellarmine . Hyperius in his Methode of diuinity lib.
3. pag. 548 : *VVhiles Elias wandred here and there, there ap-*
peared no face of the Church. Sadeel in his refutation of
the 61. article pag. 531 : *They are deceiued who think there*
is no Catholike Church , vnlesse they measure it with their eyes.
And pag.535 : *The true church may be conserued without any*
visible state . And in his repetition of Sophismes pag.
610: *it is plaine, that the Church is not so to be tyed to any out-* Wanteth
ward forme whatsoeuer , that it ought to be denyed to be a   outward
Church, as often as that forme shall not be extant.And of vo- forme.
cation of Ministers pag.543 : *The Church sometyme wan-*
teth the externall forme. Againe : *It is cleare that the Church*
hath sometymes byn without visible and personall succession. Pag.
550: *Mens wickednes doth sometymes take from vs the visible*
face of the Church. And againe : *It is sometymes so darkned,*
that it appeareth not to our eyes. Scharpe of Iustification Thewhole
Cont. 5: *The visible Church as such may perish* . The members visible
of the visible Church may perish, yea the whole visible Church, as Church
such. Bastingius vpon the Catechisme , title of the may pe-
Church, pag. 227:*VVithout doubt in euery age things haue* rish.
byn so troubled, as like a graine, couered with straw, there ap-
peared no face of the Church. Vorstius in his Antibellarm.
pag 133: *A litle before the calling of Abraham , no where ap-*
peared any visible Church. And pag.136: *Hereupon it follow-*
eth, that the visible church of Christ not only in a great part , but Thewhole
also taken whole in her vttermost extent, may for some tyme faile visible
from the true fayth, and be wholy darkned. The outward church Church
of Christ may perish. And pag. 424: *Neither did Christ pro-* may faile.
mise, that he would absolutely and perpetually hinder the peri-
shing and corruption of the outward Church. The Flemmings
Confession article 27: *The Church in the eyes of men for*
sometyme seemeth as extinguished . And Napper vpon the

K 4   11.chap.

11.chap.of the Apoc.pag. 186 : *They erre, who think that the true Church is alwayes visible*. And vpon 12.cap. pag. 195 : *The visible Church wholy imbraced the errors of merits, of indulgences &c*. And Proposit. 20. pag. 41: *The true Church was inuisible , and the true knowledge of God so couered with darknesse , that none could visibly enter*. Thus foraine Protestants. Of our coutrymen D. Whitaker Contr. 2.quest. 3.cap. 2. pag. 470: *Sometymes obscurity most of all helpeth the church . For at some tyme she could not be safe , vnlesse she lay hid.* And cap. 3. pag. 474 : *VVe say that sometyme the Church may auoyd the sight of men, & hide it selfe in corners.* Cap. 1. pag. 466: *VVe confesse , that euer more there is on earth some number of them, who piously worship Christ, & hold the true fayth and religion, but we say that this number is not alwayes visible. Their (Papists) opinion is, that there is euer more*

Not alwayes visible.

on earth a visible church. It may fall out that there cannot be found out and knowne any true and certaine visible church. And cap. 2.cit. pag. 468 : *Our aduersary would proue , that there was alwayes in the world some visible church.* And pag. 469: *Hence inferreth*(Denis the Carthusian) *not as our aduersaries do,*

The visible church may perish.

that the visible church can neuer perish, or that there is euer more in the world some visible church ; but that fayth shall neuer perish wholy , but that Christian religion shall still perseuer in some to the end of the world . This (sayth Whitaker) *is plainly that which we say and defend .* Marke how plainly he professeth , that they do not teach, that the visible Church

Note.

cannot perish , or that there is alwayes some visible Church on earth , but only that some shall alwayes belieue the Christian religion. The same doctrine he teacheth pag. 470. 473. 475. 476. and 479. And q. 6. cap. 2. pag. 559. And in his third booke against Duræus sect. 5. 6. 7. 11. M. Perkins in his problem. title of the church : *The ancients do acknowledge, that the church on earth is not alwayes visible.* D. Willet in his Synopsis

Cont.

Cont.2 q 1.pag.67: *VVe say the church is not always actual-*
ly visible to the world : nay it may sometyms be so hid and secret In Elias
that the members know not one another. Againe : *In the dayes* a tyme not
of Elias the church was not visible. And quest.2.pag. 74 : *A* visible.
visible church we define , to be a congregation of men , amongst
whome the word is truly preached, and the Sacraments admi-
nistred. Such a church hath not alwayes byn, neither can we be
assured that it shall alwayes be found vpon the earth. There was
a tyme when as the visible church failed vpon earth. This inui- The visi-
sibility of the Protestant Church, which I haue hi- ble church
therto proued by their manifold Confessions, I will failed.
also proue by sequels out of other their sayings. First
therefore D. Morton in his Apology part. 1. book. 1.
cap. 31. disliketh not these words of Bellarmine:
Protestants when they say the churchcannot faile or perish, meane
the inuisibible church. And many of them in expresse
words deny, that the Promises of perpetuity, which Protestāts
in the scripture are made vnto the church, Math. 16. say the
and other where, be made to the visible church. D. promises
Whitaker Cont. 2. quest. 3. cap. 3. pag. 468 : *It is most* belong
false, that it is the visible church, against which the gates of hell not to the
shall not preuaile. And Daneus Cont. 4. lib. 3. cap. 12. visible
pag. 717: *There* (Math. 16.) *is not meant the visible church.* Church.
To whome assenteth D.Willet in his Synopsis cont.
2. quest. 2. M. Powell of Antichrist lib. 1.cap. 10. Beurlin in his Refutation of Sotus, cap. 53. Moulins of
the vocation of Ministers lib. 1. c. 4. & in his Buckler
part. 1. pag. 49. And D. Morton lib.cit.cap. 13. addeth
that those three places Math. 16. & vlt. and psal. 47.
which promise the perpetulty of the Church , *Are* Protestāts
euery one of them vnderstood, almost by euery Father, of the only belieue
company of the elect , which the Protestants call the in- not the
uisible Church. Besides, they all generally teach, that visible
by the Catholike Church, which they professe to church.

belieue in the Creed, they meane not the viſible Church, but only the inuiſible. Luther in his booke of abrogating Maſſe, tom. 2. fol. 247 : *VVho ſhall ſhew vs the holy church, ſeeing it is hidden in ſpirit, and is only belieued, according as I belieue the holy church.* Zuinglius in his explication of the 31. article : *The church, which conſiſteth of thoſe which are knowne to God alone, in that which we profeſſe in the articles of our creed.* Danæus lib. cit. pag. 713 : *The queſtion is of the true church of God whereof it is ſayd in the creed: I belieue the holy church. Bellarmine vvill haue it to be the viſible, vve deny it.* The like he ſayth pag. 789. 717. 718. and 725. Vorſtius in his Antibellarm. pag. 144 : *VVe profeſſe not in the creed to belieue the viſible church, but the inuiſible.* D. Whitaker lib. 3. againſt Duræus ſect. vlt : *You ſee vvhat Catholike church vve belieue, not the viſible multitude of Chriſtians, but the holy company of the elect.* The ſame he ſayth Cont. 2. queſt. 2. cap. 2. Brentius in Prolegominis pag. 2. and others commonly. Furthermore they ſay, that the viſible Church is not the true Church in the ſight of God. For Caluin in his 4. booke of Inſtitutions cap. 1. §. 7. and the reſt graunt, that both wicked and reprobate Chriſtians may be of the viſible Church, but deny that they can be of the true Church in the ſight of God. Now ſurely if the viſible Church be neither the true Church in the ſight of God, nor ſhe to whome he hath promiſed perpetuity, nor ſhe which Proteſtants do belieue; what reaſon can they haue to belieue that the viſible Church ſhall alwayes remayne, or (which is all one) that the Church ſhall be alwayes viſible. Againe, their common doctrine is, that preaching of true doctrine is the note of the viſible Church; for ſo teacheth the Confeſſion of Auſpurg cap. 7. the Engliſh Confeſſion artic. 19. and all the reſt. To which his

Maieſty

They ſay the viſible Church is not the true Church before God.

Maiesty in his epist. to Cardinall Peron, D. Whitaker Contr. 2. q 5. c. 17. D. Morton part. 1. Apol. l. 1. c.
6. M. Willet in his Synopsis Cont. 2. quest. 3. pag. 102.
Sadeel to Turrians Sophismes loc. 5. Vorstius in Antibellarm. pag. 145. and others do adde, that it is an
essentiall note of the visible Church. And it is manifest that they must say so, because they vse to define
the visible Church, to be a company, *vvherein the pure*
vvord of God is preached, & the Sacraments rightly administred.
For so it is defined of the English Confession and of
Sadeel lib. cit. of Whitaker quest. 5. cit. cap. 20. of Me-
lacthon tom. 2. in cap. 15. Matth. and of others generally. But before Luther there was no preaching of
Protestantisme, as we shall heare them confesse cap.
7. therefore there was then no visible Protestant
Church. Finally, sometymes they say that not only
preaching of the word, but that also a lawfull ministery; or, that not only what true preaching soeuer,
but also such as is made by a lawfull Minister, of the
word, is of the essence and substance of the visible
Church. For thus writeth D. Whitaker Cont. 2. q. 5.
cap. 19. pag. 550 : *Stapleton sayth, that the preaching of the*
Ghospell by lavvfull Ministers is the proper note of the church; and
vve say no othervvise And pag. 551. *That he confesseth true*
preaching by a lavvfull Ministery to be a note of the church, is no
other thing then that vve say and defend. The like hath Sadeel in the place now cited : and the Switzers Confession cap. 17. putteth lawfull preaching for *the chie-*
fest note of the church; Caluin 4. Institut. cap. 2. §. 1. for
a perpetuall note, & the conclusions defended at Geneua
pag. 845. for *an essentiall note thereof.* But before Luther
there were no Protestant Ministers at all, as we shall
hereafter heare the Protestants confesse. Therefore
no visible Protestant Church.

8. By

Summe of the fore-ſayd con-feſſions.

8.   By that which hath byn rehearſed, it is manifeſt, that very many and very famous Proteſtants haue often and plainly confeſſed that when Luther *came firſt* (as they ſpeake) *to the Ghoſpell*, the Proteſtant Church and religion was not viſible, lay hid, lurked, lay in the wildernes, in lurking holes, in darkneſſe, in Trophonius his denne, was buryed, was vnknowne, vnheard of, appeared to none, cold not be diſcerned: Her image could not be ſcene, no ſhew of, beſides a huge ſpoile did appeare; no face, no faſhion, no trace of her was extant, and ſhe was ſo hid, that he who would iudge according to the outward ſhew, would think her to be no where: And that this is ſo manifeſt, as that the experience of many ages beareth witnes thereof. With what words, I pray you, could they ſay that their Church was altogeather inuiſible, if they haue not ſayd it in theſe?

9.   Moreouer it is manifeſt, that for to maintaine their inuiſible Church, they do teach, that the Church may be vnknowne to the godly, & to thoſe who are of it; that it may be not viſible, not appeare, not be ſcene by corporall eyes; that the externall knowledge therof may be taken from men, that it may conſiſt of no apparent forme, be without any viſible condition, without viſible ſucceſſion, and deſtitute of outward forme. That the viſible face thereof may be taken from vs, that it may ſeeme to haue vtterly periſhed, that the viſible Church may periſh, the outward Church periſh, that it may wholy leaue to be viſible, and the whole viſible Church periſh, and finally that there be no true viſible Church in the world.

10.   Beſides, it is cleare, that they teach, that
not

not only some part of the visible Church, but also
(as they speake) *the whole and all the visible Church may pe-*
rish, and that it may fall out that there be none, *none at* De grat.
all, no visible Church in the world. Certainly (as S. Austin *& lib. arb.*
speaketh) *these words need no witty interpreter, but only an* c. 8.
attent hearer.

    11.   Whereby also it is euident, that D. Proteſtāts
White in the defence of his way cap. 38.and 40 ſayd vntrue
vntruly, that Protestants imagine not the Church to ſhifts re-
haue byn at any tyme ſimply inuiſible. For as we futed.
haue heard, they oftentymes profeſſe openly the contrary. Vntruly alſo D. Whitaker auouchceth Cont.2.
queſt. 3.cap.2.pag.472. that we ſlaunder them, when
we ſay they make ſuch a Church, as ſometymes can
be ſeene of none. For as hath byn ſeene, many, and *Num.5.6.*
he amongſt the reſt, haue taught ſo. But D. Whitaker by the name of a viſible Church, vnderſtandeth
not a company viſibly profeſſing their fayth, but
one or two, or ſome few viſible men, who keep their
fayth ſecretly in their harts. But this, is not the
church to haue byn viſible, but the men to haue byn
viſible. Beſides that, it is inough for vs, that the
Proteſtant Religion and manner of worſhipping
God was before Luthers tyme altogeather inuiſible, and only ſecret in the hearts of ſome few. For
thence it will follow, (as ſhall appeare hereafter)
that it is not the religion of God, which can neuer
be kept ſo ſecret and inuiſible. Vntruly alſo ſayth Iunius Cont.4.lib.3.cap.16. when he writeth : *This only*
we ſay, the viſible manner of the Church may ly hid, or faile to
the vngratefull world, not that it can become inuiſible init ſelfe.
For that which is ſo inuiſible, as the Proteſtants
haue ſayd the Church may be, is in it ſelfe inuiſible.
Laſtly ſome do vntruly expound the foreſayd words

of

of Protestants, as if they had only sayd, that their Church had byn inuisible in some sort, not simply and absolutely; because their words were most absolute: and it is sophisticall to expound so many absolute speeches, only in some sort: Besides, hereafter we shall see, that sometymes they confesse, that their church was so inuisible, as it implyed contradiction to haue it seene, and those who limitate the former speaches, agree not togeather in their expositions; For D. Whitaker loc.cit.sayth they only meane, that the Church is not alwayes to be seene glorious and of euery one. D. White lib. cit. cap. 37. that they meane that the Church is not alwayes to be seene a part and free from all errour. D. Morton Apol. part. 1.lib.1.cap.13.that they only meant, that the church is not alwayes to be seene publikely of all men by her visible rites, and visible succession: which shift he calleth the *Bulwarck of Protestants*. But this Bulwarck is built of him without all foundation, and is manifestly ouerthrowne by the former Confessions. D·Feild sayth they meane not, that the Church is wholy inuisible, at any tyme; but that it is not alwayes to be esteemed by outward appearance. But what more manifest, then that they teach that the Church may be wholy inuisible, as appeareth by their words already rehearsed, and shall yet more appeare by and by?

12. For they not only confesse that their Church was altogeather inuisible before Luther arose, but also they affirme, that it is a most vniust and impudent demaund, to request them to shew it before that tyme. Hutter in his Analysis of the Confession of Auspurg pag. 448 : *It is an impudent demaund of*

the Romanists, to request to haue shewed vnto them such a church

in

in former ages, which touching the publike ministery and visible
forme, agreed in all things with Luther . For we haue demonstrated that the true Church then lay hid . D.Fulke in his
booke of Succession pag. 19 : *But you bid me bring forth*
those elect (Protestants) which lay hid through all the world.
Good God how vniust a thing do you demaund, that I should bring **Vniust.**
forth them, whome I say lay hid ? And Sadeel to the Repetition of Turrians Sophismes pag.766 : *But I promised*
not as you say, that I would answeare to this your question,
where those inuisible remnants lay hid ? as if I had not sufficiẽtly
answeared, when I sayd that they lay hid by the vnsearcheable
counsaile of God. And in his answere to Theses Posnan.
cap. 8. He will haue them to haue layne so closely,
that it cannot be knowne what they did. And in his
booke of Vocation of Ministers pag. 551 : *At last came*
that generall Apostasy , which the Apostle foretold. For then the **Only sha-**
outward light of the Church being quite extinct , there remay- **dow and**
ned the only shadow and name of the visible Church. The same **name of**
also intimateth Plessy Mornay in the Preface of his **visible**
Mystery of iniquity, when he sayth : *VVe are not bound* **Church.**
to shew the Church , it sufficeth that God knew his owne . And
Iohn Regius in his Apology pag 176 : *You deny that*
Luther found a company of his sect. I say there was an ecclesiasti-
call company of true religion , and which agreed with Luther in
all points. But when the Iesuits vrge to shew a follower of reli-
gion , they would that Luther shew , that which implieth , and **Implied**
proue the inuisible to be visible. Napper vpon 12.cap. Apo- **to be visi-**
cal. pag. 294: *From the yeare 316. God with drew his visible* **ble.**
Church from the open assemblies of men , to the hearts of particu-
ler men , and from that tyme the Church lay hid and was inuisi-
ble. The same he sayth pag.188 : *But if so it be an im-*
pudent and vniust demaund to haue their Church
shewed before Luther, if it were withdrawne from
open assemblies to the hearts of some, if her outward
light

light were quite extinct, and the only ſhadow and
name of the viſible Church remayned, and laſtly if
it implyed contradiction that ſhe ſhould be ſhewed;
it is moſt euident, that ſhe was altogeather inuiſible.
The ſame alſo they intimate, when they ſay, that
the Church either hath byn at any tyme, or may be
thus inuiſible. Luther vpon the 90. pſalme tom .3.

Church no where but in the ſight of God.

fol. 495: *The Church was then (in Elias tyme) but ſo hidden, as it was no where, but in the ſight of God.* Hyperius in
his Methode of diuinity, lib. 3. pag. 349: *VVas not the
true Church at that tyme (of Elias) altogeather inuiſible to
men, and knowne to God alone?* The Switzers Confeſſion

Knowne to God alone.

cap. 17: *The Church hidden from our eyes, and knowne to God
only, doth often fly the iudgement of men.* Beſnage in his
booke of the ſtate of the viſible and inuiſible church,
cap. 4: *The Church is eftſones knowne to God alone.* Sonis in
his anſwere to Spondè cap. 2. pag. 32: *VVe ſay the ſtate
of the Church is ſuch, as is ſometymes known to God alone.* And
D. Whitaker Cont. 2. queſt. 3. cap. 3 pag. 478: *VVe ſay
that the externall ſtate of the Church doth ceaſe, and that the
ſayihfull and godly may be ſo ſcattered, that they worſhip God*

Worſhip God in heart on-ly.

only in heart and mind. But who ſeeth not, that it implieth manifeſt contradiction, that a Church which
is no where but in the ſight God, which is knowne
to God alone, which flyeth mans iudgement, and
which worſhippeth God only in heart and mind,
ſhould be viſible or ſeene of man?

How long the Proteſtāts Church was inui-ſible.

13.　If any aske them, how many ages their
Church was thus inuiſible? Luther vpon the 1. cap.
to the Galat. tom. 5. fol. 214. ſayth that ſhe lay hid
aboue 300. years. To whome commeth neere Danæus in his 3. book de Roman. Pontif. cap. 8. ſaying,
the Church *was in baniſhment 350. years.* But Luther
better thinking on the matter, in his booke of the

Popery

Popery tom.7. maketh her to haue lurked 600. yeares.
And with him agreeth Hospinian in his epistle dedicatory of the 1. part of his History. Melancthon in
his oration for Luther tom.2. will haue this lurking
to haue byn 400. yeares. But Caluin his booke of
Scandals, Perkins and Bale in the places before cited, will haue it to haue continued 900. years. Parcus
aboue cited will haue it to haue begon in Constan-
tines tyme; and Napper from the yeare of our Lord
316. With whome consenteth Brocard vpon the 11.
Chap. Apocal. pag. 110. Fuccius in his Cronology
fetcheth the beginning of this lurking a litle higher,
from the yeare 261. and finally Curio of the large-
nesse of Gods Kingdome pag. 33 : *Almost from the Apo-*
stles ages euen to our tym. Which they also intimate, who
say that Popery began in the Apostles tyme. *O Christ*
most patient Lord (that I may cry out with Tertullian)
who so many years (yea so many ages) *diddest suffer thy do-*
ctrine to be turned vpside downe till Luther *came to helpe thee.*

14. Of all things which haue byn related in
this Chapter, it is most cleare, that Luther was at
least author of the Protestants visible Church, and
if not the first which founded it, yet the first which
after it was fallen & in substance perished, did rayse
and restore it againe. For when Luther began first to
preach, there was no visible Protestant Church at
all, and by his preaching there became such a visible
Church. Therefore vndoubtedly be was the author
thereof. And if any Protestant against so many and
so open Confessions of his Fathers and brethren,
will say that there was a visible Protestant Church
before Luther, he shall first gainesay so many witnesses without all exception in this matter, who hauing searched all corners, and enquired of all men.

Luther
Author of
the visible
Protestāt
Church.

L   haue

haue neuerthelesse confessed, that at that tyme no such visible Church appeared. Besides, he shall say that, without all either diuine or humane testimony; which to do of tymes before his age, is to play the Prophet, or rather the mad man. For it is not the part of a man in his wittes, to affirme without all kind of testimony, especially such a thing and so manifestly false, as that so many, and such kind of men, as had most need to affirme it, were neuerthelesse forced to deny it. That it wanteth all sufficient humane testimony is euident, because neither the forelayd Protestants, nor any yet to this day, could bring forth any sufficient witnesse, who would depose that he had seene such a Church before Luthers reuolt. That also it is destitute of diuine testimony, is manifest by what hath byn before rehearsed. For Protestants (as we haue heard) teach, that the promises of perpetuity, which in the scripture are made to the church, are made only to the inuisible church, that is to a society of men in election and Iustification, out of which Church they exclude the reprobate and wicked; and not to the visible Church, that is, to the society in Profession of true doctrine and lawfull vse of Sacraments. And in truth they most needs say so, sith they commonly teach, that the inuisible Church, whereof the elect and iust alone are members, is the true Church before God: and that the visible Church, whereof the wicked & reprobate may be members, is but a Church in sight of men, that is a shadow and outward shew of the Church. And it is cleare, that God promised perpetuity to that Church only, which in his sight is the true Church; and not to her which is no Church, but only in sight of men. When as I say they teach

that

Sup. num 2.

that God promised perpetuity and continuance only to the inuisible Church, out of his promises they
cannot inferre, that the visible Church hath or shall
euer continue. *Of whome therefore* (that I may vse S.
Augustins words) *hast thou heard this? whence diddest
thou learne it? where hast thou read it for to beliue it? whereupon hast thou presumed for to affirme it, where there is neither
any authority nor reason?* If Protestants cry out, that it
is most absurd, to say in Elias his tyme there was
any Church visible amongst the Gentils beside the
Synagogue, which now after so many thousands of
years we cannot name; how much more absurd
ought they think it, to say that before Luther arose,
there was a visible Protestant Church, which yet
none neither of that Church, nor out of it, neither
at this tyme, nor at that, could euer name?

*Lib. 2. cōt.
Maxim. c.
3. l. 3. c. 17.*

*Whitak.
cont. 2. q. 3.
c. 3.*

    15.   It being thus manifest, that Luther
was the Author of the visible Protestant Church, it
followeth like wise that he was the author of all and
Euery Protestant Church. For (as shall be shewed
hereafter) there can be no such inuisible Church as
Protestants meane, that is, such as believeth and
worshippeth God only in hart and mind, and no
way professeth outwardly her fayth and religion.
Yet before we come to that, we will first refute
those, who when they consider how absurd a thing
it is to affirme such an inuisible Church, especially
for so many ages, they begin to shufle and either send
vs to others, or themselues name vs such, as only in
part or in some sort held Protestantisme, but imbraced not all the substantiall points thereof, and therefore were but halfe Protestants. For to vs it sufficeth,
that we shew Luther to haue byn the Author and
beginner of whole and true Protestants, such as held

all points that are necessary to the making of an absolue Protestant.

Those confuted who say there were some visible Protestants when Luther arose.

CHAP. V.

What a mã Illyricus was.

Colloq. Aldeburg Hosp. part 1. fol. 104. Beza epist. 55. in Mat. 26. ver. 15. in 4. Ephe. Scultet. Præfat. in tom. 1. Pareus lib. 5. de Amiss. grat. cap. 1 Melancth. tom. 2. Hesk. in Antid. Schusselb. Praf. to. 2 Kemnit. loc. p. 263.

1. SOME Protestants, when we aske of them who were the visible Protestants before Luther began, do not themselues name any, but send vs to Illyricus or M. Fox. So playeth D. Whitaker lib. 3. against Duræus sect. 12. and lib. 7. sect. 1 D. Fulke of Succession pag. 324. Schusselburg in 8. tom. of his Catalogue of Heretiks pag. 365. Vorstius in his Antibellarm. pag. 159. Lubbett lib. 5. of the Church c. 2. and others: These men do manifestly shew that themselues know not of any such visible Protestants. For they would neuer lay the burden of answering this question vpon others, if they could haue answered it themselues. And besides, they declare that they know no author worthy of credit, to whome they might send vs, for the answere of this so important demaund, else they would neuer haue referred vs to Illyricus or M. Fox. For Illyricus in the iudgement of most Protestants both Lutherans and Sacramentaries, *was a vagabond, a hell hound, an heretike, a Manichee, deceitfull, a lyar, an impostor, a falsifier, a Cauiller, a sclaunderer, a singular inuenter of sclaunders, a sycophant in his own iudgement, impudently blasphemous, a broacher of doctrine which bringeth in Epicurisme and mortality of the soule, and ouerthroweth all religion; and who had nothing to impugne truth withall,*

withall, besides an audacious ignorance, and a very diuilesh spirit. This and much more write the Protestants them-selues of Illyricus; wherefore to send vs to such a man, is plainly to confesse that they know no man of credit to whome they may referre vs. And of the like stuffe is Fox, a most impudent patcher of lyes, who in his false Martyrologe proposeth theeues, traytors, sorcerers, murderers of themselues, Ana-baptists, Papists, professed enemies, and some then aliue, for Protestant Martyrs, as Allen Cope sheweth in the sixt book of his dialogues. Beside, those whom Illyricus nameth before Luther, himselfe dares not cal Protestants, but *VVitnesses of truth*; because forsooth they disliked some doctrine or fact of the Pope. And such witnesses also they are, as some of them be Popes themselues, as (a) Pius 2. some famous Papists, as (b) Peter Lumbard, and Gratian, whome himselfe cal-leth the (c) *Pillars of the Religion of the Roman Antichrist*, and sayth they *renewed Popery euen from the foundation*; some professed aduersaries of Protestâts, as (d) Clich-toueus; some of the holy Fathers, who (as before was seene) condemned the very soule and summe of Protestancy; some those, who only disliked the cor-rupt manners of some Popes, as (e) Richard Hampell; some Atheists, as (f) Machiauell; some who any way (g) gainsayd either the doctrine or deed of any Pope. Surely for Illyricus to bring such witnesses, after he had searched in all corners, and raked in all chanels, doth manifestly bewray, that there can no true Protestants be found before Luthers tyme. For Illy-ricus, though neuer so impudent, would haue byn ashamed to haue bragged of such silly witnesses, if he could haue found any true Protestants whatsoeuer. Besides, such fellowes, may be only sayd to haue byn

(a) *Lib.* 19.
(b) *Lib* 15.
(c) *Lib.* 15. & 16.

(d) *Lib.* 19.

(e) *Centur.* 6 *cap.* 1.
(f) *Lib.* 19.
(g) *Præf. Catal.*

Prote-

Proteſtants, and can no way be proued to haue byn ſimply and abſolutely Proteſtants, ſuch as we ſpeake of. And we care not whom any one may ſay to haue byn Proteſtants (for as Luther ſayth, *what is more eaſy then to ſay any thing?*) but whome he can proue & conuince to haue byn ſuch ; without which his ſaying is but voluntary and ridiculous, and the beliefe therof rath and ynreaſonable.

Tom. 1.
Fol. 437.

2.   And as for thoſe, which M. Fox produceth for Proteſtants before Luther, they liued in the year of our Lord 1521. as himſelfe writeth pag. 749. in the edition of 1596. that is, in the 4. year of Luthers new preaching, and we aske for Proteſtants before Luther. Beſides they all abiured their ſayth, as himſelfe confeſſeth pag. 750. and ſoone after dyed for ſorrow, or lingered away with ſhame ; and we aske for Proteſters not Abiurers. Moreouer no one of them is found to haue held that cheife and fundamentall article of Proteſtancy of Iuſtification by ſpeciall faith, albeit, as Fox writeth pag. 550: There was ſuch diligent inquiſition made as that no article could be ſo ſecretly taught amongſt them but it was diſcouered. Wherefore theſe wretched Abiurers were no Proteſtãts, but ſome reliques of the Wicliſiſts or Lollards, whereof we will intreat anone.

The wal
denſes
were no
Proteſtãts

3.   Others ſay, that the Waldenſes were the viſible Proteſtants before Luthers riſing, but there is no apparent reaſon to ſay, that they were true & abſolute Proteſtants, to wit, ſuch as held all the whole ſubſtance neceſſary to a Proteſtant. For firſt, there is no writer before Luthers tyme who ſayth that they belieued to be iuſtified by only ſayth. Neither can any ſuch thing be gathered, either out of their own opinions, or out of the writings of Catholiques
                                                against

against them at those tymes. And Illyricus in his Catalogue of witnesses printed at Geneua 1597. lib. 15. pag. 544. writeth their opinions out of an ancient Catholique writer, and pag. 559. out of Aeneas Siluius, and pag. 539. relateth their Confession out of Sleidan, and himselfe pag. 536. reckoneth 13. of their articles, of which he hath these words : *These are the articles of the VValdenses, albeit others part them into more branches, and make them more.* But in none of them is there any trace of only iustifying fayth. The same I say of their Confession which the sayd Illyricus hath in his Catalogue printed at Geneua 1526. yea there col. 1832. he sayth, that Husse and Hierome of Prage did add vnto the doctrine of the Waldenses the article of free iustification by only fayth, as (sayth he) Syluius intimateth: wherein albeit he belye both Husse and Hierome & also Syluius, because neither they knew *Num.7.* of any such iustification, (as shall straight appeare) neither Syluius intimateth any such matter; yet it clearly bewrayeth, that the waldenses belieued not iustification by only fayth. Moreouer Luther (as we shall now rehearse) confesseth that the Waldenses knew nothing of his imputatiue iustice by only fayth : How then can they be sayd to haue byn true and absolute Protestants, who wanted the very soul, summe, and definition of a Protestant? Secondly they not only belieued not iustification by only fayth, but belieued the contrary; that is, to be iustifyed by good works. For thus sayth Luther of them in his table-talkes chap. of Suermers : *The VValdenses are holy workmen and belieue not that fayth without works doth* Coccius *iustify, and know nothing at all of imputatiue iustice.* And *to.1. lib.8.* Bennet Morgenstern in his treatise of the church p. 124. speaketh thus vnto them : *Yee confirme the doctrine*

of *Antichrist, touching good works, iuftification, &c.* And thē-
felues in their Apology printed at Hanow togeather
with the hiftory of Bohemia pag.256. plainly fhew,
that they belieue a man to be iuftified by fayth, charity, hope, penance, and works of mercy, and do
fay: *That deuout prayer doth purge, and pennance cleanfe a
man.*

    4.   Thirdly, the Waldenfes are condemned
of Proteftants, both Lutherans and Sacramentaries.
Melancthon in his Counfailes part.2.pag.152. wri-

*See Refut.
Orthod.
Confenfus
pag. 418.*

teth: *I reioyce that you agree with vs in the fumme of doctrine.
I know the VValdenfes are vnlike.* And in Carions Chronicle printed at Paris 1557. he fayth that they *fowed
errors, denyed all oathes, and all forme of prayer, befides the Lords
prayer.* Morgenftern in his fornamed booke pag. 79.
giueth this verdict of them : *They haue proudly neglected
the light of doctrine which is kindled from heauen in this age ; &
haue with tooth and naile by writing among their own men fe-
cretly defended thofe moft groffe errors, which in the year 1523.
were difcouered by Luther.* Befides Selnecer (as he reporteth) affirmed, that they *had groffe errors, and fuch as were
not to be borne withall.* Leonicus Antifturmius alfo in
Danæus in his anfwere to his Sondè pag. 1516. pronounceth them to be impious ; and Schuffelburg in
his 3.tome of the Catalogue of heretiks pag.188. reiecteth them as heretiks. Camerarius in his booke of
the Church in Bohemia, Poland, &c. pag. 273. writeth thus : *VVe can fay that the VValdenfes were neuer one
with our Churches, nor our men would euer ioyne themfelues to
them.* Whereof he giueth thefe two reafons : becaufe
the Waldenfes would not haue extant any publike
declaration of their fayth ; and for peace fake did vfe
the Popifh maffe. *For thefe two caufes (fayth he) our men
did not ioyne themfelues to them, neither did they think that they
could*

could so do , with good conscience . Caluin also epist. 278.
thus writeth to the Waldenses themselues : *VVe abide
in one opinion, that the forme of your Confession cannot be absolutely admitted without danger.* And M. Iewell also in defence of the Apology part. pag. 48. sayth plainly of
the Albigenses: *They are none of ours.* D. Humfrey to the
third Reason of F. Campian pag. 371 : *They are not
wholy ours.* And Osiander in his 13.Century lib.1. cap.
4. Pantaleon in his Chronicle pag. 98.& Melancthon
in the foresayd Chronicle of Carion, reckon them a-
mongst heretiks: But the Albigenses were all one for
religion with the Waldenses , as D. Fulke sayth in
these words, lib. de Successi. pag. 232: *That epistle of the
Arch-bishops, doth proue that the Albigenses & VValdenses were
all one.* The same also confesseth Illyricus in his Catalogue in 4. to. pag. 536. Where also pag. 561. he speaketh in this sort : *The VValdenses or Albigenses .* Yea the
Waldenses themselues , in the Bohemian Confession
(if it be theirs) do insinuate that they are condemned
of the Sacramentaries , wheras they say in the 13. article, that they, who deny the supper of the Lord to
be the true flesh and bloud of Christ, do call them
Idolaters, Antichrist , and men branded with the
marke of the beast. Besides Illyricus in his forecited catalogue writeth, that the Thaborites, who indeed (sayth he) followed the opinions of the Waldenses , were grieuously vexed and persecuted of
Rokesana and other Hussites . Wherefore , sith Protestants commonly challenge the Hussites for their
brethren, they ought not to claime also the Waldenses, whose doctrine the Hussites did persecute. Certainly the Confession of Bohemia (which is sayd to
be theirs) doth plainly distinguish them from Protestants, especially from Sacramentaries . For art. 2.

they

they say: *VVe must keep the commandements in hart & deed.* Art. 5. that thole which repent mult confelle their sinnes to a Priest, and aske ablolution of him. Art. 9. that Priests ought to be single. Art. 11. that Sacraments are neceffary to faluation. And art. 13. that the Eucharift is the true body of Chrift, as (say they) Chrift plainly fayth : This is my body; of which words we ought to belieue the plaine sense, not declining to the right or left. Whereupon it is no mertuayle, that Caluin in his 249. epiftle denieth it to be lawfull for a Chriftian man, to imbrace the Waldenfes Confeffion, in thefe words : *Confider you whether it be lawfull for a Chriftian man to imbrace the forme of the Confeffion (of the Waldenfes) who without any diftinction bind vp all in one bundell of damnation, who precisely confeffe not, the bread to be prefently the body of Chrift. Surely we think not.*

5.   Fourthly I proue the same, becaufe the Waldenfes hold many errors, which the Proteftants condemne. Illyricus in his forefayd Catalogue pag. 545. relateth out of an ancient writer aboue 300. years agoe, that they taught, that a Prieft being in mortall finne cold not confecrate the Eucharift; that euery oath is a mortall finne; that they difallowed matrimony. And likwise out of Aeneas Syluius, that they sayd it was lawfull for euery one to preach; & that he who was guilty of mortall finne, was not not capable of any secular or ecclefiafticall dignity. Neither auayleth it any thing, that now in the Cöfeffion of Bohemia (which is fayd to be the Waldenfes Confeffion) there is found the article of iuftification by only fayth, becaufe that Confeffion was prefented in the yeare 1525. as the very title thereof declareth, & in the Preface mention is made of Charles 5. Emperour,

5. Emperour, which was after Luther had preached some years. As also becauſe Hoſpinian part. 2. Hiſtor. fol. 11. ſayth, that the Waldenſes Confeſſion was re- *Sacramē-* uewed or rather corrupted by the Sacramentaries, as *taries* the Waldenſes themſelues ſay in the Preface of their *haue cor-* Confeſſion printed anno 1538. as witneſſeth Schuſ- *rupted* ſelburg, lib. 2. Theol. Caluin. art. 6. fol. 55. Moreouer *the Wal-* Illyricus in his Catalogue in fol. col. 1502. writeth, *denſes* that after *Luther was knowne, the VValdenſes did greedily* *Cōfeſſiō.* *purchaſe greater knowledge.* Morgenſtern in his foreſayd booke pag. 79. ſayth, that *they borrow the beſt part of their* *doctrine from the Lutherans.* And D. Fulke in his booke of Succeſſion pag. 360. that *they learnt of thoſe of Baſle, to* *amend certaine errors, which they had receiued from their an-* *ceſtors.* Why then ſhall we not think, they receiued the doctrine of iuſtification by only fayth from Lu- ther? eſpecially ſith (as I befor ſayd) there is no men- tion of it amongſt them in former tymes? Againe Iurgeuicius in the 2. chap. of his warre of the 5. ghoſ- pell, affirmeth that the Authors of the Bohemian Confeſſion do profeſſe in the beginning thereof, that they would neuer conioyne themſelues to the Wal- denſes; and therefore the Bohemian Confeſſion is not the Waldenſes Confeſſion. Nor albeit therein be mention of iuſtification by only fayth, can it be in- ferred, that therefore the Waldenſes did belieue it. Finally (as I haue often ſayd and it muſt be alwayes inculcated) I regard not, whome any one ſayth to haue byn Proteſtants, but whom he proueth to haue byn ſuch. Neither whome he can proue to haue byn Proteſtants in part and in ſome ſort; but whome he can proue to haue byn abſolutely and wholy Pro- teſtants, at leaſt for the ſubſtance of Proteſtancy. Nei- ther will it auaile any whit, to complaine, that we

haue

haue burnt the writings of the Waldenses, by which
they might proue that they were true Protestants.
For if they haue not wherwithall to prouethey were
true Protestants, they in vaine do feigne it. Besides,
we asked of Luther & his followers to produce one
man, Waldensian or other, who had byn a true Protestant, before Luthers preaching; for which end
there was no need of writings, but of liuing men.

Wiclif
was no
true Pro-
testant.

6. In likesort I proue that Wicliffe and his
followers were not true and absolute Protestants.
First because the Wiclifists are by name condemned
togeather with other heretiks of Protestants in their
Apology of the Confession of Auspurg, chap. of the
Church in these words: *VVe haue plainly inough sayd in
our Confession, that we disalow the Donatists and VViclifists.*
Secondly because neither in Wiclifs booke, nor of
any of his schollers, is there any signe of sole iustifying fayth; neither did euer any Catholike writer
contend with them thereabout. Thirdly, because as
Melancthon writeth in his epistle to Myconius in his
1.tom. printed at Basle pag. 416: *VViclif neither vnderstood, nor held the iustice of fayth.* Yea Husse his principall
follower, (as we shall anon rehearse) belieued that
works did iustify. And Wiclif himselfe in Thomas
Walden.tom 3.tit.1.cap.7. bid euery one hope in the
proper iustice of his life, and men to trust in their
merits: which thing alone doth separate him farre
inough from the Protestants campe. Fourthly, because the Wiclifists are reckoned amongst Heretiks
of many Protestants, as of Schusselburg tom.3. Catal. pag.190. of Kemnice in fundamentis Coenæ pag.
114. of Pantaleon in his Chronicle, and of Matthias
Hoe disput.27. they are termed *most monstrous monsters.*
And D.Cay in his 2.booke of the antiquity of Cam-
bridge,

bridge, obiecteth Wicliffe to the Oxford men, as a
staine of their vniuersity. Fiftly wiclif taught diuers things, which Protestants dislike. And to omit
these things which Catholikes obiect vnto him,
Rokesana Prince of the Hussites, in his dispute
with Catholiks before the King of Bohemia, hath
these words: *These are the articles of VViclif: That tithes
are meere almes: That the Clergy ought to haue no ciuill gouernment: If a King be in mortall sinne, that he is no more a
King:* Which last article Osiander in his 15. Century repeateth thus: *There is no temporall Lord, no Prelate,
no Bishop, whiles he is in mortall sinne.* And Melancthon
in his foresayd epistle: *VViclif doth plainly, sophistically
and seditiously wrangle vpon ciuill dominion.* And in his dispute of the right of Magistrats: *VViclif is mad, who
thinketh the wicked to haue no Dominion.* And in his Commentaries vpon Aristotles Politiques: *VViclif would
haue those, who haue not the holy ghost, to loose their Dominion.* So that I meruaile how D. Andrews in his
answere to the Apology of Bellarmine, could say
that it is a sclaunder, that Wiclif taught so; when
as not only Catholiks, but euen Hussites and Protestants do affirme it. Moreouer Wiclif (as Osiander reporteth in the place aforecited) did condemne
lawfull oathes, and taught, that all things fell out
according to absolute necessity. And Melancthon
in his sayd epistle giueth this sentence of him: *I haue
looked into VViclif, but I haue found in him many other errors,
by which one may iudge of his spirit. He at all vnderstood not,
nor held the iustice of fayth. He fondly confoundeth the ghospell
and politique affaires; would haue Priests to haue nothing proper, &c.* And in his common places chap. of Ecclesiasticall power: *That superstition of VViclif is pernicious
and seditious, which driueth the ministers of the Church to beg-
gery.*

*Canisius
to.3 antiq.
lectionum.*

Wiclife
held not
iustice of
sole faith.

gery, *and denyeth that it is lawfull for them to hold any thing proper.* M. Stow also in his Cronicle anno 1376. writeth, that he taught that, *Neither King nor Lay man could giue any thing to the church for perpetuity.* Finally Vadianus in his fift book of the Eucharist, pag. 168. confesseth that *in many things he fouly erred.*

7. Husse likewise and his partners we proue, not to haue byn true and absolute Protestants. First, because it cannot be proued, that they held the foresayd article of iustification by only fayth, and the other fundamentall points of Protestancy. Secondly, because Husse is by name reiected of Luther, who in the defence of his 30. article tom. 2. thus writeth of him: *He agreeth not with me. He gaue not a litle to the idol of Rome. He seemeth not to repugne against the Popes Monarchy.* And vpon the 2. psal. tom. 3. fol. 295: Husse did not condemne the sacrifice of Masse, as we do. And vpon the 9. chapter of Isaias tom. 4. fol. 108. he sayth, that Husse held a doctrine most pestilent, most pernicious, horrible, and wholy impious, yea very diuelish. And in his Lypsicall dispute tom. 1. fol. 260: *I know, and that very well, that an euill Prelate is not to be reiected, and therefore I damne the article of Husse.* And both there and other

where, oftentymes denieth himselfe to be a Bohemian, by which he meant an Hussite. And in his table-talkes chapter of Suermers sayth: *Husse belieued that works with fayth do iustify*; which point alone

excludeth him from the number of Protestants. And in the chapter of Antichrist: *Husse departed not one iot from the Papists, but only reproued vices and naughty life.* Which also affirmeth Hierome of Prage, Husse his fellow, in M. Fox, vpon the 11. chapter of the Apocal. Where also M. Fox himselfe writeth, that

Husse

Husse agreed with the Papists touching transubstantiation, Masse, Vowes, Predestination, Free
will, formed fayth, cause of iustification, and merits of works: which plainly declare how litle he
held of Protestancy. Lastly when Bellarmine wrote,
that there was not in the world, when Luther began, any religion but Paganisme, Iudaisme, Mahometisme, Grecisme, Nestorianisme, Hussites heresy, and the Romane fayth; D. Whitaker Cont. 2.
quest. 5. cap. 3. pag. 502. denyeth these to haue byn
all; For (sayth he) *our Church was then.* In which words
he protesseth the Protestants to be a different church
from the Hussites. Iunius also lib. 4. de Eccles. cap.
6. acknowledgeth that some Protestant deny Hussites to be of their Church. And Luther vpon the
53. Chapter of Isaias tom. 4. fol. 220. thus writeth:
There is no religion in the world which receiueth this opinion of
iustification (by only fayth) and we our selues in priuate do
scant belieue it, though we publikely defend it. By which
words he sheweth, that neither Hussytes, nor Waldenses, nor any Christians besides Protestants, and
scarce they also, do belieue the principall and most
fundamentall article of Protestancy, howsoeuer
openly they professe it.

That

*That the Church cannot be so inuisible, as Pro-
testant confesse teirs to haue byn before Luthers tyme .*

CHAP. VI.

1. BY the name of the Church, we vnderstand
not (as I sayd before) only the men, but men
sociated, or the society of men, in the fayth & worship of God. Wherfore that a church be sayd visible,
not only the men, but their worship of God must be
visible. Neither by this word *visible*, do I vnderstand
here, that only which can be seene, but whatsoeuer
is sensible; according both to the vulgar phrase of
speach, wherewith we say : *See how it soundeth*, as S.
Augustine noteth, and also after the phrase of scripture, wherein, as the same holy Doctour obserueth:
All sensible things are called visible. And Protestants, (as is
before shewed) do confesse that before Luthers rising
their Church was simply inuisible, and vnseene of
any, either of those within or without her. And necessarily they must say so, because they can name
none at all, who before Luther arose, did see a company of men, who professed to belieue iustification
by only fayth, and the rest of the fundamentall principles of Protestancy : yea they affirmed, that it was
so inuisible, as it implyed contradiction to haue byn
seene of any.

2. Now that the Church Militant or liuing
on earth cannot be so inuisible, I proue; first, because
it is against an article of fayth of diuers Protestants.
And if perhaps any hereupon imagine, that either

Prote-

Lib. 10.
Confess.
c 35.

Lib. 1. de
mor. Ma-
nich. c. 10.

Ca. 4. n. 11.

That the
Church
cannot be
inuisible.

Proteſtants neuer graunted the contrary, or that if they did graunt it, their teſtimonies againſt themſelues are not to be accepted; let him read what hereafter I write touching that matter, in the laſt chapter of this booke. Wherefore in the Confeſſion of Saxony cap. 15. they profeſſe in this ſort: *God will haue the Miniſtery of the ghoſpell to be publike, he will not haue the voice of the ghoſpell to be ſhut vp only in corners; but will haue it heard of all mankind. Therefore he will haue publike and ſeemely meetings; and in them he will haue the voice of the ghoſpell to ſound. He will alſo haue theſe ſame meetings to be witneſſes of the Confeſſion and ſeparation of the Church from the ſects and opinions of other Nations. God will haue his Church to be ſeene and heard in the world, and will haue her deuided by many publik marks from other people.* And the ſame they repeat in the Conſent of Polony cap. de Cœna. And the ſame Confeſſion of Saxony cap. of the Church: *VVe ſpeake not of the Church as of a Platonicall idæa, but we ſhew a Church, which may be ſeene and heard. The eternall Father will haue his Sonne to be heard in all mankind. VVherefore we ſay, that the Church is in this life a viſible company &c.* Secondly it is againſt their owne definitions of a militant Church. For the foreſayd Confeſſion of Saxony defineth the Church in this life to be a viſible company. The Magdeburgians in their 1. Century lib.1.c.4. col. 170. do thus write: *The Church may be thus defined: The Church in this life, is a company of thoſe, who imbrace the ſincere doctrine of the Ghoſpell, and rightly vſe the Sacraments.* And the very ſame definition giueth Melancthon tom.4. in cap. 3.1. ad Tim. pag. 298. Hutterus in his Analyſis of the confeſſion of Auſpurg pag. 444. ſaith: *This Church, which is ſayd to be, and to be belieued, is not a Platonicall idea, but the viſible company of thoſe, that are called.* Zanchius alſo in his treatiſe of the Church cap. 2:

Proteſtãts definitiõs of the Church.

The Church in this life.

The Church which we belieue.

M   The

Church
militant.

The militant Church is the compauy of the elect, and truly fayth-
full, profeſſing the ſame fayth, partaking the ſame Sacramentt,
&c. Hereof properly ſpeake the ſcriptures, when they call the
Church the ſpouſe of Chriſt, the body of Chriſt, redeemed with
the bloud of Chriſt, ſounded vpon a rock. Gerlachius tom. 2.
Diſput. 22 : *Defining the Church, as it is on earth, we ſay that*

Church
on earth.

it is a congregation of men, who called by the voice of the Ghoſ-
pell, heare the word of God, and vſe the Sacraments inſtituted of
Chriſt.

3. Thirdly it is againſt the properties and
markes of the true Church aſſigned by the Proteſtants themſelues, to be altogeather inuiſible. For

The
proper
Church.

thus their Confeſſion of Auſpurg cap. 7: *The Church of*
Chriſt properly ſo called, hath her marks, to wit, pure doctrine,
&c. The Confeſſion of Saxony cap. 12: *The true church*
is diſcerned from other nations, by the voice of true doctrine, and
lawfull vſe of Sacraments. The French Conteſſion art.

The true
Church.

27 : *VVe belieue that the true church ought to be diſcerned with*
great care VVherefore we affirme out of the word of God, that
the Church is the company of the faythfull, who agree in follow-
ing the word of God, and imbracing true religion : wherein alſo
they daily profit, growing and confirming themſelues mutually in
the feare of God. The Conteſſion of the Low Countries art. 29: *By theſe markes the true Church ſhall be diſcer-*
ned from the falſe, if in her the pure preaching of the Ghoſpell be
of force: by theſe markes it is certaine that the true Church may
be diſtinguiſhed. The Confeſſion of Scotland art. 18:
It is neceſſary that the true Church be diſcerned from the falſe,
by euident marckes, leaſt being deceiued we imbrace the falſe
for the true, to our eternall damnation Againe: *VVe belieue the*
markes of the true Church to be true preaching of the word. &c.
Melancthon in his anſwere to the Bauarian articles
tom. 3. fol. 362 : *It is euident, that the true Church is a viſible*
company. And vpon the 16. to the Romans tom. 1. pag.
486:

486 : *She is the true Church, who teacheth the Ghospell aright,* *and rightly administreth the Sacraments.* Danæus in his booke of Antichrist, cap. 17 : *This is the proper definition* *of the Church, that the true Church is the company of the faythfull, who serue God purely, and keep the notes of adoption instituted by him such as are the heauenly word, the Sacraments and discipline. By these 3. marks the false Church is distinguished from the true.* Lubbert in his 4. booke of the Church cap. 2 : *VVe say that the Church doth shew her selfe to be the true Church, by the sincere preaching of the word of God* And Beza wrote a booke of this title : *Of the true and visible marks of the Catholike Church.* D. Whitaker in answere of the 3.reason of F. Campian : *That we iudge to be proper to the true Church, that it increase and conserue Christs word, that it vse the Sacraments entirly and purely. These we defend to be the most true and essentiall properties of the Church. Take these away and you will leaue nothing but the carcasse of the church.* Againe : *They containe the true nature of the church, which if they be present, they make the church, and take it away, if they be taken away* And D. Feild in his 1.book of the church cap. 11 : *VVe say, that that society wherein that outward profession of the truth of God is preserued, is that true church of God, &c.* Finally to omit the words of others, the same teach Wigand in his method of doctrine cap. 19. Gesner in his 24. place of the Church, The Magdeburgians in the Preface of their 6. Cetury, Heshusius in cap. 1. 1. ad Cor. Soterius in his method, title of the church, Pelargus in his Compend. of diuinity loc. 7. Sohnius in his Thesis of the Church, Bullinger in his Catechisme fol. 44. Arctius in his places part. 3. fol. 50. Theses of Geneua disput. 74. Thus thou seest (good reader) that according to the manifold iudgement of Protestants, a part of the definition, of the essence, the marke of the Church in this life,

life, of the Church militant, of the Church which
is belieued, of the proper Church, of the Church
whereof the Scripture properly speaketh, when it
calleth her the spouse of Christ, the body of Christ;
of the true Church, of the Church properly so termed, and finally of the Catholike Church; that (I
say, it is of the definition and essence, a marke of this
church, to be a visible company professing the faith,
partakiug the Sacraments, mutually confirming
themselues, and that otherwise it is (as they say) but
a carcasse of the Church. Wherefore it implieth manifest contradiction, that there should at any tyme
haue byn a true Church, and not a visible company:
because nothing can be without all its essentiall
parts. The Protestant Church therefore, which (as
we head) was before Luthers tyme altogeather inuisible, was no true and proper Church, but (to vse
their termes) a Platonicall idæa, or a carkasse of a
Church, If any reply, that when Protestants affirme
the foresayd definitions, properties, and marks of
the true Church; they meane not by the name of the
true Church that which is simply and absolutely the
true Church, but that which is the true visible
Church; I aske, why then do they simply call it the
true Church, if they do not so meane? why are not
their words conformable to their meaning? Besides,
the Church whereof they giue the foresayd definitiõs
and marks, they call not only the true Church, but
also the Church properly so termed, the spouse and
body of Christ, the Catholike church, and such like,
which cannot agree to any, which is but a Church
in appearance only, and in the sight of men, but only to that which is the Church in very deed, and in
the sight of God. Further more, according to the
opinion

opinion of Proteſtants theſe two termes *True* and *Viſible*, in the nature of the Church do one deſtroy the other; as theſe two, *True* and *Painted*, exclude each other in the nature of a man. For they imagine that the true Church is a ſociety in ſomething that is inuiſible, to wit in iuſtification and predeſtination. Whereupon they deny any ill or reprobate Chriſtians to be of the true Church. Wherefore, as he ſhould ſpeake fondly, who ſhould ſay *A true painted man*; ſo, according to their owne opinion, they ſpeake as fondly, when they ſay *The true viſible Church.* But as we can only ſay, the true picture of a man, attributing the word *True*, to the picture, not to the man; ſo they ſhould only, *The true appearance or ſhew of the Church*, giuing the word *True* to the ſhew, not to the Church it ſelfe. But they are aſhamed to ſpeak ſo, leaſt when they inquire the marks of the true viſible Church, it ſhould appeare, that they ſeeke not the marks of the true Church indeed, but only of the ſhew, ſhadow, or ſhape of the Church. And yet in very truth they ſeeke but the marks of the ſhadow of the church. For the inuiſible Church, conſiſting only of the iuſt and elect, which alone they will haue to be the true Church; hath no certaine marks; elſe we ſhould know certainly who were the iuſt and elect. And this themſelues confeſſe; for thus writeth D. Whitaker Cont. 2. queſt. 5. cap. 8: *The queſtion is not of the marks of the inuiſible Church.* Againe: *VVe ſay the marks of the Catholike Church ſimply ſo called, are knowne to God alone.* And D. Humfrey to 3. reaſon of F. Campian pa. 281. ſayth that the marks *do not reach vnto the nature of the true Church.* And the reaſon is manifeſt, becauſe (as I ſayd) otherwiſe we ſhould know who were the iuſt and elect.

Why Proteſtāts ſomtyme call the viſible viſible Church the true Church.

Proteſtāts giue no marks of the true & Catholike Church.

M 3   4. If

4.   It any againe reply, that when Prote-
stants say, *The true visible Church,* they meane the visible
Church true in doctrine, in which speach there is
no contradiction according to their owne opinion,
because they admit, that the visible Church, (that is,
the society in true doctrine and right vse of Sacraments, into which Church or society the wicked or
reprobate may enter,) may be true in doctrine,
though they graunt not, that such a Church or society be the true Church in nature or essence. Which
perhaps Vorstius meant, in his Antibellarm. pa. 180.
when he sayd: *The outward Church is not without cause
called the true church of Christ by reason of the profession of true
doctrine.* I answere, if they so meant, why did they
not speak so? were they ignorant, that it is one thing
to be true in doctrine or in speach, and another to
be true in nature? as a lyer is a true man in nature of
man, but not true in his speach. Or if they did know
this, why did they abuse the words and their hearers? Moreouer, though in this sense their words did
not destroy themselues, as they did in the former,
yet fondly should they (as they vse to do) assigne the
truth of doctrine for the marke of the true Church
in doctrine. For this were to assigne a thing for a
mark of it self; as if to know a true man of his word,
one should giue this marke, that it is such as speaketh
truth. Besides this were rather to define what is a
true man, then to giue the marke to know who is a
true man. And yet marks are giuen to know which
is the true Church, not what is the nature of the true
Church.

5.   If yet any reply, that the visible Church
or society in profession of true doctrine and right
vse of Sacraments, is termed of Protestants the true
Church,

Church, nor because this Church or society is of it
self the true church or the society instituted by God,
but because alwayes in, or vnder it there is the true
Church, to wit the society in iustice and predestination; by reason that in euery company of them
that professe true doctrine and rightly vse the Sacraments, there are some, who are sociated and vnited
in iustice and predestination. Which D. Whitaker
intimateth, when Cont.2.quest.4. cap.1.pag.485. he
sayth: *The visible Church, which holdeth and professeth true*
fayth, is the true Church only of the part of the elect and prede-
stinated: I answere, that this supposeth a thing doubtfull, and perhaps false. For what certainty can there
be, that in euery particuler company of them who
professe the true fayth & rightly vse the Sacraments,
there is alwayes a company of the iust and elect; when
as Christ sayth : *Many are called but few are chosen,* espe- *Matt.20.*
cially, if (as Protestants say) one or two make a
church. Surely Danæus Cont.4.pag. 689. seemeth to
deny this, saying : *These visible companies are sometymes a*
part of that (true) Church, sometymes none. But admit that
in euery company of true professors there be alwayes
a company of iust and elect, what reason were this,
to terme the society in profession of true fayth, the
true Church, if indeed the society in iustice & predestination be the only true Church. This would
suffice to say, that the apparent Church could neuer
be separated from the true Church, but not to call
that society the true Church, which indeed is only
the outward appearance of the true Church. And
much lesse would it suffice, to call it the church properly so termed, the spouse and body of Christ, the
Catholike Church, the Church which we professe
to belieue; as the Protestants haue termed the visible

Church.

Church. Neither can these epithets or names be giuen to any other society, then to that which hath the true nature and substance of the Church indeed; because they signify as properly and expresly that only Church; as she can be expressed of vs by any words whatsoeuer. And sith Protestants haue giuen them all to the visible church, they must needs confesse that shee hath the nature and substance of the very true Church indeed; and consequently that an inuisible Church is no true Church indeed.

6.   Fourthly I proue that the Church cannot be inuisible, because oftentymes Protestants do confesse it. The Apology of the Confession of Ausburg chap. of the Church: *The Church is principally the society of fayth and of the holy Ghost in the hearts, which yet hath her outward markes, that she may be knowne.* Luther vpon the 4.chap. of Genesis tom.6 fol. 56: *The Church was neuer so voyd of externall marks, that it could not be not knowne where God was certainly to be found.* And vpon 51.psalm.tom.3. fol. 474: *For Christ will not lye hid in the world, but will be preached; not between wals, but vpon the house top.* Melancthon vpon the 11.of Daniel tom.2.pag.511: *It is necessary, that the Church be a visible company.* Againe: *VVe feigne not an inuisible Church, like to a Platonicall idea.* And in the Preface of his 3.tome, he thinketh it so absurd to put an inuisible Church, as he sayth: *To what tendeth that perdigious speach, which denyeth that there is any visible Church.* We must needs confesse a visible Church. And vpon the 3.chap.1.Tim. tom.4.pag.398: *Others (sayth he) setting aside wholy the externall shew, do speake of an inuisible Church, as of a Platonicall idea, which is no where seene or heard.* Kemnice in his common places title of the Church cap. 3: *God will haue vs to know, where and which is the Church. Therefore she must be knowne, not to God only,*

Protestáts somtyms say that the church cannot be inuisible.

Monstruous to say the Church was inuible.

only , but also to vs; and therupon is defined to be the visible company of them , who imbrace the Ghospell of Christ , and rightly vse the Sacraments: Iames Andrews in his book against Hosius pag.2 10 : *VVe are not ignorant , that the church must be a visible company of teachers and hearers.* Againe : The *Church is , and is called a company of men, chosen of God, in which the word of God soundeth incorrupt, &c.* Hunnius in his treatise of Freewill pag. 9 1 : *God in all tymes hath placed his Church as in a high place , and hath exalted it in the sight of all people and Nations.* Hutter in his Analysis of the Confession of Auspurg, pag. 4 3 0 : *The elect are not the whole Church, no if you speake only of the true church. For the church consisteth not only of inward sayth in Christ , but also of the outward administration of the word & Sacraments. Now as farre as this in outward rite is performed , so farre the true Church truly is visible.* Beurlin in the Preface of his Refutation of Sotus : *I confesse the Church of Christ is alwayes to be acknowledged visible.* And he addeth, that all confesse the same. The same doctrine is taught by Gesner loc 24. by Adam Francis in his 1 1. place, and by other Lutherans. Amongst the Sacramentaries thus writeth Vrsin in Prolegomenis ad Catechesin pag.2 : *The Church must needs be seene in this world, that the elect may know vnto what company they must adioyne themselues in this life.* Iunius Cont.4. lib. 3. cap. 1 3. affirmeth, that it is impious to say that the Church can wholy want a visible forme. Keckerman in the 3. book of his Theologicall systeme writeth, that the Church *must always be sensible, that other nations may know to what church they ought to adioyne themselues;* and that Confession of sincere doctrine can neuer faile wholy, nor the visible church wholy erre. Danæus in his booke of the visible Church dareth to say, that *who denieth the true church of God , and that visible , to haue byn from the beginning of the*

world,

world, he without doubt sheweth himselfe to be ignorant in holy
scripture. Amongst our English Protestants M. Hocker
in his 3. booke of Ecclesiasticall policy pag. 126 : God
hath had euer, & euer shall haue some Church visible vpon earth.
D. Feild in his 1. booke of the Church cap. 10 : For
seing the Church is the multitude of t em that shall be saued, and
no man can be saued vnlesse he make Confession vnto saluation
(for fayth hid in the heart and concealed doth not suffice) it cannot be, but they that are of the true Church, must by profession of
the truth make themselues knowne, in such sort that by their profession and practise they may be discerned from other men   And
D. White in defence of his Way cap. 4. pag. 390: I acknowledge the prouidence of God, who hath left the records of
history to confirme our fayth, and freely graunt our religion to be
false, if the continuall descent thereof from Christ cannot by such
record be shewed. Moreouer at sometyms they not only
confesse that the Church is alwayes visible, but also
graunt that the scripture teacheth the same in those
parables of the barne and the net. For out of them

Protestāts
confesse
that the
Scripture
affirmeth
that the
Church is
alwayes
visible.

Caluin 4. Institut. cap. 1. § 13. inferreth that the Lord
pronounceth, that the church shall be vexed with this euill till the
day of iudgemēt, to be burdened with the mixture of the wicked.
Of the same opinion is D. Whitaker Cont. 2. quest.
3. cap. 2. pag. 471. and others. But that church which
contayneth the wicked, is the visible Church, for
the inuisible they will haue to hold only the good.
The Scripture therefore testifieth that the visible
Church shall euer be. Yea Protestants now and then
take it so ill, that it should be sayd, that they teach
that the visible Church perished for many ages, that
D. Sutliue in his answere to Exceptions cap. 7. sayth
that Bellarmine lyeth in saying so. And D. Whitaker
loc. cit. pag 472. sayth, we slaunder them, when we affirme
they put such a Church, as at sometymes can be seene of none.
                                                                    And

And sayth, that in this matter there is no controuer-sy about the thing, but about the manner, to wit, no quettion whither the Church be alwayes visible or no, but in what manner it is visible; becaue forsooth we will haue the Church to be at all tymes visible clearly, and of all men ; and they will haue it to be at sometymes visible but obscurely, and of few. The like sayth Kemnice in his Common places title of the Church cap. 3. Reineccius in the 4. tome of his Armour cap. 8. and D. Morton in the 1. part of his A-pology lib. 1. cap. 13. But yet that in this matter we neither bely nor sclaunder them, is manifest by what we haue rehearsed in the 4. chapter before going in the 5. number, and those that follow. To which I add, that Caluin in the Preface of his institutions setteth the state of this question betwixt vs & Pro-tettants in these words : *Vpon this hinge hangeth our con-trouersy, that they (Papists) will haue the forme of the church to appeare and be visible at all tymes : On the contrary we say, that the church may consist of no apparent forme.* And I would to God, that Protestants would constantly agree, which vs in this matter of doctrine, that the church of God is alwayes visible to some, either of those that are in it, or out of it; that the debate might remaine only about the matter of fact, whither the Protestat Church before Luther appeared, were seene of any either Protestant or other. But Protestants standing betwixt truth and lyes, whiles they consider the na-ture of the Church of God, especially as it is descri-bed in scripture, confesse that it must needs be visi-ble, not only to her children but to others also. But when they look back vpon the state and condition of their owne church before Luther began, are com-pelled to deny the same, as before we most euidently shewed:

VVhy Protestats contradict theselues about the inuisibili-ty of the Church.

shewed : which thing alone, if it were well confi-
dered, would difcouer fufficiently, that in their own
confciences they acknowledge their Church not to
be the true Church of God.

Inuifibili-
ty cōtrary
to the
ends of
the
Church.

7.   Fiftly, I proue that the Church cannot be
inuifible, becaufe that were contrary to the ends for
which the Church was inftituted of God : whereof
one was, that men fhould worfhip him after that entier manner of worfhip which man is to giue, which
is to honour God not only with heart and mind, but
alfo with tongue and deed, as it is euident ; and Caluin in his Confutation of a Hollander, many wayes
proueth that the Church muft render to God, not
only inward but alfo outward worfhip. But an inuifible Church worfhippeth God only in heart and
mind, as Whitakers words are. Another end of the
Church is to feed her children with the word and
Sacraments, to correct and gouerne them by difci-
pline, and to defend them from enemies ; as alfo is
manifeft and fcripture teacheth. Which offices, a
Church, which neither feeth her children, nor is
feene of them, cannot performe. Likewife another
end is to conuert the world, and thofe who are out
of her, to the fayth and worfhip of God ; which
fhe can no way do, if neither her doctrine nor example be feene of them. And yet as Luther fayth
vpon the fixt chapter of Ifaias tom. 4. fol. 234 : *The
Church is in perpetuall practife of conuerting others to the
fayth.*

8.   Sixtly, it is againft the nature of a fociety
of men amongft themfelues, for to be inuifible. For
as men confift of a body which is vifible by the co-
lours, and of a foule which is feene by the actions
thereof ; fo it is neceffary that the fociety in which
they

they ioyne, be visible, either by it selfe, or by some
other thing. Whereupon well sayd S. Augustin : *Men*
cannot ioyne in any religion true or false, vnlesse they be bound to-
geather by some fellowship of visible signes or Sacraments. And
the same, confesseth Gerlachius in his 23. disput. of the
Church pag. 995. saying : *VVe willingly confesse & graunt,*
that the church cannot be, except there be some outward and vi-
sible signes, by common communion and participation whereof so-
ciety amongst men may consist. And seauently it is contrary to the example of all other societies amongst men
whither religious or prophane, whereof none consisteth in a thing which is altogeather inuisible, and
whereby the members of that society cannot be
knowne the one to the other.

9. Seauenthly, it is contrary to the continuance and conseruation of the Church on earth to
be visible. For if the Church which was in the former age had not byn seene of that which is in this
age, how could the Church of this age haue receiued
the fayth ? We aske therefore, how the Protestant
Church of our age learned the fayth of the Church
of an other age, if in the ages before Luther she were
so inuisible as you haue heard them confesse : Protestants scared with this question like men with a
thunder clap, leape a sunder, and euery one answeareth, not what he knoweth or can proue, but what
seemeth to him least absurd, that hereby we may
perceiue, that all their talke of their Churches being
before Luthers tyme, is but as the scripture sayth, fables and vaine speaches, or fancies and fictions of
men, speaking without either testimony or reason.
Some of them say, that before Luther their Church
receiued the fayth immediatly from God alone. *Du-*
ring Popery (sayth Boysseul in his Confutation of
Spondé

Spondé pag. 75) *the holy Ghoſt taught fayth without a prea-cher.* The ſame alſo intimate Iunius Cont. 4. lib. 3. ca. 13. M. Perkins in his expoſition of the Creed Col. 788. The Author of the church in Danæus Opuſcles pag. 1029. D. Fulk of Succeſſion pag. 320. and others, who ſay, that the Church *VVas propagated and receiued fayth by extraordinary meanes.* And they alſo, who write, that their Church was preſerued *miraculouſly, meruei-louſly, by wondrous meanes, or by meere miracle*; as Luther of priuate Maſſe tom. 7. tol 240. Caluin 4. Inſtit. cap. 1. §. 2. Sadeel ad Repetit. Sophiſm. Turriani pag. 763. Danæus of Antichriſt pag. 1021. & Sonis againſt Spondé cap. 2. pag. 36. But this their aſſertion they neither do, nor can proue otherwiſe, then becauſe God can in ſuch manner preſerue the church.

10.   Thou ſeeſt (gentle reader) vpon what a vaine foundation this imaginary church is built, for the ſpace of many ages, in which it lay inuiſible and lurcking in holes & corners. For they confeſſe, that for many ages it was not ſeene of any man; and if at any tyme they confeſſe not ſo much in words, in deeds they confeſſe it alwayes; becauſe they can ne-uer name any, whom they can proue to haue ſeene it in former ages; and neuertheles they will, that for al thoſe ages it learnt their fayth miraculouſly and im-mediatly from God alone. When we aske teſtimony hereof, they produce neither diuine nor humane worthy of credit; when we demaund proofe, they giue vs no other then this, that God could ſo teach it fayth. As if God did, or doth all that he can do. We ſpeake of an effect, or a matter of fact, of Gods will; and they anſwere of his power. When we af-firme any thing, they exact demonſtrations, that is, plaine teſtimonies of Scripture, or at leaſt pregnant
                                                          proofes

proofes deduced thence . And when they affirme a
matter of so great weight and so incredible, as is that
the church was so many ages taught her faith of God
alone, they will haue vs to belieue it, not only without any testimony of God or man, but euen contrary
to the testimony of them both, for one silly sophisme,
ridiculous to the very children, and scorned euen of
themselues in other matters , as shall by and by appeare. Surely that I may vse Saint Augustins words:
They seeme to thinke, that they haue not to do with men , but as *Cõt. Adi-*
mant.c.4.
if they were meere beasts , who heare the or read their writings,
they abuse the ignorance or dulnesse of them, or rather their blind-
nes of mind. Or as Caluin sayth: *These masters need haue a* *Antid ;*
Conc.c.15.
heard of Oxen , if they would haue auditors to whome they may
perswade what they will. But to their Argument I say
with Tertullian against Praxeas cap. 10: *Surely nothing*
is hard to God . But if in our presumptions we will so rashly vse
this sentence, we may feigne any thing of God ; as if he had done,
it because he could do it . But we must not belieue he hath done
that, which he hath not, because he can do all things: but we must
seeke whether he hath done it or no. Luther also vpon the
46.cap of Genesis tom.6 fol.624.saith: *God can gouerne*
the church by the holy Ghost, without the Ministery ; but he will
not do this imm-diatly. And vpon the 32 .chap. fol. 454:
He could by the holy Ghost inwardly enlighten the hearts and for-
giue sinnes without the Ministery of the word and Ministers ; but
he would not. And the Confession of Suitzers cap. 18:
God by his power can immediatly gather a church of men , but he
chose rather to deale with men by the ministery of men. Caluin
vpon 3.chap. 1. Cor.v. 6: *Nothing hindereth God that he*
may not inspire sayth into men asleep ; but he hath otherwise de-
termined, to wit that , that sayth should come by hearing. And
vpon 1.chap. of S. Luke v. 37 : *They raue peruersely who*
imagine of Gods power without his word. It is a dangerous dispute
what

what God can do, *vnlesse withall we find what he will do.* And
4. Inttitut. cap. 17 §. 24. he faytn : *VVe aske not here what
God could, but what he would do.* The like words he hath
cap. 1. §. 5. lib. 2. cap 7. pag 5. and de vera Eccles. Reform. pag. 326. Beza in the 2. part of his anſwere to
the Acts of the Conference at Montbelgard pag. 97 :
*An argument taken from the power of God needeth no anſwere,
vnleſſe his will alſo appeare to vs by his word.* The Author of
the orthodoxall conſent in the Preface : *it is ridiculous to vrge the omnipotency of God, where we know not his
pleaſure.* Sadeel ot Sacramentall manducation pag.
272. ſetteth downe this as a Theologicall principle :
*VVe may not in diuinity argue from the omnipotency of God, vn-
leſſe his will be before declared by his expreſſe word.* Let Proteſtants therfore produce Gods expreſſe word, wherin he ſayth, that he hath, or will for many ages miraculouſly by himſelfe alone teach the Church her
fayth. Danæus alſo in his 4. booke de amiſſ. grat. cap.
15 : *It litle auaileth to proue Gods power, vnleſſe his will alſo be
proned.* And D. Whitaker cont. 2. queſt. 6. cap. 1 p. 617:
*VVhat a kind of argument is this? This may be done, becauſe no-
thing is impoſſible to God, therefore it is done, or ſometymes hath
byn? Doth our fayth rely vpon ſuch foundations?* Finally Caſaubon in his 7. Exercitation againſt Baronius: *it is a
ſaying of the Fathersthat Gods power is the refuge of Heretikes.*
Thus thou ſeeſt how vaine, euen by the Proteſtants
iudgement, is this proofe of the Churches learning
immediatly from God. They are wont to ſcoffe at
the Miracles done by Saints, albeit we proue them
by ſufficient teſtimony of man : & themſelues feigne
a continuall miracle, yea ſo many miracles, as they
feigne men, whome they ſay for many ages learnt
their fayth immediatly of God ; which they can
proue by no ſufficient teſtimony, either of God or
man.

man. Yea we will most manifestly hereafter disproue
it. Here I will only note, that those Protestants seeme
to haue byn some Enthusiasts or heauenly Prophets,
as Luther scoffingly termed some, who in his tyme
challenged such immediat learning from God; and
that the Protestants themselues do sometymes condemne this immediat learning from God, as Fanaticall, Anabaptisticall, Suenckfeldian, and Enthusiasticall.

11.   The Confession of Auspurg art. 5. (as
Fabritius relateth out of the originall copy) sayth
thus: *They condemne the Anabaptists and others, who think
that the holy Ghost cometh to men without the outward word.*
Martin Luther vpon Genesis tom. 6. fol. 117 : *The
holy ghost doth not teach new reuelations besides the ministery of the word, according as the Enthusiasts and Anabaptists
true Fanaticall Doctours do dreame.* And in the 8. art. of
Smalcald : *In this we most constantly stand, that God will not
otherwise deale with vs then by the vocall word and Sacraments.*
Schusselburg also in the 10. tom. of his Catalogue
pag. 30. rehearseth it is an errour of Suenckfeld, that
men may be saued without the outward word of
God and Ministery. And Melancthon in his answere
to the Bauarian Articles tom. 2. fol. 372. affirmeth,
that it is the opinion of Suenckfeld and the Anabaptists: *That God communicateth himself to men without the ministery of the word.* Kemnice in the 2. part of his examen
title of the Sacrament of Orders pag. 291 : *Iustly we
disallow of Enthusiasts and Anabaptists who imagin the exercise
of the outward ministery not to be needfull.* And title of P e-
nance pag 316: *The Enthusiasts are condemned, who feigne
that God forgiueth sinnes immediatly, and without the vse of the
ministery* D. Whitaker Cont 2. quæst. 3 c. 11. pag. 328:
VVe wholy reiect reuelations, which are besides the word, as Fa-

N   *naticall,*

*Protestars
reiect im-
mediat
teaching
of God.*

naticall, Anabaptisticall and altogether hereticall. And in his
1. booke of the Scripture cap. 3. sect. 1. pag. 44: *VVe
must expect no more immediat reuelation. It is so.* And he addeth, that Protestants hisse out all those who pretend
these kind of reuelations. And in the 2. book cap. 10.
sect. 4: *VVhy are the Anabaptists held for Heretiks, if the church
do know matters of fayth without all externall meanes by the only instinct of the holy Ghost?* Pareus in his 3. booke de Iustificat. cap. 3 : *The exception which they make of speciall reuel-
lation, is a meere iest. For besides the Prophets, Apostles, & some
few Apostolicall men, God doth not deale, nor hath dealt with
speciall reuelations; but with ordinary, and will haue the Church
to be content with the word and the holy Ghost working in the
hearts of the faythfull.* And cap. 8: *God will not haue his church
to be taught and confirmed by Enthusiasticall reuelations; but by
hearing of his word and ordinary vse of the Sacraments.* Finally Beza in the Conference of Montbelgard pag. 407.
sayth : *That we haue no testimony in scripture of extraordinary
meanes of infusing fayth.* Besides, it was the fashion of
both old and new heretiks to boast of speciall reuel-
lations. Of old heretiks witnesseth S. Augustin in his
booke of heresies; and Caluin in his booke of true
Reformation pag. 322. Of Munster, Carolstade, and
the Sacramentaries Luther testifieth the same vpon
the 22. of Esaiæ tom. 4. fol. 280. Of Gentilis, Caluin
in his booke against him. Of Storcke, Manlius in his
Common places pag. 482. Of Peucer and Bergius,
Schusselburb. lib. 4. Theol. Caluin art. 1. pag. 172.
that I may say nothing of Luther, Zuinglius, and
Caluin.

The
Protestant
Church
not taught
by ordi-
nary
meanes.

12.   Others therefore teach that the Protestant
church before Luther, receiued the fayth, not by any
extraordinary way, but by ordinary meanes, to wit,
by hearing some true doctrine of Popish preachers,
and

and some by reading scriptures : Thus D. Whitaker Cont. 2. quest. 3. cap. 2. pag. 424. Behold new fables and fictions (for we are like to heare no other kind of ftuffe of Proteftants in their matters of fact) not only leffe proued then the former, but alfo leffe probable or poffible. For it was at leaft poffible, that God alone fhould haue taught his church ; but that before Luthers reuolt either Popifh or Proteftanticall preachers, or the Scripture fhould haue taught Proteftan-cy, hath neither fhew of probability nor poffibility. Not Proteftant preachers, becaufe before Luther there were none at all, as hereafter both D. Whitaker and others fhall confeffe. For the prefent it may fuf-fice, that Luther vpon the 22. pfalm. tom. 3. fol. 344. writeth : *That there was left only the fcripture, and that comprifed not in voice, but in letters, by which we might reftore our felueste the fayth.* And Againft Catarine tom. 2. fol. 140. he fayth, that *the vocall ghofpell, being cho sked and extingui-shed by Papifts, was filent in all the world.* Neither could the Scripture teach Proteftancy, not only becaufe it tea-cheth no fuch doctrine, but alfo becaufe it plainly profeffeth, that none can come to fayth but by hea- *Rom. 10.* ring of preachers lawfully fent, as hereafter we fhall fee Proteftants do confeffe. In the meane tyme it may fuffice, that Dauæus in his book of the vifible church pag. 1069. writeth, that *S. Paul fayth that fayth commeth by hearing, not by priuate reading* ; and that we open a gap to Fanaticall fpirits for to contemne their Paftors, if we fay that reading alone will fuffice to get fayth ; which Proteftants haue experienced. For thus wri-teth Luther in the Preface of his Catechifme tom. 5. fol. 645 : *There are found fome this day euen of the Nobility, who dare fay, we need no more Paftors or preachers ; that bookes fuffice out of which euery one may learne the fame things by him-*

felfe

selfe without any mans teaching. And Caluin vpon the 2.
Thess. cap. 4: *Certaine phanaticall fellowes do bragge, that they
need no more the help of teachers, because reading may abundantly suffice.*

13.   Neither cou'd those imaginary Protestants learne Protestancy ot Popish preachers. First,
becaule Protestants, (as before his shewed) cōplaine,
that Papists had extinguished all their fayth. Againe
because now no man learneth Protestancy of Popish
preachers, and besides because Papistry and Protestancy are directly opposite, as Luther sayth in cap.
3. Micheæ tom. 4. fol. 446. and tom. 7. epist. ad Esslin-
genses, and against King Henry tom. 2. fol. 497: Or
(as Brentius speaketh in his Apology of the Contession of Wittenberg pag. 703) *they differ in the very principle s:* or (as Beza writeth in his Contession cap. 7. pag.
56) *In the very summe of saluation.* And as D. Whitaker
affirmeth in his oration that the Pope is Antichrist,
*Papistry is more repugnant to Protestantisme, then hoat to cold,
black to white.* How then is it possible that they should
haue learnt Protestancy of Papists, who teach so cōtrary doctrine. Lastly because Protestants themselues
deny it. For Luther vpon the Graduall psalmes tom.
3. fol. 516. thus writeth : *In Popery there was neuer heard
one pure word of sinne, of grace, of the merit of Christ.* And fol.
568 : *Vnder the Pope all pulpits, all Churches did sound out nothing but wicked doctrine.* And in cap. 2. ad Galat. tom 5.
fol. 297 : *Seeing Papists know not what fayth is, it is impossible
that they should haue fayth and much lesse teach it to others.*
And the Apology of the Contession of Auspurg in
the Preface: *No man taught, that sinnes were remitted by
fayth in Christ.* Caluin 4 Institut. cap. 2. § 2. sayth, that in
Popery *the doctrine without which Christianity cannot stand,
was all buryed & cast out.* And in Respons. ad Versipellem

pag.

(margin) Protestā-
cy & Po-
pery quit
opposite.

pag 360 : *In Popery there soundeth the bare and empty name of*
Chrst. And vpon the 2. cap. 2. Tim : *there is a horri-*
ble destruction of the gospell in Popery. Wherfore none learnt
the Protestant Ghospell either in Popery, or of Popish preachers. Besides althogh they cold haue learnt
the faith of Popish preachers, yet they shou'd be ashamed to say, that they had learned it of them, whom
they account the bondslaues and ministers of Antichrist.

14. Ninthly, I proue that the Church could
not be inuisible, because there is nothing which can
make that the Church professe not her fayth. For if
any thing, most of all persecution. But as the waters did lift vp the Arck of Nöe, which was a figure
of the church; so do persecutions raise vp the church,
and make her more knowne. And as the heauen in
day tyme all shineth, but at might glittereth in the
starres, so the church in tyme of peace flourisheth in
all her members, but in tyme of persecution is most
glorious in her constant soldiers. And there are many
and most excellent testimonies of the holy Fathers,
how that the Church is by persecution made more
pure, more famous, and more plentifull, which one
may read in SS. Iustin, Irenæus, Tertullian, Gregory Nazianzen, Hilary, Ambrose, Hierome, Augustin, Leo, Theodorete, Gregory the great, & others.
I according to my purpose will alleage only the testimonies of Protestants. Luther vpon the 1. psalme
tom. 3. fol. 125 : *The faythfull, whiles they are killed do en-*
crease, while they are diminished do multiply. And vpon the
9. of Isaias tom. 4. fol. 84 : *The Church is made fruithfull*
with the bloud of the Godly, and increaseth. Caluin against
Seruet. pag. 595 : *The true and proper church rising vnder per-*
secution, flourished vnder the same. The like he hath vpon

Nothing can make the church inuisible.

the 2. Tim.cap.2. and Philip 1. Lubbert lib.5.de Ecclef. cap. 3 : *The true Church grew vnder suffering persecutions.* And the Apology of the English Church in the end : *This flame the more it is kept downe, so much the more with greater force and strength doth it breake out and fly abroad.* D. Fulke of Succession pag. 255 : *I acknowledge that the Church is so farre from being extinguished by the persecution of the materiall sword, that I graunt it giueth her occasion to delate and extend her bounds. For so, as Tertullian sayth well, the bloud of Martyrs is the seed of the Church. Thus all that are not starck blind do see to haue happened to our Church. For how much the more Antichrist raged with fire and sword, so much the more famous she became.* And D. Whitaker Cont.2 quest.5.cap. 4. pag. 501 : *Persecutions destroy not the Kingdome of Christ, but make it more famous.* And Cont.4.quest.5.cap.2.pag. 669 : *VVhen tyrants raged against the church, religion suffered no losse; yea then most of all flourished.* How then could the Proteſtant church, if it were the true church of God, become inuiſible before Luther aroſe, by perſecution?

15.   If any reply, that this is true of violent perſecution of the heathens, but not of perſecutions by fraud & deceit, as is the perſecution of Antichriſt, which made the Proteſtant Church in former tyms to become inuiſible : I anſwere that firſt he ſpeaketh voluntary without all proofe. Againe, that the Engliſh Apology and D. Fulke ſpeake namely of Antichriſts perſecution, meaning the Pope, which they ſay hath ſince Luthers tyme made their church more famous. How then could it before his tyme make it inuiſible? Moreouer, the ſcripture and holy Fathers teach, that Antichriſt ſhall rage moſt cruelly againſt the Church : and Proteſtants affirme that the Pope, whome they will haue to be Antichriſt, hath byn ſo

cruell

cruell against Protestants, as any Herode, Nero, Domitian, may seeme to haue byn mild if they be compared to him. Finally, heretikes do by fraud persecute the Church, and neuerthelesse the Apostle saith: *There must be heresies, that those who be tryed may be made manifest.* So farre is fraudulent persecution from making the Church inuisible, as it maketh the tried faythfull to be manifest. And both S. Augustin oftentymes, & others obserue, that heresies haue byn occasion of great increase of knowledge vnto the Church.

    16.   Tenthly I proue, that the Church cannot become inuisible, because Protestants do often inferre such and such a Church or company not to haue byn, because it was not seene; as in the Preface of the Protocoll of Frankentall, they proue the Anabaptists were not before the year 1525. *Because* (say they) *if you read all stories you shall find no people from the beginning of the world, who had a Confession of fayth like vnto yours.* But by the same manner it were easy to proue that Protestants were not before Luther. For as Spalatinus in his relation of their Cōfession of Auspurg boasteth: *One shall not find such a Confession neither in any history, neither in any ancient Father or Doctor.* And Fox in his Protestation before his Acts sayth, that of their Church there is no mention made in Histories. Luther also vpon the 3. chap. ad Galat. tom. 5. fol. 358. writeth that of his principall opinion *nothing is read in books of Monks, of Canonists, of Scholmen, yea nor in the books of ancient Fathers. There was a wonderfull silence of it for many ages in all schooles and Churches.* Likewise, when one sayd, that the Roman Church was a member of the Catholike Church, Caluin in his Answere ad Versipellem pag. 259. sayd: *I do not gainsay that the Roman Church is a member of the Catholike, if he could shew a Church*

                     N 4   at

Marginal notes:

1. Cor. 10.

Protestāts inferre an inuisible Church to be no Church.

In Luther tom. 9. German.

at *Rome.* Which supposeth that no Church is where it cannot be shewed. When Bellarmine sayd, that beside the Synagogue of the Iewes there were in Elias tyme Churches amongst the Gentils, D. Whitaker Cont.2.quest.3.cap.3.pag.475. thus answered: *If they say that God had other Churches, let them shew them, and tell which they were, and where they were.* And D.Rainolds, in his 12. Prelection vpon the scripture col.106. inferreth, that none of the Synagogue did belieue those bookes of Scripture which they deny to be canonicall, because we cannot name any. When D. Harding sayd that there was such an heresy, M. Iewel art.2.diuis.8.pag.75. denying it, sayth: *It must needs be a very straung heresy that neuer had neither beginning nor ending, nor defender nor reproouer, nor mouth to speake it, nor eare to heare it, nor pen to write, nor tym to last in, nor place to rest in.* And if an heresy must be heard of, certainly much more the Church of God. When Beza impugned the Arians, thus he discourseth epist. 18. pag 98 : *If their opinion be true, we bid them shew where there Church hath byn, sith from the propagation of the ghospell it is easy to demonstrate, that neuer any one held any such thing, who was not condemned by the perpetuall consent of the Church.* And he addeth epist. 82 : *Certainly there hath byn no true Church, if these men teach truth.* When the Bohemians would proue that they had borrowed nothing of the Anabaptists, thus they write in the Preface of their Confession : *Our Congregation was long tyme before any thing was heard of the Anabaptists, or their name knowne in the world.* Finally M. Bancroft in his Suruey of the pretended discipline cap,2. auoucheth, that the Geneuian discipline began of Caluin, because before him it was neuer seene or heard of. And if they think that a discipline, or an hereticall company could be, and not be seene or

heard

heard of in the world; how much more ought they
to think the fame of the Church of God?

17. Laftly I proue that the Church of God
could not be inuifible, becaufe thereupon would en-
fue many and great abfurdities. For firft, if the vifible Church fhould faile, it is manifeft that it is not
the Church of Chrift, againft which he hath pro-
mifed, that the very gates of hell fhall not preuaile.
And if it be graunted, that the vifible Church is not
the Church inftituted by Chrift, it muft needs be but
a humane fociety inftituted by man. How then fhold
it come to paffe, that one cannot be faued, vnleffe he
be in the vifible Church, if fo he can be, as commonly all Proteftants do teach? Who contemne all ordi-
nances of men as vnneceffary to faluation, why mak
they fuch account of this humane inftitution? At the
laft the Proteftants haue felt this mifcheife, as ye may
fee in Caluin in his 3. homily in his Opufcles pag.
548. and Danæus in his booke of the vifible church;
where they bring many reafons to proue, that it is
neceffary to be of the vifible church. But feing themfelues do teach that the vifible church is not the true
Church in the fight of God, and confequently a humane inftitution, how can they proue, that God hath
commaunded, or men can appoint fo ftrictly to ob-
ferue this one humane Inftitution, vnder paine of
damnation? Another inconuenience is, that Chrifts
promifes touching the continuance of his church are
expofed to the laughter and mockery of Iewes and
Infidels. For fith (as the Law fayth, and Proteftants
acknowledge) among men, there is no other account
made of things that appeare not, then of things that
are not; what man will reafonably perfwade himfelfe, that Chrifts Church hath euer continued in the
world,

Abfurdi-
tiesfollow
of the in-
uifibility
of the
Church.

world, if she for many ages appeared in no one corner of the world? Surely this seemeth so incredible,
that I think not, that any man well in his wittes belieueth it, howsoeuer for to defend the Protestants
Church he may say it. But farewell rather such a
Church which cannot be defended but by such improbable paradoxes.

18.   The 3. inconuenience is, that the church
of God should haue byn much more miserable then
hath byn the Synagogue of the Iewes, euen since it
hath byn forsaken of God. For the Synagogue hath
euer since Christs tyme byn visible vnto the world,
and protested her fayth both before her owne and o-
thers. *The Iewish nation* (sayth S. Augustin) *whether vnder*
Pagan or Christian Kings, hath not lost the signe of her law, wher-
with it is distinguished from other nations and people. The same
testifieth S. Hierome epist. 129. ad Dardan. And Peter Martyr iu his Common places title of the Iewes
§. 47: *The Hebrews, albeit subdued of the Romans, yet neuer*
tooke their lawes, rites and customes; they keep their own yet as
well as they can. And Sadeel in his Answere to Theses
Posnan. cap. 8. graunteth the same. And the Magdeburgians in euery Century make speciall mention of
the Iewes. To this some Protestants say, that it is no
meruaile that the externall condition of the Church
was more miserable thē of the Synagogue. But whosoeuer shall read the Prophesies of the glory and am-
plitude of the Church, will think this strange. But
besides, not only the externall, but also the internall
state of the Church was more miserable then the Synagogue, if the Synagogue durst in all ages, euen before her enemies, professe her faith; and the Church
of Christ for long tyme durst mutter nothing euen
before her owne children; yea (as we shall hereafter

heare

Lib. 22. cōt.
Faust. c. 11.

Iunius &
Daneus l.
4. de Eccl.
c. 5.

heare the Protestants teach) adored Antichrist, and
obserued Antichristian and idolatricall rites & wor-
ships. The 4. inconuenience is, that if we say that the
Church may be, and yet not be seene of any, we giue
occasion to euery new start vp heretik, to say, that his
church hath euer byn: neither can we refute this his
dotage, vnlesse we do maintaine that the church
must be euermore visible, & professe her faith; which
(as we haue seene) Protestants themselues do suppose,
when they proue that any Church or company hath
not byn in former tymes.

19. Out of all which hath byn sayd in this
chapter, it appeareth euidently, that whither we put
the forme of the Church in some visible thing or inuisible, whether we say that the only elect and iust
be of the church or not they alone; of what kind soeuer (I say) the forme of the Church be, and whosoeuer be of the Church (of which matter I dispute not
now) it is euident I say, that the Church of God neuer is at any tyme, but she professeth her fayth before her children and before the world; and consequently that the Church her profession of fayth, or
(which comes all to one) that the Church according
to her profession of fayth, is euermore visible, or sensible, which sufficeth to my purpose; because before
Luther arose, there was no Church visible in profession of Protestant fayth. Wherefore I frame my 3.
demonstration for to proue Luther to haue byn the
Author of the Protestant Church in this sort: *VVhen-*
soeuer the Church is, she is visible in profession of her fayth: (whether this profession be an essentiall forme, or a property or accident inseparable) *But the Protestant Church*
immediatly before Luther arose was not visible in profession of
her fayth; Therefore immediatly before Luther she was not at

aa9

all. *And by his preaching became to be: Therefore he was the Au-*
thor thereof. The Maior or first proposition of the Syllogisme is euident by all that hath byn sayd in this
chapter. And the Minor or second proposition by all
the verball Confessions which we haue reheased in
the former chapter, & by reall confessions of all Protestants whatsoeuer, who neither in Luthers tyme
nor since, could bring forth any man worthy of credit, who had seene any company professing Protestancy before Luther began to preach it. Then the
which yet nothing had byn more easy to do, especially in Luthers tyme, if any such company had byn
extant.

That Protestants confesse, that before Luther
their Church had no Protestant
Pastors.

CHAP. VII.

1. THE 4. demonstration for to proue that Luther was the Author of the Protestant church
and Religion, we will take out of that Protestants
acknowledge their Church before his tyme to haue
wholy wanted Pastors. First therefore they confesse,
Protestāts that their Pastors in former tymes were vnknowne
Pastors to the world, and to Protestants themselues. D. Fulk
vnknown in his booke of Succession pag. 26: *God hath raised vp*
to the *Pastors in all ages, howsoeuer they were vnknowne to the world.*
world. And pag. 22 : *I deny* (sayth he) *this Succession* (of Pastors)
to be alwayes notorious to the world. And in his answere to
Stapletons Cauillat : *who will acknowledge that she alone is*
the true Church, who can shew her Pastors in a continuall succes-
sion?

fion? D. Humfrey to 3. Reason of F. Campian p. 288. confesseth, that not so much as the names of the Pastors, who taught their Church, were extant. D. Whitaker Cont. 2 quest. 5. cap 6. page 508. thus writeth: *VVhat then? was the succession of our Pastor always visible? No. For this is not needfull. Though therefore our Pastors were not in tymes past manifest, neither can we name then, yet &c.* D. Morton in the first part of his Apology lib. 1. cap. 2 1. fayth, that *the Catholike church cannot alwayes shew the ordination of Pastors.* D. White in his way to the church pag. 410: *I haue shewed the teachers of our fayth do lawfully succeed, and so alway haue done, though not outwardly and visibly to the world.* The like he hath pag. 411. and 436. Sadel wrote his book de vocatione Ministrerū against such Protestants, as thought that their ministers wanted all lawfull calling, *because (sayd they) they haue no perpetuall visible succession from the Apostles vnto these tymes.* And himfelfe there pag. 560. confesseth, that *visible succession hath byn broken of for many years in the church.* Thou seest (good reader) how they plainly confesse, that before Luther start vp, their Pastors were vnknowne to the world, not manifest, their succession not alwayes visible, their names not extant, nor they can be named of Protestants. And indeed and effect they all confesse the same, when as none of them can produce any one man worthy of credit, who heard any Protestant preacher, who before Luther arose preached iustification by only fayth, and the other fundamentall points of Protestancy.

2.   Secondly Luther eyther complaineth or boasteth for sometyme he alone preached Protestancy. In his Preface vpon his 1. tome: *At first I was alone.* And in his booke of the captiuity of Babylon tom. 2. fol. 63: *At that tyme I alone did role this stone.* And against the

Luther alone.

the King of England fol. 497: *I alone stood in the battell. I alone was compelled to cast my selfe vpon the weapons of the Emperour and the Pope. I stood alone in danger forsaken of all, helped of none.* And vpon the graduall psalmes tom. 3. fol. 555 : *In the beginning of my quarrell I took all the matter vpon my selfe, and did think that by Gods help I alone should sustaine it.* And otherwhere, (as before is reported) he sayth, that without him others should not haue knowne one iot of the Ghospell. Melancthon in the Preface of the Acts of Ratisbon tom. 4. pag. 730: sayth: *Luther alone durst medle with the errors of the Popes & schooles.* Zuinglius in his Exegesis to. 2. termeth Luther Ionathas, *who alone durst set vpon the campe of the Philistians.* And Caluin in his Admonition to Westphalus pag. 787. saith: *Luther alone doubted not to set vpon all Popery.* Besides, Luther (as before we haue rehearsed) writeth, that the only scripture was left, whereby men might recouer the fayth. But if at that tyme there had byn other Protestant Pastors, the scripture had not byn alone, and without Luther men might haue learnt the gospell. Neither had Luther byn left alone and forsaken of all, but some of them would haue stept out and seconded him especially after they saw that the preached without all danger.

The Protestant Ministery wholy perished.

3.   Thirdly Protestants do sometyme plainly say, that their ministery was wholy perished before Luther arose. Luther in his booke of priuate Masse tom. 2. fol. 249: *Papists haue taken out of the Church the true Ministery of the word.* And of the Institution of Ministers fol. 372. he writeth, that Protestant ordination *was by Papists abolished and extinguished.* And vpon the graduall psalm. tom. 3. fol. 568 : *The Church had no true Ministry vnder Antichrist.* Vpon the 25. of Genesis tom. 6. fol. 319: *In our tyme after those Popish monsters the true knowledge*

Taken away.

Abolished.

No true Ministery

ledge of the word, and of diuine ordination was extinguished. And vpon the 49. chap. fol. 655 : *VVe are not the church for any ordinary succession.* Caluin epist. 190 : *Because the true ranck of ordination was broken of, by the tyranny of the Pope, now we need haue new help to raise againe the Church.* And in Answere to Sadolet pag. 132. he writeth, that when the supremacy of the Pope was set vp, *the true order of the Church perished.* And of true reformation p. 322 : *Not without cause do we auouch the Church of God for some ages to haue byn so torne and scattered, that it was destitute of true Pastors.* Beza in his Catechisme, title of the Church, cap. 5. sect. 18: *In our tyme it came to passe, thinges being so fallen downe, that there was left no place for ordinary vocation.* And epist. 5. pag. 39 : *In our tyme ordinary vocation, which no where was, neither could, nor ought to be expected.* And Epist. 24: *Ye know, being taught by fresh examples, how the publike ministry being as it were ouerwhelmed for a tyme, yet the church of God remaineth.* And epist. 81 : *The matter came to that passe, that the Ecclesiasticall order was wholy ouerthrowne euen to the foundation, the vaine names therof only remayning.* And lib. de Notis Eccles. pag. 82: *They, who in our memory haue freed the church from the tyranny of Antichrist, had none of whome they might lawfully aske or receiue imposition of hands.* And epist. 86: *It is manifest, that for some ages lawfull order was quite abolished in the Church; none not so much as the slenderest shadow of the cheifest part, of ecclesiasticall calling, remayning.* The French Confession art. 31 : *Sometymes, as in our age, the state of the Church being interrupted, it was needfull that some (Pastors) should be extraordinarily raysed of God.* Sadeel also de Vocat. Ministrorum p. 556. sayth, *that true Order (of Pastors) was interrupted.* D. Whitaker Cont. 2. quest. 5. cap. 6. pag. 510: *VVe say, that our mens calling was not ordinary, but extraordinary; because ordinary calling was wholy corrupted.* Againe: *The state of the Church was*

[marginal notes:] Extinguished. Broke of. Perished. Destitute of Pastors. Ordinary vocation no where. Ouerthrowne to the groud. Quite abolished. Wholy corrupted.

was fallen and wholy ouerturned. Ano pag 612 : VVhen ordinary succession was corrupted, God found an extraordinary way, by which the Church might be restored . For God would that this restauration should be made, not in the old foundation, that is, in succession of Bishops, but after a certaine new extraordinary manner. And D. White in defence of his way cap 49. pag 421 : Finding no other kind of Pastors, sayth, that the Protestant Pastors were euen those, who liued in communion of the Roman, Greek, Armenian, and such like Churches; and addeth that his aduersary doth deceiue the reader when he intimateth, that Protestants goe about to shew any other kind of Pastors. Finally all those, who affirme that the vocation or Mission of Luther and their first Ministers was extraordinary, must needs say, that there were no former Protestant Pastours, of whome they could haue byn sent or approued .

Protestäts say the Church may be without Pastors.

4.   The same also they insinuate, when they teach, that the Church may be without Pastors, which they affirme, that thereby they may defend the being of their own Church before Luther, when it had no Pastors. Luther in cap.4. Oseæ tom.4. fol. 295 : *As if the Church were tyed to any certaine order (of Ministery ')* The Confession of Saxony cap 12 : *Godest-soones restoreth the Ministery.* Caluin of true Reform. pag. 332 : *I graunt indeed that it can neuer fall out that the Church perish ; but when they referre that to Pastors which is promised of the perpetuall continuance of the church, in that they are much deceiued. For the Church doth not perish streight, if Pastors be wanting* Beza of the notes of the Church pag. 55 : *Ordinary succession and vocation of Pastors was not always needfull or perpetuall* Sadeel in Answere to the abiured articles pag 533: *It is false that the outward Ministery must be perpetuall.* The same he hath in Repetit. Sophism. Turriani

pag.

pag.763. Iunius and Danæus lib. 4. de Eccles. cap. 8.
Bucan. in his 41. place de Eccles. queit. 19 : *Sometyme
the outward and vsuall ministry of the church being interrupted,
the Church is extraordinarily nourished of God, as it were in the
desert.* Keckerman in his Theologicall Systeme lib. 3.
pag. 397 : *The Church is often pressed so, that the order of succession (of Pastors) must be somewhat interrupted.* And Vorstius in his Antibellarm. pag, 158 : *The ordinary succession
vseth oftentymes to be interrupted for some tyme.* Lubbert in
his 5. booke of the church cap. 5 : *VVe say that the church
may for a short space be depriued of Pastors.* D. Whitaker c. 6.
before cited , pag. 510 : *I gather that true and lawfull succession may be broken of, and that it is not a true, but only an accidentall note of the Church; because it pertaineth not to the essence of the Church; but only to her externall state.* And pag.
512 : *VVe say that ordinary succession hath oftentymes byn interrupted, and cut of, in the true Church.* D. Morton lib. cit.
cap. 17. writeth thus : *The matter of the proposition, to wit,
where there is no succession there is no Church, ye know to be
weake.* And cap. 18. he affirmeth this saying to be
false: *Succession of doctrine cannot be deuided from succession of
persons.* And cap. 23. sayth : *Succession of fayth may be without succession of doctrine; and succession of doctrine without succession of persons.* D. Fulke lib. de Succes. pag. 319: *Yea
euen the very publike preaching of the word may be silent for a
tyme; and the Church being depriued for a tyme of this ordinary
meanes of her saluation, may be preserued so long of God.* And
D. VVhite in his way to the Church pag. 87: *All the externall gouernment of the Church may come to decay, in that the
locall and personall Succession of the Pastors may be interrupted.*
And pag. 403: *For the externall Succession we care not; it is
sufficient that in doctrine they succeded the Apostles and primitiue
Churches, and those faythfull witnesses, which in all ages since imbraced the same.*

O   5.   By

5.   By the forelayd Confessions of Protestants
it is most cleare, that when Luther began to play the
Pastor, there was no Protestant preacher at all. For
they acknowledge, that they are no Church for any
ordinary succession; that the true order of the church
perished, that the true Ministery was taken out of
the Church, true knowledge of diuine ordination
was extinguished, and ordination abolished and decayed: That the Church had no true Ministery, and
that she was destitute of true Pastors. And that they
meane these words both of a substantiall & vniuer-
fall destruction of true Ministry, is manifest both by
the selfe same words and others alfo. For they adde
withall, that the state of the church was quite ouerthrowne, ordinary vocation wholy corrupted, that
ordinary vocation was no where, no place left for
ordinary vocation, and there were none, of whome
those who freed their Church from Popery, might
receiue imposition of hands: that the state of the
Church was fo interrupted, that God must raife vp
Pastors extraordinarily, that the true ranck of ordination was fo cut of, as that their needed a new fuc-
cour and a new foundation; lastly that the Ecclesia-
stical order, the vaine names therof only remayning,
was ouerthrowne from the foundation, and lawfull
order quit abolished: that there was not left fo much
as the slenderest shadow of the cheifest parts of ecclesiasticall vocation. In which words either they say
that there was neuer a Protestant Pastor at all, or that
can be fayd by no words whatsoeuer. And such was
the state and condition of the Protestant church, not
for a small tyme, but as themselues say, for some ages.
And for this cause vsually they call Luther & his first
partners, their (a) *first ministers, first* (b) *teachers, first* (c) *re-*
storers.

(a) *Plessie*
l. t. de Eccl.
c. 11. Napp.
in 14.
Apocal.
(b) *Sadeel*
de Vocat.
pag. 556.
(c) *Gualt.*
Præfat. in
ep. ad Rom

storers of the ghospell, first (d) *preachers of the ghospell, first re-*
storers of the house of God, Apostles and Euangelists.

(d) Perkin 1. Galat. cap. 11.

6.   Finally I proue that there was no true
Protestant preacher before Luther, out of the reall
cōfession of all Protestants. For none of them all can
by any sufficient testimony or argument proue, that
there was any such Pastor. Wherefore this is rashly
affirmed and fondly belieued. *Either proue* (sayth Tertullian) *that which thou belieuest, or if thou prouest it not, how*
doest thou belieue it? And that common argument of
theirs, wherewith they vse to proue, that they had a
Church and Pastors at all tymes, because they bring
the Scripture to proue their doctrine to be true; we
shall hereafter shew to be a most vaine Sophisme.
And besides themselues do ouerthrow it, in teaching
as we haue seene, that the Church may be without
Pastors; wherby it would not follow that they had
Pastors, albeit they could by the Scripture proue that
before Luther they had a Church. Moreouer euen
those who endeauour to name some Protestant preachers or Pastors before Luthers tyme, do plainly shew
that there was no true and absolute Protestant Pastor, to wit such as taught iustification by only faith,
and the rest of the fundamentall opinions of Protestancy. For the Apology of the Church of England
pag. 103. sayth, *That they gaue not so cleare a light, but light-*
ned as it were some sparck. The Confession of Saxony
cap. 12.: *That they ioyned stuble vnto the foundation.* Cruci-
ger and Rorarius in Luther. tom. 1. fol. 202: *That they*
had some litle light. D. Fulke of Successe pag. 121: *That per-*
haps in all points they knew not the Apostolicall doctrine. And
D. Whitaker de Scriptura lib. 2. cap. 8. sect. vlt: *How-*
soeuer they were enuironed with most grosse darknesse, yet they
held some sparckes of truth, and shewed them to others. And

Lib. 5. cōt. Marc. c. 16

O 2   what

what other thing I pray you is this, but to confesse,
that such were but Protestants in part and in some
sort . Yea they name some , whome they confesse to
haue reprehended only certaine abuses amongst the
Papists , as Melancthon in his Answere to the Bauarian articles tom. 3. fol. 369. and Illyricus in his Catalogue lib. 15. confesse of Hilten . It remayneth yet
for the accomplishing of this demonstration , that
we also shew by the Confessions of Protestants, that
the true Church of God can neuer want Pastors ; as
they haue confessed theirs to haue wanted for the
space of some ages.

That the true Church cannot be without Pastors.

CHAP. VIII.

1. THAT the Church can neuer be without Pa-
     stors, I proue first out of the Confessions of
the Protestant faith. For thus professe they to belieue
in the Confession of Saxony cap. 12: *The Sonne of God
hath giuen ministers of the Ghospell vnto the Church , to the end
it do not quite perish.* Againe : *He would haue alwayes a company in mankind , in which the Sonne himselfe appointed and
conserued the Ministery of keeping and spreading his doctrine.*
The Confession of Switzers cap. 18: *God hath alwayes
vsed ministers for to setle and gather him a Church , and also for
to gouerne and preserue it ; and vseth the same now, and further
will vse them whiles the Church shall be on earth.* The French
Confession art. 25 : *VVe belieue the Church cannot consist if
it haue not Pastors, who haue the office of teaching.* The Confession of the low Countries art. 30: *VVe belieue that the
true*

true Church ought to be gouerned and ruled by that ſpirituall po-
licy, which God hath taught in his word, ſo that there be Paſtors
and miniſters in it. And the Confeſſion of Straſburg:
ſeing the Church is the Kingdome of God, it hath diuers functions
of miniſters.

2. Secondly I proue it, becauſe for the church
to be without Paſtors, is to want ſome part of the eſſence and definition giuen by the Proteſtants themſelues. For Luther Propoſition 15.to.1.fol. 385. thus
defineth a Church : *It is a number of baptized perſons and*
belieuers vnder one Paſtor. And tom.2.fol. 366. he ſayth :
The publike Miniſtery of the word whereby the Myſteries of God
are diſpenſed, muſt be inſtituted by holy ordinaticn, as the thing
which in the Church is the cheifeſt and principalleſt of all. Kemnice in his Common places title of the Church pag.
146 : *The Church conſiſteth of Paſtors and learners.* Gerlachius in his 22. Diſput. pag. 966 : *The Church is not a*
company meeting by chance or diſordered, but called by the voice
of the cryers of the word for to heare the doctrine of the Ghoſpell.
Caluin 4.Inſtitut.cap. 2. §. 7: *The Miniſtery is the cheifeſt*
ſinew and ſoule of the Church. Beza of the Notes of the
Church pag. 9 : *By the name of the Church properly ta-*
ken, it is certaine that not only Paſtors but alſo flocks are vnder-
ſtood. Iunius Cont. 5.lib.1.cap. 15: *God inſtituted or-*
ders in the Church, for the eſſentiall outward conſtitution
therof. D.Whitaker Cont.2. queſt. 5. cap.6. pag.508:
The Church cannot ſubſiſt without Paſtors of whome it is taught.
For doctrine doth make and conſtitute the Church, and is her
ſoule and life. And cap.18. pag. 546: *The Church is no other*
number, then that which holdeth the pure preaching of the word
and right vſe of the Sacraments. And cap.17.dag 541: *Sin-*
cere preaching of the word and lawfull adminiſtration of the Sa-
craments do make the church; in ſo much as wherſoeuer they be,
there the Church is; and where they be not, the Church is not.

D.Feild

D. Feild in his 2. booke of the Church cap. 6: *The Miniſtery of Paſtors and teachers is abſolutely and eſſentially neceſſary to the being of the Church.* And lib. 1. cap. 10: *Bellarmine laboureth in vaine in prouing that there is and alwayes hath byn a viſible Church, and that not conſiſting of ſome few ſcattered Chriſtians without order of Miniſtry or vſe of Sacraments; for all this we do moſt willingly yield vnto.* Yea the Philoſophers by the light of reaſon perceiued, that *it is impoſſible ther ſhould be a Common wealth without Magiſtrates.* This ſame alſo is manifeſt by many other definitions which Proteſtants haue made of the Church, and we haue rehearſed them before, in which they place true preaching and adminiſtration as eſſentiall parts of the true Church; which yet cannot be without Paſtors.

3.   Beſides, this were againſt the definitions of the Church giuen by the holy Fathers. For thus writeth S. Cyprian epiſt. 79: *The Church is the people vnited to the Prieſt, and the flock cleauing to the Paſtor.* And this he proueth out of thoſe words of our Sauiour Math. 16: *Thou art Peter, and vpon this rock will I build my Church.* S. Hierome alſo in his dialogues againſt the Luciferians: *It is no Church which hath no Prieſt.* S. Ignatius in his epiſt. ad Trallianos: *Without theſe (Prieſts) the elect Church is not, no congregation without theſe, no meeting of Saints.* And whereas Danæus lib. 4. de Eccl. cap. 8. ſayth, that theſe Fathers define only a viſible church, that auaileth nothing: becauſe indeed there is no Church on earth which is not viſible in profeſſion of faith. Againe, Paſtors ſhall be at leaſt of the eſſence of the viſible Church, and conſequently the Proteſtant Church, which before Luther wanted Paſtors, was no viſible Church. Furthermore, S. Cyprian proueth his definition out of thoſe words of Chriſt

Matt.

Matt. 16. which (as is certaine and Protestants confesse) are spoken of the true Church in the sight of God. And S. Ignatius sayth, that there is no elect church, no congregation of Saints, without Priests: which he must needs meane of the true Church. And Saint Hierome simply sayth it is no Church, which hath no Priests: which he could no wayes say, if the true Church in the sight of God could be without Priests. And hereby also is refuted Sadeel in Repetit. Sophism. Turriani pag. 652. when he sayth: *The definition of S. Cyprian is not essentiall, nor properly teacheth what the Church is, but what a one it ought to be.* For S. Cyprian inferreth out of his definition, that if one be not with the Bishop, he is not in the Church. And Saint Hierome pronounceth one Hilaries sect to haue perished with him, because he left no Pastor behind him. And for this cause the Fathers do still obiect vnto heretiks the want of succession of Pastors, as an euident marke that they are not the Church; as euen Protestants themselues confesse. For thus writeth D. Whitaker Cont. 2. quest. 5. cap. 6. pag. 509: *The Fathers rebuked heretiks that they wanted succession of Bishops.* Sadeel of Vocation of Ministers pag. 546: *S. Augustin oftentyms opposed this succession against the Manichees and Donatists.* Zanchius of the Church pag. 138: *I admit that succession of true Bishops is a marke of the Church; and of this speake the Fathers.* The like confesse Caluin Respons. ad Versipellem pag. 358. and 4. Institut. cap. 2. §. 3. Beza epist. 1, Plessy de Eccles. cap. 3. Fulke de Succes. pag. 36. D. Morton Apol. part. 1. lib. 1. cap. 13. Iames Andrews cont. Hosium pag. 89. and others. Neither is it true which D. Whitaker and Sadeel say, that the Fathers did not think that they conuinced the Heretiks not to be the Church, because they wanted succession of

O 4　　　　Pastors.

Pastors. For S. Irenæus sayth that hereby he confoundeth heretiks, and that this is a most full demonstration. S. Augustine writeth, that this argument of succession held him in the Church. S. Athanasius calleth it a notable and admirable argument. And Sadeel himselfe loc. cit. sayth that *with this battering ramme S. Cyprian did especially vanquish the Nouatians.* And Peter Martyr in his Common places tit. de Schismate, writeth that *S. Augustines argument taken from the succession of Pastors was very euident against the Donatists.*

4. Thirdly I proue that the Church cannot be without Pastors, because eftsoones the Protestāts confesse it. Luther vpon 10. chap. of Genesis tom. 6. fol. 125 : *The Church cannot consist without continuall vse of the word.* And of the Notes of the Church tom. 7. fol. 151: *The Church cannot be without Pastors.* Melancthon vpon the 3. cap. of Math. tom. 1. fol. 258: *God will always haue some publike Ministery. He will not suffer the publike ministery to be destroyed.* And in cap. 16. pag. 489 : *There is no Church where there is no true Ministery.* And ibidem in his sermon vpon the rock pag. 176: *The Church is built vpon the Ministery.* And tom. 1. in loc. cap. de Ecclef. fol. 227: *We must not feigne a Church without the Ministry.* And cap. de numero Sacramentorum fol. 334: *The Ministry cannot be quite destroyed.* And in his dispute of Ecclesiast. policy tom. 1. Lutheri fol. 442: *The Church cannot exist, this ministry being extinguished.* Kemnice in his Common places tit. of the Church cap. 4 : *There are promises extant of the perpetuall conseruation of the Ministry in the Church.* Gerlachius Disput. 22. pag. 940: *The publike Ministry is always conserued.* James Andrews against Hosius pag. 230 : *No man denieth that the Church cannot be without Bishops.* Oecolampadius vpon the 62. cap. of Isaias pag. 305: *God raiseth vp at all tymes Apostles and preachers.* Pola-

nus

Protestāts confesse necessity of Pastors

nus in his Syntagme lib. 7. cap. 11 : *The function of ordinary Ministers after the Ecclesiasticall order is one setled, is perpetuall, and to endure to the end of the world.* Caluin 4. Institut. cap. 2. §. 4: *For neither the light and heat of the Sunne, nor meat and drinck are so necessary to cherish and sustaine the present life, as the Pastorall function is for to conserue the church on earth.* And §. 3 : *God hath setled foreuer the way of gouerning and holding his Church by Ministers.* And § 4: *The church can neuer want Pastors and teachers.* Beza de Notis Eccles. pag. 60: *The church can neuer want either the seed of the word, or sowing, or sowers.* Vorstius in Antibellarm. pag. 197: *The Ghospellers acknowledge the 2. other orders to be perpetuall in the Church, to wit, Pastors, Priests, and Deacons.* D. Whitak. t cont. 2. quest. 3. cap. 2. pag. 469: *I answere that there were alwayes Pastors and sheepe, and that there shall be euer Pastors to the end of the world.* And quest. 5. cap. 6. pag. 508: *I confesse the succession of Pastors to be necessary.* Againe: *I answere that the Church cannot stand without Pastors.* D. Fulke de Succes. pag. 22: *I graunt that the succession of Pastors is necessary in the church.* And pag. 95: *The true doctrine of Christ and the Apostles neuer wanted cryers.* D. White in defence of his way cap. 35. pag. 381: *The Church shall neuer want Pastors.* And his Maiesty in his Monitory epistle pag. 61: *Neither can hell stand without some order and distinction. The Diuels are deuided into Legions and haue their Princes, how then can any company on earth stand which is confused and disordered without all difference of orders or dignity.* You see how confused a thing Protestants account the Church to be without Pastors, and that they speake far otherwise of the Church, when they consider the true nature thereof, then when they looke vpon the condition of their owne Church in former tymes before Luther. Neither do they only sometymes confesse that the Church cannot be without Pastors, but also

O 5 acknow-

Scripture
requireth,
Pastors.

acknowledge that Scripture so h teach so . For thus
Melancthon in his foresayd dispute fol. 483 : *VVhere
the Church is , there must needs be lawfull ordination of Ministers; which ordination is one of the proper giftes of the Church,
according to that of the 4 chap. to the Ephesians : He hath giuen
Pastors &c.* Kemnice in the 2. part of his examen tit.
de Sacramento ordinis pag. 191 : *The Sonne of God himselfe will conserue in the Church with perpetuall calling the Ministry of those who teach the Ghospell . So sayth* Paul Ephes. 4.
Caluin. 4 Institut. cap. 3. §. 2: *In these words (*Ephci. 4)
*he sheweth the Ministry to be the cheife sinew , wherewith the
faythfull hung togeather in one body, and insinuateth also that the
Church cannot otherwise be safe, vnlesse it be propped with these
helpes, in which God would place her safety.* The like he hath
in cap. 4. Ephes. and 1. Cor. cap. 6. and 12. and 1 . Tim.
cap. 3. D Whitaker Cont. 2. quest. 5. cap. 19. pag. 549:
Thuplace of Esay cap. 59: *My spirit &c. sheweth that the true
preaching of the word shall be perpetuall in the Church .* D.
Whitgift in his Answere to the Admonition pag. 17:
The place of Mathew 9. *sheweth that Ministers are necessary in
the Church.* D. Fulk ad Cauillat. Stapl: *You do that which
is done already, whiles you proue out of the Apostles writings that
the continuance of the Pastors and Doctors is of no lesse certainty, then the continuance of fayth and doctrine.* And de Succes.
pag. 180: *The Scriptures promise perpetuall succession of Pastors
and Doctors.*

Preaching
necessary
to fayth.

5.   Fourthly I proue this same because Protestants sometymes do teach, that preaching (which
cannot be done without Pastors) is necessary to in-
graft fayth in men. For, as before we rehearsed, they
condemne the Anabaptists and Suenckfeldians in
that they teach , that men can come to fayth without preaching . And Luther tom. 1. fol. 54. writeth
that the administration of the word by a Priest is
                                                     needfull

needfull for faith. And Cont. Caterin tom.2.fol.140. fayth, that by the vocall word the Church is conceiued, formed, nourished, begotten, and conserued. And de instituendis Ministris fol. 372: *Seing the church is brought forth, nourished, and conserued by the word of God, it is manifest that she cannot be without the word; or if it be without the word, that it leaueth to be a Church.* In cap. 17. Ioannis tom. 5. fol. 203: *For God hath not determined to conserue them (the faythfull) without outward meanes, albeit he could do it.* Also vpon the 1. chap. of Zacharias: *Although God can teach men the Ghospell without sermons, yet he will not do it.* And of the Notes of the church tom.7.fol. 149: *What could or would the people of God belieue, vnlesse the word of God sounded there.* Melancthon in locis tom. 3. cap. de libero arb. fol. 311: *God gathereth a true Church by the voice of the Ghospell and not otherwise.* Kemnice in the 2. part of his examen tit. de Sacramento ordinis pag. 391: *God by his certaine counsell hath determined, that he will dispense those things, which belong to the matter of our saluation, not immediatly by infusing new and peculiar reuelations into the minds of men without any meanes, but by the outward Ministry of the word.* Caluin. 4. Institut.cap. 1. §.5: *Howbeit Gods power be not tyed to outward meanes, neuertheles he hath tyed vs to the ordinary meanes of Preaching. Many are pusht on by pride, disdaine and emulation to perswade themselues that they can profit inough by priuate reading and meditating.* And §. 4: *The knowledge of her (the visible Church) is profitable to vs; yea necessary, for we cannot come to life vnlesse she conceiue vs in her wombe, beare vs, nourish vs with her duggs.* And in 1. Tim. cap. 3: *The office of preaching which God hath left in his church, is the only instrument of truth, that it goe not out of mens minds. The Ministery of the word being taken away God truth will fall downe.* Beza epist. 20: *It is cleare that fayth cometh of hearing, and therefore preaching must goe before fayth.* Tayé in

his

his Enchiridion disput. 60 : the necessity of ecclesiasticall Ministry appeareth in that without it we can not know the word of God, nor his will therein reuealed vnto vs. D. Whitaker lib.1.de Scriptura cap.9 lect.9. pag. 106: *The ministry being taken away, neither fayth, nor Charity, nor obedience, nor any vertue will remayne safe.* And cap.2. lect.6. pag. 37: *VVe cannot at all belieue without the Ministry of the church.* And lib.3 cap.15 lect.20.pag.478: *I affirme, determine, and hold, that there is no entrance to saluation without the Ministry of the word.* Againe : *by the Ministry of Pastors we belieue the Scripture, neither is it to be hoped that without this Ministry fayth can grow in our minds.* And cap.5. sect.2 : *I confesse the Ministry of the Church to be most necessary.* And Cont.2.quest.5.cap.19.pag.550: *VVe neuer come to fayth without preaching of the word.* D. Fulke de Succes. pag.30: *The peoples saluation cannot be procured without preaching.* And pag 162: *No Christian will deny preaching of the word to be necessary for the edification of the church.* M. Latimer in his sermons fol. 38: *Take away preaching and take away saluation.* Fol. 99 : *The office of preaching is the only ordinary meane, whereby God hath determined to saue vs.* M. Cartwright in M. Hooker lib.5. of Ecclesiasticall policy p. 41: *Reading may set forward, but not begin the worke of saluation, fayth may be nourished therewith, but not bred; herein mens attention to the Scriptures and their speculation of the creatures of God haue like efficacy, both being of power to augment, but neither to effect beliefe without sermons.* And the Puritans in D. Whitgifts Answere to the Admonitions: *Reading is no feeding.* How then could there be any Protestant Church or fayth at all before Luther, when (as we heard before) there was then no Protestant preacher? And in like sort sometymes they confesse, that the Scripture it selfe teacheth, that preaching is necessary to haue fayth. The Confession of Auspurg.

Scripture requireth preaching

cap.

cap. de potest. Ecclef. pag. 59: *Euerlasting iustice, the holy Groft, eternall life, cannot be had but by the ministry of the word and Sacraments, as Paul sayth.* The Confession of Bohemia art. 10: *They graunt that none can attaine to right fayth, vnlesse he heare the word of God, according to that of S. Paul; Fayth is of hearing.* And againe: *How shall they beleiue in him of whome they haue not heard.* And the Protestants in their conference at Marspurg agreed, as reporteth Hospinian part. 2. Histor. fol 77: *That the holy Ghost, if we speake of the ordinary course, giueth fayth to none, vnlesse preaching or the vocall word goe before; but by and with the vocall word he worketh and maketh fayth, where and in whome it pleaseth him,* Rom 10. Caluin also 4. Institut. cap. 1. §. 5: *God inspireth fayth into vs by the instrument of his Ghospell, as Paul admonisheth, that fayth is of hearing.* Againe: *VVe must hold that which I haue set downe out of Paul, that the Church is not otherwise edified but by outward preaching,* and in 1. Tim. cap. 3: *Paul meaneth simply that which in other words he deliuereth* Rom. 10. *because fayth is of hearing, that there will be no fayth vnlesse there be preaching.* The like he hath 1. Cor. 3. v. 6. Heb. 4. v. 12. and Ephes. 4. v. 12. Beza in the Conference at Montbelgard pag. 407: *The ordinary manner whereby fayth is infused, is by hearing the word,* Rom. 10. And Bucer in cap. 10. Rom: *The Apostle knew that God could call men without the ministry of men, neuertheles he absolutely wrote: How shall they beleiue in him of whome they haue not heard.* Hyperius also vpon the same place: *That is, that all beleiue and call vpon God, it is needfull that before they heare the Ghospell and be taught.* D. Whitaker lib. 1. de Scrip. cap. 2. sect. 4: *That of the Apostle, how shall they beleiue without a preacher, conuinceth this much, that preaching is necessary to conceiue assured of fayth God.* And c. 10. sect. 4: *The Apostle doth plainly say, that fayth is of hearing.* And Cont. 2. quest. 5. c. 19. pag. 549: *This place (of Isay 59.) sheweth*

sheweth that true preaching of the word shallbe perpetuall in the Church. M. Perkins in his expoſition of the Creed col. 787: *I anſwere that place* Rom. 10. *Faith is of hearing, to be vnderſtood of iuſtifying fayth.* So that neither the viſible nor inuiſible Church could euer haue byn without preaching.

6.   Out of all that hath byn ſayd in this and the former chapter I thus make my fourth demonſtration, for to proue that Luther was Author of the Proteſtant Church. *If before Luther the Proteſtant Church had no Paſtors, she was not then at all: But then she had no Paſtors at all: Therefore then she was not at all: And by him she came to haue both Proteſtant Paſtors and sheep: Therfore by him she had her beginning.* The Maior is euident by thoſe Confeſſions of Proteſtants which we haue rehearſed in this chapter; and the Minor by thoſe that were repeated in the former.

That the Proteſtants Church and Religion before Luther was no where.

CHAP. IX.

1.   THE firſt demonſtration, for to proue that Luther was Author of the Proteſtant church **Proteſtãts name not the place.** and Religion, ſhall be taken from want of place; to wit, that it was no where before Luther began. And this I proue, firſt, becauſe they oftentymes ſay, that before Luthers tyme their Church was in the deſert, in darknes, in lurking holes, in Trephonius denne; neuertheles they tell not where this deſert, this darknes, this lurking hole, this denne was. Secondly ſome of them confeſſe, that they know not where their

their Church was in tyme past. D. Whitaker Cont.
2. quest. 3. cap. 3. pag. 475 : *They are angry with vs that* Know not
we cannot shew , and as it were point with our finger the place.
where our Church was in tymes past. The same insinuateth - Sadeel ad Repetit. Sophism. Turriani pag.
766. saying , that he answered this question , *VVhere*
there Church lurked, when he sayd, *That it lay hid by the vn-*
searcheable iudgement of God ; as if he sayd: It lay so close
hid , that it cannot be knowne where it lay. Also D.
Hail in his Rome Irreconcileable sect. 1 , when he
calleth this our demaund , *VVhere their Church lurked,*
an idle demaund of Pettifoggers. But that it is no
idle demaund, is manifest. For first, what man in his
wittes seeth not, that she, who is pretended to be the
Catholike Church , that is , spred ouer the world,
was not at all , if no place can be found where she
was for many ages. Againe, because the holy Fathers
and Protestants themselues demaund this of here-
tikes. *VVho are yee* (sayth Tertullian) *when, and whence* *Præf. 32.*
came ye? where lurked ye so long? Againe : *Let them bring forth* *37.*
the o spring of their Churches. S. Athanasius: *VVhence came*
these things? yea what hell hath vomited them out? And S.Au- *Lib. de Ni-*
gustine: *VVhere appeared Donatus?Out of what ground sprung* *cen. Synod.*
he? Out of what sea arose he? from what heauen sell he ? And *& de Syn.*
Beza epist.18.demaundeth the like of the Arians say- *Selenuc.*
ing: *If their opinion be true, we bid them shew then where was* *Lib 3 de*
their Church. Besides, the Confession of Saxony chap. *Bapt. c. 2.*
of the Church, professeth , that *the true Church knoweth*
where she is. And Kemnice in his Common places, tit.
de Ecclef. cap. 3: *God will haue vs to know which, and where is*
the true Church. Wherefore it is no idle but a most necessary thing, to know where the Church is: and if
Protestants immediatly before Luther arose, knew
not where the Church was; it must needs follow

that

that she was not the true Church.

2.   Thirdly I proue it, becaufe euen thofe who take vpon them to tell where their Church was in former tymes, do shew indeed, that they know no place where she was. For as M. Iewel sayth art. 1. diuif. 7. pag. 10: *Eckius, Pighius, Hosius and others haue often cryed out a mayne in their bookes and pulpits, where was your religion before Luther first began to preach?* And that the same hath byn demaunded by Catholiks, confesseth Peter Martyr in locis tit. de difceffu ab Eccl. Rom. col. 1492. Beza de Notis Ecclef. pag. 78. and in his 132. queftion. D. Whitaker Cont. 2. queft. 3. cap. 3. M. Perkins in his Reformed Catholik tract. 22. cap. 1. and others. And it is manifeft by the writings & speaches of all Catholikes. Yea Luther in cap. 19. Ifaiæ tom. 4. fol. 125. writeth, that this was our first argument againft them, and will be our laft: *Art thou alone wife, or doeft thou thinke that all our auncestours saw nothing? Did all those, who were before thee, erre?* Becaufe he saw, that this argument did moft preffe him, and that he could neuer anfwere it. Let vs see therefore, what they anfwere to this our first and laft demaund fo often and with such earneftneffe and fo great cryes propofed of vs. D. Whitaker cont. 2. queft. 3. cap. 2. propofeth their

anfwere in thefe words: *Stapleton sayth, that Caluin and we say, that the true Church was in Popery, but that Popery was not the church: That indeed we all say.* And the same in fubftance anfwereth Luther lib. de feru. arbit. tom. 2. fo. 438. in pfalmos graduales to. 3. fol. 589. And de Miffa priuata tom. 7. fol. 236. Iames Andrewes cont. Hofium pag. 326. Herbrand in Compend. Theol. loc. de Eccl. pag. 502. Hunnius Præfat. tract. de Iuftific. Huberus in Antibellarm. lib. 4 cap. 2. Hutter in Analyfi Confeff. Auguft. p. 447. Geriachius difput. 22. p. 952.

Lobechius

Lobechius diſp. 10. pag. 202. Geſnerus loc. 24. Reineccius lib. 4. armaturæ cap. 3. And amongſt the Sacramentaries Caluin 4. Inſtit. cap. 2. §. 11. Peter Martyr, Beza, and M. Perkins locis cit. Sadeel in Refut.
Theſ. Poſnan. cap. 8. Polanus part. 3. Theſ. de Eccl.
Daneus de Antichriſto cap. vlt. Iunius lib. 4. de Eccl.
cap. 166. Vorſtius in Catechiſm. queſt. 54. art. 2. Sohnius in method. Theol. pag. 213. Bucanus loc. 4. de
Eccl. and others commonly.

   3.   But this anſwere ſatisfieth not our queſtion, for many cauſes. Firſt, becauſe to ſay that the
Church was in Popery, but Popery was not the
Church, doth not ſeeme an anſwere, but a ridle, &
perhaps put of purpoſe, becauſe as Bucer ſayd: *Pro-*   *Lib. 1. epiſt.*
teſtants myſteries muſt not be expounded to Papiſts. Secondly *Zanchu.*
they agree not among themſelues what they meane
by Popery. For Boyſſeul in his Côfutation of Spondé pag. 723. will haue it to be Popiſh doctrine, ſaying: *He knoweth not what we call Popery. He imagineth, that*
it is men. But we ſay, that it is hereſies and errors, the abuſes &
idolatries of the Roman Church. And D. White in defence
of his way cap. 32. pag. 305: *The Papacy is nothing elſe but*
a diſeaſe or excrement breeding in the Church. Moulins of
Arnolds flights cap. 6: *Popery is a maſſe of errors, and cor-*
ruption of Chriſtianity. And Caluin in 1. Galat. v. 9: *Pope-*
ry is a horrible ouerthrow of the Ghoſpell. Others by Popery vnderſtand the company of Papiſts. Schuſſelburg
tom. 8. Catal. heret. pag. 480. writeth that Popery
ſignifieth a company. And Iames Andrewes Cont.
Hoſinm pag. 326. ſayth: *Popery, that is, the Pope, Biſhops,*
and they who conſent to their impiety. Thirdly Popery
whereby you vnderſtand ſuch a company, or ſuch
doctrine, is no place; & we aske for the place wherin Proteſtants were before Luthers tyme. Fourthly,

         P   becauſe

because we aske not wher only they say thier church
was, (for what can they not say?) but where they
proue their Church to haue byn. Wherefore that I
may imitate S. Augustins words, I demaund whither
God told them that their Church was in tymes past
in Popery, or man? If God, let them read it out of
the Scripture. If man, let them bring him forth that
we may iudge, whither he be worthy to be belieued
or no. If neither God nor man told them this, then
it is, (as the Scripture speaketh) an vnlearned fable,
which cannot be proued by any diuine or humane
testimony, a fiction, a dreame, which they would
be ashamed to vtter, if they were not compelled by
necessity to say somewhat. But (as S. Hilary sayth) *he
is not ashamed of folly, who hath lost religion*. Fiftly I proue
this, because Protestants euen by their manner of
speach do bewray, that they are not certaine that
their Church was in Popery. For D. White in his
Way cap.33.pag.338. sayth: *It is more then probable*. O-
siander in his Manuel englished pag. 65. sayth: *It is
Credible.* Gerlachius tom.2.disput.22.sayth: *How many shall we think there were*. Others confesse, that they
know not those Protestants whome they say to haue
byn in Popery. Luther in psalm.45.tom. 3. fol. 447:
*Vnder Popery there were alwayes and yet are some belieuers,
whome we know not.* D. Whitaker Cont. 2. quest. 3. cap.
3.pag. 476: *VVe say there were in tymes past many thousands
of men in Popery, who professed our fayth and adored not the
beast; whome albeit we cannot name, yet God knew.* Besides,
some of them say, that there was no face or shew of
their Church in Popery. D. Whitaker loc.cit.p.477:
*VVe say, that there were so few good in Popery, as they appeared
not.* And Cont.4.quest.5.cap.3.pag.682:*VVe surely say,
that in tymes past the Church lay hid in Popery.* And Luther
vpon

Lib. 1. cot.
Gaud.c.33.

2.Pet.1,

Lib.7.de
Trinit.

Know
not.

Can not
name.

Appeared
not.

vpon the 90. pſalm. fol. 495 : *The Church was in Popery, but truly ſo hidden, as to him, that would iudge of the outward appearance, it might ſeeme to be no where.* Caluin alſo 4. Inſtitut. cap. 2. §. 12 ſpeaketh in this ſort of his Proteſtants, whome he imagined in Popery: *In whome all things are ſo out of order, as there may rather ſeeme the face of Babylon then of the citty of God.* By what appearance then iudge they, when then ſay that their Church was in Popery:

4. Sixtly, I proue that the Proteſtant church was not in Popery ; by the Perſons whom they challenge. Luther cont. Caterin. tom. 2. fol. 140. writeth thus : *Where ye ſee no ghoſpell, as we ſee none in the Synagogue of the Papiſts, there doubtles is no Church ; vnleſſe you except infants and ſimple folke.* And tol. 155 : *whome in all the world hath not the Pope ſubdued, except perhaps infants and ſilly perſons, ſaued by an vnknowne Counſaile.* M. Bale Cent. 1. cap. 74. writeth, that their Church ſince Phocas the Emperours tyme, *Was in lurking holes and amongſt idiots.* Gerlachius diſput. 22. ſayth that Infants *were no ſmall part of their Church* Oſiander loc. cit. pag. 65. that they *were a great part.* And as Lobechius addeth diſput. 10. pag. 202: *The nobleſt part.* A worthy Church vndoubtedly, which for many ages conſiſted of infants, idiots, and ſuch ſilly perſons. And they more ſilly who giue credit to ſo ſilly an affirmation of Proteſtants without all proofe ; and they moſt ſilly of all who relinquiſhing the Catholike Church, adioyne themſelues to ſuch a childiſh and ſilly Church, ſo ſillily affirmed and without proofe. Seauenthly Proteſtants themſelues do plainly profeſſe that the entire ſubſtance and eſſence of their Church was not in Popery, but only ſome part thereof. And we, (as hath byn often ſayd) ſpeake not of a Church in part, or in ſome ſort, but

What kind of Perſons they challenge.

Infants & ſilly ones.

Idiots.

of a

The whole essence of a protestāt Church not in Popery.

of a Church which hath all the essentiall and substantiall partes, and may be simply and absolutely tearmed a Church. Caluin 4. Institut. cap. 2. after he had sayd §. 1. that it is certaine there is no Church where lyes and falsity haue gotten the vpper hand; he straight sayth §. 2 : *Seing matters go so vnder Popery, VVe may gather how much of the Church remayneth there.* And addeth, that vnder Popery. *That doctrine without which Christianity standeth not, is all buryed and thrust out.* And Respons. ad Sadolet. pag. 128. writeth : *That in Popery there appeareth scarce any scattered and torne remnants of the church.*

Scarse any remnants.

Only rubbish.

Peter Martyr in locis tit. de discessu a Rom. Eccl. col. 1493 : *Now there are left among Papists only some rubbish and parcels of old walles, togeather &c.* Sonis Resp. ad Spondeum cap. 2. pag. 32 : *Antichrist hath left nothing in all the building, but some old wals.* Sadeel Præfat. lib. de Verbo

But old wals.

scripto : *The Roman Church is so depraued and corrupted, that whiles we seeke the Church, in the church ; we are forced to behold only ashes of the Church.* The Apology of the Church

Only ashes.

of England part. 4. cap. 9. diuis. 3 : *These men now haue left nothing remayning in the Church of God that had any likenesse of his Church.* And part. 6. cap. 17. diuis. 1 : *VVhen we saw*

Nought but ruins.

that nothing remayned in the temple of God but pittifull spoiles and decayes, we &c Finally Luther in Psalm. 22. tom. 3.

No trace.

fol. 132 sayth, that in Popery *there was no trace of the Church.* And in psalm. 17. fol. 285: *They haue brought mat-*

Name only.

ters to such passe, that where the Church of God was heretofore, there is nought but heathenish superstition and the name only of the church remayning ; the substance is quite lost. The same also meane those, who say that in Popery were some small footsteps, some reliques, and parcels of the church, albeit they had not this exclusine terme, *Only.* But if in Popery the doctrine without which Christianity cannot stand were wholy buryed and shut out ;

out; If therein scarse appeared torne parcels of the Church, only ashes thereof were seene; if nothing remayned but old wals, rubbish and ruines; nothing entire and like to a Church; and the name only remayning, the substance were quit lost, doubtles there was no absolute and true Protestant Church in Popery, but only in part and in some sort. Which Daneus plainly intimateth when he saith Cont. 4. lib. 3. cap. 13. pag. 387: *Some footsteps of the Church remayne yet in that (Popish company, as if the ruines of a house cast downe and the bare walls were called a house equiuocally.* Or as Caluin speaketh Respons. ad Versipeliem pag. 357: *In some part the Protestant Church was heretofore in Popery.*

5.   That I may therefore gather togeather all that Protestants say of their Church in Popery befor Luthers tyme; Concerning the persons whereof it consisted, they were infants, idiots, silly ones, and perhaps not they neither; Concerning the substance, it was only ruines, rubbish, old walles, ashes, and name only of the Church. Concerning the number, it was (a) *Very small, slender reliques, few remnants, and scarce a few reliques, so small reliques, one or two persons.* Touching the place wherein she was, that was lurking holes, or rather none at all. For so sayth D. Whitaker Cont. 2. quest. 3. cap. 2. pag. 468: *The holy and pious men were togeather with their Pastors dispersed into this or that place without any certaine aboad or Succession.* And quest. 5. cap. 4. pag. 503: *Our men were in tymes past scattered here and there.* Touching the state of their Church, that was (b) quite fallen downe. Touching the face or shew thereof, that was rather of Babylon then of the Church. As for the Condition, it was afflicted of Antichrist, with sauadge domination, was misera-

(a) *Luther in psalm. grad. f. 508 de Missa lot. 7. fol. 236. Gerla. disput. 2a. A contine h. 1. Strat. p. 25. Sadeel ad Sophis. pag. 596. d Thes. Pos. nan 18.*

(b) *cap. e. 2.*

bly brought to naught , and all her affaires most desperat. For profession of fayth , she made none at all. For externall rites and worship, she was compelled to keep very Babylonicall , heathenish, idolatricall, and Antichristian rites. For piety, that was all driue out. Touching fayth, that was quite extinct. As for her Conseruation, that was by meruailous and miraculous meanes, & by meere miracle. And lastly for the testimonies whereby either her being, are any of these points are proued, they are pure Pythagoricall, that is, their owne words , which is (as themselues say) arguments of fooles , or rather lyes, for who so speaketh of himselfe speaketh lyes.

6.   My eighth reason is, because Protestants should haue sayd that their Church had bene in any company rather then in Popery. For Luther lib. cõt. Regem Angliæ tom. 2. fol. 334. writeth, that *Popery is the most pestilent abomination of Satan , which hath byn , or hereafter shalbe vnder heauen.* And in cap. 15. Genet. tom. 6. fol. 342: *Popery is a Congregation of diuels and of most wicked men.* And lib. cont. Papatum. tom 7. fol. 479. saith: *It is the last mischeife of the world , and to which all the Diuells* *with all their cunning & power cannot bring a greater.* Others say that Popery is *the body of Satan and Antichrist, the dungeon of errors, & heresies, that it is worse thē any sect of heretiks; yea then Paganisme, or Turcisme;* And almost all of them cry that it is the Synagogue of Satan and Antichrist. Moreouer Luther in Actis exustionis decretalium tom. 2. fol. 123. pronounceth, *that it were safer liuing in the wildernes, to see no man, then to conuerse in the Popish Kingdome.* And in cap. 2. Galat. tom. 5. fol. 227: *VVhosoeuer is earnestly affected towards Godlines, let him tremble at the name of Popery.* And Protestants commonly gather out of that saying of the Apocalips : *Go out my people, that it is*
the

the commaundement of God, that, all pious men
should goe out of Popery. If then Popery be the Synagogue of Satan and Antichrist, & worse then any
hereticall, Turkish, or heathenish company; or any
other, whom all the diuels which all their cunning
could raise; If all pious men ought to tremble at the
hearing of the name thereof, and rather liue in a desert then therein; If finally it be the Commandemēt
of God, that all godly men should goe forth of Popery, how came it to passe, that in former tymes the
godly (forsooth) Protestants liued in Popery, and in
Popery alone, & that for so many ages? Would godly men abid in that company, and only in that company, and so long tyme, which was the worst that
could be, before which they shold haue preferred the
wildernes, haue shaken at the name thereof, & were
commanded to come out from thence by Gods expresse commandement? Surely the Protestants must
not only haue byn children and simple, but also impious and vngodly. What! could not, or would not
the spouse of Christ lurke for so many ages, but in
the stewes of the diuell? Could Christ be no where,
but with Antichrist? Would only Antichrist for so
many ages affoard Christ and his church a harbour
or lurking place? *O straightes* (sayth S. Austine) *O in-* l.1.de mor.
credible absurdities! For what greater straights, what Manich.c
more incredible absurdity can there be, thē to thrust 16.
Christ and his Church into the diuels stewes, and
that for many ages togeather? But as Caluin himself 4.Instit.c
sayth: *There is no meruaile if these reprobate spirits, as if they* 16.§.31.
were frantique, do thrust in most grosse absurdities for to defend
their errors, for God iustly punisheth their pride and obstinacy
which such giddinesse.

7.   Ninthly, I argue, and aske what is the

meaning of the forelayd ridle: *The Church is as in* Popery
but Popery *was not the Church.* First, I suppose that by Popery heere, they meane not (as did Boysseul) popish
doctrine; as if the sense were, that the Protestant
Church consisted of Popish doctrine, as we say that
the Popish Church consisteth (to wit formally) of
Popish doctrine; the Iewish Church of Iudaisme, &
the Turkish of Turcisme; because this sense were too
far from the question, which demaundeth the place,
and not the forme, or doctrine of the Protestant
church in former tyms. Besides, it were too too absurd to say that the Protestant Church consisteth in
the contrary doctrine, which he condemneth. Sup-
posing therfore, that hereby Popery they vnderstand
the company of Papists, their meaning cannot be,
that their Church was in the company of Papists, as
in a multitude of men amongst whom they liued only, but did no way participate of their doctrine or
worship; both because in this manner, it had byn
knowne to Papists, which notwithstanding they
deny, as before we shewed, and anone shalbe proued
to be false; as also because in this sort their Church
may be sayd to be in Iudaisme, Turcisme, & the like,
if they liue among Iewes or Turcks; which is so absurd as Protestāts deny their meaning to be such. For
thus Beza epist. 10. quest. 4: *The Church was in* Popery,
which can no way be sayd of the Turks. And M. Perkins lib.
cit. after he sayd that the Church was long tyme in
Popery, addeth, *VVhich cannot be likewise sayd of Turks and
other Infidels, that the Church was conserued, or that yet any
hidden Church is conserued amongst them.* Neither can their
meaning be, that the Protestant church was in tymes
past in Popery, as a part in the whole, to wit, because
it consisted of some that belieued both Protestancy
and

and Popery, or if they did not belieue Popery, yet
they professed it; because after this manner Popery
should no lesse haue byn the Church, the Church
should haue byn in Popery. For as the church should
haue byn in Popery, because it consisted of such a
part of Popery; so Popery shold haue byn the church
because such a part of Popery had byn the Church.
Besides, it implieth contradiction, that one should
belieue both Popery and Protestancy, which as Protestants say, are right opposite in many fundamental
points. If any reply, that those Papists in whom the
Protestant Church of old tyme did consist, did not
belieue all fundamentall points of Popery, nor were
absolutely Papists, but only in part and in some sort:
first he mocketh the Reader in saying absolutely, that
the Protestant church was in Popery, because Popery absolutely taken, doth signify absolute Papists or
Papistry. Besides he feigneth and deuiseth those Papists in part & in some sort, and cannot proue by any
sufficient testimony that there were any such; Wheras according to S. Augustin, *He must proue, not speake at
random*. Nor can he say, that the Protestant Church *2. Cont.
consisted of such, who though they belieued litle or *Petil. c.18.*
no Papistry at all, yet outwardly professed it. For if
outwardly they professed only Papistry, how know
you that inwardly they belieued Protestancy? Will
you, as S. Augustin sayd to the Donatists, iudge of *Lib.2.de
mens harts and not of their open deeds? Besides such *Baptis.c.7*
Papists are feigned and not at all proued. And if there
had byn any such, they should haue byn termed Denyers not Protesters. Lastly such men cold not haue
byn the visible Church of Protestants, because they
denied their fayth and professed Antichristianity;
and consequently were no holy men, of whom only

P 5   their

their inuisible Church consisteth.

8.   Tenthly I argue by enquiring the manner, how the Protestant church in former tyms was in Popery; to wit, whether it professed the substance of the Protestant fayth, or no : and whether it communicated with Papists in their Popish worship or not? Protestants, like men vncertaine answere diuersly to this question. D. Whitaker Cont. 2. quest. 3. cap. 3. pag. 474. sayth : *Our Churches were alwayes in the middest of Papists churches, distinct from Papists in Communion and Profession.* But this is soone refuted . First, because

Cont. Parmen. ca. 38. it cannot be proued. *And to cast out words and proue naught, what is it* (as S. Augustin sayth) *but to dote?* Besides if the Protestant Church had professed Protestancy, she had byn knowne to Papists ; and the same had also byn if she had not communicated with them. For as D. Andrews writeth of the Catholikes in England : *They come not to seruice, they heare not sermons, they refuse to take the Communion, without this or any other oath one may know them to be Papists.* But she was not knowne to Papists, because not only all Papists ; but also Protestants deny that. Besides otherwise Catholiks would not haue so earnestly enquired of Protestants, where their Church had byn heretofore. Moreouer Catholikes had persecuted them as they persecuted Luther, so soone as he was knowne for a Protestant. Lastly, because Protestants cannot name any Papists, who knew of their Church before Luthers tyme . Others therefore say, that those imaginary Protestants professed their fayth, if not at other tymes, yet at least at the point of death. D . Whitaker loc. cit. pag. 473: *Many at the point of death, if not before, professed their fayth.* The same sayth Luther of priuate Masse tom. 7. fol. 237. and Lobechius Disput. 10. To which D. White

in

in defence of his way cap. 4. pag. 424. addeth, that *they renounceth Papiſtry alſo in the agony of their conſcience.* And Hunnius before cited, not knowing what certainly to determine, ſayth: that *they did either openly gird at Papiſtry, or ſecretly with themſelues deteſt it, or at leaſt in the laſt examen of tentations (the ſtuble of errour being fired) did hold the foundation of ſaluation.* But to ſpeake with S. Auguſtin: *VVho ſayth this, but he that ſayth what he will, and will not heare what is true?* They ſay that in the Scripture alone that ſaying of Pythagoras Schollers (he ſayd it) taketh place. But if they vſed not this Pythagoricall priuiledge, they would be more dumbe then fiſhes. What man or diuell told them this profeſſiō of their men at the houre of death? How learnt they that, which at that tyme no man could fiſh out? Againe, if only at the houre of death they profeſſed Proteſtancy, they were Proteſtants no longer then they lay a dying; and conſequently the Proteſtant church endured no longer then ſome of her children were dying. A ſtrange Church certes, that liued no longer then her children dyed; nor at any tyme drew breath, but whiles they gaue vp the ghoſt. Wherefore they find out other deuiſes to ſay, that thoſe feigned Proteſtants communicated with Papiſts and profeſſed their fayth in things lawfull, as in Baptiſme, reading of the Scriptur, and ſuch like; but not in things vnlawfull. Thus Reineccius in the 4. tome of his armour cap. 4. Thou ſeeſt reader, that as theſe Proteſtants had their being only by theſe mens imaginations, ſo they did, or did not, what, or in what manner they will haue them. *O great fabuloſity,* (that I may cry out which S. Epiphanius) *of them, who vtter theſe things? ſo manifeſt it is, that this is a ſhop rather of iuglers, then of thoſe who haue the ſhape of the promiſe of life and of vn-*

lib. 5. cont.
lul. c. 4.

Bulling. in
Compend.
fidei l. 1. c. 3.

derſtan-

derstanding. For who besides his owne imagination, told Reineccius, that those Protestants deuided thus their Communion with Papists? who besides him-selfe heard euer of such a halfe-communion?

9. Wherefore others of them do absolutely say, that their imaginary Protestant Church in Popery communicated with Papists, and professed their fayth. For thus writeth Luther in psalm.Grad.tom. 3.fol.568: *The Church vnder Antichrist had no true Ministery or worship, but was forced to keep the very Babylonicall and heathenish rites of Papists.* The same he intimateth tom. 7. lib.de Missa priuata fol.236.& 237.and lib cont.Papatum fol.456.Osiander also in the epist. dedicatory of his 8. Century sayth of those Protestants, that *although from their heart they disallowed the Popish errors, yet they durst not professe their owne opinions; but neglected not the externall rites, and were carryed away with the common custome as it were with a torrent, for to do those things which others did; whose weaknesse (sayth he) God did beare withall and pardon.* And the same pardon Luther de Missa priuata fol. 237. bestoweth vpon them saying: *No sinne could hurt them; but God must pardon the miserable, afflicted, oppressed and captiue Church.* Thus these men haue Gods pardon in their hands, that when they please, God must pardon those, who all their life tyme denyed their faith and serued Antichrist and idolatry. Iunius also lib.4. de Eccl.cap.5.sayth, that the Church in former tyms *was all one with the Roman.* Againe: *She communicated with the Roman Church in worship of God euery where, so long as she was suffered to communicate in pure worship, in right fayth, and good conscience.* Forsooth the Synagogue of Antichrist, (as they account the Roman church)vseth pure worship, or the Church of Christ communicateth with her in right fayth, and good conscience. And D.Whi-
taker

How impious their church in Popery was.

taker Cont. 4. queſt. 5. cap. 3. pag. 682. writeth, that
thoſe feigned Proteſtants, *Perhaps vſed Popish ceremonies
for customes ſake.* And pag. 689: *Antichriſt deceiued the elect
and ſeduced them. The very elect erred.* And Cont. 2. queſt.
3. cap. 3. pag 474: *In Popery there were many (*Proteſtants*)
who communicated with* Papiſts. Gerlachius tom. 2. diſp.
22: *They were driuen into the common opinions with an vniuerſall and fatall ouerflow* of ſuperſtitions. And Caſaubon
epiſt. ad Peron pag. 10. writeth, that *the godly communicated with Babylon.* D. Feild lib. 3. de Eccleſ. cap. 13 : *The
authors of thoſe (*Popiſh*) errours, and thoſe that were free from
them were of the ſame Communion.* D. White in his way
pag. 171 : *The children of God abode in the communion of the
Roman Church.* And in the defence cap. 44 pag. 394:
*VVe do not hold a definite number of perſons, diſtinct from the
members of the Church of Rome, and liuing apart in another ſociety by themſelues in ſecret, as it were the 7. ſleepers lying hid in
a mountaine : but we affirme this company liued in the middeſt of
the Church of Rome it ſelfe , and were the viſible Profeſſors therof.* This alſo is that, which Caluin would, when 4.
Inſtitut. cap. 2. §. 12. he ſayth, that his Churches in
Popery *were prophaned with ſacrilegious impiety , corrupted
and almoſt killed with pernicious doctrines; in which lay halfe
buryed, the ghoſpell ouerwhelmed, godlines baniſhed, and all things
ſo out of order, as there ſeemed rather the face of Babylon then of
the citty of God.* And vpon the 23. of the Acts : *VVe com-
plaine that the Church was corrupted of them (*Papiſts*) the
temple of God prophaned , that it differed litle from a ſwines-
cot. See, ſayth* S. Auguſtine, *to what a precipice, the difficulty to find where to get out hath brought theſe men.* They ſayd
their Church was in Popery, and afterward found
not how to creep out, but by this moſt ſteep & crag-
gy precipice. For what ſteeper precipice, what greater abſurdity can there be, then to ſay that the church
of

*Li. 2. cont.
Creſc. c. 17.*

of God (which the Protestants will haue theirs to be)for many ages denyed her fayth, professed infidelity, forsook Christ, worshipped Antichrist, or to vse their owne words, *Did vse very Babylonicall and Antichristian rites, was corrupted with pernicious doctrine, prophaned with sacrilegious impiety, and out of which godlines was banished? God forbid* (sayth S. Cyprian) *that a company of fallen persons should be called the Church.* Againe: *God forbid, & his mercy and inuincible power neuer permit, that a company of fallen persons be called the Church.* And Beza himselfe : *The Church is a community of Saints, not a company of excommunicated or sacrilegious persons.* And shall we think , that before Luther arose the Church of God for many ages was nothing else but a company of fallen, sacrilegious, hypocrites, denyers of Christ, and worshippers of Antichrist ? Is such a company the holy Church? Is the Communion of such, the Communion of Saints which we belieue in our Creed? Is such a society the spouse and mysticall body of Christ, the wife of the lambe, the Kingdom of God? Surely a fit Church for protestants, and a fit company, to which the forsakers of the Catholike Church may adioyne themselues, and most worthy to be eschewed & detested of all that loue Christs or their owne honour. For who is he, either pious or well in his wits, who will make himselfe of that company which for many ages consisted all of lapsed Hypocrites, denyers of Christ, and worshippers of Antichrist? The whole Scriptures and Fathers say that the spouse of Christ is honest and chast, and cannot be deflowed. But this protestant harlot did for many ages prostitute her selfe to Antichrist.

     10. Moreouer this kind of company which thus communicated with Antichrist and professed

his

his doctrine, could not be the viſible Proteſtant
Church. For her they define to be a company *which* Conf. An-
profeſſeth Chriſts true doctrine, and rightly vſeth his Sacraments. glic.art.19
But this foreſayd company, as themſelues write,
Durſt not profeſſe their opinion, had no Miniſtery, & did obſerue
Babylonicall and heatheniſh rites. Nor were they their inuiſible Church, which alone they will haue to be
the true Catholike and proper Church, becauſe ſhe
according to all their opinions, is the company of
Saints & elect only. The Confeſſion of Auſpurg. art.
7 : *The Church properly ſo called, is the congregation of Saints,*
who truly belieue and obey Chriſt. And D. Whitaker cont.
2.queſt.1.cap.3: *Thus we define the Catholike Church; It is a*
company of holy men, whome God hath choſen in Chriſt, to euer-
laſting life. This definition (ſayth he) excludeth all hypocrites.
But thoſe who worſhipped Antichriſt were no
Saints, obeyed not Chriſt, were hypocrites. Therefore they were no Catholike or true church. Againe,
it is the common doctrine of Proteſtants that naughty & great ſinners are no mē ers of the true church.
For thus the Confeſſion of the Low-countries art.
29 : *Hypocrites belong not properly to the Church.* Caluin 4. Ill mē not
Inſtitut.cap.1.§. 7: *Into that Church, which is indeed before* the true
God, none are admitted but ſuch as both by grace of adoption are church by
the ſonnes of God, and by ſanctification of the ſpirit true members Proteſtāts
of Chriſt. Peter Martyr in his places tit. de Eccleſ. col.
1368: *VVe affirme that ſuch (wicked) men are not indeed &*
before God members of the Church. Aretius in locis part.3.
fol.50: *The Church, properly ſo called, conſiſteth only of the true*
members of Chriſt. Bucer lib.de vi & vſu Miniſterij pag.
558.: *The true Church conſiſteth only of thoſe that are borne a*
new. D. Whitaker cap.3.cit: *VVe all belieue that Catholike*
Church, which we profeſſe in our Creed, to conſiſt of no euill or
reprobate perſons, but only of the elect, iuſt, and holy. And c. 7:

VVe

VVe deny ill men to belong to the Church, which is the body of Chriſt. M.Perkins in his expoſition of the Creed col. 795: *An ill man cannot be a member of the Church.* Adā Francis loc. 11. de Eccl: *Ill men are only in name members of the Church.* And finally Muſculus in locis tit. de Eccl. pag. 299: *Not ſo much as the name of the Church ought to be giuen to the wicked.* But they who were ſuch as the Proteſtants before deſcribed, were no Saints, were not iuſt, were not ſanctified; but ill, wicked, hypocrites, if euer there were any: therefore they could not be the true Catholike and proper Church before God. Furthermore Proteſtants vſe to teach, that thoſe who communicate with Papiſts do cut themſelues from the true Church. The French Confeſſion art. 28: *VVe think all thoſe who adioyne themſelues to theſe (Popiſh) actions and communicate with them, do ſeparat themſelues from the body of Chriſt.* Luther in cap. 13. Geneſ. tom. 6. fol. 163: *VVho acknowledgeth the Pope for maſter, he hath no part with Chriſt.* And in cap. 28. fol. 396: *If the Pope muſt be worſhipped, Chriſt muſt be denyed.* And de Miſſa priuata tom. 7. fol. 475: *VVhoſoeuer is vnder the Pope and obeyeth him cannot be ſaued.* Caluin againſt Seruet. pag. 607: *Is it not a profanation of the ſacred vnity, to profeſſe one God and faith with an impious and prophane company?* And Reſponſ. ad Verſip. pag. 362: *How wicked and foule treachery is it to abide in that ſacrilegious company (of Papiſts)?* And D. Whitaker ad Rat. 3. Campiani: *None abide with the lambe in the mountaine, who haue any commerce with Antichriſt.* And Caluin in Confutat. Hollandi & lib. de vitandis ſuperſtitionibus, bringeth many proofes to ſhew that the faithfull may not communicate with the falſe Church, and therto citeth the letters of Melancthon, Bucer, peter Martyr, and thoſe of Zurich: and the ſame is commonly taught of proteſtants. How then did not
those

those protestants separate themselues from the body of Christ? how were they saued, who in tymes past communicated with Papists? How were they saued vnlesse God be an acceptour of persons and tymes, that he will cut of some from his body, and from hope of saluation, who communicate with Antichrist, and not others, at these and not in former tymes. Againe, protestants teach that the Church ought to professe her fayth, as besides the testimonies before repeated, the Preface of the Confession of Saxony sayth: *They that are demaunded must needs tell the doctrine.* And the Confession of Bohemia art. 2: *They teach, that they must indoubtedly belieue all the articles of the Creed, and confesse them with the mouth.* Luther in 1 Petri cap.2.tom.5.fol. 464: *If any now, as the Emperour or other Prince should aske me my fayth, I must plainly confesse it to him.* And de Seru. Arbit. tom. 2. fol. 432: *Truth and doctrine must alwayes be preached openly, and neuer kept secret or crookt and turnd awry* D. Feild lib. 1. de Eccl. cap. 10: *For seeing the Church is the multitude of them that shall be saued vnlesse he make confession vnto saluation, for fayth hid in the heart and concealed doth not suffice, it cannot be but they that are of the true Church must by the profession of the truth make themselues knowne in such sort that &c.* And the Preface of the Syntagme of Confessions: *When euery one ought, according to the Apostles precept, giue a reason of his hope; how much more the Church?* And D. Whitaker Cont.4.quest.6.cap.2.pag:696: *True fayth can no more be separated from confession with the mouth, then fire from heat, or the sunne from its brightnes and beames.* What fayth then had those protestants, which, as is sayd, durst not professe their mind? And Cont.2.quest.3.cap.2.pag. 472: *It is not lawfull for the godly to dissemble true Religion or make shew of false; nor to conceale what they think of Religion, if they be examined of them who haue authority to aske them of*

Q

their

their fayth. But it is not credible that in so many ages, in no part of the Christian world, no Catholike Magistrate should aske any Protestant of his fayth, especially if it be true that Luther writeth in psalm. 22. tom. 3. fol. 344. that *Papists do so examine the body of the Church, that all her bones may be counted, that is, none of them can by hid. VVherefore we must not imagine that there are any hidden bones of Christ, all are bewrayed and counted, wheresoeuer they are, either by the espials of secret confession, or by the tortours or examiners.* Which sheweth, that if there had byn any true Protestants heretofore, they would haue byn discouered.

11.   Finally they are brought to these straights, that sometymes they say, that the Protestant church, (which they imagine was heretofore in Popery,) did consist of those who were papists both in opinion and profession. This Caluin intimateth in the words before cited, when he sayth that his church was corrupted with pestilent doctrine. And Luther de Missa priuata tom.7.fol.231.saying: *The very elect were seduced in that great darknesse.* And in cap.9. Isaiæ tom.4.fol.95: *Behold* (sayth he) *the whole face of the Churches vnder Popery. Did not they all who truly felt the burden of sinne imagine that they should by good works satisfy for their sinnes?* Which thing alone would suffice to blot them out of the role of Protestants. D. White in defence of his way cap. 36.pag.350.sayth those imaginary Protestants were corrupted, some more some lesse, with those errors, which (sayth he) now we fly. And cap.40. pag. 394. graunteth, that they were infected with damnable heresies. D. Whitaker lib. 2. de Scriptura cap. 8. sect. vlt. sayth: *They were beset with most thick darknes.* Napper in cap.12. Apocal.pag·195. that their visible Church in tymes past: *VVholy embraced the errors of merits and in-*

dulgen-

dulgences &c. And Morgenſtern tract. de Eccl. pag. 41:
*Theſe things were in tymes paſt to be forgiuen the godly, that they
beliued the Pope to be Chriſts vicar, and head of the church, Popery to be the church , Saints to be prayed vnto, Maſſe to be the
Lords ſupper.* Are theſe men (think you) in their wits,
who call them godly, and ſay they muſt be pardo-
ned, who belieued Antichriſt to be Chriſts vicar,
Antichriſts Synagogue to be the Church of Chriſt,
and horrible idolatry (ſuch as they account Maſſe &
prayer to Saints) to be ſeruice of Chriſt? The ſame
alſo they meane, when they challenge the ſimple &
ignorant Papiſts for theirs, or confeſſe the vulgar Roman Church to be the true Church ; or (as others of
them ſpeake) graunt the Roman Church ; but deny
Popery, the Popiſh, or Roman Popiſh Church. For
they imagine, that the ſimple Catholike people neither doth now, nor in former tyms did belieue thoſe
points of fayth, which themſelues deny. But this
they feigne of the ſimple Catholike people, and cannot proue it . Beſides , there is no Catholike ſo ſimple, as doth not vertually belieue all points of Catholike fayth, which Proteſtants deny, ſith he actually profeſſeth to belieue whatſoeuer the Catholike
Church teacheth . Neither is there any at all, who
doth not belieue iuſtification by good works, which
point alone would ſuffice to make them no Proteſtants. Beſides, Caluin 4. Inſtitut. cap. 8. ſayth that
we affirme him *to be no Chriſtian, who doth not vndoubtedly
agree to all points of doctrine , as well affirmatiue as negatiue* .
And the ſame ſayth D. Whitaker Cont. 2. queſt. 5. cap.
8. pag. 519. D. Morton part 1. Apol. lib. 1. cap. 9. and
D. Willet in the preface of his Synopſis. Yea , as before we rehearſed, they confeſſe that before Luthers
reuolt all from head to foot were drowned in the *Cap 2.*

Q 2   pudles

pudles of Popery, that none dreamed of that which
is the cheifest point of Protestancy. Wherfore Schuf-
selburg tom. 8. Catal. Hæret. pag. 440. seemeth to say,
That befor Luther arose popery was the true church
like as the Synagogue of the Iewes was before the
comming of Christ, for thus he writeth: *Popery, as Iu-*
daisme heretofore, signifieth that company, which at least in her
tyme had the true Church with it. Such were the Iewes before
the comming of Christ, and the Papists before the comming of Lu-
ther. His meaning (as I suppose) is that as the Christian Church is in state another church from the Synagogue; because it hath other Sacraments, other Sacrifice, and more points of fayth, and Christ another
founder of the Church distinct from Moyses; so the
Protestant Church is a distinct Church from the ancient Christian Church, and Luther not only another Elias, as they call him, but also another Messias,
a founder and beginner of another Church, distinct
from that of Christ, at least as far as his church differed from the Synagogue. Behold Christian Reader
wherto all their winding, turning, and doubling
about the being of their Church in Popery, is come.

L. 20. cont.
Fauft. c. 12. *Surely* (as S. Augustin sayd, against the Manichees)
their imaginations haue lost all wayes. For they are nothing, but
the visions of frantike men . For their remayneth no probable way to defend, that their Church was heretofore in Popery. It is mere frenzy to think, that it was
in Popery virtually and implicitly, like as a plant is
in the seed, or a man in a child, as the Christian
Church once was in the Synagogue, or that it was
openly distinct in Communion and Profession from
Papists: or that it consisteth of such, which either in
hart, or at least in Profession were Papists ; or finally, that the Church of God (such as they will haue
the

the Protestant to be) was for many ages in a discreet, yea a most opposite church; where neither by diuine nor humane testimony it can be proued to haue byn; neither can there any way be imagined, by which it may with any appearance or probability be sayd to haue byn there, Thus (sayth S. Augustine) *do they dote, who not abiding true doctrine, turne to fables* . *lib 20. cõt. Faust.c.vl.*

12, And out of these, wherewith we haue shewed, that the Protestant Church heretofore was not in Popery, is refuted also Zanchius Præfat.lib.de Natura Dei, where he sayth that their brethren in tymes past liued in some obscure vallies and Mountaines, and met at night. And D. Fulke lib.de Succes. pag. 324. saying, that in Europe the Church was by Antichrist thrust into obscure places; but least they should be tript in their lying, they name neither those mountaines, nor vallyes, nor places, nor their night-owle-brethren, nor finally proue any thing. But as S. Augustin sayd of Faustus : *They say it & away, they neuer seeke to proue it* . Or as Christ sayd of the aduersary man, they sow cockle and depart. It sufficeth for these new Pythagorians, to powre out lyes like oracles : for they assure themselues that with retchlesse men they will find credit of themselues, & like weeds grow without tilling. Hence also is refuted the same Fulke in cap. 10. Apocal . Where he affirmeth his brethren hertofore haue liued in the Alpes, in the Appenine Mountaines, and in the Hercinian Forest . He might better haue sayd they liued in the Wildernes of Vtopia, for he proueth nothing. O man (that I may cry out which S. Augustine) *thincking only of his owne talke, and not thinking of any gainesayer* ! Againe: *Doest thou not know , or doest thou not feele with the heart* ,of *what man soeuer , that in dispute where truth is sought , where* *L.14.cont. Faust. c.9.*

L.16.cont. Faust.c.16

l b.4 cont. Cres. c.54.

Q 3

proofe

proofe followeth not , the talke is vaine and foolish. Wherefore
now let vs heare their arguments, or rather Sophismes, wherwith sometymes they endeauour to
proue, that their Church was in tymes past in Popery.

The Sophismes , wherwith some Protestant
ma e shew to proue that their Church
was heretofore in Popery , refuted.

CHAP. X.

1. THE first argument, wherewith Protestants
would seeme to proue, that their Church in
former tymes was in Popery, is grounded vpon that
saying Apocal .18 : *Goe out of her (Babylon) my people.*
Therefore Gods people were in Babylon , that is,
(say they) in Popery. Thus argueth Luther in cap.
12. Genes. tom. 6. fol. 144. And in cap. 19. fol. 234. The
Magdeburgians in Præfat. Centur. 8. Plessy lib. de
Eccles. cap 10. and others commonly. Yea M. Perkins
in his reformed Catholike tract. 22. writeth that by
this commandement , it may be gathered that the
true Church is, and was long tyme in the Roman
Church . Wherein he speakes more truly then he
meant . For the true Church is and was alwayes in
the Romane ; but the Protestant, neither is , nor was
there . To the argument I answere, that this place
can be no sufficient ground of fayth among the Pro-
testans, because their Angel , their Apostle, and E-
uangelist Martyn Luther, denyeth the Apocalipse to
be Canonicall Scripture. Againe, though indeed it
be canonicall Scripture , yet for the most part it is so
obscure,

obscure, as but very few places therof are fit to groūd
any point of fayth; as is euident both by the booke it
selfe, which is wellnigh all Mysticall and allegoricall, and by the iudgement of the Fathers and confession of Protestants. For thus sayth S. Denis Pa- *Euseb. l.7.*
triarch of Alexandria of the Apocalipse: *I verily think,* *cap. 20.*
that almost in euery sentence there lyeth some mysticall and mer-
ueilous sense. Likewise S. Hierome : *The Apocalipse hath as* *Epist. ad*
many mysteries as words. And S. Augustin: *In the booke of the* *Paulin.*
Apocalipse many obscure things are told, and there are few things
therein , by light whereof the rest may be sought ought with la- *lib 20. de*
bour   And with Protestants D. Andrewes in his an- *Ciuit.c.17.*
swere to Bellarmines Apology cap. 9: *Is he ignorant, that*
concerning the Apocalipse nothing certaine or of fayth is yet pre-
scribed by the Church, that it may be lawfull to vse one only kind
of interpretation and no other ; as if it were so cleare and euident
that it were a hainous offence to leaue it , or to dissent any way
from it. Yea as any may with greatest probability shew the pro-
phesies there to be fulfilled, so is it free for any to vse his iudgement
& to follow his own opinion in explicating them. And D. Whitaker Cont.4.quest.5. cap.3 pag. 677 : *It is well inough*
knowne that Iohn in the Apocalipse speaketh not of cleare and
open matters, but of obscure and hidden . M. Brightman in
his Preface of the Apocalipse: *In so great abundance of an-*
cient and new expositions, the Apocalipse yet, as all agree, needeth
an Apocalipse. And M. Sheldon in his booke of the miracles of Antichrist cap.4.pag.54 calleth it *a darck &*
Mysticall prophecy, in which (sayth he) quot verba , *tot latent*
Mysteria. And pag.226: *The Apocalipse is a booke wholy my-*
sticall, which doth (excepting some few doctrinall rules and ex-
hortations to vertue) in types, figures, formes, and resemblances,
describe and foretell the future euents of the church. How then
can Protestants gather certainly out of the Apocalipse , that their Church heretofore was in Popery ?

　　　　　　　　　　　　But,

VVhy
Protestãts
accoũt so
much of
the Apoc.

But, as Luther in cap.9. Genef. tom. 6.fol. 114. fpeaketh of the Anabaptifts and others: *The Anabaptifts
make fo much of obfcure books as the Apocalipfe, becaufe there
they may feigne any thing.* And in cap. 11. fol. 136: *Ambitious
headstounk it a great matter, if they giue their iudgment freely
of obfcure places, and after ftubbornly maintayne their opinion.*
And Præfat. in Cantica tom. 4 fol. 47: *Some do put all
their labour in hard places, thinking it a commendation of their
wit to medle with thofe matters, which others by reafon of their
obfcurity do fly, & becaufe in obfcure places euery one may diuine
and follow his owne head.*

2.   Thirdly I anfwere, that the forefayd place
is allegoricall, myfticall, and obfcure, and therefore
not fit to ground fayth vpon. That it is myfticall and
allegoricall, is manifeft, becaufe Babylon doth not
litterally, but at moft myfticall; fignify Popery. That
alfo the fenfe which Proteftants frame thereof is obfcure, is euident, becaufe they cannot either by any
part or by any circumftance therof, clearly fhew, that
by Babylon is meant Popery. Befides, neither any of
the Fathers, nor of thofe imaginary Proteftants before Luther, did perceiue this fenfe; otherwife fome
of them would haue obeyed Gods commandement,
and gone out of Popery. But it were playne madnes
to vrge an incredible thing, (as is that Proteftants
were heretofore in Popery) to be belieued certainly,
for one myfticall & obfcure place. *VVho* (fayth S. Auguftin) *without great impudency will goe about to expound for
himfelfe, any thing fpoken in Allegory, vnleffe he haue manifeft
places, by which the obfcure may be lightned.* Let them bring
therefore fome euident place, wherein Babylon fig-
nifieth Popery. Luther alfo fayth: *If in the new teftament
the fignification of a figure be not cleare, we muft not rely vpon it,
becaufe the diuell, an excellent craftfman, playeth with figures, &
if he*

Epift 48.

*Morton
part. 2. l. 2.
c. 5.*

if he catch a ſoule which without certaine ground wreſteth the Scripture to allegories, he vſeth to caſt him here and there like a dye. And *in cap.3.*Genel.*tom.6. fol. 52: An Allegory ſerueth nothing for proofe.* Kemnice *alſo 1.part.exam. tit. de cō*ſtit.Apolt.*pag.79: VVe ſay, that a ſentence is not to be builded vpon any obſcure places of Scripture, which cannot be proued out of other cleare places.* Peter Martyr *in locis tom. 2. tract. de* Miſſa : *An opinion is not to be founded in doubtfull words,* Sadeel *ad* Sophiſm. Turrian. *loc. 11. pag. 597: The moſt learned interpreters do teach that* Anagogicall *arguments muſt rely vpon cleare and expreſſe teſtimonies, if they will breed faith.* And Pareus *lib.4.de* luſtificat.*cap.15. pag. 1120: Teſtimony for a falſe opinion is in vaine ſought out of an Allegoricall and moſt obſcure place.* But as the Fathers haue noted, it was euer the humour of heretiks, to ſeeke ſome pretext of allegoricall and obſcure places. Of the Gnoſtiques, thus writeth S. Irenæus *lib. 1.cap. 1: VVhereas many parables and Allegories are recited, which may be drawne into diuerſe ſenſes, they craftely accommodating that which is ambigious vnto their deuiſe, do lead into captiuity from the truth, thoſe which haue a weake fayth in Chriſt.* Heretikes ſeeke out obſcure places. And S. Auguſtin *lib.de* Vnitat.*ca.24.*ſayth to the Donatiſts: *Yee willingly abide in obſcure matters, that you may not be compelled to confeſſe cleare matters.*And of heretiks in generall thus ſpeaketh Tertullian : *Diuers preſumptions of neceſſity* Præf.c.17. *will not acknowledge thoſe things, by which they may be ouercome ; and relye vpon thoſe, which they haue falſely forged, and haue taken out of vncertainetyes.* Againe : *This is the cuſtome of* De pud. c. 6. *froward men, idiots, and heretikes, by occaſion of ſome doubtfull paſſage to arme themſelues againſt an army of the whole teſtament.* And Clement *7.*Stromatum : *They ſeek out doubtfull ſpeaches, and turne them to vphold their opinions.* The like writeth Luther of Anabaptiſtes. And others, as hath byn now rehearſed. Wherfore Proteſtants do follow

the

the custome of Gnostikes, Donatists, Anabaptists, froward idiots, and heretikes, whiles they fit the Allegory of Baoylon to their turne, whiles they willingly abide in obscure matters, and make such account of the Apocalipse because there they haue leaue to feigne any thing, whiles they rely vpon thoie things which they take out of vncertainties, and by occasion of one ambiguous and doubtfull place, are armed against an army of sentences of the Scripture, which teach that neither Popery is Babylon, nor Protestants the people of God. Moreouer Donatists for the very like place Isaiæ 52: *Goe backe againe out of the midst of her*, would proue that they ought to go out of the Catholik Church of their tyme, as witnesseth S. Augustin, and Danæus confesseth lib. 3. de Eccl. c. 9. who also in lib. 1. August. cont. Parmen. hath thefe words: *The argument of the Donatists out of Isay the 52. is: That we ought to goe backe and goe out of the midst of Babylon.* And the Anabaptists in Zuinglius tom. 2. in Elencho fol. 21. Out of this selfe same place of the Apocalipse, did gather that they ought to goe from Protestants. Why then may wee not say with D. Whitaker: *Our aduersaries serue themselues of the same weapons, whereof most wicked heretikes did; and herein shew themselues to be nothing lesse then Catholikes.* Moreouer I say, that if I list to expound Scriptures at my pleasure, I might say, and more probably too then Protestants, that by the foresayd words God commandeth Protestants to goe out of Protestancy. For Protestancy may well be called Babylon, because it is a Masse and confusion of opposite heresies, where almost euery one hath a fayth of his owne, and speaketh a peculiar language, nor vnderstandeth the tongue or doctrine of another. And Protestants may be called the people of God in that
they

lib. de vnic.
bapt. c. 14.
l. 2. cont.
Parmen. c.
18. l. 2. côt.
Gaud. c. 9.

Cont. 2. q.
6. c. 23.

they are baptiſed, and therein dedicated to his ſeruice; and pretend the fayth of Chriſt as did Iſrael
euen after it had forſaken the Synagogue: And as *De prouid.*
Caluin ſayth that God calleth euen the diſobedient, *art. 11.*
his ſeruants, as Nabuchodonozor in Hieremy, and
as God hath both good and faythfull ſeruants, and
naughty and vnfaythfull; ſo hath he good & naughty people.

3.   Secondly I anſwere, that the argument
which can be framed out of this place, to proue that
which the Proteſtants write of their churches being
in Popery before Luther aroſe, to wit: *Goe you my peo-*
ple out of Babylon, Therefore before Luthers tyme the church was
in Popery, and ſo ſecret as for many ages ſhe was not ſeene either
of her own or of others; is a meere Sophiſme. Firſt becauſe
one vnknown thing is here proued by another more
vnknown, a falſe thing by another not only falſe, but
alſo impoſſible. For more vnknowne it is, more incredible, more impoſſible that the Proteſtant church
ſhould be the people of God, or that Babylon, out of
which Gods people is bidden to goe, Popery: then
that Proteſtants haue byn heretofore amongſt Papiſts. For this, although it be both falſe and incredible, yet it is not impoſſible, as the other is. How
then can they proue vnto vs, that they were heretofore in Popery, by affirming that they are that people of God, and Popery that Babylon, ſith this is to
vs farre more incredible, then the other. Let Baby-
lyn ſometyme in Scripture myſtically ſignify the
citty of Rome; let it alſo ſignify the number of the
wicked both faythfull and Infidels; but in Scripture
it neuer ſignifieth a certaine religion, and leaſt of all
Popery. Beſides his Maieſty in his Epiſtle to Cardinall Peron, hath thoſe words: *VVhat that Babylon is, out*
of

of which Gods people is commanded to go, the King enquireth not in this place, nor pronounceth any thing of that matter . And if his Maiesty will not pronounce what that Babylon is, why should Ministers do it ? Secondly, it is a Sophisme, because there are many things in the consequent, which are not at all in the antecedent, although it be vnderstood as Protestants would. And therefore herein they not only proue an vnknowne thing by another more vnknowne; but some things they proue only by themselues, that is, they affirme them, and proue them not at all. For let the Protestants be the people of God; and let Popery be that Babylon (which they can neuer proue) neuerthelesse that the Protestant Church had byn in Popery so long tyme, to wit, so many ages, and in such manner, to wit so secret as she was altogeather inuisible either to her own or to others, can no way be gathered out of the foresayd words. though they were expounded according to the Protestants mind.

4.   Their second argument they ground vpon that, 2. Thessal. 2. that Antichrist shall sit in the temple of God, which they expound, as that the Pope should sit in the true, that is, according to them, the Protestant Church, and consequently that heretofor the Pope ruled ouer Protestants. To which I answer, that this argument is a Sophisme like to the former. First, becaus it proueth an vnknown thing by another more vnknowne; and one vntruth, by another both vntrue and impossible. For it is more incredible to vs, that Protestants are the temple of God, or the Pope Antichrist, then that they were heretofore amongst Papists. Secondly if hence they Inferre, that their Church was so long in Popery, and in such manner as we haue recited out of their words, they will

will inferre that in the confequent, whereof there is
no figne in the Antecedent, although it were expounded to their defire. Thirdly I fay, that there can
be no certainty gathered out of this place, becaufe it
is obfcure, as appeareth both by it felfe, and by the
different expofitions thereof, and by the iudgement
of S. Augustine, who writeth thus: *In what temple of* *Lib.* 20. *de*
God Antichrist is to fit as God, it is vncertaine, whether in that *Ciuit.c.*19.
ruine of the temple which Salomon built, or in the Church. A-
gaine: I truly profeffe my felfe not to know, what he fayd; yet I
will relate the fufpicions of men, which I haue heard or read of
this matter. And againe: One in this fort, another in that,
gheffeth at the obfcure words of the apoftle. Yea D. Andrews
intimateth, that it cannot be certainly gathered *Refpon. ad*
hence, that the Pope is Antichrift, when he fayth]: *It* *Apol.*
is probably gathered out of the 2.*chap.*2. *Theffal. That the Bishop* *Bellar.c.*5.
of Rome is Antichrift. But we regard not, whence they
probably gather what they pleafe, but only whence
they can certainly & vndoubtedly proue what they
fay. Fourthly I fay, that whatfoeuer is the temple of
God wherein Antichrift fhall fit, this place it felfe
fheweth, that the Pope is not Antichrift, becaufe he
fitteth not in the Church of God as God, but as Bifhop, and as Gods vicar. Fifthly I adde, that the Prote- Proteftāts
ftants themfelues do not firmly belieue, much leffe as not cer-
a point of their fayth, that the Pope is Antichrift, taine that
howfoeuer they vfe the name of Antichrift as a bugg the Pope
to feare children. For Melanchthon, as Schuffelburg is Anti-
reporteth!, *feemed to doubt whether the Pope were Antichrift,* chrift.
or no. D. Whitaker lib. 1. cont. Dureum fect. 33: fayth:
In the meane tyme, we muft needs probably and iuftly fufpect the *l.* 4. *Theol.*
Pope to be Antichrift And Cont. 4. queft. 5. cap. 3: *Many* *Cal. p.*1661
who care not much for the Pope, do not think, that it can be pro-
ued that he is Antichrift. And his Maiefty in his Monitory
epiftle

epistle pag. 70: *Surely for so much as pertayneth to define Antichrist, I would not vrge a thing so obscure and hidden as a matter necessary to be beleeued of all Christians.* And the same sayth Moulins in his defence of that Epistle. To which his Maiesty addeth pag. 142. these words: *If any list to refute this my ghesse concerning Antichrist, &c.* Behold how the Protestants themselues doubt, account it but a suspicion, a ghesse, an obscure matter, and not needfull to be beleeued, that the Pope is Antichrist. How then can they certainly gather out of the foresaid place, that the Pope sat among Protestants? Yea some of the deny the Pope to be the true Antichrist. For thus Luther in cap. 9. Genes. tom. 6. fol. 122: *We hold the Turck for the true Antichrist.* Zanchius lib. 1. Epist. ad Stuckium: *I am perswaded that the name of Antichrist agreeth rather to the Turck then to Pope.* And in his answere to an Arian, Antithel. 21. col. 879 : *The Bishop of Rome is not that Antichrist whereof is meant 2. Thessal. 2.* And in his Disceptation betwixt two Deuines pag. 637. and respons. ad calumnias pag. 217. he plainly denyeth, that the Pope *is that notable and singular Antichrist, whereof the Fathers speake* And his opinion herein many Protestant vniuersities do iudge probable, namely the vniuersity of Marspurg, Heidelberg, Zurich, & Basle, among which, that of Zurich hath these words : *The 2. Thesis of Antichrist, cannot be reiected as hereticall, seeing it is very probable. For almost all the Fathers are of that mind. Againe: Since malice daily increaseth, nothing letteth but at the last some notable one may come who in impiety surpasseth all the enemies of the Ghospell.* Vorstius also in his Antibellarm. pag 79: *Who discourse more aduisedly of this matter, do graunt that it is very likely, that yet some one shall arise, to whom all the qualities of Antichrist may agree in the highest degree.* What certainty then can Protestants haue out of the foresayd place,

for

for their purpose, sith some of their best learned doe
but doubt, and others deny, that the Pope is that Antichrist, wherof S. Paul speaketh?

5.　　The third argument they wring out of
the 12. Apocal. where it is sayd, that the dragon shall
cause the woman, that is, the Church, to fly into the
wildernesse. This also is a fallacy, not vnlike to the
former. First, because it is more vnknowne that the
Protestant church is the woman, or the true church,
or the Pope that Dragon, or the Popery the desert, hē
that Protestants were heretofor amongst Papists. A-
gaine, there is no speach at all, that the Church shold
be so long tyme and so secret as Protestants say their
church was in Popery. Yea the tyme which this woman was to abide in the wildernesse, is set downe, to
be 1260 dayes, or (as it is sayd cap. 20.) a small tyme.
And as Luther vpon Daniel tom. 4. fol 265. and Bullinger conc. 46 in Apocal. write: *Almost all Doctours at-*
tribute but 3. yeares and halfe to the persecution of Antichrist.
Wherefore these kind of testimonies, by which Protestants make shew to proue that their Church was
heretofore in Popery, are but as S. Augustin speaketh
of the like testimonies vsed by Donatists: *Slender snares* De vnit. c.
of delayes, wherewith you vnderprop an euill cause, by delaying. 19.23.
But we demaund some manifest testimony. Therefore bring out
some manifest, produce some thing that needeth no interpreter, or
if you cannot performe that which so iustly we demaund of you,
belieue truth, hold your peace, sleep a nap, and after waken to sal-
uation.

6.　　Their 4. Sophisme they draw out of reason in this sort: As soone as Protestancy was publikly preached, many came out of Popery, and followed
it. Therefore there were who in Popery did belieue
it. This fallacy is nothing better, then the former. For
　　　　　　　　　　　　　　　　　　　　　　if

if it be reduced to a Syllogisme, it will be found to rely vpon this principle: It any in a company do follow the preaching of a new doctrine, there were some therin, that before tym belieued it; which principle is manifestly false. For neuer any heretiks preached, whome some vnsetled Christians did not follow; and yet who will say that there was neuer any heresy preached which before had not byn belieued of some Christians. Besides Protestants account it for a wonderfull miracle, that at the beginning so many Papists came out of Popery vnto them; but it had byn no shadow of miracle, if before they had byn Protestäts. Moreouer the number of Papists forsaking Popery argueth not, that before tymes they had byn Protestants, but that they were vnsetled Papists, who as the Scripture speaketh, were carryed about with euery wind of doctrine; and that protestancy is a voluptuous and licentius doctrine, because (as Caluin sayth) *deceitfull doctrines do soone bewray themselues, whiles they are admitted of all men with gentle eares, and are heard of the world applauding thereto.*

Epist. Monitor. pag. 107.
Whitak. cont. 2. q. 5. c. 6. Pless de Ecclef. c. 11. Sadeel. Refutat. Posnan. c. 10.

Ephes. 4.

Praef. Inst.

7.   Of all which hath byn sayd in this and the former chapter I frame my fist demonstration in this manner: *If the Protestant Church and Religion were no where before Luther arose, it was not all But before him it was no wher. Therfore not at all.* And by him it got to be some where. Therefore by him it got to be. The minor is manifest by all that hath byn sayd in the former chapter. And the maior is euident by it selfe. For no company of men, much lesse a Catholike or vniuersall Church, can be, and be no where. And these 5. demonstrations which hitherto we haue made, haue byn taken out of the state wherein the protestants confesse their Church to haue byn before Luther arose.

The case of the Protestant Church before Luther.

arose. For by them hath beene shewed, that before him according to the most free, most frequent, and most euident confessions of the famousest Protest- (a) *Cap. 8.*
ants, it had no (a) Pastours to gouerne, no (b) sheep (b) *Cap. 3.*
to be gouerned, no (c) appearance to be seene, no (d) (c) *Cap. 5.*
place to abide, no (e) being to be. What then could (d) *Cap. 9.*
it be but a siction of lying men, or an imagination of (e) *Cap. 1.*
phrantike men, vainely deuised, vntruly auouched,
and soundly belieued.

*That all the Protestants first heard of, had
beene in former tymes Papists .*

CHAP. XI.

T H e 6. demostratio for to proue Luther to haue
bin the Author of Protestacie shall be grounded
vpon that all Protestats who were first heard of had
bin al Papists before Luther began to teach. Of him- Luther
selfe, thus writeth Luther Prefat. in tom. 1. *Before all* before a
things I request the godly reader, that he read all with iudgement, Papist.
and consider that I was once a monck, and a most madde Papist,
when I began this cause; so druncken and drowned in Papistry,
that I was most ready to kill all, if I had bin able, &c. And in
psalm. 45 tom. 3. fol. 441: *I was baptised in the Popes*
house, I was catechised, &c. And in psalm. 51. fol 476:
I wholy liued so in trust of my iustices, as if any had then taught
that which I now teach, I thinck I should haue torne him with
my teeth. And in cap. 1. Galat. tom. 5. fol. 291 : *If*
any at any time, surely I before the light of the gospell, did thinck
piously, and was zealous for Popish lawes and traditions of Fa-
thers, and did in great earnestnes vrge and defend them as holy,
and the obseruation of them as necessary to saluation. I purely

R   *adored*

adored the Pope , and what soeuer I did , I did of a simple heart, a good zeale , and to the glory of God. The authority of the Pope was so great with me, that I iudged it a crime worthy of eternall damnation to dissent from him ; and would haue subministred with fire and sword for the defence of the Popes authority .

2.   Melancthon, who, as Caluin writeth, was a principall Minister of God in doing great matters, and was indeed Luthers chiefest instrument, in his dispute of Matrimony tom. 2. Luther. fol. vlt. giueth

Melan-
cthon first
a Papist .

God thackes, that he was deliuered out of the king-dome of Antichrist and Popish errors; and sayth, as reporteth Scusselburg tom. 13. Catal. Hær. pag. 625. of himselfe: *I moued not these controuersies , but fell into them after they were moued , which being many and not explicated , I began to consider them with a desire of truth* And the Saxonicall Ministers in the Coference of Alburg. Scrip. 7. pag. 349. write that Melancthon of his owne accord acknowledged himselfe a scholler of Luther. yea the

The Vni-
uersity of
Wittem-
berg first
Papist ,

whole Vniuersity of Witterberg, out of which almost al Luthers first champions came, was in former times Popish ; as appeareth by their epistle ad Militi-tium tom. 1. Lutheri fol. 205. where thus they write: *VVe are so affected both to all the Christian Religion and the sea Apostolike and holy Church of Rome , that if we were certaine, that D. Martin Luther were fallen into so foule and impious errours , we first of all would not only yield him vp to the law, but also would punish him and cast him out.* And in their Epistle to Pope Leo 10. ibid. fol. 206. *Most holy Father we deuout and obedient children of your Holynes, do most humbly & earnestly beseech &c.* And below : *Neither would we euer seeme such, as would pertinaciously hold any opinion contrary to the Catholike doctrine, ready at all tymes to obey yours and the holy Churches behests in Christ .* And in another letter to Fredericke the Elector fol. 227. *Aboue all thinges we ex-*
ceedingly

ceedingly like that your highnesse simply and purely honoureth the holy Church and the Pope . Neither wil we euer be of any other mind. VVe *preferre nothing before the iudgment of the Roman Church.* And not only the Vniuersity, but the people of VVittemberg were also Catholiks, as Luther declareth in these wordes, to Fredericke Electortol. 330. *It cannot be denyed that the Reformation of doctrine and religion in this Church (of* VVittemberg *) began by me.*

3. Fredericke also the Elector and Luthers chief Patron was a Papist. For thus himselfe writeth to Cardinall Raphael. tom. 1. Lutheri fol. 228. *Your kindnes God wilting shall neuer see that I haue any other mind or will then to shew my selfe obedient and officious vnto the Catholike Church.* And his Counsailers tom. 2. fol. 116. profesfe that he *is an obedient sonne of the Holy Catholike Church.* And likewise tom. 1. tol. 101. *Fredericke the Elector aboue all loueth the Catholike and Apostolike truth.* Besides (as Luther writeth tom. 7. sermone desimulacris) he put siluer statuaes in the Church, thinking thereby to merir at Gods hands. And tom. 2. lib. de abroganda Missa fol. 268. *He deceaued by Papists, did greatly increase and adorne the house of All Saints.* He founded also a Colledge of Canons, where he kept Masse vntill the end of the yeare 1524. as Chytreus testifieth lib. 11. histor. Saxon. and Luther intimateth in formula Missae tom. 2. fol 387. saying. *Be not you or any other afraid, that in our* VVittemberg *that sacrilegious Tophee remayneth as yet, which is the wicked and lost mony of the Princes of Saxony, I meane the temple of All Saints.*

4. Bugenlage the Pomeran and first Protestant of VVittembrge had beene before a Papist. For as Scultet. concione saecul.pag. 15. reporteth when he first read Luthers booke de captiu. he sayd : *Since the beginning of the world the Sunne neuer beheld a greater heretike then*

Fredetike Elector first Catholke.

Pomeranus.

R2

Osiander.

then *Luther*. Of Osiander thus writteth Danæus responſ. ad Leonicum pag.1518. *He was a moſt wicked Frãciſcan Frier: His proper name was Hoſen, that is hoſe or hoſier, but of hoſier he would be called Hoſion, that is a holy man.*

Zuinglius.

5. The ſame alſo we manifeſt of the Captains of the Sacramentaryes, among whom Zuinglius writeth thus of himſelfe epiſt. ad Fratres tom. 1. fol. 341. *I will not deny, that in tymes paſt I receaued guiſts of the Pope. For then I thought it lawfull to vſe the Popes liberality, when I thought it a pious and godly matter to defend to my ſtrength his Religion and fayth*. And Luther lib. de Cœna writeth that Zuinglius *was become ſeauen tymes worſe, then when he maintayned Popiſh religion*. Likewiſe Oecolampadius

Oecolampadius.

Zuinglius his cheiteſt partener thus witneſſeth of himſelfe reſponſ. poſter. ad Porkeymerum pag. 108 . *I entred into a Monaſtery being of a good age and a man & Doctor, and with mature aduiſe*. To which Hoſpin addeth part. 2. hiſt. fol. 35 . *He entred two yeures before into the Monaſtery of our Sauiour neere to Auſpurge, and there became a Monke, fearing ſome danger of the common wealth by Luthers writings*. And ibidem fol. 42. he ſayth that Pellican

Pelicanus.

was a Franciſcan. And fol. 213. that Bucer became a Dominican in his childhood, of whome alſo and

Bucer.

Peter Martyr D. Andrewes Reſponſ. ad Apol Beilar. ſayth : *They left their monkiſh life*.

6. Of Caluin thus teſtifyeth himſelf lib de ſcandalis pag. 100. *Vnder the Popes tyranny I was free to marry, ſince God deliuered me from thence &c*. And reſponſ. ad Sa-

Caluin.

dolet. pag. 122. *If I would haue prouided for my matters, I ſhould neuer haue left your faction*. In his Teſtament : *God deliuered me from the deep darknes of Idolatry, wherein I was drowned*. And Pareus lib. 2. de amiſſ. grat. cap. 1. *VVhence were Luther and Caluin but of Papiſts ?* The ſame appeareth out of his life writte\n by Beza, where he

ſayth

fayth that he had a benefice in the Cathedral Church
of Noyon, and the cure of a Parish thereby, and that
he was firſt put in mind of Proteſtancy by Robert Peter
Oliuetan. That Peter Martyr was long tyme both Martyr,
Catholike and Canon regular, Simler teſtifyeth in
his life, which alſo he affirmeth of Zanchius ſaying, Zanchius.
that he was one of the 18. companions that forſaking
Popery followed Peter Martyr, who alſo in his preface *de Natura Dei* ſayth that he was 35. yeares of age
when he left Babylon.

7.   Concerning the Lutherans in generall thus Lutherãs
writeth Luther epiſt. ad Erford. fol. 500. *In which* in general
(errour of Antichriſt) *we being all ſtifled enthralled with
a grieuous and miſerable ſlauery, did ſerue the God and Prince
of this world, ſeruing the ſame in ſinnes and all kind of impiety.*
And tom. 4. in cap. 43. Iſaiæ fol. 179. *VVe are accounted
heretikes of the Pope, as who haue deuided our ſelues from that
Church wherein we were baptized and inſtructed.* In cap. 4.
Galat. tom. 5. fol. 377. *VVe old men were brought vp in
that (Popiſh fayth) and haue ſo ſwallowed it, that it hath
entred the moſt inward ſinewes of our harts. And therefore we
forget it with no leſſe paynes, then we learne the true fayth.* Ye
heare how hardly the very firſt Proteſtants could become Proteſtants, & leaue to be Papiſts. And in cap.
11. Geneſ. tom. 6. fol. 129. he thus boaſteth: *VVe are
holy Apoſtataes, for we haue fallen from Antichriſt and the
Church of Satan.* Melancthon likewiſe in cap. 7. Math.
tom. 1. fol. 406. *VVe were heeretofore ſubiect to the Popes
kingdome.* Tom. 2. cont. Suencfeld pag. 200. *VVe departed from the Popes Churches.* Tom. 3. ad Art. Bauar.
fol. 364. *There was neceſſary cauſe, that we ſhould forſake the
Papiſts.* And tom. 4. in Act. VVormat. pag. 403. *VVe
haue iuſt cauſe of departure from the Popiſh congregation, and
with good conſcience we forſooke the conſent of ſo many Nations.*

R 2   Iames

Iames Andrewes cont. Honum pag. 322. *The more aged doe gratefully acknowledge , that they came from you , that is, left you, and your doctrine* . And Schuſſelburg in Epiſt. dedicat. tom. 8. Catal. hærer. hath theſe wordes : *It is behoofull to haue before our eyes the cauſes whereon our conſciences may in the ſtormes of tentations rely, why in this our age Anceſtours would and ought to deuide themſelues from the Roman Church* . Behold how their conſciences were toſſed as with a ſtorme, for that they had forſaken the Roman Church Lobechius alſo diſput. 10. pag. 224. ſayth : *Our Anceſtours did well, that they went out of the Roman Babylon.*

Sacramē-
taryes in
generall. 8. Of Sacramentaryes alſo in generall thus writeth Zuinglius in Præfat. lib. de ver. & falſ. relig. fol. 159. *VVe were alas long tyme ſo beſieged with the iuglings of men* . And Caluin in confeſſ. Fidei pag. 111. *VVe diſſemble not that we alſo were of the number of them (who honour Maſſes) vntill the abuſes of Meſſe were diſcouered* . And 4. Inſtit. cap. 6. §. 6. *VVe departed from the Roman church.* cap. 15. §. 16. *VVe were chriſtened in the Popes kingdome.* Reſponſ. ad Verſipel. pag. 360. *Of our owne accord we went from the table of Popery.* Reſp. ad Sadolet. pag. 122: *That I may not make any long role, this I ſay, there was none of thoſe who were beginners of this cauſe, but might haue beene in better eſtate and condition among you then that he needed therefore to thinke of any new kind of life* . Peter Martyr in locis col 1459. propoſeth this queſtion : *VVhether the Ghoſpellers be Schiſmatikes, becauſe they ſeparated themſelues from the Papiſts* . And col. 1465. concludeth thus: *Seeing there were ſo many and ſo iuſt cauſes of our departure from Popery, our ſeparation ſeemeth to be very laudable & not to be diſliked* . Zanchius tract de Eccleſ. cap. 18. *It is manifeſt that we departed from the Church or rather from the ſect of the Pope. And this we willingly confeſſe* . Bullenger tom. 1. decad. 5.

ſerm.

ſerm. 2. fol. 282. *VVe willingly confeſſe that we went from the Roman Church.* Muſculus in locis tit. de Schiſmate p. 620. *VVe are termed Apoſtataes of the Romaniſts, as many haue forſaken the Communion of the Roman Church. This we are ſo farre from denying as we thinke that we ſhould rather glory theereof.* Pleſſie de Ecclef. cap 11. pag. 361. writeth that *Luther, Zuinglius, Oecolampadius, Bucer, Capito, Martyr and others out of whoſe ſchoole ſayth he the Miniſters who gathered the Church from Antichriſt did come were Prieſts, Curats, Doctours of diuinity &c*, To whome Beza. lib. de Notis pag. 8. adioyneth Pellican and Haller and others more. D. Whitaker lib. 9. cont. Duræum ſayth: *Luther was a Prieſt according to your order, and ſuch were Zuinglius, Bucer, Oecolampadious and others without number.* M. Perkins in cap. 4. Galat. v. 26: *All the firſt renewers of the Ghoſpell were either Prieſts or teachers of Schooles.* Paræus lib. cit: *Are we worthy of blame or heretikes becauſe we left the Popes Church?* And in the end of his booke de Iuſticatione: *Our Anceſtours 97. yeares ago had neceſſary cauſe for to forſake Popery.* And Sculter. in concione ſæculari pag. 4. *This is the hundreth yeare ſince God pluckt our Anceſtors out of Popiſh darknes.* Finally Polanus in præfat. Theſ. de Eccleſ: *VVe haue ſeparated our ſelues from the falſe Catholike Synagogue.*

9. The ſame alſo is manifeſt of the Engliſh Proteſtants by their owne wordes. For thus they ſpeake in their Apology part. 5. cap. 12. diuiſ. 1. *It is true we haue departed from them.* Item: *True it is we were brought vp with theſe men in darkreſſe and in the lacke of the knowledge of God.* And part. 6. cap. 20. diuiſ. 2. *As for vs truly we haue fallen from the Biſhop of Rome.* Cauſabon alſo Epiſt. ad Card. Peron cap. 16. *The king confeſſeth, that his church hath forſaken no few points of that ſayth and diſcipline, which at this day the Roman Church doth profeſſe.* And pag.

17. *The English haue gone from that* Church *.* M . Hooker lib. 4. de Polit. Ecclei. pag. 181 . *VVe were a part of the* m. M. Powel. lib. 1. de Antichriſto cap 21. *VVe confeſſe we haue ſeparated our ſelues from the Biſhop of Rome, and his Synagogue .* M . Perkins in cap. 5 . Galat. verſ. 21. *VVe haue ſeparated our ſelues from the* Roman Church *.* D . Whitaker cont. 2. queſt 6 . cap. 3 . ſayth: *The Roman Church was iuſtly left of vs.* And D . Morton part. 2. Apol. lib. 2. cap. 10. *The former booke tould a iuſt cauſe of our ſeparation from you .* In like manner thoſe of Zurich in Sleidan lib. 4. hiſtor. ſay : *After the riſing of the Goſpell we haue caſt of that burden which the Pope had put vp̄ vs idiots.* And adde withal that *before they had heard nothing of Pro-*

Suitzers . *teſtancy.* And the Suitzers in their confeſſ. cap. 17. confeſſe that their Churches had parted themſelues from the Roman Church . And the Scotsin their

Polonians confeſſ. write that *the truth was lately borne amongſt them.* And the Polonians in their conſent, that *God hath deliuered their Churches out of the groſſe darcknes of Popery .*

The whole Proteſt. Church .   10. Furthermore of the whole Proteſtant church or of Proteſtants in general, thus they write. Lobechius diſp. 12. pag. 254. *Our confeſſion (of* Auſburg *was the belieſe of the whole orthodoxall Church gone out of* Roman Babylon *.* And in like ſort ſpeaketh Daneus de Antichriſto cap. 17. Pareus Proæm. l. de Iuſtificat. *The Euangelicall Church was compelled aboue* 96. *yeares ago to make a diuiſion from the Popiſh Church .* The like he hath lib. 2. cap. 1. & lib. 3 . cap. 8. Schuſſelburg tom . 8. catal. pag. 727. *Our Church departed from the Church of the malignant .* Polanus part. 2. Epiſt. ad Bezam . *The reſormed Churches did well that they did ſeparate themſelues from the Popiſh Church .* Aretius in loc. part 2. fol. 10. *Our reſormed Churches departed from Popery.* D . Andrewes reſponſ. ad Apoll. Bellarm. cap. 14. boaſteth that *almoſt halfe of the*
Chriſtian

Christian world is gone out of the Roman Babylon . And D . Whitaker cont. 2. queſt. 3. cap. 3. ſayth: *England, Germany, Scotland long agoe haue fallen from the Pope .* And the Engliſh Apology glorieth in this ſort, part. I. cap. I. diuiſ. 3. *For they be not all made at this day ſo many free citties ſo many Kings, ſo many Princes which haue fallen away from the ſeat of Rome.* Daneus cont. 4. lib. 4. cap. 12 . *All Scotland, England, Saxony, Denmarke, a great part of Germany, all Suitzerland, the greater part of the Griſons haue fallen from the Church of Rome.* D . Sutliue lib. 2. de Eccleſ. cap. 2. p . 251. *Our Church hauing ſhaken off the filth of the Roman church is returned to the Catholike ſayth.* And pag. 254. *England, Scotland, Ireland, Denmarke, Norwey, Saxony, Pomerania & the chieſeſt parts of Germany , France, Flandres, Poland haue fallen from the Pope.* Moalins lib. de . fug. Arnoldi cap. 2. *Our Churches be called reformed, becauſe they be Chriſtian Churches purged from Popery.* D . Rainolds amongſt his concluſions putteth this for the ſixt : *That the reformed Churches in England, Scotland, France , Germany, and other kingdomes and Common wealths haue iuſtly ſeparated themſelues from the Roman.* And addeth with all that, *All reformed Churches haue departed from the Roman Church .* Brentius in his Apology for the confeſ. of Wittemberg pag. 873. ſpeaking of Proteſtants ſayth : *VVe alſo once were all fooles ſeduced and ſeducing and ſeruing idolatry and Antichriſt .* Serauia defenſ. lib. de Grad. Miniſt . cap. 2 . pag. 33. *I marke that the Authours of all Reformations which were made in our age were Prieſts of the Roman Church.* To al which I adioyne that Luther in cap. 2. Oſex. tom. 4. fol. 279. ſayth that theſe be the ſpeeches of Papiſts. *VVere yee not Chriſtned in the Popes Church ? VVhy therfore go yee from her?* And he acknowledgeth that the Roman Church is their Mother , but ſayth that they haue left her, becauſe ſhe is a harlot and an adultereſſe .

R 5　　　　　　　　And

And Scrauia de diuerf. Minift. grad. cap. 6. pag. 30.
hath thefe wordes: *The Roman Church is our Mother in
which and by which God regenerated vs ; but becaufe she is a
harlot and an adultereffe , we tuftly conteft againft her.* The
like hath Iunius lib. fingulari de Ecclef. cap. 17.
and others commonly. So that they acknowledge
themfelues to be the children of an harlot, and confequently baftardes, & not begotten of God, becaufe
God begetteth not children of harlots , but only of
his chaft fpoufe the Church. Let them therfore heare
the Romá Church fpeaking to them in thefe words
of S. Hierome: *If an Angel or Apoftle haue rebaptifed thee I*

*breake not that which thou followeft. But if thou borne in my
lappe , nourished with the milke of my breafts . doeft draw thy
fword againft me , reftore what I gaue thee , and be if thou
canft, a Chriftian by other meanes: I am a harlot but yet thy mother : I keep not chaftity to one hufband , fuch I was when thou
wert begotten.* Or els let them harken to S. Athanafi-
us : *It remayneth that they find fault with the bafeneffe of their*

*ftock, and fay that they came not of pious , but of heretikes , nei-
ther feare they that which is written in the Prouerbs, An ill brood
curfeth their father .* Or elfe let them giue care to S .Au-
guftin thus fpeaking to the Manichees : *doe fo flaues of*

Cham. Get you gon who defpife the naked flesh wherof you fprung.
Againe : *Yea thou often maryed to elements or rather harlot
proftitute to deuils and great with facrilegious vanities dareft thou
reuile Catholike maryage of thy Lord with the crime of vnchafti-
ty.* But omitting this, becaufe Proteftants regard not,
how farre they difgrace themfelues, fo that they reuile the Church of Rome; out of that which we haue
rehearfed in this Chapter , it appeareth how impudently D. Morton 1. part Apol. lib. 1. cap. 10: wrote
that Melancthon, Pellican, and others were Proteftants before Luther arofe, and much more impudently

dently D. Feildiayd lib. 3. deEcclei. cap. 8 : that before Luthers time thole who defended the Popiſh
errors, were but ſome faction like to thoſe in the
Church of Corinth, who in S. Paules time denyed
the Reſurrection : which vntruth is ſo apparant,
as to haue related it only, is to haue confuted it. But
hereby the Reader ſeeth how needfull it is for me to
heap vp many teſtimóies of Proteſtants, for to proue
euen thoſe things which are moſt manifeſt.

11. My ſixt demonſtration therfore I frame in
this manner : *If all Proteſtants who were firſt knowne , whe-*
ther people or perticuler perſós, were Papiſts before Luther began
to preach , then were there no Proteſtants before him , and he
author of their Church : But all the firſt knowne Proteſtants
were ſuch. Ergo. The Maior is manifeſt by it ſelfe, &
the Mimor oy that which hath bin recited in this
chapter.

That no Proteſtant ancienter then Luther did
come forth and adioyne himſelfe to his com-
pany when Luther ſafely preached.

CHAP. XII.

THE ſeauenth demonſtratió for to proue Luther
to be the firſt Beginner of Proteſtancy, ſhall be
taken from thence, that after that Luther ſecurely
preached Proteſtancy, no Proteſtant ancienter then
he peeped out, and adioyned himſelfe vnto him.
This I proue : firſt out of the reall Confeſſion of all
Proteſtants, who neither then, nor hitherto could
name one ſuch Proteſtant. Whereupon it followeth
neceſſarily, that Luthers company was altogether
new,

new, & no one member thereof before him: neither
did he adioyne those whome de drew out of Popery
vnto any company before extant; neither did any
company which had bin before, adioyne it selfe
vnto him. Secondly this may be proued by the silence of D. Whitaker Cont. 2. quest. 5. cap. 3. where
being vrged with this argument, he answeareth it
with silence only, and standeth mute, as confessing
the accusation to be true. Thirdly I proue it by the
sillinesse of the Answeares of other. Iunius lib. 4.
de Eccles. cap. 5. sayth only, that some ancienter
Protestants came forth, and adioyned themselues to
Luther, but nameth none, nor proueth any thing;
& therfore giueth words & nought else. He should,
as Tertullian said to old heretikes, *haue feignes the na-*

Præscrip. *mes of some. For after blasphemy what may not they doe?* But I
c. 32. know not how it cometh to passe, that wheras Protestants feigne many things and persons, yet they
dare not feigne names. As D. Sutline, when in the
Preface of his book of the Church he had sayd only,
that Bollec (who wrote Caluins life) doth insinuate
that he wrote for hire; after growing more bould
in his answeare to exceptions cap. 4. pag 120 deui-

D. Sutcli- seth a synode, in which (as he sayth) *Bollec publikely re-*
ue feig- *canted the book which he had writtē of Caluins life.* Of which
neth a Sy- Synode none before him euer heard, but since D.
nod. Morton and M. Beard write that they haue heard of
it, perhaps by D. Sutliue, but yet durst not feigne
1. part. A- the names either of the men who held this synode,
pol. lib. 2. or of the place where it was held, nor yet specifie the
cap. 33. yeare of our Lord when it was held. This he left to
Beard Mo- others to feigne, or to himselfe at more leasure
tiue. 12.

    2. Fourthly it may be proued by the ridiculous
nomination and prouing made by some. D. Morton
part.

part. Apol. lib. 1. cap. 16. writeth that Melancthon, Pellican, Lambert, Capito, Osiander, Sturmius, Bucer came forth, which he proueth becaufe
Alphonse a Caftro in the epiftle dedicatory of his
booke againft herefies hath thefe words; *Neither did
Luther in this age come forth alone, but accompanyed with a
great troupe as with a guard*, and nameth thofe before
cited. But firft it is ridiculous to fay, that the forefayd perfons were Proteftants before Luther, fith
partly themfelues, partly Proteftants deny it, as we
fhewed in the former chapter. Againe, it is ridiculous to proue this by Caftroes teftimony, who being
a Spaniard, and thofe all Germans except Lambert
who was a French mã, it is moft likely that he neuer
knew thē nor heard of their names before Luther had
reuolted. Moreouer ridiculous it is, to imagin that in
the forecited words Caftro fhould fay, that the fornamed perfons did come forth in fuch fort as we
mean, that is, came out of the proteftãt lurking holes,
or to haue bin fecret Proteftãts before Luther appeared; feeing he only faith, that they came forth in fuch
fort as he faith Luther came forth, to wit forth of the
Catholik church & of Catholiks became heretiks.

3. Fiftly I proue it out of the common doctrine
of Proteftants, wherin they teach that euery one
ought to adioyne himfelfe to the vifible Church if
fo he can conueniently. For fo teacheth the Confeffion of the low countryes art. 28. the French art. 26.
Melancthon in cap. 8. Matth. Caluin 4. Inftitut. cap.
1. D whitaker Cont. 2. queft .3 cap. 2 and others
commonly. But thefe former Proteftants (if any
fuch had bin) might conueniétly haue ioyned themfelues to Luthers cõpany after that they faw him to
preach fecurely and out of danger. Seeing therfore,
no

no such came to him, it is manifest that there were no such at all. Finally this is manifest otherwise. For suppose, that before Luther they lay so close, as that they worshipped God only in hart and soule, yet when rhey saw Protestancy to be preached publiquely and securely, and that they might liue openly and amongst men, who will imagine, that they would preferre darcknes before light, and lurking holes before townes and citties, and alwayes keep in deserts? Certaidly such kind of fellowes should be rather batts or owles, then men. Besides being iust men, forsooth, why did they not afford God externall worship whē they might securely doe it? Why did they not according to Christs commandement celebrate the memory of his Passion by receiuing of the Sacraments?

4.   Out of these I compose the seauenth demonstration: *If after that Luther securely preached Protestancy, neuer any ancienter Protestant came forth and adioyned himselfe to his company, there were no Protestants before. But no such euer came forth. Ergo.* But if there were no Protestant before Luther, vndoubtedly he was the beginner of that company.

That the Protestant Church, and Religion is new.

CHAP. XIII.

THE eighth demonstration with which we will proue, that Luther was the beginner of the Protestant Church and religion, we will frame out of Protestāts Confessions of the nouelty therof. First therefore therfore they say, that in the iudgment almost of all men it is new, and that it is almost impossible, to wipe away from it the spot of noueltie. Thus Illyricus in the Preface of his Catalogue : *VVhen Doctours rayfed of God preach the (Proteftant) gospell and doe inueigh against contrary errors, they feeme in the iudgement almost of all men to bring a new doctrine vnheard of before and to impugne the old.* Againe: *It is very hard and almost impossible to remoue the hatefull marck of nouelty from the (Proteftant) doctrine.* To which D. Fulke lib. de Succeff. pag. 454.addeth, that the Proteftant religion,*VV as altogether new to most nations.*

2. Secondly in equiualent words they oftentymes call their Religion new or begun of new. For as we fhal ftraight rehearse they terme it *in the blade, renafcent, reuiuing, borne a new, renewed, repayred, reftored, rayfed againe, refufcitated.* And what can be meant by thefe termes, but a religion either new or newly erecteth, fuch as Chrifts religion is not? For neither is it new in it felfe, neither can it be begun or rayfed anew, becaufe it can neuer fall. Luther in cap.22.Genef. tom. fol. 208. writeth thus : *In the beginning of the gospell borne a new, Monetarius &c..* In cap. 31. fol. 434: *Nine affemblies haue beene held since the Ghofpell began to be borne a new.* In cap. 32. fol. 458 *After the light of the Ghofpell was borne againe.* In cap. 48. fol. 643. *At the beginning of the Ghofpell rising againe.* In cap. 49. fol. 662. *They defire to extinguish the light of the Ghofpell rising againe.* In cap. fol. 342. *I remember that before thefe tymes of the Ghofpell borne a new.* And in the Praefat. Deuter. tom. 3. Ienen.fol. 75. *The rising againe or rather springing Ghofpell.* Thus fpeaketh Luther. Melancthon Apol. pro Luthero tom. 2. Lutheri fol. 194. *You oppose against the rising light of the Ghofpell.* And refponf. ad Clerum Colon. tom.2. pag. 97.

The

The beginning of the pure doctrine rising againe . And in cap ᷒

renewed. 7 Matth. tom. 1. fol 398 : He termeth *it renewed doctrine.*
Carion in Chron . pag . 706 . calleth their Church
the renascent Church . Iuftus Ionas Epift. dedicat . lib.
Lutheri de Iudæis tom. 7. fol. 166. *God would that in our
time the Gofpel should be borne againe vnder the house of Saxony.*

reuining. Befoldus in his Preface of the 4. part of Luthers Có-
métarie vpon Genef. hath thefe words: *In the begining
of the Church borne anew.* O fiander in his Manual engli-
fhed pag. 62 : *Our doctrine is renewed* . And his fonne
Lucas Epift. Euchar: *The doctrine of the gofpel borne againe.*

Chriftia- The author of the Sponge in Daneus pag. 13. calleth
nity it *the light of the Ghofpell borne againe, the Euangelicall doctrin*
greene . *reuiuing or quickning againe.* Kemnice in locis part. 2. p.
106. *In the beginning of the Ghofpell borne againe.* Amongft
the Sacramentaryes Zuinglius fpeaketh thus in fup-
plicat. ad Suithenfes fol 121 : *Chriftianity being greene,
chriftianity rifing againe.* And in Ecclef· fol. 41. *New born
truth* . Which phrafe he repeateth difput. tom. 2. fol.
607. Gefnerus in Bibliotheca fayth of Luther: *The*

Recalled *new borne Church doth owe much vnto him* . Mufcle Epift.
Ghofpell. dedicat. locorum. *I was in the beginning of the new rifing E-
uangelicall truth.* Bucer in Retract . pag. 642 . viewh.

beginning thefe words: *Among the Minifters of the recalled Ghofpell.*
of the Beza in cap 3. Rom. v. 20 . *They by whofe Miniftery God*
new born *in our age hath recalled to light Chrifts Ghofpell almoft buryed* .
Ghofpell. Gualter. Præfat. in Rom . *How much harme the Anabaptifts did at the beginning of the new borne Ghofpell* . Martyr in

Quick- locis tom. 2 . pag. 228 . *In the beginning of the Ghofpell*
ning a- *born againe.* And in Epift. dedicat. comment. ad Rom.
gaine. *The Ghofpell quickning againe.* Hofpin. Epift. dedicat. 1.
part. hiftor. *The Euangelicall truth borne againe.* Sohinus
in Methodo Theol. pag. 215. *Among the Doctours of the
Church borne againe.* And Caluin 4. Inftitut. cap. 7. §.
24. *The*

24. *The doctrine of the Ghoſpell borne againe*. lib. de ſcand. pag. 76. & 94. *The ghoſpell borne againe*. Admonit. 2. ad Weſtphalum pag. 784. *The Ghoſpell is borne againe*. And cont. Seruetum pag. 592 : *Of the Ghoſpell borne againe*. And in like manner he ſpeaketh ordinarily . Sadel reſpo. ad Arthurum cap. 7 . *The Church borne againe* . Paræus in Miſcellan. Vrſini pag. 26. *The light of the Ghoſpell borne againe* . Danæus reſpon. ad Solnec. pag. 1565: *In the very beginning of the Ghoſpell borne againe*. pleſ-ſie de Eccleſ. cap. 11: *Chriſt borne againe*. Cambden in apparatu Annalium : *The riſing religion of Proteſtants* . V-Chriſt ſher de Succeſſ. cap. 8. *In the beginning of the Ghoſpell born* againe . Scult. in Præfat. 4. partis Medullæ : *Thou wert in the floure of the Church borne againe*. Moreouer Luther tom. 1. in diſ. fol. 410. calleth his doctrine, *A doctrine repayred in this age*. And Præfat. ad Galat. tom. 5. fol. 270. ſayth: *In theſe later tymes the holeſome knowledge of Chriſt was againe reſuſcitated* Iames Andrewes lib.cont. Hoſium pag. 1 *The Lord by the Miniſtery of Luther hath re-ſuſcitated the doctrine of the Ghoſpell*. And pag. 349 : *Among our men after the doctrine of the Ghoſpell was reſuſcitated*. Ké-nice Præfat. in lib. de vnione hypoſtat : *It is now three ſcore yeares ſince the ancient ſerpent raiſed againe the hereſy of Berengarius for to oppreſſe as they ſay in the blade the doctrine of the Ghoſpell then firſt reſtored by Luthers Miniſtery*. Caluin l. de Cœna cap. 10 : *This controuerſie began betweene them, who were the chiefeſt captaines in reſtoring the doctrine of the ghoſpell, and bringing it backe as it were when it was loſt*. Lib. de libero arbit. pag. 147. *The purity of the Ghoſpell was re-ſtored by Luthers labour eſpecially*. Et epiſt. ad Ducem So-merſeti : *God would haue me to be one of thoſe by whoſe labour he reſtored this tyme the ſincere doctrine of the Ghoſpell* Da-næus in method. ſcripturæ pag. 400: *There are 54 years paſt ſince that tyme that the pure light and doctrine of the Ghoſ-*

borne a-gaine.

In the floure of the Church.

Repaired.

Reſuſcita-ted.

Ghoſpell in the blade.

Reſtored.

S   *pell*

pell *was first restored to the world.* Apol. Ecclef. Angl. part.
pag. 64. *It is no new thing though at this day the religion of
Christ be entertained with despits and cheks being but lately
restored and as it were comming vp againe a new.* Ibid. cap.
17. *Our desire was to haue the temple of the Lord restored a new.*
Iezler de bello Euchar. fol. 72 : *Euen from the beginning
of the restored Euangelicall light.* M. Bancroft in his Suruey cap. 8. *In this later age of the world it hath pleased God to
restore vs the light of the Ghospell.* And M. Alenson in præf.
contro. 4. Whitakeri : *After the restauration of the Ghospell.*
And many more (as we see in the chapter following)
call their ghospell *restored Religion*. By which it may
appeare that D. Andrewes Responf. ad Apol. Bellarm. cap. 1 did vntruly deny, that their men call
their fayth a *restored fayth*. But whiles he denyeth
that their men termeth it so, he clearely sheweth,
what those meane who terme it so, to wit, that they
meane *a religion borne or framed a new*, according to the
very substance thereof. And in truth what els could
they meane by so many termes and so often repea-
ted *of a religion greene in the blade, borne againe, rising a-
gaine, resuscitated, renewing, reuiuing, recalled, repaired,
brought backe againe, restored,* but a religion substantiall
produced, inftituted and founded a new.

    3.   Thirdly this is proued, becaufe they write,
that in the tyme of Luther, of Melancthon, of Zuinglius, of the Anabaptists and such others, was *the beginning, the very beginning, the first beginning, the originall, the
entrance, the cradle, the dawning, the new rifing* of their
Church and religion, as appeareth in the aforefayd
teftimouies of Luther, Melancthon, Befoldus, Kem-
nicius, Musculus, Gualter, Peter Martyr, Danæus,
Vfferius, Gezler. And befides, Luther in cap. 3. Genef. tom. 6. fol. 33. hath thefe words : *In the beginning*
                                       of

of the Ghoſpell, *Caroloſtadius &c.* Georgius Fabritius lib.
8. Orig. Saxon. pag. 13. *God would that true and beleſome
doctrine ſhould haue her beginning in the vniuerſity of* VVittem-
berg. Caluin epiſt. ad Montisbelgardenſes col. 590.
edit. 1617: *In this our age the ghoſpel did flow out of the church
of* VVittemberg. Brentius Præfat. lib. Andreæ contra
Hoſium : *Did not we all in the beginning of the reuealed ghoſpell with one mouth diſproue your Popiſh impietyes?* And in
Recognit. pag. 327: *They cannot deny, that, euen from the
beginning of the reborne ghoſpell, the Zuinglians &c.* And l.de
Maieſt·Chriſti pag. 109: *Euen from the beginning of the reuealed ghoſpell, Melancthon &c.* Wittebergenſes in Reſut.
Orthodoxi conſenſu: pag. 22. *Luther recated ſome things
which in the beginning of the reborne doctrine of the ghoſpell he
graunted to the Papiſts.* Lobechius diſput. 12. *Straight after the beginning of the ſhining truth, in the yeare* 1520. *&c.*
Pappus defenſ. 1 cont. Sturmium pag. 19. *Thou ſaydſt
that there were no ſuch Theſes publiſhed ſince the beginning of religion. I ſhew thee the contrary that Luther and Philip held the
ſame.* Sleidan præfat. hiſtor: *The beginning (of Proteſtancy) was ſlender and almoſt contemptible, and one only* (Luther)
bore the brunt of all the world. Zanchius lib. de perſeue-
rat. 192: *In the beginning of the Ghoſpell the ſect of Anabaptiſts
aroſe.* Caluin epiſt. 63 *If in the firſt beginning of the church
riſing againe, this example of tyranny doth now peep , what will
be ſhortly?* And epiſt. 178 : *In the beginning of the ghoſpell
borne againe.* Epiſt. 269. *The beginnings of the kingdome of
Chriſt euery where in our ages were almoſt baſe and contemptible.* Reſponſ. ad Sadolet p. 133: *After the new riſing of
the ghoſpell.* Pleſſie de Eccleſ. cap. 11. VV*hat ſhall we thinke
that the new ſtarre anno* 1572.*)did ſignify but the new birth of
Chriſt on earth by preaching of the word.* And he addeth
that as Chriſt firſt borne put the Idols oracles to ſi-
lence, ſo borne againe he hath made the Popiſh mi-

*Proteſtã-
cy had its
beginning
in Witté-
berg.*

*Anabap-
tiſts in the
beginning
of Prote-
ſtãtiſme.*

*New ry-
ſing.*

*New
birth.*

racles

racles to vanish. Scultete part. 1. Medullæ in Irenæo

The dawning. cap. 9. *In this age the dawning of the Euangelicall truth hath shined a new vnto vs.* Zuinglius lib. de Prouid . tom. 2.
fol. 352: *The Lantgraue laboureth that the infancy of Religion*

The infācy. *be piously nourished .* And Gelner in Bibliotheca layth: *Luther did happily set forward the infancy of Religion.* The Alogy of the Church of England part. 2. c. 2. diuil. 1.
writeth, that Anabaptists, and Libertynes *haue beene stirring in the world euer since the ghospell did first spring .* M. Powel de Antichristo c. 32 . *How many wars haue beene since the light of the ghospell arose, the Heluetian, the Protestant warre &c.* Vsterius l. de Succest. Eccl. c. 8. *At the beginning of the ghospall borne againe,* Thomas Bilney &c. M. Bale cont. 8. cap. 68. speaking of the beginning of protestancy,

Second birth. calleth it, *The rising of the new Hierusalem .* Horne in his harbour, *The second birth of Christ.* And Brocard in cap. 2. Apocal: *the second comming of Christ .* But surely if the yeare

Second comming 1520. *were straight after the beginning of Protestancy:* If Luther, Melancthon, Zuinglius, the Anabaptists, and such like were from the beginning, at the beginning, and straight after the Rising of Protestancy: If the dissention amongst Protestants, were in the first beginning of their Church : If finally Protestant doctrine had its beginning in the Church of Wittemberge & flowed from thence, without doubt it is a new doctrine and Church, which either had neuer been before, or was newly founded and restored. Besides what other thing can signify *The new rising, the new birth, the second comming of Christ,* but another substantiall beginning and repayring of Christs religion and Church after it had been quit ouerthrowne. The same also they insinuate, when they say, that the light of the ghospell was in their tyme new kindled, or lightned a-

Kindled againe. gaine. Luther tom. 2. fol. 305. alias 307 . *God in this last tyme hath kindled againe the light of the ghospell.* And in
cap.

cap. 17. Genef. tom. 6. fol. 210. *He hath kindled againe for vs the light of the Ghoſpell.* Melancthon in cap. 11. Dan. tom. 2. fol. 314. *God hath againe kindled for vs the light of the ghoſpell,* which againe he repeateth in his common places tit. de gratia. The ſame hath Vitus Theodorus Præfat. Comment. Luth. in Pſalm. Kemnitius in locis tit. de Iuſtificat. pag. 109. 247. The Electot in Edicto de lib. concord. & Zuinglius Præfat. Elench. tom. 2. fol. 5. ſayth: *Chriſt hath lighted againe in our tyme the lanterne of his word .* Wherefore falſly doth Boyſſeul in confutat. Spondæi pag. 25. deny, that their men ſay they kindle a new the doctrine of ſaluation . But (as before I ſayd of D. Andrewes) Boyſſeul by denying that their men ſay they kindle againe the doctrin ſheweth vs, that thoſe who indeed ſay ſo, do meane of a ſubſtantiall production of light , as in truth the word kindling doth ſignify .

4. Fourthly I proue the nouelty of the Proteſtant Church and religion , becauſe they doe ſometymes in plaine termes call it *new , freſh, vnuſed, vnacuſtomed newly planted, altogeather new, and newly erected .* Luther Præfat. formulæ Miſſæ tom. 2. fol. 284. *I was alwayes ſlow and fearefull for the weaklings in fayth from whome could not ſuddenly be taken ſo old and intured, nor ingrafted ſo freſh & vnaccuſtomed manner of ſeruing God.* In Pſalm. 45. tom. 3. fol. 439. he ſayth: *Neither was there euer any new word reuealed without miracles.* Which after he had proued by the example of Abraham, Moyſes and Chriſt, he addeth : *So we alſo haue our Miracles .* And in cap. 19. Gen. tom. 6. fol. 278. he ſayth , that Papiſts do ſore vrge them ſaying : *Your doctrine is new and vnknowne to our forefathers,* which he anſwearing, denyeth not that his doctrine is new, but rather granteth it, ſaying: *VVhat belongeth it to vs what God hath iudged of thoſe who dyed heeretofore .*

Freſh and and vnac-cuſto-med.

S 3

rofore. Now the word is preached vnto vs, we must not be Inquirers who aske God why he hath reuealed his doctrine at this tyme and not in former ages. And in cap. 12. fol. 148. he writeth in these words: Heere surely Abraham doth shew no small trouble of conscience which euen in his banishment is wounded with this dart, to thinke in this sort: Looke to it, Thou art all alone a stranger, wheresoeuer thou goest thou carryest with thee a new and strange religion. Art thou alone holy? hath God care of thee only, and hath he cast off so many people and nations? The like (sayth Luther) we also suffer when our aduersaryes with open mouth demand of vs, Are all who went before vs, and followed the Popes religion damned? Yee see how plainly he intimateth his trouble of conscience about the newnesse and strangenes of his religion. And in Appendice confess. in Hospin. part. 2. fol. 188. he sayth:

Seemed very new to the whole world. Because our doctrine seemed at that tyme very new and wonderfull scandalous to the whole world, it behoued me to deale moderatly. And in the Epitaphe of his tombe is engrauen this verse:

A new light of the Ghospell he spred throughout the world.

Melancthon Præfat. in tom. 2. Lutheri thus speaketh of him: He did so illustrate these writings, that after a long & **New in the iudgement of al wise men.** darcke night there seemed to the iudgment of all pious and prudent men to arise a new light of doctrine. The vniuersity of Wittembrg in Sentent. de Missa in Luthero tom. 2. fol. 349. writeth that the abolishing of priuate Comunion: Is in this tyme a thing altogeather new, As Luther ibidem fol 285. sayth that Communion vnder both kinds, is a rite ouer new. Spalatine whome Protestāts account a very graue man in his relation of the Con- **Neuer such a cō-fession.** fession of Auspurg sayth: Such a confession was neuer made not only a thousand yeares agoe, but not since the beginning of the world, neither in any history nor in any ancient Father or Doctor is such a Confession to be heard of. Huber in Antibellar-
minum

minum libro 4. capite . 3. *Our Church hath a new forme not vſed at that tyme when the Pope had all.* Wittembergenſes in Prefat : Refutat. Orthodoxi Conſenſus call the Proteſtant Church lately planted, and as yet tender. George Fabritius libro 7. Orig. Saxon. pag. 858. ſpeaking of proteſtancy ſayth: *Duke George was greatly againſt this new doctrine , who was deceiued by the anetenter vſe of his forefathers.* And lib. 8 pag. 21. writeth that euen the Prince Electour himſelfe at the firſt did not much defend Luthers reformatiō *as being new .* And Freſchelius Archdeacon of Wittemberg Preface in Comment Melancthonis in Math. calleth the Proteſtants company according to the age therof *a Childiſh camp .* In like ſort doe the Sacramentaries ſpeake, for thus Zuinglius Pareneſ ad ciuitatem Suithenſem tom . 1. fol. 110. *Firſt of all in humble manner we entreat this , that our cauſe doe not ſeeme to you abſurd by reaſon of the newneſſe therof.* And in Supplicat. ad Suithenſes he doth almoſt openly confeſſe that *he goeth about to giue men new precepts and lawes* And thoſe of Zurich in Sleidan lib. 4. write that *their miniſters doe teach them now fiue yeares,* and that at the begining this kind of doctrine ſeemed new, becauſe they had neuer heard any ſuch thing before. Sadeel de vocat. pag. 543: *Godhath brought into light the reborne Church as a youngling,* and pag. 555. that he hath layd a new foundation of the Church, and erected againe the Church. Caluin Reſpons. ad Sadolet pag. 131. maketh a man ſpeake thus to God in defence of his becomming a Proteſtant: *I being offended at the nouelty , did hardly giue eare vnto it.* Baſtingius epiſt. dedicat. Catechiſ : *It ſeemed good to God in our time to erect his Church a new .* Beza in Confeſſ cap. 4 ſect. 49: *God would preſerue the reliques of his Church in Poperie till he had erected it againe.* The Apologie of the Engliſh Church part. 4. cap. 4. Diuiſ. 2:

Lately planted.

New doctrine.

A childiſh campe.

Seemed new.

A new foundation.

Erected a new.

Erected againe.

S 4

forty

Forty yeares agoe and vpward it was an eaſy thing for them to deuiſe againſt vs theſe accurſed ſpeeches and others too, when in the midſt of the darckneſſe of that age it firſt began to ſpring and to giue ſhine ſome one glimmering beame of truth vnknowne at that time and vnheard of, when as yet the thing was but new & the ſucceſſe therof vncertaine, and when there could be imagined againſt vs no fact ſo deteſtable but that the people then would ſoon beleiue it for the nouelty and ſtraungeneſſe of the matter. Ibid. diuiſ. 1: *How often haue they ſet on fire Princes houſes to the end they might quench the light of the goſpell in the very firſt appearing of it.* M. Fox in his Acts ſet forth anno 1610. pag 788. writing what paſſed anno 1523 ſpeaketh

But in the blade.

thus: *Then the doctrine of Luther firſt beginning to ſpring and being but in the blade, was not yet knowne wherto it tended, nor to what it would grow.* D. Rainolds in his Conference cap. 5. ſect. 2. ſayth that Proteſtants *haue not had long tract of time.* And a late Chronicler, thought to be M. Goodwin writing the life of K. Henry 8. 1521. ſayth: *In the meane time our king moued at the nouelty of Luthers doctrine* &c. To all which I adde, that Eraſmus (whome Proteſtants as is before ſhewed doe challenge as one of theirs) writeth thus to the Brethren of the low coûtreis: *do not they bring a new Goſpel,*

New Ghoſpell.

who expound it otherwiſe then the Church hitherto hath don? But Why I pray you ſhould the Proteſtants religion ſeeme new to all the world, and in the iudgement of all pious and prudent men, if indeed it were not new? How ſhould ſo many, ſo famous Proteſtants, ſo often, and in ſo many different kinds of writings, to wit in proſe, in verſe, in peaceable, in contentious writings, in Hiſtoricall, in dogmaticall, in ſpeech to men & to God himſelfe haue ſayd ſo plainly and ſo many wayes, that Proteſtant religion was *new, freſh, vnwonted, vnuſed, wholy new, newly planted, & erected*

erected anew if they had not thought that it was in-deed new . For as Luther fayth : *It is impoffible but that the confcience will fome time betwray it felfe* .

5.   If any anfweare that the fore fayd Proteftants doe not meane , that their religion was abfolutely new . Firft I aske , why then doe they abfolutely fay fo , and that fo often and in fo many kind of wri-tings ? Why do they fo often and in fo weighty a matter write otherwife then they think ? Befides , it cannot be proued , that they did not meane that it was abfolutely new when they fpake fo , otherwife then becaufe perhappes at other times they fayd the contrary . Which kind of proofe in Heretikes is friuolous , as partly hath bin fhewed before , partly fhall be more hereafter . Moreouer this is like the ex-cufe of the Marcionifts , who whē they had brought in a new God , yet would not haue him to be called abfolutely new , but *only newly knowne or difcouered* .

6.   Fiftly I proue the nouelty of Proteftant reli-gion becaufe euen then when in words they deny it to be new , in very deed they confeffe it to be new in fuch fort as fufficeth for me to proue that Luther was the Author therof , and that it is not the religion of Chrift , to wit , that it is ofnew erected , built & fet vp according to the very fubftance and effence therof in fuch forr as a houfe fallē downe but newly raifed in walls , roofe and other fuch fubftantiall , parts may be called a new houfe ; Becaufe Chrifts Church and religion cannot be new in this fort , being fuch as can neuer fall . For they confeffe , that the antiquity of their Church was abrogated , and that it is a religion refined and reformed , and that they are refiners and reformers . D . Morton 1 . part . Apol . lib 1 . cap vlt · writeth that Proteftants *Chal-lenge*

lenge the first antiquity, but abrogated by mens fault. Iunius
Cont. 4. lib .4. cap . 7 sayth : *The continuance of the old
and Catholike doctrine is renewed*. But surely that thing
whose antiquity hath bin abrogated and broken of,
is new. For the kingdome in Cæsars time was new
in Rome although it began with the citty it selfe,
because it had bin abrogated for diuers ages. Wherupon Riuet Epitom - Cont . tract . 3 cap , 21 sayth:
*Things are called new, when they are renewed and vsed after
interruption*. Besides whether a thing once abrogated
and taken away and afterward restored be to be called new or no, it sufficeth to me, that the Protestant
religion is in such sort new, as a house fallen downe
and newly raised may be called new : because the
Church & religion of Christ cannot be new in this
manner, nor the antiquity therof, abrogated, and
cut of. In like sort Muscle in locis tit . de noua doc-
trina pag . 417 : Albeit he deny that they make new
doctrine yet he confesseth that they renew doctrine,
And that he meaneth of a substantiall renouation
wherin the very substance of a thing is renewed, it
appeareth by the precedent page where he sayth that
old matters abrogated & fallen down for some ages are renewed.
A Church therfore and religion fallen downe they
doe renew, that is, erect a new. Wherupon the
French Confession, Beza, & Bastingius as is before
recited say that their Church *is againe, & a new erected,*
and others cal her a Church *Reuiued, resuscitated, reborn*
and assigne a new birth and begining of her, which
words doe manifestly signifie a new substantial production or making of her : which whether it be called a nouatiõ or renouatiõ, maketh not much to the
purpose, seing it is either a substantial production or
first making of that which neuer had bin before, or
a re-

a reproduction and ſecond making of that, which though it had bin before, yet was fallen, and the ſubſtance therof corrupted and periſhed. Of which nouation or renouation Luther was the Author, Beſides they call themſelues *Renewers or Refiners,* and their Church or religion *Reformed or refined*. D. Andrewes Reſponſ. ad Apol. Bellarm. cap. 1: *VVe are Renewers. VVe call our religion reformed*. Caluin Epiſt. 341: *VVe carry the name of the reformed Church*. Iunius lib. 4. de Eccleſ. cap. 16: *VVe hold the Reformed Chriſtian faith*. And in the ſame ſort ſpeaketh the Scots Confeſſion, the Conſent of Poland, D Whitaker Prefat. cont. & cont. 1. queſt. 2. c. 16· & 17. & cont. 2. queſt. 5. c. 2. & others commonly. I aske therfore what kind of forme of religion haue they taken away by their reformation, and what a one haue they giuen? Surely they haue changed the very ſubſtantiall forme. For (to omit al other points) they haue taken away the former manner of obtayning remiſſion of ſinnes by the Catholike faith and good workes, and brought in a new of obtayning the ſame by ſpecial faith only, and vndoubtedly the way to obtaine remiſſiõ of ſins, is ſubſtantiall to a Church and religiõ. But they who take away the ſubſtantiall forme and bring a new, doe make a new thing, and ſuch a mutation ought rather to be termed a formation, then reformation. But whether it be called a formation or reformation, it skilleth little, it ſufficeth (as I ſayd) that it is a ſubſtantiall mutation of religion, the Author whereof Luther was, and ſuch a mutation, as cannot happen to the religion and Church of Chriſt. Moreouer, it is the ſhift of old and new heretiques to bring in new religions vnder the name of Reformation. Of the Marcioniſts thus writeth Tertullian: *They ſay that Marcion*

Proteſtãts call themſelues reformers.

Marcion did not ſo much innouate the rule (of faith) as reforme that which heretofore was corrupted. And he himſelfe after he was become a Montaniſt : *This is ſhewed of vs, that the diſcipline of Monogamie is neither new nor ſtrange, yea both ancient and proper to Chriſtians, that yow may thinck the Paraclete (Montanus) to haue bin rather the Reſtorer then beginner therof.* And of Seruetus thus write thoſe of Zurick in Caluin cont Seruet. pag. 626. *He goeth on to thruſt vpon the Church a moſt corrupt doctrine vnder the ſhew of reſtitution of Chriſtianity.*

7. Sixtly, becauſe the Proteſtants deſigne the place, the occaſion, the yeare, day, and hower, when Proteſtancie began : The place we haue heard already out of Caluin and Fabritius was Wittemberg, & the ſame doth Luther inſinuate in cap. 49. Iſaiæ tom. 4. fol. 192 ſaying : *Now VVittenberg is blaſphemed as the fountaine of all hereſies, but it will come to paſſe ſome yeares hence that it ſhall be praiſed of Poſterity, as Gods garden from whence the Goſpell was propagated into Germanie and all parts of the world.* And Matthew Iudex in Edicto æterni dei : *That clamour againſt Antichriſt came out of the durty townes of barbarous and baſe Germany.* A fit place no doubt from whence ſo durty, filthy, and barbarous an hereſy ſhould ſpring. Forſooth Wittemberge is the Proteſtants Syon, from whence their law ſhould come. S. Auſtin thought it ridiculous madneſſe, that the Donatiſts ſhold ſay that the Church was to be renewed out of Africa the third part of the world, & ſhall we think it wiſedom to imaginthat it ſhould be renewout of a durty and barbarous corner of Duchland ? The occaſion of it was Tezelius his preaching of Indulgences, for thus writteth Cruſius l.10. Anal. Sueu. pag. 5 ‘8. *Tezelius boldneſſe ſtirred vp Luthers mind to ſet vp concluſions againſt thoſe indulgences on the gates of the temple of*

L. 1. cont.
Mar. c. 20.

L. 1. de
Monogam
c. 4.

The place
where
Proteſtā-
cy began.

Proteſtan-
cy began
in a durty
towne of
a barba-
rous coū-
try.

De vnit. c.
7.

The occa-
ſion of the
beginning
of prote-
ſtancy.

All

Saints in VVittemberg the last day of October which was satur-
day . Hence now came the occasion & beginning (sayth he) of **The day**
correcting the christian religion. Schutlelburg Præf. tom. **of the**
8. Catal. hæret: *Old men remember & it recorded in writing* **weeke &**
for remembrance for euer and publiquely extant , that this was **month.**
the cause that the Gospell flourished againe in our age , that Iohn
Tetzele carryed about pardons of sinnes to be sold in the Popes na-
me. And Kemnice 4. part. Exam. tit. de Indulgentijs
pag. 78 : *It is knowne to all the world, that the impudent, and*
impious sale of pardons aboue 50. yeares ago gaue entrance to
the holesome repurging of heauenly doctrine . And Manlius
in Calendario: *On All Saints eue first of all conclusions against*
Indulgences were fastned by Luther vpon the gate of the Church
of VVittemberg castle in the yeare 1517 .at twelue of the clocke.
The same say Melancethon præfat. in tom. 2. Luthe- **The year**
ri, Sleidan , Carion, and others. We haue then the **& houre.**
place where, to wit, Wittemberg, the yeare 1517.the
day of the month, the last of October,the day of the
weeke, Saturday, and finally the very houre, to wit,
twelue of the clocke , when first Protestancy began
to arise , And as Vincent , Lyrin.sayth : *VVhat heresy e-* *Cap. 34.*
uer was there which sprung not vp vnder some certaine name in
a certaine place, and tyme .

8.   Seauenthly I proue the nouelty of Protestan- **Lutherãs**
cy by the mutual testimony of the Lutherans against **say that**
the Sacramentaries,and of the Sacramétaries against **the Sacra.**
the Lutherans. For of the Sacramentaries doctrine **doctrine**
thus testifieth Luther in defens.verború Cœnæ tom. **is new .**
7 fol. 381. *Neither doth any thing set forth this heresie more*
then noueltie. And tom. 2. Zuinglij fol. 383. *Carolstadi-*
us first raised his errour. Melancthon Epist .ad Mico-
nium , calleth it *new doctrine* , and addeth that *Carol-*
stadius first raised this tumult . Heshusius lib . de reali
præsentia fol. 2: *Carolstadius the vnhappy author of this dis-*
cord

cord . Kemnice in fundamentis Cœnæ pag . 116: *Carolſtadius was the firſt author of this ſtrife.* And Hoſpin. part . 2. Hiſtor. fol. 68. writeth that Melancthon impugned the Sacramentaries doctrine *as a thing altogether new* , and fol. 46. that Pomeran *diſallowed Zuinglius doctrine as a noueltie.* And in Narrat. diſſipatæ Eccleſ. Belg. pag. 179. The Lutherans ſay to the Caluiniſts , *your doct:ine is new:* and pag. 213. *your doctrine is of late.* And Confes. mansfeld: *The Sacramentary doctrin is iuſtly ſuſpected of vs . Firſt for the nouelty therof becauſe it aroſe in our tyme.* Neither ought the Sacramentaries to accept againſt theſe teſtimóies, as if they were the teſtimonies of the aduerſaries. For ſuch aduerſaries they are as themſelues account them their brethren in Chriſt , and members of the ſame Church . Beſides, though themſelues be aduerſaries both to Catholiks and Lutherans , neuertheleſſe they will haue their teſtimonies to be také againſt thé in matters of fact . Moreouer , becauſe the Sacramentaries themſelues doe ſometime confeſſe the ſame. For Zuinglius tom. 2. Reſponſ. ad Struthionem fol . 303. calleth Carolſtadius: *The firſt teather of the truth of the Eucharist.* And in Subſidio fol. 244. he calleth his opinion, *the expoſition of the ancients brought back is it were after it was loſt.* Laſco Epiſt . ad Reg . Poloniæ , *Aboliſhed byiniury of times and reſtored as it were after it was loſt* . Lauather de diſſidio Euchar . fol. 2. writeth that the Senate of Zurich *VV as troubled which the newneſſe of the matter.* And fol. 5. that when Occolampade had ſet forth his booke, *the Senate of Baſle moued with the nouelty of the matter, forbid his book to be ſold, vntill it had bin examined by Cenſors.* And fol. 1. that Zuinglius opinió *was not heard of by the common petple.* In like ſort the Sacramentaries write of the proper opinions of the Lutherans. For of their im-

panation

panation or mixture of Chrifts body and bread in
the Eacharift Caluin Defenf. 2 . cont Weftphalum Sacramé-
pag. 786. fayth : *It is a new doctrine , and till now vnheard* taryes fay
of, that bread is substantially the body of Chrift . Oecolam- the Lu-
padius responfione poster. ad Perkeymer pag. 18. theran
Those new Doctours grant to bread that it is substantially the opinions
body of Chrift . And of the Lutherans vbiquity, wher- are new.
with they make Chrifts body to be euery wher, Caluin pronounceth Admonit. vlt. ad Weftphalum pag,
829. *that it was not borne long since* . And Alcfius apud
Hofpin part. 2. fol. 201. fayth: *I know both the tyme when
this opinion was firft broached to the Church, and who was Author thereof* . Authores Admonit. de lib. concord. cap.
3. pag 95. *No man taught this their opinion before Luther. Do
they not bring forth new deuises and not heard of before in the
Church?* Beza alfo lib. de Omnipræfentia carnis Chri-
fti pag. 509. calleth it *a doctrine vnheard of in the Church* .
Finally Clenuitius apud Hefhuf. lib. cit. calleth the
very Confeffion of Aufpurg, *A new and fifth Ghospell* .
Thus Proteftants teftify the uewneffe of each other
doctrine.

9. Eightly I proue the newneffe of Proteftancy
by the new and before vnheard of nams, which pro- The na-
teftants giue to themfelues, and to their Church and mes of
religion . For they call themfelues *Proteftants, or Ghof-* Proteftats
pellers: and their Church and Religion *Euangelicall and* are new .
reformed . D. Andrewes refponf ad Apol. Bellarm. c.
1. *Proteftants is our name*. D. Willet in the Preface of his
Synopfis: *VVe refuse not the name of Proteftants. This name
agreeth fitly to our profeffion* .Præfat. confenfus Poloniæ:
VVe are termed Ghospellers . Iezler lib. de bello Euchar.
fol. 31. *VVe will be called Gospellers, and woe be to them who
call vs otherwise.* His maiefty in his declaration againft
Vorftius pag. 49 : *The men of our Religion doe eftfoones take*

to them the name of Goſpellers. D. Morton *part.* 1. Apol. *lib.* 1. *cap.* 7: *If ye aſke where is the Euangelicall and reformed Church, all will ſtraight point their finger to the Proteſtãts aſſembly.* But ſurely all theſe names are new and neuer heard of before Luther, neither can there be any name deſigned, which before Luthers time was proper to the Proteſtant company. But it is incredible that there ſhould haue bin ſuch a company, and yet that it neuer had any proper or peculiar name giuen either by thoſe of that company or of any others.

10.   Laſtly I proue the nouelty of the Proteſtant Church by that, that Proteſtants knowing well the newneſſe therof, deny that the greateſt antiquity among Chriſtian Churches is a marck of the true Church of Chriſt, as doth Iunius *lib. de Eccleſ. cap.* 16. yea ſome of them are ſo offended at this marck of Antiquity, as they bid vs (a) ſhut our eyes at it, and ſay that it is a (b) baſtardly marke, and rather a mark of the (c) Synagogue of Antichriſt, thẽ of the church of Chriſt. Neuertheles ſeeing it ought to be vndoubted amongſt Chriſtians, that ſince Chriſts Church was founded by him, it neuer failed or periſhed, and that it is manifeſt, that he founded his true Church before any falſe Chriſtian in imitation of him began a falſe Chriſtian Church, it ought alſo to be certain that ſhe which amongſt all Chriſtian Churches is the moſt ancient, is the very true Church of Chriſt. Neither would euer Proteſtants deny this, if they did not too wel know, that their Church is far yonger then the Roman, as being (according to their ſaying) her daughter.

(a) *Luth. tom. 2. fol. 357.*
(b) *Raino. Confer. c. 5. diuiſ 2.*
(c) *Ples l. de Eccleſ. c. 3.*

11.   Out of all which hath beene recited in this chapter, I make my eight demonſtration in this ſort: *If the Proteſtant Church and Religion were in Luthers ſyme*

tyme new or builded or begun a new, he was the Authour and beginner thereof. But so it was, as hath beene made manifest by the aforesayd confessions of Protestants. Therefore Luther was the Author thereof.

That Proteftants do plainly confeffe, that Luther was the Author and Beginner of their Church and Religion.

C H A P. XIIII.

THE ninth demonftration, that Luther was the Author of the Proteftant Church and religion, fhallbe taken out of Proteftants open confeffions thereof. Firft therefore they fay, that he was the firft who openly preached Proteftancy. Luther Præfat. in tom. 1: *The Duch men did looke what would be the euent of fo great a matter, which before none either Bishop or Deuine durft touch.* ibi. fol. 159. It is faid, *Luther firft of all in our age did taxe the Popes abominations, and illuftrate the ancient and pure doctrine of the Church.* And Præfat. difput. fol. 370. *I firft allowed the marriage of Bishops.* In cap. 3. Galat. tom. 5. fol. 233: *Many gaue God thankes, that by the Ghofpell, which by Gods grace we then firft of all preached, &c.* In cap. 4. fol. 387. *God in this later tyme hath againe reuealed the truth of the Ghofpell by vs vnto the vngratefull world.* Epift. ad Argentinenfes tom. 7. *VVe dare boaft, that Chrift was firft published by vs.* Melancthon Præfat. in tom. 3: *VVith what ioy did men receaue the firft fparckle of light difcouered by Luther.* præf. in tom. 2. Lutheri: *God by him reftored the Ghofpell to vs.* Againe: *He recalled the minds of men to the Sonne of God, and as the Baptift shewed the lambe that taketh away the finnes of the world.* And præfat. in tom. 3: *VVhen there was great darcke-*

Luther the firft that preached his Ghofpell.

Firft publifhed Chrift.

Firft fpark of Proteftancy.

T

darcknes in the Church, and the light of the Ghospell was oppres
sed, Luther layd open the iuſtice of fayth. The vniuerſity of
VVittemberg in Hoſpin. part. 2. hiſtor. fol. 250: *Out*

The firſt
light.

of this Church and ſchoole did ſhine the firſt light of pure doctrine
touching God and Criſt, which our new aduerſaryes are forced to
graunt, though they burſt with enuy. Amſdorfe, Alber and others write, that Luther *was the firſt vnder heauen, who*
impugned externall ſacrifice & Prieſthood in the new teſtament.
Schuſſelburg lib. 2. Theol. Caluin. fol. 130. ſayth that
Vtenhonius a Caluiniſt *was impudent, when he wrote that*
he heard Conrad Pellican ſay, that many learned men in Germa
ny held the doctrine of the ghoſpell before Luther appeared, and
that Pellican himſelfe had reiected Purgatory before Luthers na
me was heard of. This lye (ſayth Schuſſelburg) *the later*
Caluiniſts haue refuted. And fol. 228. he affirmeth, that
Luther *began the refining of the doctrine of the Ghoſpell. This*
praiſe (ſayth he) *we truly and with good right giue to Luther,*
though the Caluiniſts take it in very ill part. Mergerſtern
tract. 145. ſayth, *It is ridiculous to thinke that before Luther*
any held the pure doctrine, and that Luther receaued it of them,
and not rather they of him. Milius in explicat. confeſſ. Auguſt. art. 17. *If Luther had had orthodoxall forerunners in his*

Had no
predeceſ
ſours.

office, there had beene no need of a Lutheran reformation. The
Author of the booke entituled Prognoſtica or Finis
mundi pag. 12. *Luther* (as is confeſſed) *firſt brought in the gho*
ſpell at the end of the world. Brentius lib. de Cœna in fine.

The firſt
that
brought
in the
Ghoſpell.

God raiſed vp Luther to carry before vs the torch of the knowledg
of Chriſt. And Smedenſted apud Hoſpin. part. 2. hi
ſtor. fol. 232 : *He firſt in our age brought into the world the*
light of the Ghoſpell, after it had beene extinguiſhed. Thus the
Lutherans: And in like manner the Sacramentaryes.
Zuinglius reſponſ. ad Luther tom. 2. fol. 380. thus
ſpeaketh Luther : *Thou firſt cameſt into the field.* Ibidem
in Exegeſ. fol. 335. *VVe willingly acknowledge thee to be the*
                                                        cheiſeſt

chiefest defender of the Ghospell, the Diomedes who durst set vpon the Roman Venus, the Ionathas who durst alone assaile the campe of the Palestins. Bucer de Cœna pag. 675. calleth Luther *our first Apostle of the pure Ghospell*, and 673. sayth, *Luther first in our age did impugne superstitio̅.* Caluin writeth that *he began to take the cause in hand, and first shewed the way.* Danæus lib. de Baptismo cap. 15: *Luther first gaue others occasion to thinke rightly of mans iustification before God.* Lauather de distid. Euchar. anno 1546. *Luther first in our age did by diuers writings openly inueigh against Popish errours.* Author Orthodoxi consensus in Præfat. Apol: *Luther and Zuinglius were the first, who began to reprehend inueterate errours.* Againe: *The first teachers of Germany, Luther, Melancthon, &c.* Amongst English Protestants M. Iewell in defens. Apol. part. 1. cap. 7. diuis. 3: *Thus I say, in this later age after your so long darcknesse, Luther was the first that preached the Ghospell of Christ.* M. Fox in his Acts pag. 402: *Luther opened the veine long before hidden.* M. Wotton in his examination of the title of the Roman Clergy: *It might be truly sayd, that Luther was the first who in that tyme did publish Christ, especially in the chiese points of the Ghospell, which is iustification by fayth in Christ. And in this respect it is an honour for Luther to haue been a sonne without a father, a scholler without a maister.* Yee see how plainly they say, that Luther *first preached the Ghospell, first brought in the Ghospell, first shewed the way, first published Christ, discouered the fi̅st sparcle, first layd open the iustice of fayth, had no orthodoxall Predecessours, was a sonne without a Father, and a scholler without a maister*, and that in the article of iustification by only fayth, which the soule, hinges, and summe of Protestancy.

First
shewed
the way.

Scholler
without a
maister.

2. Secondly without Luthers help no man had knowne a iote of Protestancy. Luther cont. Regem Angliæ tom. 2. fol. 497: *Vnles we had opened the way, they*

were

were like to haue vnderstood nothing at all, either of Christ *or of*

Nothing at all.

the Ghospell . In cap. 15. 1. loc. tom. 5. fol. 134: *The gospell is by our labour and diligence brought into light, and they first learnt it of vs, without our paynes they could neuer haue learnt one word of the Ghospell.* And fol. 141 : *God hath called vs by his holy spirit, that by vs* Christ *might be manifested & knowne to the world. This prayse they cannot take from vs, that we were the first & carryed away the prize of bringing the Ghospell into light of which they would not haue knowne one iote, vnlesse by our paines and study it had beene brought forth .* And ibidem in cap. 17. Matth . he sayth that without him the Sacramentaries and others *would not haue knowne neuer so little of the Euangelicall truth .* Zuinglius in Exegesi tom. 2. fol. 358. writeth these wordes of Luther: *If they had not had it of vs, doubtlesse they would haue knowne nothing of.* And those of Zurich in their confession write thus: *Luther boasteth, that himselfe is the Prophet and Apostle of the Germans who hath learnt nothing of any, and all haue learnt of him. None knew any thing but what they haue knowne by him .*

Not one word .

Not one iote.

Neuer so little .

3. Thirdly they write, that Luther did kindle the Protestant light . Schusselburg tom. 13. Catal. hæret. pag. 897 : *By Luthers ministery the cleare light of the Ghospell is kindled againe for vs:* Lobechius disput. 1. pag. 6. *By this mans Ministery the Lord hath kindled in Germany the light of the heauenly truth .* M. Iewel defens. Apol. part. 1. cap. 7. diuis. 3. pag. 56. *Luther and Zuinglius were appointed of God to kindle againe the light which you had quenched .* Verheiden in his Images, at the Image of Luther: *Thou first didst preach the Ghospell with so great constancy. Thou didst lighten the torch of the Ghospell to the world .* And at the image of Zuinglius he sayth of him and Luther: *These two Architects laying the foundation of the Euangelicall kingdome.* D. Whitaker cont. 4. quest. 5. cap. 3. pag. 693. *Luther lighted a torch which no flouds can put out .* And in Præfat.

Luther kindled the Protestant light .

Laid the foundation .

Præfat. tom. 2. Danæi, it is sayd: *God raysed vp Luther for to kindle and restore to the world the light of his Ghospell.* And what is it to be a kindler of light, but to be Authour therof.

4. Fourthly they say, that Luther was the *renewer, the Founder, the Restorer, the setler and promulgator of their Church and Religion.* Zuinglius in Exegesi tom. 2. fol. 358. writeth, that Luther challengeth to himself *all the instauration of fayth.* Illyricus in Schusselburg. tom. 13. Catal. hæret. fol. 850: *This same religion was renewed and setled by Luther.* Hamburgenses ibidem fol. 658. *Luther truly the renewer of diuine worship.* Hethusius lib. de præsentia Christi sayth of Luther : *He is as that notable instrument by which true religion was renewed.* Saxonici in the conference at Aldburg Scripto 7. pag. 319. speake thus: *Since the tyme of the Ghospel renewed by Luther.* Hemingius in Schusselburg. lib. 2. Theol. Caluin Pap. 133. *Luther restored the ancient worship which our first parents receaued of God, and which Christ commended to his Church.* Caluin admonit. 2. pag. 147: *By his endeauour principally the purity of the Ghospell was restored :* And pag. 768. *God raysed Luther & others, by whose Ministery our Churches were founded and instituted.* The Protestant Princes in Germany in Schusselburg tom. 13. catal. pag. 877. write that the King of Nauarre *willingly affirmeth the French Churches to acknowledge Luther to be their Father in Christ.* Or as Thuanus lib. 79. histor. reporteth their wordes: *That Luther is esteemed and honoured of the French Churches as their Father in Christ, and that by his ministry truth was first pulled out.* Beza de Hæret. puniend. pag : 148: *Luther the Renewer of Christian Religion.* And in his Images: *The principall instrument of Christianity renewed in Germany.* Danæus cont 5. pag. 1135. reckoneth Luther among those, of whom (saith he) *all other men haue receaued what*

Renewed religion & setled it

Restored purity of the Ghospel.

Renewed religion.

T 3

what light of the Ghospell they haue . And lib. 1. de Euchar.

First Re-newer of the Church & truth . cap. 1. termeth him *the Renewer of the Ghospell of Christ .* And Apol. pro Eccles. Heluet : *The first renewer of the Church .* Hospin. part. 2. hist. fol. 134: *The first renewer of Euangelicall truth and doctrine.* Bucer Resp. ad Episc. Abrincen. pag. 613. writeth *that God by Luther hath merueilously and happily restored the summe of the Ghospell in our age.*

Restored the summ of the Ghospell . D. Whitaker cont. 2. quest. 5 . cap . 12. pag. 528 : *Luther only tooke vpon him to restore religion corrupted , and to renew the ancient and true doctrine.* And ad Rat. 10. Cam-

Restored Religion . piani calleth him the *Renewer of the old farth,* or as the English Apology termeth him *the promulgator of this doctrine .* D. Humphrey in Prolegomenis pag. 82 saith: *VVe reuerence Luther as a great renewer of Religion .* And what is it to be a renewer, Restorer, Setter of a thing corrupted, especially if he restore the summe thereof, as Bucer sayd that Luther restored the summe of Religion, but to be an Author or maker of it according to the very substance thereof.

5 .   Finally, they plainly graunt, that Luther was the first to whom Protestancy was reuealed, that he layd the first foundation of Protestant Religion, and that he was the captaine, Author. and Begetter

Luther first to whome Protestats was reue-aled . therof. Luther himselfe in sermone , *Quid sit homini Christiano prastandum* tom. 7. fol. 274. speaketh thus to Protestants : *I was the first whome God set in these lists. I was also the first, to whome God vouchsafed to reueale these thinges which are now preached vnto you .* Behould Christian Rea-

(a) *Theod. l. 2. c. 18.* der a new (a) Aetius surnamed Atheist, who sayd that

(b) *Basil l. cont. Eun.* those thinges were now reuealed to him by God, which hitherto he would haue to be hidden vnto all . A new (b) Eunomius,

(c) *Vinc. c. 43 .* who sayd, that he had feund *a new way to God and vnheard of which none before had perceaued .* A new (c) Nestorius, who gloried that *he first vnderstood the Scripture.* A new

Cata-

Cataphryge, (d) who sayd: *VVe haue the first reuelation*
& of vs beginneth the Christian fayth. For of thee (Luther)
began the Protestant fayth, and thou wert the first,
to whom the God of this world (as the Apostle speaketh) vouchsafed to reueueale those thinges which
haue beene preached to Protestants: *To thee alone (that*
I may vse Tertullians *wordes) hath truth been reuealed.*
Forsooth thou hast found greater fauour and more plentifull grace
at the Diuells hands. Againe in expofit. Papafelli tom.2.
fol. 398. Luther hath these words : *VVhen I layd the first*
foundation of this cause, as Bullinger Præfat. Comment.
in Ioan. writeth of Zuinglius faying: *VVhen Zuinglius*
layd the first foundation of Euangelicall doctrine. Moreouer
Luther tom. 1, fol. 206. writeth thus to his most inward fellow Melancthon : *The citty is full of the noyse of*
my name, and all men desire to see the man the Herostratus of so
great a fire. Ye fee, how in a letter to his most assured
friend, he confesseth himselfe to be the Herostratus,
that is, the Author of that fire wherewith not the
temple of Diana , but the temple of God burneth.
Melancthon also acknowledged the like, as it appeareth by these words of Luther in a letter to him tom.
9. Wittemberg. Germ. fol. 416. *Thou writest, that for my*
authorityes sake thou didst follow me as the author, and leader or
captaine in this matter. Behould how Melancthon accounted Luther the Author. And what suspicion is
there, that Melancthon should in this matter write
otherwise to him then he thought. Schusselburg
tom. 8. Catal. pag. 363. defineth true Lutherans or
Protestants to be those, *whoimbrace the doctrin of the Go-*
spell amending Popish abuses, of which amendement (fayth he)
Luther was the Author. And the fame meane they, who
call Luther the Author of the Protestant reformation. For they protest amendment or reformation is
indeed

indeed (as hath beene shewed before) a substantiall mutation or change of religion, and therefore the Authour of such an amendment or reformation is indeed the Author of a new Church and religion. D. Sutcliue lib. 2. de Eccles. cap. 3. pag. 237. writeth in this manner : *VVho were the first Authors of raysing the*

Author. *Church fallen downe, as Cranmer, and other our Bishops, also Luther, Zuinglius &c.* And cap. 7. pag. 328. *The Princes who first followed the Authours of restoring religion.* Osiander in Sleidan fol. 22. sayd that Luther & Melancthon *had*

Maker. *made a certaine diuinity which sauoured more the flesh then the spirit.* Lobechius disput. 1. pag. 26. calleth Luther *the*

Deuiser. *first deuiser of the Confession of Auspurg.* And Melchior Neofanius Pastour of the Church of Brunswich in loc. Kemnitij part. 2. sayth: *How much doth all Dutch-land owe to worthy Luther for his great deserts, who was the Author of*

Authour. *pure Religion.* D. Couel also in his defens. of Hooker art. 19. pag. 130. plainely confesseth, that *some Protestants make Luther and Caluin Authours of the religion which they hold.* And M. Horne in his harbour maketh England speake in this manner : *I am thy Country England,*

Begetter. *which brought forth blessed man Iohn VViclise, who begot Hus, who begot Luther, who begot truth.* And heereupon it ariseth, that (as Rescius in his Ministromachia p. 15. reporteth) the Lutherans call Islebium (where Luther

A new was borne) their new Bethleem. Forsooth because
Bethleem. there was borne their new Messias, the begetter Author, and founder of their religion. Mark now Reader how Luther, by his owne and other Protestants confession was, *the first to whome Protestant doctrine was reuealed, layd the first foundation of the Protestant cause, was the Authour of the Protestant amendment or reformation, was the deuiser of the first Protestant Confession, was the Herostratus of the Protestant fire, finally was the leader, maker, begetter,*

and

and Authour of the Protestant Church, and Religion. Which
is in plaine termes the very same, which in all this
booke I endeauour to proue. Iustly therefore may
Protestants sing to Luther as Lucretius did to his E- *Lib. 3.*
picure the Author & beginner of Epicorisme. Those
alle of Basle were not ashamed in the Epitaph of his
tombe to call Occolampadius, *the first author of Euangelicall doctrine in that citty*, as report Hospin. and Lauater in their Hostories an. 1531. and Iunius lib. 4.
de Eccles. cap. 8. Neither was it peculiar to Luther
to spread deuiles vnder the name of religiõ For thus
writeth Iezier . de bello Euchar. fol. 26. of Ministers:
Matters deuised of some few, we thrust vpon the whole world.
And King Henry 8. when he began to encline to
Protestancie, set forth articles with this title, *Articles
deuised of his Maiesty.*

6. And from this euidéce & acknowledgement
that Luther was the Author of Protestant religion, it proceedeth. First, that Luther oftentimes calleth it *his doctrine* , *his gospell* , *his word* , *his cause* , *his part.*
For so he speaketh tom. 1. fol. 138. tom. 2. fol. 23. Protestancy is Luthers doctrine.
39. 93. 238. 488. 493. 494. tom. 3. fol. 555 tom. 5.
fol. 290. tom. 6. fol. 79. and other where often.
Secondly it ariseth that true Protestancie is called
Lutherans doctrine , *the Lutheran cause* , *the Lutheran religion,*
the Lutheran businesse, and Lutheranisme. Of Luther himselfe tom. 2. fol. 37. and 497. Of Frederick the Protestãts terme themselus Lutherãs,
Electoar tom. 1 Lutheri fol. 237. Of his Counsailers tom. 2. fol. 116. Of the deuines of Manssfeld in
Schusselburg tom. 8. pag. 270. Of Schusselburg
himselfe Epist. dedicat. tom. 4. Of Melancthon tom.
2. Lutheri fol. 193. 197. Of Kemmice Epist. dedicat.
lib. de duabus naturis. Of Hutter in Analysi Confess. August. pag. 595. Of Brunsfelse Respons. ad

Spongiam Erasmi. Of Lobechius in Epist. dedicat.
Disput. Of George Fabritius l b. 1 & 8. Orig. Saxon.
and of other Lutherans. And in like manner of Sa-
cramenttaries also, as of Bucer in Matth. 26. & lib.
de Cura animorum pag. 261. Of Hospin. Prefat.
part. 2 Histor. Of Scultete Con. sæcular. Of D,
Morton 1. part. Apol. lib. 1. cap. 45. and others
Thirdly therof proceedeth, that the true and proper
Protestants are called Lutherans, both of themselues
and of others. For thus speaketh Luther in psalm.
118. tom. 7. fol. 551: *I graunt my selfe to be a Lutheran.*
And in like manner speaketh he ibidem fol. 79. 242.
233. 361. & 400. And tom. 2. fol. 473. and in
Hospin. part. 2. fol. 134. So also speaketh Melancthon in dominicam 8. Trinit. tom. 1. and in
Hospin. lib. cit. fol. 72. and Brentius also ibid. fol.
107. So speaketh the Confession of Saxonie in the
Preface, and the Saxon Ministers in the Conference
of Aldburg pag. 160. Vrban. Regius in Iudicio de
Conuentu Norimberg pag. 9. Amsdorfe in Bucer
in Scriptis Anglicis p. 635. Matheus Iudex in Edicto
æterni Dei. Iames Andrewes in Colloq. Montisbel.
pag. 179. Yea Grauer in the Preface of his Caluinisticall absurdities dedicateth his booke *Vnto the pro-*
per Lutherans: and pag. 61. affirmeth, that their men
are called Lutherans, that they may be distinguished
from Papists and Caluinists. Scusselburg tom. 17,
Catal. pag. 866. sayth, *The Deuines of our part call them-*
selues, and the Defenders of their opinion, Lutherans. Which
also affirmeth Reineccius tom. 1. Armat. cap. vlt.
Hutten in Expostulat cum Erasm. sayth: *I acknowledge*
the name of Lutheran. And Hailbruner: *VVe are not asha-*
med of the name. And Andrew Schafman in Prodromo
bringeth many reasons to proue, that they did well
in

in calling themielus Lutherans. And thofe of Berga
(as Hofpin reporteth in Concord . Diſcord.c .20.)
ſay that, *All the ſincere doctours of the Church call themſelues
Lutherans of Luther.* The fame alſo teſtifie the Sacramentaries. For thoſe of Newſtade againſt the booke of
Concord.cap 6. pag.213. ſay *they account none a ſincere
diſciple of Chriſt , vnleſſe he wilbe called as well a Lutheran as a
Chriſtian.* The author of the orthodoxe Conſent in
Prefat.Apologet. *They take to themſelues factious names
vpon a prepoſterous and too great eſteme of their maſters.* Parcus
in cap 2 . Galat.lect. 24 : *They doe not only call themſelues
Lutherans of Luther, but alſo willbe ſo called of all.* Beza in
Conſpicil. pag. 8: *Ye all will be named and called Lutherās.*
And pag .56: *Not content with the name of Chriſtians , they
call themſelues Lutherans, and reioyce to be ſo called.* Danæus
Apol. cont.Iac. Andreæ ſaith that, *He glorieth in Luther
as in another Chriſt , of whome euery where be thundereth , &
calleth himſelfe a Lutheran a Lutheran &c.* And Reſp. ad
Selneccer he ſaith , that Selneccer *Freely confeſſeth , that
the Ducth Churches terme themſelues Lutherans.* Vrſin in
Catechiſm . pag 494. ſaith: *This is the opinion of them who
call themſelues Lutherans.* Zauchius Epiſt . dedicat .
Miſcellan: *Many are not aſhamed euen in printed bookes to all
themſelues Lutherans.* And Iezler de bello Euchar. fol.
115 :*Some haue no ſhame euen in pulpit to ſay : VVe wilbe Lutherans conſtantly.* And at ſome times euen the ſacramē-
taries ſeeme to be deſirous of the ſurname of Lutherans. For thoſe of Newſtade in Admonit . de lib
Concordiæ pag.106.compliane,*that ſome would ſeeme
to be the only diſciples of Luther.* Muſculus in locis tit . de
hæreſi pag 604. ſaith:*No man condemneth true Lutherans,
vnleſſe be be ignorant of the truth or very naughty.* And the
Proteſtanr Princes of Germanie in Thuan .lib.79 .
Hiſtor. pag .595. relate, that the King of Nauarre
wrote

wrote to them, that *if the French Protestants, were to be termed of any man, they ought most of all to be called Lutherans. Because when this name was odious in France for almost therscore years, many by fire, by rack, by death sealed with their bloud the testimonie of that doctrin which they receiued first of Luther.* Scultete also in Concione sæculari compareth Luther with the Apostolicall men. Besides the Sacramentaries call Luthers true follwers Lutherás, as Zuinglius tom. 1. fol. 420. 436. 470. Oecolampadius ibidem fol. 479. and in Hospin part. 2. fol. 84. 112. 126. Tigurini ibidem fol. 88. Bucer in cap Rom. & in Scriptis Angl. pag. 669. Marryr tom. 2. loc. Epist. ad Caluin · Hospin. lib. cit. fol. 91. Caluin in Zancius lib. 2. Epist. pag. 78. Daneus ibidem pag: 401. Zanchius himselfe pag. 394. Pareus lib. 5. de Amiss. grat. cap. 1. & 2. lib 4. cap. 17 lib. 6 cap. 1. Vorstius in Antibellarm. pag. 561. D. Whitaker cont. 1. quest. 2. cap. 3. and quest. 5. c. 8. and quest. 6. cap. 9. cont. 4. quest. 5. cap. 3. & lib. 3. de Concup. sc. cap. 9. & lib. 3. de Scrip. cap. 2 sect. 3. D. Fulke de Success. pag. 321. M. Perkins in Explicat. Symboly col. 781. & 790. Yea Iezler loc. cit. fol. 39. & Vorstius in Collat. cum Piscatore write, *that properly and vulgarly they are called Lutherás.* Wherupon D. Humfrey ad Rat. 2. Campian. pag. 128. sayth, *Lutherans vulgarly called.*

7. Hereby we see, first that the Lutherans glory of the name of Luther, as the Donatists (which S. Augustin reporteth) did of the name of Donatus. Secondly, that they glory of a schismaticall name: for such is the name of Lutherans, as Luther himselfe confesseth in D. Morton part. 1. Apol. lib. 1. cap. 8. And Hospin Præfat. part. 2. Histor. Vorstius in Antibellarm. pag. 149 Yea D. Whitaker cont.

2. quest.

2.queſt.5.cap.2.ſayth, that *to take the name of any man at all, is Hereticall and ſchiſmaticall, and that heretikes carry the names of their maſters, and willingly acknowledge ſuch names.* Thirdly it appeareth, that the Engliſh Apologie vntruly ſayd, that Luthers diſciples are called Lutherans in diſgrace or deriſion. For Grauer lib. cit.ſayth, they are termed ſo *for diſtinction ſake.* Lauatherus and Hoſpin. Præfat. Hiſtor. ſay, they call them ſo *for doctrine ſake; that it may be knowne whome they meãe.* And Scul etc ſo termeth them for honours ſake. And ſurely ſith both Sacramentaries, the common people, and themſelues alſo terme them Lutherans, and glory alſo in that name, it cannot be ſayd, that they are called ſo in diſgrace or contemp. Fourthly it appeareth to be falſe, that D. Morton lib.cit. and D.Surliue lib. de Eccleſ.cap.2.ſay: *It is rather to be attributed to a lye then to Luthers deſert, that Proteſtants call themſelues Lutherans.* For (as we ſee) Luther himſelſe called them ſo, and therin they follow his example. Neither skilleth it, that Luther did once diſlike this name, becauſe he did oftentimes vſe it, & it was vſuall to Luther to allow and diſallow the ſame thing. Fiftly we ſee it to be falſe, which D.Whitaker writeth cont.2 queſt.5.cap.2 pag.494: *None of vs euer called himſelſe a Lutheran: we acknowledge not theſe names, nor are we delighted with them. This name our aduerſaries haue faſtened vpon vs, only vpon malice and enuie: Neither are we called Lutherans but of the Papiſts.* Falſe alſo is that, which D.Fulke ſayth de Succeſſ. pag. 188. that *they acknowledge no other name proper to their religion, but the name of Chriſtians and Catholiques.* Theſe I ſay are falſe; for Luther (whome D.Whitaker accounteth his father) and the Lutherans (whome he termeth his brethren in Chriſt) doe call themſelues ſo, and are

well

well pleafed with that name. Befides, they are fo termed of the Sacramentaries and common people, and therfore not of Papifts only, nor vpon malice and enuie, but (as Grauer fayd) truly for diftinction fake, and that moft iuftly. For as S. Athanafe fayth, *VVho deriue the origen of their faith from other then Chrift, iuftly carry the furnames of their Authors.* But Proteftants (as we haue fhewed) confeffe that they deriue the origen of their faith from Luther. Therfore iuftly they beare his name.

8.   Out of all which hath bin rehearfed in this chapter, I thus frame my ninth demonftration of this Matter: *If Luther and many other famous Proteftants fometimes indeed, fome times in plaine words do confeffe, that Luther was the Author of their Church and religion, he ought to be fo taken and efteemed. But they do foe confeffe. Ergo.* The Minor is euident by all that is fayd in this Chapter: And the Maior, by what we fayd in the Preface. For fo many and fuch principall Proteftants knew well the origen of their religion, and willingly would not lye to the difgrace and ouerthrow therof.

That Proteftants cannot proue their Church to haue bin before Luthers time, by any probable argument or fufficent teftimonie.

CHAP. XV.

THE tenth and laft demonftration for to proue that Luther was the firft Author of the Proteftants Church and religiõ I will take from hence, that albeit Proteftants doe fometimes boldly affirme their Church and religiõ to haue bin before Luthers
time

time , Yet they can neuer proue it by any reasonable
argument or sufficent testimony. Which thing alone
would suffice to shew , that (as I sayd before) it is a
fable vainely feigned , falsely affirmed , and fondly
beleiued . It hath bin alwayes the fashion of heretiques boldlyto auouch any thing , but few things to
proue euen in shew . This S . Augustin doth often
obserue in the Manichees and Donatists , and some
of his sayings we haue alleadged before . Of Eunomius S . (a) Basil noteth the same , and S . (b) Ambrose of all heretikes saying, *Heretiques are wolues , they
can howle , but proue nothing* . And this doe Protestants
confesse . For thus D . Whitaker cont . 2 quest .5 .
cap 18 : *Heretikes are wont to boast and promise truth , but
haue to proue it* . Of Luther thus writeth Zuinglius tom .
2 . fol . 473 .and 509 : *One argument he hath in all these matters , He sayd it*. And tol .447 : *Luther relyeth only vpon his toyes
and deuises* . Fol . 395 : *Thou puttest forth whatsoeuer the mo-
tion of thy affections do appoint , and when a reason of thy saying is
exacted of thee , thou standest naked , vnarmed* . And of the
Lutherans thus writeth Erasmus : *They say it , and for
that alone they will be belieued* . Of the Sacramentaryes in
like manner Luther writeth in defens. verb. Cœnæ
tom . 7 . fol . 384 . *One word not easily ouerturneth all these
thinges : for if you deny them , then as butter melteth in the sun
so they quaile* . And the same is euident to all that read
the bookes either of Lutherans or Sacramentaryes.
In the meane tyme they cry to vs , that that Pythagoricall word : *He sayd it*, hath no other place but in
(e) Christ and the Scripture : that in other it is the
proper argument of (d) fooles : that to affirme any
thing beside scripture , is to (c) trifle : that til we proue our affirmatiue , they will stand in their (f) negatiue , and exact (g) demonstrations , that is , either expresse

(a) *Lib. 1,
cont. Eu-
nom* .

(b) *Serm.
6. in psal.
118* .

In Diatrib.

(c) *VVhit
lib. 2. de
script. cap.
10. sect. 5.
Bullenger
in comp.
l. 1. c. 3* .
(d) *Vorsti-
us Anti-
bel. p. 468*.
(e) *Powel.
l. 1. de An-
tic. c. 19* .
(f) *Luth.
tom 2. fol.
437* .
(g) *Vor-
sius l. cit.
Fulke de
succes. p.
74* :

preſſe teſtimonies of ſcripture , or forcible reaſon deduced from thence. Now we ſay the ſame to them. They affirme their Church to haue bin before Luthers time . We deny it vntil they proue it . Neither let them affirme it only, which is the proofe of fooles & wilfull men, but if they cannot bring demonſtrations therof , at leaſt let them produce ſome credible teſtimonie, or ſome effectuall reaſon and argument. Otherwiſe their beliefe in this matter , is (as ſayth Tertullian) *a peruerſe beliefe which will not belieue thinges proued, and belieueth thinges which cannot be proued* .

Scorp.c.11.

2.   That in this matter they be deſtitute of all credible teſtimonie, appeareth ſufficently by what hath heretofore bin rehearſed of their owne confeſſions, and now we will ſhew, that they want alſo all probable reaſon or argument. For all their arguments herein be reduced to this one : *Our doctrine is the doctrine of Chriſt : Therfore our Church was alwayes ſince Chriſt.* For thus agreeth D. Whitaker cont. 2. q. 5. c. 3. p. 498 : *I vſe this argument : VVhat Church ſoeuer keepeth the doctrine & preaching of the Apoſtls , ſhe is the Apoſtolical Church. But our Church doth ſo , Therefore &c. Of the Maior (ſayth he) no controuerſy can be made .* And cap. 5. p. 505 : *It was our Church which was in the tyme of the Apoſtles and afterward vnto the Apoſtaſie. But how doe we proue this? By this reaſon, that our Church keepeth the ſame faith and doctrine which the Church in the Apoſtles time and afterward kept.* And cont. Dureum ſect. 1 : *If thou holdeſt Chriſts doctrine thou art a Catholike .* And ſect. 2 : *It muſt needs be the true Church of Chriſt which keepeth & conſerueth Chriſts doctrine deliuered in his word.* Dancus cont. 3. pag. 288 . *VVith vs is the true Church of God , becauſe we reſtore the true doctrine of Chriſt .* Lubbertus lib. 5 de Eccleſ cap. 1 : *If the doctrine which our Church profeſſeth , be the ſame which Chriſt deliuered , then*
our

our Church *is that which* Chriſt *inſtituted .* D. Fulke lib. de
Succeſſ. pag. 27: *Seeing we are ready to proue out of the ſcripture, that we profeſſe the ſame doctrine of fayth, and manners ,
which* Chriſt *would haue to be perpetuall by euident reaſon, our
ſucceſſion is manifeſt, althogh all* Hiſtoryes *were ſilent of the names of the Perſons and continuation of ſucceſſion .* And the like
he hath pag. 154. and 331. D. White in his way pag.
403. ſayth he knoweth his Church was alwayes, becauſe it holdeth the fayth of the Scripture, which
cannot be extinguiſhed . The like he ſayth pag. 320.
& 326. Likewiſe Luther de notis Eccleſ. tom. 7. fol.
149. Caluin in Matth. cap. 24. verſ. 28. and generally
al of them whiles they make the truth of doctrin the
infallible marke of the Church . *O proofe* (that I may
cry out in S. Auguſtins words) *O errour, o dotage.* And
with S. Athanaſe : *A worthy hereſy which wanteth probable reaſons to vnderproppe it.* For this argument on which
all their belief, that their Church was before Luther
doth rely, is a moſt fond ſophiſme, and moſt coun-
terſait ſyllogiſme, as manifeſtly appeareth, whether
it be framed in that forme wherein D. Whitaker hath
propoſed it, or whether it be reduced to this forme :
That Church which holdeth the true doctrine of Chriſt *hath alwayes beene, and conſequently before* Luther . *The Proteſtant
Church holdeth the true doctrin, holdeth the true doctrin of* Chriſt
*as (ſay they) we will proue by ſcripture . Therefore it hath bin
alway .*

    3. I anſwere that this argument is a manifeſt
ſophime for many cauſes . For if the Maior be particuler, ſo that the ſenſe thereof be , *Some Church which
holdeth the true doctrine of* Chriſt *hath alwayes beene,* it is true
becauſe the catholik church, which holdeth Chriſts
true doctrine, hath alwayes been : but then the Syl-
logiſme is ſophiſm for want of due forme, inferring

    *Lib. 2 .
contra A-
rian .*

V   a con-

a conclusion out of particuler propositiõs. But if the
Maior be vniuersall, according as it is made of D.
Whitaker, then so farre is it from being out of controuersy (as he affirmeth) that it is manifestly false,
and no way true, but only apparant, and therefore
vnfit to make a true syllogisme, but only a counterfait and a sophisme. That it is manifestly false, is euident, because that Church or company of Christiãs
which is strictly and properly termed schismatical,
holdeth the true doctrine of Christ as both the Fathers teach, and the Protestants themselues doe also
most plainely affirme, & yet it is not the true church
of Christ. Wherefore sith (as the Philosopher teacheth) those thinges are probable, which seem true
to all, or to most, or to wise men, and those either al
or most, or most approued, and such as are not probable serue only to make sophismes; The foresayd
Maior, not seeming true to all, or most, or the wisest
Christians, yea not euen to the Protestants themselues, it is manifest, that it is no probable propositiõ,
but only apparent, and therefore not fit to make a
true syllogisme, but only an apparent and counterfait.

    4.   That the Fathers teach that a Schismatical
Church holdeth the true doctrine of Christ, is manifest by S. Augustine who lib. quest. Euang. pag.
38. tom. 4. sayth: *It vseth to be enquired, wherein Schisma-*
tickes differ from heretikes, and this found, that no difference in
faytht but breach of society in communion maketh Schismatikes.
And lib. de fide & Symbolo cap. 10: *Heretikas by be-*
lieuing wrong of God violate the fayth: but Schismatickes by
wicked diuisions leape from fraternall charity, albeit they belieue
aright those thinges which we belieue. And lib. cont. Gaud.
cap. 9. refuteth him, because he had sayd, that Schis-

matikes

Protestãts
assume a
manifest
falsity.

That
Schisma-
tikes hold
true do-
ctrine.

matikes and Heretikes are the ſame; againſt which
he ſayth: *Thou art a Schiſmatike by ſacrilegious diuiſion, and*
an heretike by ſacrilegious opinion . And lib. 1. cont. Creſc.
cap. 29. and de geſtis cum Emerito affirmeth that the
ſame fayth is had out of the Church . S. Hierome in
Tit. 3. *VVe iudge this difference to be between hereſy and ſchiſm*
that hereſy holdeth a naughty opinion, ſchiſme ſeparateth from
the Church by diſſention of Biſhops . S. Gregory lib. 18. Mo-
ral. cap. 14. *Some doe belieue falſe thinges of God, others by*
Gods help belieue rightly of God, but keep not vnity with their
brethren, theſe are diuided by ſchiſme. S. Iſidor. lib. 8. Ori-
gin cap 3. *Schiſme tooke its name of breach, for it beleeueth the*
ſame religion and rites that others do, only is pleaſed to keep com-
pany a part . The ſame teach S. Ireneus lib. 4. cap. 62.
S. Chryſoſt. hom. 3. in 1. Cor. S. Optat. lib. 1. 4. &
5. cont. Parmen. and others. And it is manifeſt by
reaſon . For if Schiſmatikes did erre alſo in Fayth,
they ſhould not differ from heretikes. And it is graū-
ted both of old and new Heretikes . For thus ſayth
Fauſtus in S. Auguſtine lib. 20. cont. Fauſtum cap.
3. *Schiſme if I be not deceaued, is to belieue the ſame & to wor-*
ship God in the ſame manner that others do, only to be delighted
with diuiſion of aſſemblyes. Caluin 4. Inſtitut. cap. 2. §.5.
Auſtin putteth this difference betwixt heretikes and ſchiſmatiks,
that they corrupt the ſincerity of the fayth with falſe doctrines,
theſe ſometymes euen hauing the like faith breake aſunder the
band of ſociety And. in. 1. Cor. cap. 11. verſ. 19. *It is*
known in what ſenſe the ancient vſed both theſe nams (ſchiſme
hereſy.) they put hereſy in difference of doctrine, but ſchiſme
rather in alienation of minds. to wit. when any either vpon enuy.
or hatred of the Paſtours or of frowardneſſe departed from the
Church. Beza libro de puniendis Hæreticis pag. 89. :
Shiſm properly is the diuiſion of thoſe who belieue the ſame things
And pag. 150. *Let them remember that we terme them not*

heretikes,

heretikes, *who are properly called Schismatiques*. The same
he hath in 1. Cor. 1. v. 10. and other where. Plessie
lib. de Ecclef. cap. 1. pag. 16: *VVe call erroneous Churches
either heretikes, or schismatikes according as they erre either in
fayth or in charity.* And pag. 32. *VVhat pertaineth to schismaticall Churches, either they are simply schismaticall or when heresy also is adioyned as it vseth after schisme, as an ague after a
wound.* And cap. 10. pag. 340. *True and pure Schismatiks
are those, who holding the same doctrine yet make meetinges a
part.* Peter Martyr in iocis tit. de Schism. pag. 618.
*I thinke it more plaine to define Schisme to be a cutting a sunder
of the Ecclesiasticall peace & vnity.* And pag. 619: *There may
be schisme in the Church without heresy.* Aretius also in iocis
part. 2. fol. 10 : *Schisme sometymes in the same doctrin brea-
keth society.* Bucan in loc. quest. 33. de Eccl. affirmeth,
that schismatiks differ from heretiks because *heresy properly is dissention in doctrine.* Pol an. part. 2. Thesf. de notis
Eccl. *Albeit schismatical Churches agree in the doctrine of truth
&c.* Zanchius tract. de Ecclef. cap.: *There may be breach
in the symboles of Charity, that is in participation of Sacraments
communication of publike prayer, and such like other Ecclesiasticall exercises, to wit when one thought he agree with the rest of
the Church of Christ in the principall heades of Christian fayth,
yet I know not for what light causes withdraweth himselfe from
the rest of the Church and communicateth not with her in the sacraments. Such (fayth he) are properly called schismatikes.*
M. Perkins in cap. 5. Galat. vers. 21. *Heresy is in doctrin,
Schisme in manners, order, and gouernement.* D. Fulke de
Succesf. pag. 165: *There may be schisme in the Church, where
the same doctrine is held on both partyes, & the one wanteth lawfull succession.* D. Field lib. 1. of the Church cap. 7:
*Some professe the whole sauing fayth but not in vnity, as schisma-
tiks.* Daneus in August. de hæresf. cap. 3 *He is a schismatike, who retayning the same doctrine of fayth and that entire, yet
            without*

without probable and better reason followeth not the decent rites of the Church. The same he hath Apol. pro Heluet. Ecclef. pag. 1485. Bullinger tom. 1. Decad. 5. ferm. 2. Vorfius in Antibel'arm. pag. 190. D. Whitaker cont. 2. queft. 5. cap. 10. D. Rainolds Praelect. 1. col. 2. Hethufius in 1. Cor. 1. and others.

5. Now that proper Schifmatikes, to wit, fuch as willfully feparate themfelues from the Communion of the Church, be not members or parts of the Church, is cleare by the teftimony of the Fathers, the confeffions of Proteftants, and manifeft reafon. S. Auguftin lib. de fide & fymbolo cap. 10 fayth: *Nei-ther doth an heretike belong to the Catholike Church, nor a fchif-matike.* Tract. 3. in 1. Ioan. *All heretikes, all fchifmatikes are gone out of the Church.* Lib. 3. de Baptifm. cap. 19. *All heretikes and fchifmatikes are falfe Chriftians.* And lib. 2. cont. Crefcon. cap. 29: *I thinke not that any fo doteth to be-lieue him to belong to the vnity of the Church, who hath not cha-rity.* The like he hath in many places S. Ambrofe lib. 7. in Luc. cap. 11. *Vnderftand that all heretikes and fchifmatikes are feparated from the kingdome of God and from the Church.* S. Optatus lib. 2. *The Church cannot be with any heretikes or fchifmatikes.* S. Fulgentius de fide ad Pe-trum cap. 38 : *Belieue moft ftedfaftly and doubt nothing, that not only all Pagans, but alfo all Iewes, Heretiks, & fchifmatiks, which end this life out of the church, are to go into euerlafting fire* The fame teach S. Hierome, & S. Chryfoftome loc. cit. S. Ignatius Epift. ad Smyrnenf. S. Iren. lib. 4. cap. 62. S. Cyprian lib. de vnit. & epift. 42. 51. 55. S. Profper de vocat. Gentium cap. 4. and the reft. The proteftants confeffions of this matter we related heeretofore, amongft whom e lay, that this is an vn-doubted truth. Reafon alfo conuinceth the fame: for as Caluin confeffeth 4. Inftitut. loc. cit. The cô-

That Schifma-tikes are out of the Church.

Lib. 1. c. 1 num. 4.

V 3   munion

munion of the Church is held with two bandes, to wit conſent of doctrine and traternall charity: But Schiſmatikes breake the band of fraternall charity: therefore they are not within the Church. Againe Danæus lib. 3. de Eccl. c. 5. ſayth: This is the marke that thou art of the viſible Church, that outwardly thou profeſſe the fayth & communicate with the reſt of the Church in the ſame Sacraméts: but ſchiſmatikes doe not communicate in Sacramentes with the reſt of the Church. And D. Feild lib. 2. of the Church cap. 2. ſayth: Communion in Sacramentes vnder lawful Paſtours is an eſſential note of the true Catholike Church: but Shiſmatiks want this communion. And Caſaubon epiſt. ad Card. Peron. pag. 9. *The true Churches of Chriſt are vnited in the vnity of fayth, and doctrine, and coniunction of minds and in true charity and offices of charity, eſpecially of mutuall prayer.* But Schiſmatikes are not vnited in charity and offices of mutuall prayer. Finally only Catholikes are members of the Catholike Church, as is euident and [a] Proteſtants confeſſe: But Schiſmatikes are not Catholiks, as the very name doth declare, the Fathers doe teach, and [b] Proteſtants acknowledge.

*(a) Whi-
cont. 2. q.
5. cap. 3.
(b) Geſner
loc. 14.
Field l. de
Eccleſ c. 7.*

6. By this it appeareth that the foreſayd Maior which is the foundation of Proteſtants in this matter, is not only falſe, but alſo ſo manifeſtly falſe, as out of this queſtion, it is commonly denyed of Proteſtants themſelues. Beſides it is not only falſe, but alſo ſo improbable, that neither it is proued of Proteſtants, nor can be any other wayes, then by proofe of fooles or willfull men, that is, by their owne ſaying. For D. Whitaker (as we haue ſeene) proueth it no other wayes, then by ſaying, it is out of controuerſy. D. Fulke, that it is manifeſt. But Luther

more

more boaſtingly ſayth l. de Miſſa priu. tom. 7. ſ. 247.
Thus is our ſolid foundation and moſt ſtedfaſt rocke : VVherſoe-
uer true doctrine of Chriſt or the Ghoſpell is preached, there is
neceſſarily the true holy Church of God. And who doubteth of
this (ſayth he) *may in like manner doubt, whether the Ghoſpel*
be the word of God. A notable proofe ſurely, and fit for
Pythagoras ſchoole, and a ſound foundation, on
which ſo fayned a Church ſhould rely, and a fit rock
for them to build vpon, who haue left the rocke vpon which Chriſt built his Church. Wherefore that
I may imitate S. Auguſtine in the like matter. I aske
whether God or man hath told them, that wherefo-
cuer true doctrine is, there is the true Church? If
God, let them read it out of the Scripture, where indeed we read, that where the true Church is, there
true doctrine is : but contrarywiſe, that where true
doctrine is, there the true Church is, there we neuer
read. If men haue told you this : Behold a fiction of
man, behold what you belieue, behold what ye ſerue, behold for what ye rebell, ye run mad, ye burne.
Againe, what kind of men were they, ſurely no o-
ther then your ſelues. And what is your authority, I
ſay not with vs, but euen with your ſelues ? Is (as
one of your part ſayd) *the iudgement of Lutherans or Sacra-*
mentaryes, the ſquare of truth? Moreouer, ſeeing that three
things are eſſential or ſubſtantial to the true church,
to wit, true doctrine, lawfull Paſtours, and people
following their Paſtours, nor any thing can be, vnles all the eſſential parts be, it is ſophiſtry and madneſſe to inferre, that that company is the true Church
wherin one only of theſe parts is to be found. If they
ſay, that by the true Church they meane not her
which is true in nature, or eſſence of the Church, but
only her which is true in doctrine, of whoſe eſſence

Lib. 1. cont
Gaudent.
cap. 33.

Pareus l 3.
ce iuſtific.
cap. 18.

V 4   is

is only truth of doctrin. Firſt they deceaue the Reader. For we ſpeak only of the Church true in eſſence, not of that which is only true in doctrin, as a ſchiſmaticall Church may be. Beſides, if they meane ſuch a true Church and vnderſtand their foreſayd Maior vniuerſally, it is falſe; for not euery true Church in that ſenſe is Apoſtolicall or hath euer beene. For a ſchiſmaticall Church is true in doctrine, and yet is neither Apoſtolicall, nor hath euer beene. And if they vnderſtand their Maior particulerly the concluſion followeth not, becauſe it is deduced out of pure particuler propoſitions. And thus much of the Maior.

7. Secondly the foreſayd argument is a ſophiſm becauſe of the Minor, by which one vnknown thing is proued by another, one falſe thing by another, not only falſe, but alſo impoſſible. For it is more vncertaine, that the Proteſtant Church holdeth the doctrin of Chriſt, then that ſhe was before Luther. For albeit ſhe were not before, notwithſtanding it was not impoſſible that ſhe ſhould haue beene, but that ſhe holdeth the doctrine of Chriſt, is both falſe and impoſſible alſo. And as Luther ſayth in defenſ. verb. Cœnæ tom. 7. fol. 385. *It is a mad mans part to proue vncertaine things by others as vncertaine*. And D. Whitaker cont. 2. queſt. 3. cap. 3: *All proofe is by thinges that are more knowne*. Which alſo he hath cont. 2. queſt. 5. cap. 18. Sadeel præfat. lib. cont. Traditiones. Daneus l. 4. de Eccleſ. cap. 2. D. Morton part. 2. Apol. lib. 1. cap. 37. Pareus lib. 2. de Iuſtificat. cap. 1. Wherupon Luther tom. 2. Præfat. aſſert. Antic. fol. 95. writeth *Ariſtotle and all ſenſe of nature sheweth, that vnknowne thinges muſt be proued by thinges more knowne, and obſcure thinges by manifeſt*. If therefore, (as Pareus ſayth lib. 1. de Iuſtificat.

Marginal note: Proteſtāts proofe out of a thing more vnknowne.

ficat. c. 20.) when the Aduerſarie is brought to that,
that, eithcir he gaineſayth himſelfe, or beggs that
which he is to proue, aſſuming that in his proofe
which is in debate, or trifleth by repeating now and
then the ſame thing, he is vanquiſhed; ſurely then
Proteſtants are vanquiſhed, whom in this ſmal work
we haue ſhewed oftentymes to gaineſay themſelues,
now including theſe within the Church, now ex-
cluding them, now affirming the Chu‑ch to be inuiſible, now denying it, now to haue alwayes Paſtours, now denying it, and the like: And in this ar-
gumment, with which alone they proue the exiſtéce
of their Church before Luther, they aſſume in the
Minor, that which moſt of all is in debate: And the *Caluin.* 4.
Maior they can proue no otherwiſe, then by trifling *Inſtitut.c.*
by repeating it, and ſaying that it is out of all doubt. 1. §. 12.
I add alſo, that the ſacramentaryes ſay, that the Lu- *Narrat.do*
theran Church erreth euen in the fundamentall *Ecclef.*
points, and the like ſay the Lutherans of the Sacra- *Belg.* p.
mentaries, and ſcarce there is any Proteſtant, who 196.
doth not thinke that the Church whereof he is doth
erre in ſome points. What reaſon then haue they,
out of the trueneſſe of the doctrin of their Churches
to inferre their perpetuall exiſtence?

8.   Thirdly I adde, that the manner wherwith
Proteſtants doe proue the Minor of their foreſayd
ſyllogiſme, is ſophiſticall and not ſuch as they exact
of vs for proofe of our doctrine. For commonly they
exact of vs to ſhew, that our doctine is contained in
expreſſe words in Scripture, or (as Luther ſayth lib.
de ſeru. arbit. tom. 2. fol. 440)*inſo manifeſt teſtimonies*
as are able ſo to ſtop all mẽs mouths as they are not able to ſay any
thing againſt it. But manifeſt it is, that ſuch be not the
proofes wher with Proteſtants proue their doctrine.

V 5   For

Tom. 6. in
c. 22. Gen.

VVhitak
cont. 1. q.
4. cap. 5.

VVhitak.
loc. cit. p.
480.
Plessy l. de
Ecclef. c.9.

Protestats
conclude
against
sense.

For to omit other points, where is in expresse words
in scripture that fundamentall point of their doctrin
that we are iustified by only faith? Nay the contrary
is so expresly in S. Iames epistle, as therfore Luther
blasphemously sayth *S. Iames doted.* And the Lutherans
for that very cause deny his epistle to be canonicall.
Besides, Protestants doe now confesse, that the scripture is not of it selfe sufficient to end all questions of
faith, and that Schismatikes cannot be conuinced
by scripture. How then can they sufficiently proue al
the points of their doctrine by scripture? Againe,
themselues acknowledge, that they need certaine
meanes to attaine to the right sense of the Scripture
and that their meanes are humane and not infallible,
as knowledge of tongues, conference of places, and
such like, and with all, that such as the meanes be,
such is the exposition of Scripture. If therfore their
meanes be not infallible, how can their vnderstanding of the scripture be infallible? Moreouer, they
scarce euer proue any thing by both principles out
of scripture, but almost euermore adioyne one human principles, as easily will appeare if their proofs
be brought to a syllogisticall forme, as well obserue
the most learned Bishop of Luçon in his defence of
the Principall articles of faith cap. 3. & 5. And how
can they be infallibly certaine of the conclusion,
which they cannot know but by one human principle, whereof they can haue no such certainty?
Furthermore, because many of their proofes doe not
only consist of one humane principle, which is not
at al in the scripture, but also they inferre a conclusiõ
directly contradictory to that which the scripture
in most expresse words teacheth of that matter. As
for example, when they proue that the Eucharist is
of

not the very body and bloud of Christ, alwayes one
of their principles is humane ; and besides their con-
clusiō is that contrary to expresse words of scripture,
which affirmeth that it is Christs very body and
bloud· And who is he in his wittes, that will perswade himselfe, either that the scripture meaneth,
that the Eucharist is not the body & bloud of Christ,
which directly it neuer sayth, rather, then that it is
his body and bloud, which it as expresly sayth, as
euer it sayth any thing, or that that proofe is not
sophisticall, which out of one humane principle at
least, inferreth the contrary of that, which the scripture most expresly teacheth ? Lastly, they neuer proued any one point of their doctrine any other wise,
then euer Heretiks do, that is in their own iudgmēt
neuer before any iudge or general Councell, which
Luther himselfe confesseth in c. 27. Gen. tom 6. fol.
368. in the words: *In the affaire of the Gospell we haue decided the matter against al the impiety of the Pope without forme
of law. VVe accused not the Pope, neither could we, for there was
no iudge .* Yea their doctrin hath bin cōdemned according to all forme of law in the Generall Councel of
Trent & of the Patriarch of Constantinople, to whō
they appèaled, and of al other kinds of Christians.

9.   Fourthly I say, that the foresayd argument is
a sophisme, in that in a sēsible matter (as the Church
is) it concludeth against the sense of all men . For ne-
ther did any see the protestant Church before Luther,
neither did any mā feele or perceiue himselfe to haue
bin a member of such a Church before that time.
Wherfore, as he should manifestly play the Sophister
who would goe about to proue by scripture that the
sunne appeareth at midnight: so likewise doth he,
who out of scripture endeuoreth to proue, that there
was

was a proteſtant Church before Luther, becauſe all mens ſenſe conuince the one as well as the other. Beſides proteſtants write, that though faith commaund vs to beleiue things which we ſee not, yet it doth not commaund ys, not to beleine that which we ſee, for otherwiſe faith ſhould be contrary to ſenſe, and none ſhould become faithfull, but he ſhould firſt be ſenſeleſſe. But ſurely wonderfull is the blindnes or wilfulneſſe of Sacramentaries, who in the matter of the Euchariſt, againſt the moſt expreſſe words of Scripture, will endeuour to proue by ſenſe, that there is not the body of Chriſt, when as the body of Chriſt there is not ſenſible. And here in the matter of exiſtence of their Church before Luther, out of ſome apparent ſhew of ſcripture, againſt the moſt manifeſt ſenſe of all men, will proue, that it was before Luthers time. When as a Church is a ſenſible thing, and can be felt either of others, or at leaſt of them who are of it. How much better and more reaſonably ſhould they proceed, if in the Euchariſt where Chriſts body is not ſenſible, they would rather giue eare to the moſt expreſſe words of ſcripture then to the ſuſpicions of their ſeſes, which can iudge of nothing but of ſenſible accidents; and in the matter of the Church, whoſe being is ſenſible, they would ſubmit their vncertaine (if not falſe) expoſitions of ſcripture, not only to the ſenſe of all men, but alſo the moſt certaine expoſitions of the Church and Fathers. But this ſheweth, that in their beleife they are guided neither by ſeſe nor ſcripture but out of them both borrow a ſhew of proofe for that which of their mere wilfulnes or fancy they chooſe to beleiue.

10.   Thus thou ſeeſt (Chriſtian Reader) for how vaine a ſophiſme, whoſe Maior is manifeſtly falſe &

ſo falſe, as that out of this matter it is generally denyed of Proteſtants themſelues, and ſo improbable alſo,
as that it cannot be proued in no ſhew or colour, and
whoſe Minor is more doubtfull, then the concluſiō
it ſelfe, and the manner of prouing ſophiſticall, and
no other then the proofes of al Heretikes be: for how
vaine a ſophiſme (I ſay) then the which ſcarce any
can be more vaine, Proteſtants beleiue, or rather will
ſeeme to beleiue, a thing wholy incredible, and in a
thing ſenſible, againſt the ſenſe of al mākind, to wit,
that before Luther there was a Church which held
the whoſe ſubſtance or all the ſubſtantiall and fundamentall points of Proteſtancy; nor in ſo weighty a
matter reſpect either their owne conſciences, or the
iudgements of men, or tribunal of God, or danger
of their eternall damnation. Surely, that I may end
with S. Baſils words, *I meane and bewayle them that for
a meane ſophiſme and counterfait paralogiſme they caſt themſelues into hel.*

*Homil.
cont. Sabel.*

11.   Out of all which hath bin ſayd in this chapter, I thus frame my tenth and laſt demonſtration:
*If no ſufficent teſtimonie, nor any probable argument, but only
one fond ſophiſme, can be brought to proue that the Proteſtant
Church was before Luther, this is not to be beleiued of any wiſe
and prudent man: But no other proofe can be brought. Therfore
&c.* And if it were not before Luther, ſurely he is the
Author of it. The Maior is euident by it ſelfe, and
the minor by what hath bin brought in this chapter.
Certainely if euery one of the demōſtrations which
we haue brought, doe not conuince that the Proteſtant Church and religion was not before Luther,
at leaſt all of them together manifeſtly conuince it.
For by the firſt fiue demonſtrations was ſhewed that
before Luther it was not at all, it was in no place,

was

was vnknowne of all the world, was not seene of
any, nor had any Pastors: And with the rest hath
bin demonstrated, that after Luther arose no ancienter Protestant did euer appeare and adioyne himselfe to Luther, that all the first knowne Protestant
had bin Papists afore times, that the Protestant
company and religion is new, that Luther and other
plainly confesse, that he was autho of that religion,
and finally that no proofe besides one friuolous fallacie can be brought to shew, that such a Church or
religion had bin in former times. And if yet any protestant doubt hereof, let him at least compare al the
foresayd demonstrations, wherwith so many wayes
out of the very testimonies of Protestants we haue
shewed, that no such Church was before Luther,
with their vaine sophisme, wherewith they make
shew to proue the contrary, and he will easily perceiue on whose side this so important truth is like to
stand. And if he make any account of truth, of Gods
seruice, of his owne reputation, or eternall saluation
he will forsake the Protestants Church, & put himselfe in the lappe of the Catholike Church. Which
(as S. Augustine speaketh) euen in the testimony of
all mankind hath not only beene in all ages since
Christ, but also hath had Pastors, nor hath been visible only to her owne, but to others also, and to the
whole world, and hath most valiantly fought, o-
uercome, and triumphed ouer Iewes, Pagans, Heretikes, Schismatiks, and all the gates of hell. To preferre before this most ancient, most glorious church,
another newly start vp, many ages lurking, knowne
to none not to her owne, and destitute of Pastours,
flocke, seat, and appearance, and in truth feigned,
and deuised, and (to omit all other proofes) wounded

*De vtil.
credendi
cap. 17.*

ded deadly with so many confessions of her owne
champions, and proued by one only vaine fallacie;
what other thing were it, then to preferre lyes before
truth, darcknesse before light, death before life,
the synagogue of Satan before the Church of Christ,
and finally wilfully to cast himselfe headlong into
hell?

*What he must obserue who will answere the
foresayd demonstration.*

CHAP. XVI.

SEeing I haue yielded so much to Protestants, &
condescended to so vnequall conditions, as that I
haue vndertaken to proue that Luther was the author of their Church and religion by the only Confessions of Luther and other Protestants, it is reason,
that if any one of them goe about to answeare my
foresayd demonstrations, he hould obserue these most
iust lawes, which I will here set downe, and which
themselues haue prescribed to others.

2. First therfore touching the words of Protestants which I haue alleadged, let him either confesse that they are truely cited by me, or if he denye
that, let him not say it only, but let him shew, that
they are supposed, falsifyed, or so changed, as that
the sense which I alledge and vrge to my purpose, be
either quite altered, or else obscured. For if in any
place for breuities sake the words be so litle chāged,
as the sense which I presse, remayne whole and cleare, it skilleth not. Because I argue not out of the
meere titles or letters, but only out of their sense and

signifi-

*See Iuel.
defens. A-
pol. par. 2.
c. d. 5.
Kemnice
Exam. tit.
de script.
Epist. Mo-
nit. p. 145.
Calu. cont.
Serues. p.
643.*

signification . Besides, if at any tyme, there be some colour of cauiling about the alteratió of the sense of one or other place (for iust cause I hope there will not be, though in so many places as are here cited it were no meruaile if some were mistaké) let him not therfore cry, that all the testimonies are falsified, or think that therby he hath satisfied all the rest .

3. Secondly touching the testimonyes them-selues, let him obserue, that either he answere them all, or at least those, which are the stronger, as for the most part those are, which are noted in the margent, otherwise by the iudgment of the Fathers and Protestants also, he will shew in effect, that though he conld not hold his peace, yet could he not an-swere sufficiently. For as S . Augustine (a) sayth: *Surely that he held his peace, not his tongue, but his cause failed him .* And in another place (b): *I take your silence for con-sent .* S . (c) Hierome: *You confesse more by silence then you denie by dispute .* And againe (d): *It skilleth litle, whether I binde mine aduersary sleeping or waking, only it is easier to binde one that is quiet, then one that resisteth .* (e) Luther also: *Euill consciences speake much besides the matter, but litle to the purpose, and seldome come to it .* And he noteth that it is the art and nimblenes of Heretikes, to skip ouer the matter and difficulty . Whitaker pronounceth it *to be a signe of a most desperate cause not to touch the Matter .* And D (f) Billon: *To this thou answearest nothing, and therfore all wise men conclude that thou canst not maintaine that which I then did disproue .* D, Sutliue lib . 2 de Eccles: cap. 1: *The rest because they say nothing to it, I will take for graunted. For if there had ben any hope of refuting it, or any place of cal-muniating it without doubt they would not haue bin silent .* And M. (g) Burhill: *Amongst the wiser both of our side and yours a tergiuersatour doth no lesse hurt his cause then a bewrayer. For*

he

(a) *Lib.* 1. cont. *Gau-dent.*
(b) *Lib.* 2. cont. *Ma-xim .*
(c) *Epi.* 6t.
(d) *Epi.* 83
(e) *Tom.* 7. fol. 384. 388.

(f) *Defens. of serm. p.* 243.

(g) *Pro Tortura forti c. t.*

be seemeth to consent & graunt, who then holdeth his peace when silence is suspicious.

4.   Thirdly touching the exposition of the testimonies, let him obserue, that when the words are cleare and their sense manitest , he doe not expound them or wrest them to another meaning. For first, if cleare words must be expounded, there would be no end of expounding. Againe, to what purpose should he expound those words which need no exposition? This were, as (h) S. Augustin sayth , *no other then to goe about to bring darknesse into open light.* Besides, Protestants themselues say, that cleare words ought not to be expounded. For thus (i) Luther : *This rule (that one place is to be expounded by another) without doubt is particuler , to wit a doubtfull or obscure place must be expounded by another that is to.> .ep. ad certaine and cleare. For to expound certaine and cleare places by conference of other places is wickedly to mock truth , and to bring clouds into light.* The Ministers of Saxony in (k) Colloq. Aldeburg. say to their fellowes: *Let them remember that exposition is not to be admitted in cleare places .* And those of (l) Zurich: *Then there is need of declaration, when the words & sense thereof is obscure.* And Melancthon : *Nothing can be sayd so properly, so plainly, aduisedly, which may not be depraued by some cauillation.* Beza (m) allo: *It is easy to wrest other mens writings.* And M. Dominis: (n) *Let those words which are cleare be kept in their proper and plaine sense.*

(h) Serm. 14. de verb. Apost.

(i) Luther to.>.ep. ad Carolstad.

(k) Pa. 303.

(l) Hospin. fol. 161.

(m) Ep. 4:

(n) l. 1. c. 3.

5.   Fourthly let him obserue, that in expounding the Protestants testimonies he deuise not hyperboles or figures at his pleasure , but let him bring good reason why he expoundeth them figuratiuely. *Either deny (sayth* (o) *Tertullian) that these are written, or who art thou that thou deniest that they ought to be taken as they are written.* And the Protestants in Admonit. de lib. Concord. cap. 3. say: *If they would not that these should be*

(o) Cont. Prax. c. 13.

X   *vnder-*

vnderstood as they sound, why speake they so? And Brentius in Recognit. pag. 148. *VVhat liberty what temerity is this of abusing words and deuising a new Grammar?* For firstthe rule of vnderstanding mens words is, that they be taken according to their proper and common signification, vnlesse the writer or speaker do by some way (p)*Tom.* declare the contrary. Whereupon (p) Luther sayth: *2.fol. 473.* *VVe haue ouercome, that words are to be taken in their naturall sense except the contrary be demonstrated*. And (q) D. Rai- (q)*Colloq.* nolds: *That is the sense of words, in which they are commonly* *c.8.Diu.4.* *taken.* Besides, otherwise all force of prouing any thing by any words of God or man is quite gone. For Note. sith all the force of such proofe standeth in the sense, if this be vncertaine, and must be proper or figuratiue according as the hearers or readers will, all the force of the proofe shall depend vpon the will of the hearer or Reader. And hence it proceedeth, that the proofes which Catholikes make out of Scripture a-gainst Heretikes seeme to some not to conuince thē, which falleth out, not for defect in the proofes themselues, but for the manner of thē, to wit because they be taken from words, which Heretiks will expound at their pleasure. And if there be no rule obserued in expounding words, but they be wrested at euery ones fancy, what meruaile is there, if Heretikes cannot be conuinced either by the words of Scripture or any other whatsoeuer. Moreouer, if at the will of the Reader or hearer wordes may be expounded eyther properly or figuratiuely, he that telleth the greatest vntruths, may be thought to tel the greatest truths, & contrariwyse, he that speaketh most piously, may be (r)*Tom.2.* iudged to speake most impiously. Hereupon sayd (r) *fol. 489.* Luther: *If this licence raigne, I may interpret all things sitly,* *whatsoeuer either Heretiks or the diuell himselfe hath done or* *sayd, fayd, or can do or fay for euer. VVhere then shall be the meanes to refell an heretik or the diuell?* And (ſ) againe: *If it be lawsull to play with figures at pleasure without yelding any reason, what hindereth but that all words haue new senses?* Furthermore, it was the custome of heretiks to deuise figures at their pleasure. Thus (t) S. Athanasius: *Heretiks rashly deuise figures.* And (u) Tertullian : *These are the subtilties & slights of Heretiks to call in question the simplicity of common wordes.* And this namely he noteth of the (x) Valentinians, as (y) S. Austin doth of the Priscillianists. And the same condemneth Luther in the Sacramentaries, and the Sacramentaries in the Anabaptists. Finally Proteſtãts themselues condemne this wresting of wordes from their proper signification without iuſt cause. Luther li.cont.Ecchium tom.1.fol.354: *If words do serue thee as another Mercury at thy pleasure.* And fol.55: *To say that Auguſtin speaketh excessiuely against Heretiks, is to say, that Auguſtin almoſt euery where lyed.* And Præfat. in Artic. Smal-cald.he bitterly inueigheth against some who expoũ-ded his words against his meaning. The Ministers of Saxony in Colloq. Aldeburg pag. 343. greatly com-plaine of the Electorall Ministers, that they misera-bly crucify Luther with their glosses, and pag. 337. say: *It is vnciuill to feigne a sense, which the wordes beare not.* And pag.304: *VVhosoeuer goeth about to cloak opinions which by themselues as the words sound are false, he is guilty of them, especially if he be a Doctour of the Church and Minister of the word of God.* And in like sort the Ministers of the Ele-ctour say to those of Saxony pag.252. that they auoyd *Luthers words by sophiſticall interpretation, and by opposing other places.* And pag.447: *Let power be giuen to expound & wreſt Luthers writings according to pleasure and fancy, like the Sybills oracles or Sphinx his ridles.* Besoldus alſo Præfat.in Com-ment.Luther in Geneſ.tom.6.fol. 497. thus writeth

of

Marginal notes:

(ſ) Ib fol. 220.

(t) Epiſt. ad Serap.

(u) Cont. Hermog. c.27.

(x) Præſc.
(y) l. de Hæreſ.

ot some: *If they fall vpon any such places in Luthers interpre-*
tations by the clearnesse of whicu they may be refuted, they feigne
that they are figuratiuely spoken, they deuise tropes and figures.
And whē the Sacramentaries expounded the words
of the Confession of Aulpurge commodiously and
dextrously, as they speake, according to their opinion, the Lutherans sayd : *May not any in this manner sub-*
scribe to the Turkish Alcaron, and make the canons of Trent or
other sentences howsoeuer contrary, to be orthodoxall? M. Bancroft thus writeth of Puritans: *You must bring strang dis-*
cords of which these men will not make some harmony. Againe:
To their profit they can make Quodlibet ex Quolibet . Pareus
lib. 2. de Iustificat. cap. 13. sayth that it *riseth of a naugh-*
ty cause to depraue the nature of words. And lib. 4. cap. 1. calleth it a haynous slaunder in Bellarmine, when he
sayd that many protestants speak one thing & meane
another. The Ministers also of Zurich in Hosp. part.
2. fol. 161. affirme, *That he may iustly be condemned of mad-*
nesse of all who giueth credit not to sound and cleare words but to
some explication not of him whose the words are but of some other
whose they are not . Yee see how mad they are to be accounted, who should belieue not the plaine and euident testimonies of Protestants rehearsed of vs, but
some other mans exposition of them .   To which I
add, that Luther and other Protestants do command,
that according to the ciuill law, words be expounded against him, who could speake more clearly, and
did not. Seing therefore Protestants could haue vttered their meaning more clearly, if they had meant o-
therwise then in the forsayd testimonies their words
do signify, iustly we may interprete their wordes a-
gainst them. Lastly Luther according to his own &
other mens verdicts did vtter his mind plainly, and
did condemne all doubtfull manner of speach in
                                                              matters

Lobechius
Disput .1.

Suruey. ca.
87.

Luther to.
1. Colloq.
Aldeb. fol.
303.
Schuss. to.
4. Catal.

matters of religion. For thus writeth D. Whitaker of
him : *He was an open and plaine man.* D . White: *They speake*
not alwayes so plainly as Luther doth. And Luther himselfe:
I will be plaine. Againe : *I had neuer this dissimulation to pre-*
tend to dispute that which I meant to determine. And in another place: *I will not abide to be suspected of such hypocrisy, to*
think otherwise then I write. And yet more : *To what is this*
double-tongued and hatefull kind of speach, but vnder words and
letters to sow the seed of all heresies? The Confession of Saxony cap. 3: *In the Church we must auoyd ambiguities:* And
Caluin de vera Eccl. reform. pag. 3 3 5: *VVhen in all mat-*
ters plainesse is to be vsed especially when religion is handled it is
not lawfull to vse craft and dissimulations. And the Sacramentaries in Admonit. de lib. Concordiæ cap. 3. pag.
62 : *VVe endeuour nothing lesse then to seeme to be of one opinion*
with them with whome we are not. To conclude howsoeuer it may be, that one or other Protestant, in some
one kind of writing, had written hyberbolically or
figuratiuely when he declared it not ; yet that so many, and so principall Protestants, so often, and in so
many kind of writings as we haue cited, & in a matter of so great moment, should speake hyperbolically
or figuratiuely, and yet not declare that they meant
so, is altogeather incredible. Wherefore vnlesse Protestants will ouerthrow the very rule of vnderstanding mens speaches or words, and make the fancy of
the hearer or reader the rule of vnderstanding them,
take away al force of proofes out of any words what
soeuer, imitate both old and new heretikes, follow
that manner of expounding words which themselues haue condemned, expound Luther contrary to
his owne protestation, and confesse that Protestants
in so great a matter spak one thing and thought another, and finally affirme a thing so incredible, as euen

X 3

now

Præfat.ad
Demonstr.
Sanderi.
Defess.c.33.
Tom.2 fol
r14 215.
Epist.ad
Amsdorf.

Note.

now we shewed this to be, they cannot interprete the foresayd testimonies of Protestants hyperbolically or figuratiuely, vnlesse they yield a sufficient reason or proofe thereof. Besides, if in this question of fact they not only reiect the testimonies of Catholikes and of all other men besides their owne, but also expound their owne mens testimonies as they list, they manifestly shew, that in this matter they will heare no testimony nor abide any iudgement whatsoeuer, which is the most euident argument that can be of a naughty cause. For to admit testimonies, not according to the proper sense of the wordes, but to your owne liking, is only to admit the sound or figures of the words, and to reiect the sense or signification, which is the soule and forme of them, and in which alone the force of the testimony or iudgement doth consist.

6.   Fiftly touching the reason or argument wherewith he will proue, that Protestants in their testimonies by me alleadged meant hyperbolically or figuratiuely, let him not account it sufficient to shew, that the same Protestants in other places haue sayd the contrary. First, because this will not shew, that they sayd not that which in the places which I cite they most plainly and euidently did say, but only, that according to the manner of Heretikes and lyers they gainesayd themselues. May a man accused of crime expound figuratiuely his open Confession of that crime, because at other tymes he denyed it? Againe Protestants themselues reiect this kind of proofe. For (as we did see) the Ministers of the Prince Electour did reprehend those of the Duke of Saxony, because they auoyded Luthers testimonies by opposing other places of his.   And the Ministers of

Saxony

Saxony pag. 303. ſay: *It is a friuolous kind of argument*; *He ſayd well ſometymes, therefore heere.* Beſides, it will be as equall for me to inferre, that Proteſtants in thoſe teſtimonies which he produceth, did ſpeake figuratiuely, becauſe in thoſe which I alleage they manifeſtly ſayd the contrary. For to vſe Luthers wordes: *By this raſhnes and licence ye giue your aduerſary leaue to turne it againſt you.* Certainly if they clearly haue ſayd both, we cannot deny, but they thought both, or ye muſt confeſſe, that your pleaſure ſhall be the rule and ſquare to know what they ſpeake properly & what figuratiuely. Moreouer, Proteſtants crie, that the holy Fathers contradicted themſelues. *How often (ſayth Luther) doe the Fathers fight with themſelues. They are men that fight againſt themſelues. VVe find the Fathers to haue taught contraryes, to haue ſlumbered.* And Caluin: *The Fathers doe often skirmiſh amongſt themſelues, and ſometymes fight with themſelues.* The like ſayth Melancthon tom. 1. Lutheri fol. 341. Iacobus Andreæ cont. Hoſium pag. 282. Beza Præfat. in nouum Teſtamentum and in Schuſſelburg lib. 4. Theol. Caluin. art. 32. Pareus lib. 2. de Grat. & lib. arbit. cap. 14 & lib. 4. cap. 4. Polanus part. 1. Theſ. de Notis Eccleſ. Apologia Anglica. And D. Whitaker lib. 5. cont. Dureum. Wherefore, either they muſt ſhew ſome priuiledge whereby Proteſtants be more excepted from contradicting themſelues, then the holy Fathers in their opinion were, or they muſt not inferre, that they ſayd not that which they did in places by me alleaged, becauſe otherwhere they ſayd the contrary. Furthermore, becauſe both the Fathers and Proteſtants alſo (as I ſhewed in the Preface) doe teach, that Heretikes are wont to contradict themſelues. And the Sacramentaries both ſay and ſhew by many examples, that

Tom. 2. fol. 220.

Tom. 2. Apert. Art. 2. & cont. Cochleum. Præfat. Inſtitut.

Hoſp. to. 2. fo. 12 Beza in Cōſpicil. Buing to. 2. fol. 412. 458. 460.

X 4 Luther

Luther oftentymes hath gainsayd himselfe. And of Sacramentaries Schusselburg lib. 1. Theol. Caluin art. 20. writeth : *That it is their property to contradict them-selues.*

7.   Lastly, touching the weight of the Pro-testant Confessions which we produce, let him not think, that it is any way impaired in that they haue at other tymes sayd the contrary, as if in this matter they were not to be belieued, because they haue byn taken in two tales. For the Confessions of those that are accused be of greatest force against themselues, because (as I sayd) no man willingly lyeth against himselfe, neither can these be discredited by any words of theirs spoken in their owne behalfe. For what will it auayle a criminall person, if he deny an hundred tymes the cryme, which he once openly có-fessed. And protestants haue not once, but oftentymes, most plainly, most openly, most freely confessed those things which I alleage. Againe, though no cre-dit be to be giuen to a lyer who gainsayth himselfe in matters for his owne behalfe or against any others, neuerthelesse in a matter against himselfe, the great-est yea euen the diuels open & free Confession ought more to be credited then any other mans testimony whatsoeuer. Wherfore we alleage Protestants sayings not as testimonies, but as Confessions, neither pro-duce them as witnesses, but as Criminels confessing the truth against themselues. And as Saint Ambrose sayd : *I admit not the diuels testimony but his Confession*: so I accept not the Protestants testimonies, but their con-fessions. Let their testimony be of no credit, either for themselues, or for others, or against others, vn-doubtedly it is of great force against themselues. As the Latin Oratour sayd: *Thy testimony which in another*

Serm. 5. de Sanctis.

must

mans matter would be light, is in thine owne matter, because it is against thy selfe, most weighty. Besides Protestants crie, that it is found to produce the Criminels as witnesses in their owne cause, and that any witnesse in his owne cause is to be reiected. Whereupon in the question of Supremacy they refuse the testimonies of all Popes though neuer so ancient, neuer so learned, neuer so holy. How much better may we reiect the testimonies of Protestants, when they speak in behalfe of their religion, and yet admit their Confessions, when they speake against it. These therfore lawes of answearing so iust, so equall, and approued of the Protestats themselues, if he will not keep, who goeth about to answeare my foresayd arguments, it will easily appeare, that in very deed he could not answeare them. And if none endeauour to answeare them, it will yet more appeare, that they can no way answeare them, & that this kind of dealing with Protestants out of their owne Confessions, is the fittest of all to stop their mouthes.

Vorstius Antibel. pag. 440. 456. Iud. Def. part. 2.c.3.D. 5. VVhitak. cont. 4. q. 6.c.2.& 1. 4.c.2.

FINIS.

The Translatour to the Reader.

THE *Author adioyned hereto a Catalogue of the Proteſtant Books with their ſeuerall impreſſions, out of which he gathered the teſtimonies by him alleaged: but becauſe I thought it not needfull for thoſe that read this Engliſh copy, I haue omitted it. The Reader, if he pleaſe, may ſee it in the Authors Latin Copy.*

THE

THE
INDEX OR TABLE
OF THE
CHAPTERS
CONTAYNED IN
THESE BOOKES.

THE
SECOND BOOKE.

Of the Author or beginner of the Proteſtant Church and Religion.

THE TABLE.

FINIS.